Cycling Futures

This book is available as a free fully-searchable ebook from
www.adelaide.edu.au/press

Cycling Futures

Edited by

Jennifer Bonham

*Department of Geography, Environment & Population,
The University of Adelaide*

and

Marilyn Johnson

*Institute of Transport Studies,
Monash University*

UNIVERSITY OF
ADELAIDE PRESS

Published in Adelaide by
University of Adelaide Press
The University of Adelaide
South Australia 5005
press@adelaide.edu.au
www.adelaide.edu.au/press

The University of Adelaide Press publishes externally refereed scholarly books by staff of the University of Adelaide. It aims to maximise access to the University's best research by publishing works through the internet as free downloads and for sale as high quality printed volumes.

© 2015 The authors

This work is licenced under the Creative Commons Attribution-NonCommercial-NoDerivatives 4.0 International (CC BY-NC-ND 4.0) License. To view a copy of this licence, visit http://creativecommons.org/licenses/by-nc-nd/4.0 or send a letter to Creative Commons, 444 Castro Street, Suite 900, Mountain View, California, 94041, USA. This licence allows for the copying, distribution, display and performance of this work for non-commercial purposes providing the work is clearly attributed to the copyright holders. Address all inquiries to the Director at the above address.

For the full Cataloguing-in-Publication data please contact the
National Library of Australia: cip@nla.gov.au

ISBN (paperback) 978-1-925261-16-5
ISBN (pdf) 978-1-925261-17-2
ISBN (epub) 978-1-925261-18-9
ISBN (kindle) 978-1-925261-19-6

Editor: Rebecca Burton
Editorial Support: Julia Keller
Book design: Midland Typesetters, Australia
Cover design: Emma Spoehr
Cover image: Courtesy of Takver, licensed under a Creative Commons ShareAlike 2.0., https://www.flickr.com/photos/81043308@N00/4038650169

Contents

	Page
Preface	vii
Editors	ix
Contributors	xi

PART I Current challenges

1. Cycling: Bringing the future into the present — 1
   Jennifer Bonham and Marilyn Johnson

2. A glimpse at Australia's cycling history — 25
   Jim Fitzpatrick

3. Health benefits of cycling — 43
   Chris Rissel

4. An epidemiological profile of cycling injury in Australia and New Zealand — 63
   Julie Hatfield, Soufiane Boufous and Ros Poulos

5. Faster than the speed of bikes — 89
   Marilyn Johnson and Derek Chong

6. Economics of everyday cycling and cycling facilities — 107
   Jungho Suh

7. Cycling and sustainable transport — 131
   Simon Kingham and Paul Tranter

8. Cycle touring — 153
   Matthew Lamont

Contents

PART II Strategies for change

9. Gender and cycling: Gendering cycling subjects and *forming* bikes, practices and spaces as gendered objects — 177
   Jennifer Bonham, Carol Bacchi and Thomas Wanner

10. Making (up) the child cyclist: Bike Ed in South Australia — 203
    Anne Wilson

11. More than a message: Producing cyclists through public safety advertising campaigns — 229
    Rachael Nielsen and Jennifer Bonham

12. Spaces for cycling — 251
    Glen Koorey

13. Off-road cycling infrastructure — 283
    Narelle Haworth

14. Teaching Australian civil engineers about cycling — 303
    Geoff Rose

15. What should planners know about cycling? — 321
    Wendy Bell and Donna Ferretti

16. Skilling landscape architects and urban designers for design of bicycle parking and network facilities — 357
    Hilary Hamnett

17. Cycling and Australian law — 407
    Margaret Grant

18. Evaluating cycle promotion interventions — 429
    Jan Garrard

Preface

The genesis of *Cycling futures* can be traced to a workshop at the 2010 Australian Cycling Conference (ACC). For the past six years, Australian and New Zealand researchers, policy makers, practitioners and community representatives have convened in Adelaide, South Australia usually during the week of the *Tour Down Under* professional cycling race to share research, new ideas and contribute to a greater understanding of cycling in the region. As editors of this volume, we developed the original concept and invited the authors to contribute to this book. We appreciate the considerable effort made by each of our contributors and wish to thank them for their enthusiasm and patience as we have slowly progressed toward completion of the book. We would also like to thank the organisers, past and present, of the Australian Cycling Conference (now the Australian Walking and Cycling Conference) for providing for providing the forum to share ideas and advance our knowledge of cycling in Australia and New Zealand.

As this book goes to print, several Australian states and territories are implementing or trialling new road rules, such as minimum overtaking distances, to improve cyclists' safety. Meanwhile in New Zealand the government has flagged spending NZ$330 million in the next three years on new urban cycling infrastructure. Researchers must critically evaluate these legislative and funding changes to ensure cycling can play a key role in the future of our cities and regions.

Producing and sharing knowledge about cycling is a key element in enabling the growth of cycling. This book provides an overview of cycling research in Australasia today. It includes researchers and practitioners who have made cycling a primary focus of their work and those who have introduced cycling into their academic disciplines or professions. It draws people from a range of different fields — engineering, planning, landscape architecture and urban design, sociology, geography, public health, economics — and diverse theoretical backgrounds.

This publication will be the first book to provide an Australasian perspective on cycling. Bound by the limitations of one volume, it offers a first step in capturing the broad and diverse knowledge about cycling in Australasia while recognising

Preface

that it has not been possible to include the full breadth, depth and diversity of work currently being undertaken.

It is our intention that this book will contribute to a broader discussion of cycling in Australasia and about Australia and New Zealand internationally, informed by our experience and knowledge and help set the future cycling research agenda.

Jennifer Bonham and Marilyn Johnson
November 2015

Editors

Jennifer Bonham

Dr Jennifer Bonham is a Senior Lecturer in the School of Social Sciences, The University of Adelaide. She has a background in human geography specialising in urbanisation and cultural practices of travel. Her research draws on poststructuralist and feminist theoretical frameworks as it explores the relations between materials, bodies, rationalities and practices of travel. Since 2004 she has focused on cycling, conducting studies into gender, spatial distribution of cycling, road space and the place of cycling in Australian cities and culture. Jennifer is a Chief Investigator on the recently awarded ARC Linkage Project *Cycle Aware: Driving with Bikes*, which is examining how Australian driver licensing systems equip motorists to interact with cyclists. Jennifer is a member of the Australian Walking and Cycling Conference reference group and is a current member of the editorial board of *Transfers: Interdisciplinary Journal of Mobility Studies*.

Marilyn Johnson

Dr Marilyn Johnson is a Senior Research Fellow at Monash University. Her research focus is road safety and active transport specialising in cycling. She is also the Research and Policy Manager at the Amy Gillett Foundation (AGF). Through this unique combination of roles, Marilyn pursues research questions with academic rigour and translates scientific evidence into action on Australian roads. She has conducted numerous cycling-focused studies in Melbourne, regional Victoria and the Australian Capital Territory. Marilyn is a Chief Investigator on a new ARC Linkage grant that will investigate how urban road designs can be improved to further increase road safety. She is also a lead contributor to the Amy Gillett Foundation's campaign 'A metre matters', which has resulted in amendments to the road rules in Queenland (2014), the Australian Capital Territory (2014) and South Australia (2015).

Contributors

Carol Bacchi

Carol Bacchi is Professor Emerita of Politics, The University of Adelaide. She researches and writes in the fields of policy theory, feminist political theory, embodiment and citizenship, and mobility studies. Her work on policy theory draws on Foucauldian perspectives. She explores Foucault's position on problematisation and elaborates diverse understandings of problematisation. Currently, with Jennifer Bonham, she is developing a poststructural analytic strategy for interview analysis. This work will form part of a new book entitled *Poststructural policy analysis: A guide to practice,* written with Susan Goodwin (available from Palgrave Macmillan in 2016).

Wendy Bell

Wendy Bell is an urban and regional planner and a retired architect with qualifications from the University of New South Wales. She has run her planning practice, Bell Planning Associates, based in Adelaide, since 1986 and specialises in the social and environmental aspects of planning and urban design. Her clients have included the private sector and all levels of government in Australia and New Zealand and her career in planning started in a British New Town where she managed Landscape Design and prepared Recreation Plans. She spent several years as a sessional lecturer and tutor in planning at the University of SA.

Soufiane Boufous

Dr Soufiane Boufous is an injury epidemiologist at Transport and Road Safety (TARS) Research, University of New South Wales. Soufiane's research focuses on developing innovative methods of assessing the burden and risk factors of injury. He has extensive experience in injury surveillance and record linkage of injury data. Soufiane has led and been involved in large observational studies and randomised trials that increased knowledge and supported the development of evidence-based road safety policies, including in the area of cycling safety.

Derek Chong

Derek Chong is a computational bushfire and risk modeller at the University of Melbourne. A geospatial expert, Derek has extensive experience in modelling complex events in real time and he is the lead developer of Phoenix RapidFire, the operational bushfire modelling and tracking software used in emergency bushfire management. Derek's expertise includes analysis of big data and his contribution in this book is innovative analysis over 1 million GPS data points to determine cyclist speeds and speed relative to crash and near-crash events.

Donna Ferretti

Dr Donna Ferretti is an urban and regional planner with over thirty years of experience working in state and local government, the private sector and as an academic teaching planning at the University of South Australia. She has particular skills in strategic planning, social planning, development assessment, policy planning and community/stakeholder engagement, for which she has won a number of state and national planning awards. Donna is a Fellow of the Planning Institute of Australia, has served on numerous boards and committees, and is committed to developing and championing the planning profession across Australia — a commitment which is underpinned by an ethic of environmental responsibility and social inclusion.

Jim Fitzpatrick

Dr Jim Fitzpatrick, retired, has a long record of researching and writing on cycling history. He has taught at tertiary institutions in three countries, and worked and published in numerous disciplines. A list of his non-cycling publications in the fields of geography, history, education, health and urban planning is available at https://independent.academia.edu/JimFitzpatrick.

Contributors

Jan Garrard

Dr Jan Garrard is a Senior Lecturer in Public Health in the School of Health and Social Development at Deakin University, Victoria, Australia. Her research interests are in active transport, women's participation in cycling and cycling safety. Jan has published several articles and book chapters on cycling promotion, bicycle safety, and research and evaluation methods in public health. Jan is a member of the Expert Advisory Committee of the Cycling Promotion Fund and the Research and Policy Committee of the Amy Gillett Foundation, and she was an Australian representative on the OECD/ITF Cycling Safety Working Group, which recently released the research report *Cycling, health and safety*.

Margaret Grant

Margaret Grant is a lawyer and adviser with ARETE Group Lawyers, Attorneys and Advisers. She holds qualifications in law, physiotherapy, research and education and leads ARETE's health law and regulation practice area. Prior to commencing legal practice, Margaret worked for many years as a sports physiotherapist, including being physiotherapist for several Australian cycling teams. She now couples her passion for cycling with her interest and expertise in regulatory law. Margaret is a current member of the research and policy advisory committee for the Amy Gillett Foundation.

Hilary Hamnett

Hilary Hamnett is a self-employed landscape architect specialising in site planning, landscape architecture and urban design. Clients include local and regional councils, and education and health authorities. Hilary studied urban and regional planning in the UK followed by a Masters Degree in Landscape Design. Prior to establishing her own landscape architecture practice in Adelaide she worked in the UK, in the Netherlands for the Rijnmond Metropolitan Authority in Rotterdam, and in landscape practices in Queensland and South Australia.

Contents

Julie Hatfield

Dr Julie Hatfield is a Senior Research Fellow at Transport and Road Safety (TARS) Research, University of New South Wales. Her behavioural research focuses on informing policy and practice in the area of road safety. She is particularly interested in contributing to the evidence base for promoting safe cycling. Julie represented Australia on the Joint OECD/International Transport Forum [ITF] Transport Research Committee Working Group on Bicycle Safety and is a chief investigator on the Safer Cycling Study, a cohort study of over 2000 cyclists in New South Wales (doi: 10.1136/injuryprev-2011-040160).

Narelle Haworth

Professor Narelle Haworth is the Director of CARRS-Q and has more than twenty-five years of experience in road safety research. She was awarded the 2013 Australasian College of Road Safety Fellowship 'for her outstanding contribution as an internationally recognised researcher in the road safety field and for her major contribution as a policy advisor at the state, national and international level'. Her special interest is in improving the safety of vulnerable road users — pedestrians, bicyclists and motorcyclists — and the synergies among both risk factors and road safety measures for these three groups.

Simon Kingham

Simon Kingham is Professor of Geography and Director of the GeoHealth Laboratory at the University of Canterbury, in Christchurch, New Zealand. He is an environmental geographer whose research focuses largely on public health issues — specifically links between the urban environment and health; and he has conducted research in the fields of travel behaviour and cycling. He has presented widely at conferences, including at VeloCity and Asia Pacific Cycle Congresses. He has a BA (Hons) and a PhD in Geography from Lancaster University, UK.

Glen Koorey

Glen Koorey is Senior Lecturer in Transportation within the Department of Civil and Natural Resources Engineering at the University of Canterbury, Christchurch,

New Zealand. Glen specialises in road safety and sustainable transport, particularly speed management and cycling. He was part of the recent New Zealand Cycle Safety Expert Panel and was also heavily involved in the development and delivery of national guidelines and training on planning and design for both cycling and walking. Glen is a Member of the Bicycle Research Committee of the US Transportation Research Board and has presented on cycling at numerous international conferences.

Matthew Lamont

Dr Matthew Lamont is a Lecturer in the School of Business and Tourism, Southern Cross University. His research interests encompass the social impacts of sport, with particular reference to the social aspects of participation in sports tourism and sports-based leisure. Matt's PhD research examined independent cycle tourism in Australia, and his research is published in a variety of scholarly tourism and leisure journals. Matt has been a regular speaker at cycle tourism conferences in Australia and currently serves on the editorial boards for the *Journal of Sport & Tourism*, and *Annals of Leisure Research*.

Rachael Nielsen

Rachael Nielsen is an Honours student at the University of Adelaide. Her current area of research is focusing on driver-cyclist interaction and the influence of driver training strategies on this relationship. She is a social scientist whose research interests are in the areas of human geography, active travel and social justice. She has undertaken independent research for the Adelaide City Council and has presented the findings from her contributing chapter at the 2014 VeloCity global conference.

Ros Poulos

Dr Roslyn Poulos is a public health physician and Associate Professor in the School of Public Health and Community Medicine at the University of New South Wales. Ros teaches public health to both undergraduate and postgraduate students. Her particular research interests include injury prevention and control, and the translation of injury research into policy and practice. Ros is lead investigator on the Safer Cycling Study, a cohort study of over 2000 cyclists in New South Wales (doi: 10.1136/injuryprev-2011-040160).

Chris Rissel

Chris Rissel is a Professor in the Sydney School of Public Health, University of Sydney. He has a background in health promotion, with a particular focus on physical activity and active travel. He has an active practice role, being involved in a number of community-based intervention studies. Chris is a regular presenter and participant in cycling conferences and is a current member of the editorial board of the *Health Promotion Journal of Australia*, and the *Journal of Transport and Health*.

Jungho Suh

Dr Jungho Suh is a Lecturer in the School of Social Sciences at the University of Adelaide, Australia. His research interests range from non-market valuation to sustainable agriculture and nature-based tourism. Jungho teaches general economics, and environmental and resource economics for non-economics students. In 2012, he obtained a Permaculture Design Certificate at the Food Forest, a permaculture farm located at northern Adelaide, South Australia. Due to his interest in permaculture, he has recently visited various ecovillages, including Crystal Waters Permaculture Village in Queensland, Australia, and the Auroville Foundation in Tamil Nadu, India.

Paul Tranter

Paul is an Associate Professor in geography in the School of Physical, Environmental and Mathematical Sciences at UNSW Canberra (the Australian Defence Force Academy), where his research and teaching interests are in the areas of transport geography and global change. Paul has made a pioneering contribution to research in the areas of child-friendly environments, active transport, and healthy and sustainable cities. His research demonstrates that creating urban environments that support the child-friendly transport modes — walking, cycling and public transport — will paradoxically save time for everyone, as well as making our cities more liveable, healthy and resilient.

Contributors

Thomas Wanner

Dr Thomas Wanner is a Senior Lecturer in the department of Geography, Environment and Population at the University of Adelaide, South Australia. His research and teaching interests concentrate on the political economy of environment and development issues, with a particular focus on international environmental governance, gender and development, and education for sustainability. He is member of the research network of Australia's National Climate Change Adaptation Research Facility, and the Higher Education Research and Development Society of Australasia; and he is Associate Editor of the *International Journal of Environmental, Cultural, Economic and Social Sustainability* and *The International Journal of Climate Change: Impacts and Responses*.

Anne Wilson

Anne Wilson is a researcher in the School of Social Sciences, Department of Politics, The University of Adelaide. Her main interest is in poststructural analyses of social and environmental issues, with a particular interest in Foucauldian theory.

Part I

Current challenges

1 Cycling: Bringing the future into the present

Jennifer Bonham and Marilyn Johnson

Introduction

Inspired by the growing interest in cycling across Australasia, *Cycling futures* brings together work by both well-established and emerging cycling scholars from Australia and New Zealand. Australasian cycling research has been developing alongside the steady growth in cycling. Since the early 2000s, reported rates of cycling participation have been increasing (Department of Communications, Information Technology and the Arts, 2011). In 2015, more than 4 million Australians (17.4%) had ridden their bicycle in the previous week, while over a third (36.3%) had ridden in the previous year (Australian Bicycle Council & Austroads, 2015). In New Zealand, in 2009-13, a third of the population (34%) cycled in the previous year, with 19% of New Zealanders reporting cycling in the last month (Ministry of Transport, 2013). This increase across Australasia reflects the growing interest in cycling in towns and cities across the globe.

Cycling participation rates in the Netherlands and Denmark are well documented, and attempts to foster alternative-mobility futures are gaining momentum around the world. The implementation of cycling-friendly policies and cycling infrastructure in global (and aspiring global) cities sends a powerful message about the changing future of urban mobility. New York City has been installing cycling facilities for almost two decades (Chen et al., 2012), while some areas of

London report that cycling now comprises 16% of vehicle journeys (Transport for London, 2013, p. 5). Tokyo has continued its long tradition of cycling with an estimated 14% of journeys being made by bike (Kidd, 2013); and in Paris, the pervasive Velib bike-share scheme provides a well-patronised, practical option for the city's residents and tourists (Beroud & Anaya, 2012).

Cycling has remained a significant means of travel in China despite policies through the 1990s and early 2000s which either sought to reduce bicycle use (Zacharias, 2002; Haixiao, 2012) or eroded conditions for cyclists (Wang, 2011a; 2011b). Bicycles constitute more than 15% of journeys in cities such as Beijing and more than 50% of journeys in cities like Tianjin (Wang, 2011b; Haixiao, 2012). Perhaps more importantly, changes in central government thinking since 2005 have fostered a reassessment of the role of the bicycle in urban China, facilitating the incorporation of cycling into city planning and the spectacular development of bike-share schemes (Haixiao, 2012, pp. 163 & 169). Similar to China, the complex relationship between national policies, personal income growth and the attachment of socio-economic status to different mobility practices has seen a significant increase in automobile ownership among the urban middle-class in India. Nonetheless, more than 20% of journeys in many medium-sized Indian cities are made by bicycle (Brussel & Zuidgeest, 2012, p. 181).

A review of Latin American cities by Hidalgo and Huizenga (2013) shows that cycling and walking (combined) make up more than 30% of journeys in many large cities including Curitiba, Santiago and Rio de Janeiro. Latin American countries differ on how they are implementing the Bogotá Declaration (on sustainable transport), but the city governments of Bogotá, Buenos Aires and León (Mexico) are shaping their urban travel futures away from motorisation and toward active travel by providing bike lanes, bike paths and secure bike parking, amongst other initiatives (Hidalgo & Huizenga, 2013). Policy makers in African nations such as Nigeria and South Africa have also identified cycling as playing an important role in urban and economic development (Chidoka, 2012).

The growing interest in cycling in Australia and New Zealand, as in other parts of the world, is underpinned by three major concerns: health and fitness; congestion and liveability; and pollution and climate change. Australasian researchers, practitioners, policy makers and community members are engaged in a global discussion on the role of cycling in addressing these concerns. Contributors to this book report on, and extend, this discussion as they explore the insights generated locally and internationally on the past, present and future of cycling. The focus of the first half of the book (Part I: Current challenges) is largely on the current engagement with cycling, challenges faced by existing and would-be cyclists, and the issues that cycling might address. The second half of the book (Part II: Strategies for change) is concerned with strategies and processes of change. Contributors working from different ontological positions reflect on changing socio-spatial relations to enable the broadest possible participation in cycling. The structure of this introductory chapter broadly reflects the overall structure of the book, as it positions contributors in relation to debates within the wider field of Australian and New Zealand cycling research.

Current challenges

While cycling participation rates in Australia and New Zealand are amongst the lowest in Western countries (Pucher & Buehler, 2008) this has not always been the case. Chapter Two, 'A glimpse at Australia's cycling history' by Jim Fitzpatrick, presents Australia's forgotten history as one of the world's leading cycling nations. His chapter is introduced in full below.

The pervasive image of Australia as a healthy, sporting nation is being fundamentally challenged by representations of its citizens as overweight and obese (Australian Institute of Health and Welfare, 2013; Colagiuri et al., 2010). Cycling, as a form of active travel, has been embraced by all levels of government across Australia and New Zealand as well as by health promotion organisations such as the Heart Foundation. In Chapter Three, 'Health benefits of cycling', Chris Rissel focuses on Australia as he reviews the country's current health challenges and critically examines the role of cycling in reshaping the nation's health.

Cycling is often considered to act as a panacea to a range of societal ills, from improving individual and population health through to fostering urban social interaction and revitalising rural communities through slow tourism (Dickinson & Lumsdon, 2010). However, there is a significant human cost for cyclists in Australasia. An average of 9 cyclists has been killed each year in New Zealand for the past 10 years, while in Australia more than 50 cyclists were killed in 2013. This latter figure exceeded the previous decade average by more than 10 deaths. Further, almost 1 in 5 (18%) of the people seriously injured on Australian roads is a bicycle rider (Henley & Harrison, 2012). In Chapter Four, Julie Hatfield, Soufiane

Boufous and Ros Poulos provide a sobering account of the human trauma costs of cycling. Their chapter, 'An epidemiological profile of cycling injury in Australia and New Zealand', examines the various ways of measuring rates of road trauma and the factors that influence the nature and severity of such trauma.

One crash factor that has been well researched in road safety is speed. Typically, speed research focuses on the posted speed limit or the travel speed of motor vehicles in relation to crashes (Elvik, Christensen, & Amundsen, 2004; Aarts & Van Schagen, 2006). In addition, speed is a critical element in cycling safety and potential crashes, yet there has been little cyclist speed research in Australasia to date. In Chapter Five of this volume, 'Faster than the speed of bikes', Marilyn Johnson and Derek Chong present new findings from an innovative naturalistic cycling study in the Australian Capital Territory. The findings present the first analysis of the study's cyclist speed data generated using helmet-mounted video cameras equipped with GPS data loggers.

After road trauma, the second major issue leading to a rethink of mobility is urban congestion, which has both economic and liveability implications. The cost of road congestion in Australian cities is $9.4 billion per year (Bureau of Infrastructure, Transport and Regional Economics [BITRE], 2007) and is forecast to more than double to over $20 billion per year by 2020 if it remains unaddressed (Council of Australian Governments [COAG], 2006). Although the productivity costs associated with over-reliance on motor vehicles have been acknowledged and cycling has been recognised for its role in reducing congestion (BITRE, 2014a, p. 140), there is very little scholarly analysis of the economic contribution of cycling. Figures compiled for the European Cycling Federation show that 650 000 people are employed in cycling-related industries in Western Europe, and a doubling of cycling would increase employment to over a million people (Blondiau & van Zeebroeck, 2014). In Chapter Six, 'Economics of everyday cycling and cycling facilities', Jungho Suh reflects on the market benefits of cycling as he reviews existing economic analyses of cycling. However, his chapter focuses specifically on the tools available to decision makers when determining the non-market benefits of cycling. Congested roads impose additional costs, as they make life unpleasant and difficult for people living in adjacent areas as well as for people seeking to travel on foot or by bicycle, an issue taken up in Chapter Seven, 'Cycling and sustainable transport', by Simon Kingham and Paul Tranter.

Finally, carbon emissions from the transport sector are growing. Across Australia and New Zealand, transport accounts for 42% and 27% of average household greenhouse gas emissions respectively (for example, see Department of Infrastructure and Transport, 2013a, p. 188; Romanos, Kerr, & Will 2014, pp. 13-14). Single-occupant private automobile use is a key target for sustainable transport policy and planning. The issues of travel practices, vehicle emissions and liveability interact in complex ways. Kingham and Tranter use a scalar approach to examine the human and environmental impacts of transport systems that are motor-vehicle oriented, and the significant role that even a modest shift to cycling might play in addressing these impacts.

Most contributors to this volume explore the role of cycling as an everyday means of transport, but in Chapter Eight, 'Cycle touring', Matthew Lamont elaborates on the breadth of cycle tourism. Cycle touring is highly developed in New Zealand, while in Australia there is a strong emphasis on cycling events, including professional and elite racing and organised community rides. Lamont provides an overview of current cycling research and examines the social, economic and environmental challenges that cycling might address.

The second part of the book focuses more closely on proposals to create cycle-friendly environments. It is in this second section that the ontological differences which inform various strands of cycling research become explicit.

Ontology and cycling research

Skimming the Contents page of this volume, it will be clear that contributors are working from different ontological positions. These differences are keenly debated among European scholars (for example, Cycling and Society forums), but they are rarely discussed in the Australasian cycling literature. Nonetheless, the differences are significant, as they determine the kinds of questions researchers ask about cycling and the recommendations they make about how to proceed — for instance, in terms of policies, programs, funding, further research and so forth. In this section, we discuss both realist and constructionist ontologies. However, we provide greater detail on constructionist positions precisely because they are not well represented in Australasian cycling research and it is timely to open a discussion between researchers working from different approaches.

Most chapters in this volume are grounded in realist ontology — that is, a view that reality exists independent of the individual and it is possible to produce objective knowledge about that reality (Petersen, 2014, p. 4). From this position, definitions — such as those for cycle tourism given in Matthew Lamont's chapter, and those for cycle paths in Glen Koorey's chapter (discussed further below) — serve to describe, as accurately as possible, the object under investigation. Further, the methodology employed by Johnson and Chong in their chapter is informed by a naturalistic theory which is grounded in realist ontology. Researchers working from realist positions often see their role as providing objective knowledge to assist individuals and political representatives in decision-making processes. Jan Garrard's chapter on evaluation (discussed later) provides an accessible account of the policy-making process from a realist ontological position.

By contrast, constructionist ontologies hold that the world does not exist independent of the individual. Rather, as individuals are born into an already-interpreted world, they and their interpretations of the world are necessarily shaped by socially available understandings (Irwin, 2011). Clearly, if interpretations of the world are socially produced then the knowledge created by researchers cannot be objective, but it is shaped by how it is possible to understand the world. For convenience, constructionist approaches can be distinguished into constructivism and social constructionism. Constructivists hold that individuals are 'actively engaged in the creation of their own phenomenal world' (Vivien Burr as cited in Bacchi, 2015, p. 5), so that their research focuses on 'the meaning-making activity of the individual' (Crotty, 1998, p. 58). Many researchers working from constructivist positions are interested in how individuals relate their own experiences to socially produced understandings of such experiences (for example, Davis, 2010). Australasian researchers Simone Fullagar (2012) and Kath Bicknell (2013) are exemplars of constructivist cycling research. Fullagar explores women's experiences of a cycling event, while Bicknell examines meaning making in the mountain biking blogosphere. In this volume, Matthew Lamont's chapter describes constructivist research as he foregrounds the different understandings cyclists attach to their physical and emotional experiences of cycle touring.

From a policy perspective, constructivists focus upon 'how people ... offer an interpretation of a problem' and the 'challenges they face in developing shared understandings of a problem' (Bacchi, 2015, p. 3). Constructivist cycling policy research might focus on the cultures of different stakeholder organisations and, given the problem definition processes that exist within these organisations, how it is possible for individual policy makers to frame cycling. For example, transport authorities may frame cycling in terms of efficient traffic flow; bicycle organisations may view it in terms of citizenship; hospital emergency staff may operate within a framework of injured bodies; and public health researchers may frame cycling in terms of exercise. Following Robert Hoppe, cycling might be regarded as one of those 'messy' or 'unstructured' problems whereby

> there is uncertainty about which disciplines, specialties, experts and skills to mobilize; conflicts over values abound; and many people get intensely involved, with strong but divisive opinions. (2002, p. 310)

Constructivist research into cycling might disentangle problem definition processes within stakeholder organisations and examine how individual policy makers engage with these processes. The objective of such research would be to reach across stakeholder boundaries and produce a single shared 'problematisation' that can be addressed in policy (Bacchi, 2015, p. 7).

By way of contrast, social constructionism 'emphasizes the extent to which our understandings of the world are the product of social forces' (Bacchi, 2015, p. 5). Instead of examining the individual's involvement in meaning making, social constructionists are interested in the social processes through which particular understandings of the world are produced and become pervasive. Three chapters in this volume employ a strand of social constructionism that emphasises how practices *produce* realities — in this view, there are multiple realities, and politics is involved in the production of what is taken to be 'reality' (the real). Both Annemarie Mol (1999) and John Law and Annemarie Mol (2008) use the term 'ontological politics' to describe *how* objects and subjects are produced or, to put it more precisely, to focus on the ongoing enactment of networks of strategic relations within which objects and subjects are produced (for example, see Bacchi & Bonham, 2014). These networks of relations involve heterogeneous elements (for example, people, activities, computers, tools, materials, words, images) across a range of sites (for example, households, laboratories, streets, universities); and it is in the enactment of specific arrangements of these elements across these sites that objects and subjects are given effect.

This position is not a denial of materiality nor is it a claim that we somehow invent reality, but it is a suggestion that 'realities are practised into being in heterogeneous networks of relations' (Law & Singleton, 2014, p. 388). For example, the cyclist is enacted in the field of transport in terms of origins, destinations, purposes, timing, trip distance and so forth. The cyclist is also enacted in the field of health in terms of disease history, cardiovascular function, duration, frequency and intensity of exercise effort. Cyclists are also enacted in the field of sport in terms of biomechanics, heart rate and lung capacity. Each of these fields has instruments — surveys, traffic sensors, blood pressure machines — which, following Annemarie Mol, interfere in, rather than describe, reality. Borrowing from Mol (2002, p. 117), the term 'cyclist' can be seen as a 'coordinating mechanism' that spans disciplinary boundaries and prevents the 'pluralising' of the bike-body assemblage into 'separate and unrelated objects', but each discipline brings a different version of the cyclist into effect. Clearly, if objects (and subjects) do not precede these various networks of relations but are enacted within them, then objects (and subjects) are fundamentally political (Law & Singleton, 2014, p. 380). They are political in terms of both the forging of the strategic relations which produce each version of the object (and subject), and the version of reality (in this case the transport or health cyclist) which becomes prioritised in policy.

Research informed by ontological politics foregrounds the fragility of objects and subjects usually taken as a self-evident phenomenon. The important point for a book on cycling is that different versions of cycling and cyclists are produced within different networks of relations, and these can challenge what has come to be taken for granted. The three chapters in this volume that take ontological politics as their starting point scrutinise key conceptual categories for how they are produced and what they make possible.

In the first chapter of Part II, 'Gender and cycling: Gendering cycling subjects and *forming* bikes, practices and spaces as gendered objects', Jennifer Bonham, Carol Bacchi and Thomas Wanner draw on poststructuralist and feminist insights to demonstrate the instability of gender categories. Their chapter reflects on the potential lived effects of gendering as the authors trace the various processes through which femininity and masculinity become attached to, and then detached from, bicycles, cycling practices and cycling spaces. In Chapter Ten, 'Making (up) the child cyclist: Bike Ed in South Australia', Anne Wilson examines how children and cyclists are produced as particular kinds of governable subjects in bicycle education ('Bike Ed') programs implemented in South Australia through the early 2000s. Wilson recommends making changes to bicycle education programs so that they foster cycling mobility rather than simply focusing on cycling 'safety'. Finally, in Chapter Eleven, 'More than a message: Producing cyclists through public safety advertising campaigns', Rachael Nielsen and Jennifer Bonham apply Carol Bacchi's 'What's the problem represented to be?' analytic strategy to examine how cyclists are constituted in drink-driving commercials aimed at youth. These authors provoke cycling scholars to reflect on how they produce cycling and cyclists within their work, as well as on the potential lived effects of their research practices. In questioning categories such as 'woman', 'child' and 'cyclist', they consider what these categories 'make possible, what they prohibit, and whether their transformation would open new creative possibilities of life' (Sellar, 2012, p. 96).

Despite Eva Petersen's (2014) concern over the reinstatement of the privileged position of realist ontologies, there may be productive ways in which scholars working from different positions can engage with each other's work to achieve socially and environmentally just outcomes. Research informed by either social constructionism or ontological politics not only assists in critiquing existing categories, but also opens alternative ways of constituting objects and subjects of cycling, and these might be taken up and pursued by those working from realist approaches.

Strategies for cycling

Providing new ways of thinking about 'cycling' is one strategy for fostering cycling. Another is to remind Australians and New Zealanders of our cycling past. A considerable literature now exists on our varied cycling histories, including the role of the bicycle in unsettling gender norms (Mackay, 2012; Simpson, 2007; Kinsey, 2011); framing contact between settlers and Indigenous populations (Clarsen, 2014); providing a new sector of employment (Fitzpatrick, 1980; Kennett, 2004); and changing expectations about the construction and regulations of roads (Kennett, 2004; Mackay, 2012). Amongst the broader community, relatively little is remembered of our cycling histories, but available evidence indicates that cycling once equalled and often exceeded levels currently seen in the leading cycling cities of Europe (Knott, 1994; Kennett, 2004). Despite the work currently being undertaken into cycling histories, there is still much to be done. Recovering these histories is one step in disrupting a motor-vehicle-oriented status quo and foregrounding the micro-political processes that have shaped contemporary travel practices across Australasia.

In his aforementioned chapter, Jim Fitzpatrick, Australia's foremost cycling historian, provides a glimpse of Australia's cycling history as he focuses on the introduction of the bicycle to Australia and its central role in rural Australia. Although Fitzpatrick's chapter is located in the first part of the book, it begins the process of recovering Australia's cycling past in order to take cycling into the future.

Following on from Fitzpatrick's work, an important question is whether cycling will suffer a reversal of fortunes as it has done in the past. Zack Furness (2010) provides an overview of the rise and fall of cycling in the United States over the past 120 years, and it may well be argued that, just as in the 1970s, the current interest in cycling will be short-lived not only in the United States but across the globe. However, it is instructive to examine how the 1970s 'rediscovery' of the bicycle was handled in the Netherlands. Cycling in Dutch cities in the 1970s was as precarious as it is in many Australian cities today (Directorate General for Passenger Transport, 1999, p. 30). The development of cycling knowledge by organisations such as Fietsersbond and CROW played an integral role in the formation of a cycling culture in the Netherlands (Jervis, forthcoming).

It seems that a key difference between interest in the twenty-first century in cycling and interest in the 1970s is the level of research currently being conducted into cycling, and active travel more broadly. A search of the Scopus database[1] shows a significant change in cycling-related literature published in the past five years. Of the 47 cycling publications identified in 1995, three-quarters (35 publications, or 74%) were published in sports medicine, physiology and biomechanics journals, and were focused on sport cycling. The number of peer-reviewed publications more than doubled by 2009, but they remained overwhelmingly concerned with medical and physiological aspects of cycling.

However, since 2010, an average of 206 cycling-related articles, book chapters and conference papers have been published each year, and 50% or

---

[1] This database searches peer-reviewed literature and includes more than 20 000 journals, books and conference proceedings.

more of these have investigated cycling as an everyday activity (Bonham, 2014). Cycling research now appears across a wide range of disciplines including sociology, anthropology, psychology, engineering, transport, urban planning, road safety, geography and public health. There have also been a plethora of studies undertaken by, or on behalf of, government and non-government organisations at local, state and national levels. The authority attached to academic and government-sponsored literature about cycling elevates its status as a field of research; and as this research is distributed across the media, government departments, community organisations and so forth, cycling is brought into everyday thinking. As individuals become practised in thinking about their mobility in relation to cycling, a space is opened up for more people to take up cycling. Beyond its policy impacts, the production and distribution of cycling research will itself bring about change.

Cycling journeys are often categorised in terms of transport, recreation, sport and so forth. However, like all journeys, the journey by bicycle is often many journeys in one. The habit of prioritising 'transport' as the essential meaning or element of the journey operates to marginalise other qualities and possibilities of the journey. The process of excising and creating knowledge about particular characteristics, qualities and practices over others — such as distance of a journey rather than calories used, people encountered, serotonin produced — is political. Such apparently innocuous processes have profound effects. Drawing on the governmentality theorists (Miller & Rose, 1990; Dean, 1999), the knowledge created through these processes — both the 'how' and the 'what' — both shapes how individuals can think about their journeys and renders mobility governable (Bonham, 2006). Scholars conducting research into cycling and active travel more generally are challenging traditional transport studies as they incorporate a new range of embodied responses, social engagement and environmental interactions into the journey. These discussions serve to demonstrate how the bicycle is integral to the process of reconstituting 'the journey' to include health, economic and social opportunities, as well as environmental interactions. As these scholars constitute journeys in new ways, they enable a shift in how the mobility of populations is governed.

Turning to more explicit strategies for bringing about change, in recent years researchers have directed attention away from 'anticipating' the future toward a critical interrogation of *how*, at different scales of analysis (from the sub-cellular level through to society level), practices of anticipating the future bring that future into the present (Clough, Goldberg, Schiff, Weeks, & Willse, 2007; Anderson, 2010). Geographer Ben Anderson is fundamentally concerned with socio-spatial relations when he describes three practices of anticipating the future: 'calculating', 'imagining' and 'performing' (2010, pp. 783-787). All three practices are widely used in 'anticipating' mobility futures, and they are not mutually exclusive. For instance, the enumeration which informs calculating practices (such as trend analysis, cost-benefit analysis and impact assessment) is also used to inform imagining practices (for example, CAD models, visioning and scenario planning) and performing practices (for example, simulations, exercises and games). It is precisely these practices that bring the future into the present. As an example, the graph that tracks and then forecasts levels of motor vehicle use (see, for example, BITRE, 2014b) brings the future of motor vehicle use (whether high, low or static) into the present. Although these practices do not necessarily *cause* a particular future to come about, Anderson argues they give us pause to consider what life (or lives) and ways of living are valued in these futures and how the places we live in are gradually shaped by the constant folding of the future into the present (pp. 787 & 793).

Following Anderson, the future of cycling in Australia and New Zealand is already being created. The decisions taken on a day-to-day basis provide opportunities, or not, for cycling. Tactics such as budgeting for cycle tracks as an integral part of all new freeway projects, reducing speed limits, resuming car parking spaces for cycle parking spaces (City of Adelaide, 2012), and creating standards which invert the road hierarchy so that walking, cycling and public transport are fostered ahead of private automobile use (City of Yarra, 2006) operate to alter existing socio-spatial relations and make a different future possible. The final chapters of this book pay particular attention to measures that re-engineer relations between people, vehicles, buildings, street furniture, paint, vegetation, tarmac and so forth, and how these new arrangements produce new effects. There is a steadily growing literature on shared cycle-pedestrian spaces (for example, Haworth & Schramm, 2011; Brooks, 2013) and creating on-road conditions for cyclists (for example, Patterson, 2010; Cumming, 2012; McDonald, 2012). In Chapter Twelve, 'Spaces for cycling', Glen Koorey addresses on-road cycling treatments and how the familiar features of roads (signs, lines, surfaces and so on) can be, and are being, reordered to produce more inclusive travel spaces. Koorey's practical advice is informed by a wealth of research from engineering and related spatial disciplines. By contrast, in Chapter Thirteen, 'Off-road cycling infrastructure', Narelle Haworth brings a psychological perspective to the infrastructure discussion as she examines the role that off-road infrastructure can play in facilitating cycling.

Chapters Fourteen, Fifteen and Sixteen, by Geoff Rose, by Wendy Bell and Donna Ferretti, and by Hilary Hamnett respectively, explore the cycling-related knowledge required by professionals working in key spatial disciplines. In 'Teaching Australian civil engineers about cycling', Rose has made a detailed analysis of the university courses available to engineers wanting to pursue careers in traffic and transport planning. His work demonstrates the need to rethink our current efforts to educate professionals working in the areas of traffic and transport policy and planning. Wendy Bell and Donna Ferretti continue the focus on socio-spatial relations in Chapter Fifteen, 'What should planners know about cycling?', as they demonstrate how strategic plans across Australia and New Zealand are using health, environmental and economic discourses to make the case for increasing cycling. However, Bell and Ferretti argue that strategic planning goals are not being adequately or appropriately written into planning policy and, consequently, cannot be used to implement change in the development assessment process. They provide a guide on what planners need to know to translate strategic objectives into local contexts and transform mobility in cities and towns. In 'Skilling landscape architects and urban designers for design of bicycle parking and network facilities', Hilary Hamnett provides practical advice for landscape architects and urban designers on how to address the needs of cyclists at the beginning and end points of the journey. Hamnett has examined the plethora of 'bicycle design codes' to identify treatments appropriate to the Australasian context. Many of the treatments she recommends could be written into development plans to assist land use planners when they assess development applications. In each of these chapters, the authors emphasise the need for collaboration amongst built environment professionals.

Alongside infrastructure and professional development, further research is required into the role of legal processes and knowledge in establishing and continuing to stabilise current mobility norms. A considerable body of historical research exists on how certain mobility practices (such as the efficient journey) and affordances (such as motor vehicles) have been normalised as they have been incorporated into statutes and court processes (see for example, Bonham, 2000; 2006; Jain, 2004; Norton, 2008). However, this research has been undertaken by geographers, historians and anthropologists rather than academics in law, and there is very little work on the ongoing, day-to-day enactment of statutes and court processes which stabilise or disrupt prevailing travel practices. Studies have been undertaken by market researchers and social scientists into community responses to particular cycling-related laws, such as the Queensland Government's trial of the legislative amendment to specify a minimum distance when drivers overtake cyclists in 2014 (Queensland Government, 2014)[2]. Australasian law academics (for example, Butler, 2008) have examined the relationship between the law, the production of norms, and road users/road space; but only Dent (2012) explicitly includes cyclists in his study. In Chapter Seventeen of this book, 'Cycling and Australian law', Margaret Grant, a legal practitioner, opens another front in the conversation on cycling and the law. Grant's chapter addresses current debates within the Australasian community, such as the law's impact on, and role in, cyclist safety and the issue of liability.

The substantive chapters in this volume are brought to a close with a contribution by Jan Garrard. In 'Evaluating cycle promotion interventions', Garrard discusses the importance of evaluation in developing an evidence base for action which aims to increase community-level cycling participation. Evaluation is essential if we are to determine the effectiveness of a program, yet often it is 'tacked on' at the end of a program and insufficiently funded. Garrard focuses on the evaluation of cycling interventions that specifically target cycling for transport, and highlights the importance of a reflective practice in cycling intervention evaluation. She identifies the need for evaluation to assess whether an intervention has been effective as well as, importantly, the reasons *why* the outcomes were achieved. Her chapter provides a critical review of evaluation approaches, and demonstrates the need for evaluation to be built into program planning to ensure that the effectiveness (or ineffectiveness) of actions are adequately determined.

---

[2] This legislation requires that drivers leave a minimum distance when overtaking cyclists (1 metre in speed zones up to 60 km/h and 1.5 metres in speed zones over 60 km/h). For more information, see http://www.tmr.qld.gov.au/Travel-and-transport/Cycling/Parliamentary-inquiry-into-cycling-issues.aspx.

Bringing the future into the present

The discipline of transport developed after World War II with tools of trade — investigative techniques, models, concepts and language — conducive to a motorised mobility future. Today a new set of social, environmental and economic issues demands innovation in our tools of trade. Cycling research in Australia and New Zealand is engaged in developing these new tools, and the field has rapidly expanded over the past decade. This volume provides an overview of the current status of cycling research for scholars, practitioners, cycling advocates and policy makers already working in the field. Some contributors have focused on reviewing cycling research in their discipline and provided suggestions for further work. Other contributors have undertaken new research specifically for this book or reported the latest findings from their current work.

Cycling futures also provides a starting point for people new to cycling studies, as each contributor recommends questions for further investigation within her/his particular field. Cycling research is being conducted by scholars from a range of disciplines including geography, public health, anthropology, engineering, sociology, road safety and psychology. We would encourage many more disciplines to join the conversation, and to this end we have invited practitioners from law, urban and regional planning, as well as urban design and landscape architecture, to take up the discussion in their respective fields. We anticipate that the chapters in this volume will bring more participants into the global conversation on cycling.

References

Aarts, L, & Van Schagen, I. (2006). Driving speed and the risk of road crashes: A review. *Accident Analysis & Prevention*, 38(2), 215-224.

Anderson, B. (2010). Preemption, precaution, preparedness: Anticipatory action and future geographies. *Progress in Human Geography*, 34(6), 777-798.

Australian Bicycle Council and Austroads. (2015). Australian cycling participation 2015. Retrieved 10 November 2015 from https://www.onlinepublications.austroads.com.au/items/AP-C91-15.

Australian Institute of Health and Welfare [AIHW]. (2013). *Overweight and obesity*. Retrieved 28 October 2013 from http://www.aihw.gov.au/overweight-and-obesity.

Australian Sports Commission. (2011). *Participation in exercise, recreation and sport: Annual report 2010*. Australia: Standing Committee on Recreation and Sport.

Bacchi, C. (2015). The turn to problematization: Political implications of contrasting interpretive and poststructural adaptations. *Open Journal of Political Science*, 5(1), 11 pages. doi: 10.4236/ojps.2015.51001.

Bacchi, C, & Bonham, J. (2014). Reclaiming discursive practices as an analytic focus: Political implications. *Foucault Studies*, 17, 179-192.

Beroud, B, & Anaya, E. (2012). Private interventions in a public service: An analysis of public bicycle schemes. In J Parkin (Ed.), *Cycling and sustainability* (pp. 269-301). Bingley, UK: Emerald Group.

Bicknell, K. (2013). Everybody's writing. *Proceedings of the Fifth Australian Cycling Conference*. Retrieved 13 April 2015 from http://www.australian cyclingconference.org/images/proceedings/ACC-2013-proceedings.pdf.

Blondiau, T, & van Zeebroeck, B. (2014). *Cycling works: Jobs and job creation in the cycling economy*. Brussels: European Cyclists' Federation.

Bonham, J. (2000, April 13-15). Safety and speed: Ordering the street of transport. In C Garnaut, & S Hamnett (Eds.), *Fifth Australian Urban History/Planning History Conference — Proceedings* (pp. 54-66). Adelaide: The University of South Australia.

Bonham, J. (2006). Transport: Disciplining the body that travels. *The Sociological Review*, 54 (Supplement 1), 55-74.

Bonham, J. (2014). Rethinking urban mobility: Street spaces and cycling futures [blog post with video, Research Tuesday public lecture series, The University of Adelaide]. Retrieved 13 April 2015 from http://blogs.adelaide.edu.au/researchtuesdays/2014/09/09/the-streets-are-alive.

Brooks, C. (2013). Shared paths: Perceived and actual conflicts. *Proceedings of the Fifth Australian Cycling Conference*. Retrieved 13 April 2015 from http://www.australian cyclingconference.org/images/proceedings/ACC-2013-proceedings.pdf.

Brussel, M, & Zuidgeest, M. (2012). Cycling in developing countries: Context, challenges and policy relevant research. In J Parkin (Ed.), *Cycling and sustainability* (pp. 181-216). Bingley, UK: Emerald Group.

Bureau of Infrastructure, Transport and Regional Economics [BITRE]. (2007). *Estimating urban traffic and congestion cost trends for Australian cities*. Working paper 71. Canberra: BITRE.

Bureau of Infrastructure, Transport and Regional Economics. (2014a). *Trends: Infrastructure and transport to 2030.* Canberra: BITRE.

Bureau of Infrastructure, Transport and Regional Economics. (2014b) *Long term trends in Urban Public Transport.* Canberra: BITRE.

Butler, C. (2008). Slicing through space: Mobility, rhythm and the abstraction of modernist transport planning. *Griffith Law Review*, 17(2), 470-487.

Chen, L, Chen, C, Srinivasan, R, McKnight, C, Ewing, R, & Roe, M. (2012). Evaluating the safety effects of bicycle lanes in New York City. *American Journal of Public Health*, 102(6), 1120-1127.

Chidoka, OB. (2012). Cycling as an urban transportation solution: Federal road safety corps effort in Nigeria. *Proceedings of the Fourth Australian Cycling Conference.* Retrieved 13 April 2015 from http://www.australiancyclingconference.org/images/proceedings/ acc-2012-proceedings.pdf.

City of Adelaide. (2012). *Smart move: Transport and movement strategy 2012-2022.* Adelaide: City of Adelaide.

City of Yarra. (2006). *Strategic transport statement.* Richmond: City of Yarra.

Clarsen, G. (2014). Pedaling power: Bicycles, subjectivities and landscapes in a settler colonial society. *Mobilities.* doi: 10.1080/17450101.2014.927201.

Clough, P, Goldberg, G, Schiff, R, Weeks, A, & Willse, C. (2007). Notes toward a theory of affect-itself. *Ephemera: Theory & Politics in Organization*, 7(1), 60-77.

Colagiuri, S, Lee, CM, Colagiuri, R, Magliano, D, Shaw, JE, Zimmet, PZ & Caterson, ID. (2010). The cost of overweight and obesity in Australia. *The Medical Journal of Australia*, 192(5), 260-264.

Council of Australian Governments [COAG]. (2006). *Review of urban congestion: Trends, impacts and solutions.* Canberra: Commonwealth of Australia.

Cresswell, T. (2006). *On the move: The politics of mobility in the modern west.* London: Routledge.

Crotty, M. (1998). *The foundations of social research: Meaning and perspective in the research process.* London: Sage Publications.

Cumming, B. (2012). A bicycle friendly roundabout: Designing to direct cyclists to ride where drivers look. *Proceedings of the Fourth Australian Cycling Conference.* Retrieved 13 April from http://www.australiancyclingconference.org/images/ proceedings/acc-2012-proceedings.pdf.

Davis, K. (2010, July 13). Accounting for disappointment: Biographical choices re-visited. *XVII ISA World Congress of Sociology: The Role of Transnational Public Intellectuals*, Gothenburg, Sweden.

Dean, M. (1999). *Governmentality: Power and rule in modern society*. London: Sage.

Dent, C. (2012). Relationships between laws, norms and practices: The case of road behaviour. *Griffith Law Review*, 21(3), 708-727.

Department of Infrastructure and Transport. (2013a). *State of Australian cities 2013*. Canberra: Commonwealth of Australia.

Department of Infrastructure and Transport. (2013b). *Walking, riding and access to public transport: Supporting active travel in Australian communities*. Canberra: Commonwealth of Australia.

Dickinson, J, & Lumsdon, L. (2010). *Slow travel and tourism*. Washington DC: Earthscan.

Directorate General for Passenger Transport. (1999). *The Dutch Bicycle Master Plan*. Netherlands: Ministry of Transport, Public Works and Water Management. Retrieved 23 July 2015 from http://www.fietsberaad.nl/library/repository/bestanden/The%20Dutch%20Bicycle%20Master%20Plan%201999.pdf.

Elvik, R, Christensen, P, & Amundsen, A. (2004). *Speed and road accidents: An evaluation of the Power Model*. TØI report 740. Institute of Transport Economics [TOI].

Fitzpatrick, J. (1980). *The bicycle and the bush: Man and machine in rural Australia*. Melbourne: Oxford University Press.

Fullagar, S. (2012). Gendered cultures of slow travel: Women's cycle touring as alternative hedonism. In S Fullagar, & KW Markwell (Eds.), *Slow tourism: Experiences and mobilities* (pp. 99-112). Bristol: Channel View Publications.

Furness, Z. (2010). *One less car: Bicycling and the politics of automobility*. Philadelphia: Temple University Press.

Haixiao, P. (2012). Evolution of urban bicycle transport policy in China. In J Parkin (Ed.), *Cycling and sustainability* (pp. 161-180). Bingley, UK: Emerald Group.

Haworth, N, & Schramm, A. (2011). Adults cycling on the footpath: What do the data show? *Australasian Road Safety Research, Policing and Education Conference*. Retrieved 13 April from http://casr.adelaide.edu.au/rsr.

Henley, G, & Harrison, J. (2012). *Serious injury due to land transport, Australia 2007-08*. Injury research and statistics Series no. 59. Cat. no. INJCAT 135. Canberra: AIHW.

Hidalgo, D, & Huizenga, C. (2013). Implementation of sustainable urban transport in Latin America. *Research in Transportation Economics*, 40(1), 66-77.

Hoppe, R. (2002). Cultures of public policy problems. *Journal of Comparative Policy Analysis: Research and Practice*, 4(3), 305-326.

Irwin, A. (2011). Social constructionism. In R Wodak, B Johnstone, & P Kerswill (Eds.), *Sage handbook of sociolinguistics* (pp. 100-113). London: Sage.

Jain, S. (2004). Dangerous instrumentality: The bystander as subject in automobility. *Cultural Anthropology*, 19(1), 61-94.

Jervis, C. (forthcoming). *Cycling practices: A comparative approach to policy development in Australia and the Netherlands* (Doctoral Thesis, The University of Adelaide, Australia).

Kennett, J. (2004). *Ride: The story of cycling in New Zealand*. Wellington: Kennett Brothers.

Kidd, B. (2013). How many Japanese cycle to work? Retrieved 6 February 2015 from http://www.tokyobybike.com/2013/10/how-many-japanese-cycle-to-work.html.

Kinsey, F. (2011). Stamina, speed and adventure: Australian women and competitive cycling in the 1890s. *The International Journal of the History of Sport*, 28(10), 1375-1387.

Knott, J. (1994). Speed, modernity and the motor car: The making of the 1909 motor traffic act in New South Wales. *Australian Historical Studies*, 26(103), 221-241.

Kuschel, G, Metcalfe, J, Wilton, E, Guria, J, Hales, S, Rolfe, K, & Woodward, A. (2012). *Updated Health and Air Pollution in New Zealand Study, Vol. 1*. Summary report prepared for Health Research Council of New Zealand, Ministry of Transport, Ministry for the Environment and New Zealand Transport Agency. Retrieved 13 April 2015 from www.hapinz.org.nz.

Law, J, & Singleton, V. (2014). ANT, multiplicity and policy. *Critical Policy Studies*, 8(4), 379-396.

Law, J, & Mol, A. (2008). The actor-enacted: Cumbrian sheep in 2001. In C Knappett, & L Malafouris (Eds.), *Material agency: Towards a non-anthropocentric approach* (pp. 57-78). Düsseldorf: Springer.

Mackay, J. (2012). Bicycles — Cycle clubs, advocacy and accidents. Retrieved 17 January 2015 from http://www.TeAra.govt.nz/en/bicycles/page-4.

McDonald, A. (2012, January 16-17). A car is 1.9m wide. How much extra space does it really need? *Proceedings of the Fourth Australian Cycling Conference*. Retrieved 13 April 2015 from http://www.australian cyclingconference.org/images/proceedings/acc-2012-proceedings.pdf.

Miller, P, & Rose, N. (1990). Governing economic life. *Economy and Society*, 19(1), 1-31.

Ministry of Transport. (2013). *New Zealand household travel survey 2009-2013 — Cycling*. Retrieved 24 July 2015 from http://www.transport.govt.nz/assets/Import/Documents/Cycling-2013.pdf.

Mokhtarian, P, Salomon, I, & Lothlorien, R. (2001). Understanding the demand for travel: It's not purely 'Derived'. *Innovation: The European Journal of Social Science Research*, 14(4), 355-380.

Mol, A. (1999). Ontological politics: A word and some questions. *Sociological Review* 47 (Supplement 1), 74-89.

Mol, A. (2002). *The body multiple: Ontology in medical practice*. Durham and London: Duke University Press.

Norton, P. (2008). *Fighting traffic: The dawn of the motor age in the American city*. Cambridge, MA: The MIT Press.

Oddy, N. (1996). Bicycles. In P Kirkham (Ed.), *The gendered object* (pp. 60-69). Manchester: Manchester University Press.

Oddy, N. (2007). The flaneur on wheels? In D Horton, P Rosen, & P Cox (Eds.), *Cycling and society* (pp. 97-112). Aldershot, UK: Ashgate.

Patterson, F. (2010). Cycling and roundabouts: An Australian perspective. *Road and Transport Research*, 19(2), 4-19.

Petersen, EB. (2014). What crisis of representation? Challenging the realism of post-structuralist policy research in education. *Critical Studies in Education*, 56(1), 147-160. doi: 10.1080/17508487.2015.983940.

Pucher, J, & Buehler, R. (2008). Making cycling irresistible: Lessons from the Netherlands, Denmark, and Germany. *Transport Reviews*, 28(4), 495-528.

Queensland Government response to the Transport, Housing and Local Government Committee's Report No. 39 — Inquiry into cycling issues: A new direction for cycling in Queensland. Retrieved from http://www.parliament.qld.gov.au/documents/committees/THLGC/2014/INQ-CYC/gr-28May2014.pdf.

Romanos, C, Kerr, S, & Campbell, W. (2014). *Greenhouse gas emissions in New Zealand: A preliminary consumption-based analysis*. Wellington, NZ: Motu Economic and Public Policy Research.

Sellar, B. (2012). Occupation and ideology. In G Whiteford, & C Hocking (Eds.), *Occupational science: Society, inclusion, participation* (pp. 86-99). Chichester: Wiley-Blackwell.

Simpson, C. (2007). Capitalising on curiosity: Women's professional cycle racing in the late nineteenth century. In D Horton, P Rosen, & P Cox (Eds.), *Cycling and society.* (pp. 47-65). Aldershot, UK: Ashgate.

Transport for London. (2013). *Central London cycle census: Technical note*. London: Transport for London.

Wang, R. (2011a). Shaping carpool policies under rapid motorization: The case of Chinese cities. *Transport Policy, 18*(4), 631-635.

Wang, R. (2011b). Autos, transit and bicycles: Comparing the costs in large Chinese cities. *Transport Policy, 18*(1), 139-146.

Zacharias, J. (2002). Bicycle in Shanghai: Movement patterns, cyclist attitudes and the impact of traffic separation. *Transport Reviews, 22*(3), 309-322.

2 A glimpse at Australia's cycling history

Jim Fitzpatrick

Introduction

The island continent of Australia and the bicycle seem almost to have been made for one another. The machine was widely adopted from 1890, and over the next three decades was routinely ridden over greater distances as part of daily rural life than anywhere else on earth.[1] By 1896 there was an extensive and well-used bicycle path network in Western Australia that linked communities over an area of some 350 000 km^2, one and a half times the size of Victoria — the largest such bicycle path system in the world at the time (Fitzpatrick, 1980a, pp. 110-116). At the turn of the twentieth century, cycle racing — centred in Europe and North America — was the most popular, lucrative and widely followed sport internationally. Yet, half a world away, Australia sponsored the world's richest race and still hosts the oldest continuous track race, the Austral Wheel, and the second-oldest road race, the Melbourne to Warrnambool, in existence (Fitzpatrick, 2011, p. 85). As well, the

---

[1] In 45 years of researching and writing about cycling history I am unaware of any published material or suggestion that the bicycle was used in any other rural environment in the manner, to the extent, or across the distances it was used in Australia over that period. For example, in personal correspondence (cited in Fitzpatrick, 1978b, pp. 20-21) Robert Smith, author of *A social history of the bicycle, its early life and times in America* (1972), stated that he had seen no evidence of a comparable rural use in the United States.

bicycle saw its first significant military use during the Boer War of 1899-1902, in which experienced Australian bush cyclists demonstrated the machine's wartime value (Fitzpatrick, 1998, pp. 67-70).

This chapter presents an overview of Australian cycling history, from the early high wheeler to the present day. It considers the machine's utilitarian nature and effectiveness in the Australian environment. It reviews its social impact, both rural and urban, and role in the development of modern tourism and road maps. It surveys the bicycle craze of the 1890s, and its unique employment on the West Australian goldfields, including the cycle messenger services and camel pad interaction. It looks at the bicycle's widespread adoption by rural workers through the early twentieth century, the machine's decline in use by 1970, and its subsequent resurgence.

A remarkable cycling history

Australia's first cycling phase was occasioned by the introduction of the high wheeler or penny-farthing cycles (also known as ordinaries) in 1875, with Melbourne the premier centre. In 1884, Alf Edward became the first person to cycle from Melbourne to Sydney, taking eight and a half days. Australia's most famous high wheeler cyclist was George Burston who, with HR Stokes, undertook a round-the-world journey in 1888, and was among the few world cyclists to do so (Burston & Stokes, 1890). By a combination of ship and overland travel they went via Java, Singapore, Penang, Rangoon, India, Egypt, Palestine, Asia Minor, Sicily, Europe, the British Isles and America. However, being very expensive and difficult to ride, high wheelers were essentially limited to a small segment of society.

In contrast, in 1885 came the relatively affordable safety bicycle, so named because with its two equal-sized wheels and low seating position it was much easier and safer to ride. It was a technological marvel. The deceptively delicate-looking device encompassed such recent innovations as the ball bearing, tubular steel frame, roller bearing chain, and tangentially spoked wheel. In 1888, the pneumatic tyre was invented. The bicycle was lightweight and proved strong, durable, reliable and capable of operating with a minimum of maintenance. Although it was the product of some advanced manufacturing processes, any reasonably competent handyman could assemble and repair it. Of great importance, the bicycle could, where necessary, function with makeshift repairs (see Bijker, 1997, for a fuller discussion of cycle technology).

A glimpse at Australia's cycling history

The first safety bicycle recorded in Australia was one that Joseph Pearson imported into New South Wales in 1887 (Pearson, 1925, p. 14); and by 1890, pneumatic-tyred bicycles were commercially available in Melbourne. The safety bicycle's speed and progressively decreasing cost resulted in its quickly capturing the Australian imagination. By 1895, the colonies found themselves in the midst of the world bicycle boom and the concurrent cycling craze (Fitzpatrick, 1992, pp. 111-112), and the changes the machine wrought in colonial society caught the public up in debates and arguments that were already going on abroad (Smith, 1972; Oddy, 2007).

Riding schools were established, with imported European cycle instructors to help aspiring cyclists learn to ride properly. Arguments were mounted and countered as to which was the best food and drink for cyclists; some contained cocaine. Some clergymen questioned the morality of Sunday cycling; to counter them, scores of churchgoers were quickly organised to ride to church. Mrs Hotson Tate's Massage Boudoir promised to develop cyclists' strength and elasticity and banish fatigue, with testimonials from leading Melbourne doctors. Cyclistes, as female riders were then commonly known, took to the streets, raising many questions about the wearing of bloomers versus skirts, and about the morals and physical effects of cycling on women, especially their womanhood. Another issue was the question of who would chaperone women on the 100-kilometres-a-day trips that had now become possible (Fitzpatrick, 1980c, pp. 12-17).

Cycle racing became big business and gripped the public imagination to a degree almost incomprehensible today. In Melbourne, crowds of 40 000 to 65 000 turned out for the two-day annual Austral Wheel and Australian Natives' Association cycle races (Figure 2.1). However, women were not professional participants Down Under (Fitzpatrick, 1979a, pp. 326-342), in contrast to women in some other countries.[2] The publishing world saw the creation of many cycle magazines, every colony having at least one, and several being in print in Victoria. Most newspapers and magazines had a cycling column and an occasional editorial discussing the machine. The bicycle was advocated, lampooned, criticised, supported or denounced through cartoons, stories, poems and articles, and thus added new elements to the Australian language (Fitzpatrick, 1981, pp. 65-69).

---

[2] See Simpson (2007) for a discussion of overseas experiences.

Current challenges

Figure 2.1: Cycle racing crowd, late 1890s. Exhibition Ground, Melbourne, Victoria. (Source: La Trobe Collection, State Library of Victoria, CB5/6/14/6.)

The pneumatic-tyred safety bicycle opened up mass tourism in Australia. With men and women able to pedal 100 kilometres a day and more, weekend and holiday trips were feasible, unconfined to railway, riverboat or coaching routes. An immediate result was that many found themselves on country roads — until then the province of local residents, coachmen, teamsters and commercial travellers who knew where they were going — with few signs indicating which road led where, or how far it was to the next community. There was also little information available as to eating and sleeping facilities. The early riders quickly built up a store of information, and groups such as the New South Wales Cyclists' Touring Union were established. They enrolled members, contracted for local representatives in country towns to assist tourists passing through, negotiated discounts at hotels for club members, offered tips on touring and advised on the care of bicycles.

The modern road map — designed specifically to inform travellers of road surface conditions, distances, directions and facilities *en route* — was developed by and for cycle tourists. In the process, cyclists established the basic principles upon which later motoring organisations, such as the Automobile Association in England, were founded. In 1896, Joseph Pearson produced the first New

South Wales road map[3], and was instrumental in producing the two-volume *Cyclists' handbook and guide to the roads of New South Wales* in 1898 (New South Wales Cyclists' Touring Union, 1898), which was the most comprehensive, and astonishingly detailed, touring guide in Australia. In 1896, George Broadbent also published his first road map of Victoria, and with continual revisions his maps became the Victorian standard for many decades.[4] Close to 200 000 road maps had been printed in Australia by 1910, at which time there were only about 5000 motor vehicles in the country. Both men provided the impetus for the establishment of their respective state tourist bureaus (Fitzpatrick, 1980b; 1982).

The utilitarian machine

The climate over much of Australia permits year-round cycling. Even in settled areas, only a few railway lines existed (there were none over some three-quarters of the country), and inland water transport was essentially limited to the Murray-Darling River system in the south-east. That left vast spaces to be crossed by walking, riding a horse, travelling by horse-drawn vehicle, or (to a minor extent) using a camel. Teamsters and carting contractors routinely trod thousands of miles annually alongside their bullock or horse teams or pack camels. Rural workers such as shearers, rouseabouts, prospectors, commercial travellers, ministers and others who served the scattered population were perennially on the move, often walking between various properties and mining centres. In 1893, two riders cycled from the Gulf of Carpentaria to Sydney (a distance of over 2600km), demonstrating the bicycle's practicality in difficult outback conditions. With so many people travelling so far as part of their work routine, the machine quickly proved itself a superb personal transport device.

The concept of 'bicycling' is fundamental to understanding the role of the energy-efficient machine in Australia (and elsewhere). A cyclist is not a person on wheels, but a person with wheels. There is an immense difference. While 'riding a

---

[3] This map was provided as a photographic plate in the July 1896 issue of the *Review of Reviews* (p. 26), currently available for viewing at the Mitchell Library Reading Room in the State Library of New South Wales.

[4] Both men were also pioneer cyclists. Broadbent was among the first to pedal into the Alps in south-eastern Australia from the Victorian side, and Pearson estimated that he rode 180 000 miles during his lifetime, including the first full bicycle ascent of Mount Kosciusko (elevation: 2229m) in 1900.

bicycle' is the usual image, bicycling is essentially a human-machine combination that allows mode to be matched to terrain, optimising the use of wheel and foot. When sand, mud, obstacles, high winds or a steep incline make pedalling difficult, the rider can get off and walk. The cycle can be pushed, carried, lifted over fences and floated across rivers. Moreover, man and machine can be readily carried on wagons, trucks, cars, boats or trains. It was this combination that added a new element to the human travel equation in the 1890s.

Travellers often carried considerable weight on their bicycles. Luggage was initially secured on the handlebars and within the frame, as fixed wheel riders kept the rear wheel clear for a safe backward dismount if they lost control of rapidly spinning pedals. By 1899, freewheels with backpedal brakes were coming into use, enabling much bulkier loads to be carried over the rear wheel. Weights of 25 to 35 kilograms were common and sometimes cyclists carried much more (one imperial gallon weighs 4.5 kilograms, and waterbags hanging under the crossbar were a standard item for rural travel).

The bicycle's utility lay in not being restricted to formed roads. Cyclists rode on dry lake beds as level as billiard tables, and on rough, dried clay surfaces. Bush tracks padded down by the passing of strings of camels provided paths so smooth they could be walked on barefooted. In contrast, bullock teams and wagons could severely cut up road surfaces. Sand provided the worst riding conditions for most cyclists, though after rains set it, it could provide a good riding surface. Nonetheless, over a variety of surface conditions, the riders pushed on to wherever they were going.[5] In the process, the pneumatic-tyred machine added a new dimension to plant dispersal across the countryside (Fitzpatrick, 1979b, p. 61).

The West Australian goldfields

In September 1892, gold was discovered 550 kilometres east of Perth at Coolgardie, and over the next few years the Western Australian goldfields were the scene of the world's largest gold rush. The fields covered an area of some 350 000 square kilometres, one and a half times the size of the state of Victoria. Most of the area was flat, arid and hot — the town of Marble Bar now holds the world record of

---

[5] Cyclists' experiences of various Australian riding surfaces are described in great detail in many sections of Fitzpatrick, 1978b and 1980a.

Figure 2.2: Cyclists in Kalgoorlie, Western Australia, 1895.
(Source: West Australian Newspapers Limited.)

100 °F (37.8 °C) or more for 160 consecutive days — and the scarcity and high cost of water and stockfeed made the upkeep of horses often difficult. This was reflected in the columns of the early newspapers, where there were comments on the number of dead and dying animals in the streets.

In those circumstances, the bicycle played a role unlike anywhere else in the world at the time. Kalgoorlie's *Western Argus* editorialised that '[o]ne of the great institutions in the district is the trusty bicycle, a machine which is daily becoming more useful' (see Figure 2.2).[6] It was quickly adopted for travel and prospecting throughout the fields. After one man pegged his claim, the *Coolgardie Miner* commented that 'he was surrounded by the usual crowd of peggars on bike, buggy, cart and shanks' pony'. At a deep lead discovery, the roads were described as crowded with 'cyclists, buggies, etc.'. A Coolgardie writer estimated that the town 'had more bicycles in proportion to population than any other Australian town'. A visitor to Cue, which lay 650 kilometres north-west, commented that '[t]he first thing that struck [me] ... was the number of bicycles in use ... [E]veryone seemed in too much

---

[6] All quoted material in this paragraph is as cited in Fitzpatrick 1980a, pp. 166-171.

of a hurry to walk'. Another writer's first impression was that 'bustling merchants and clerks were hurrying past on bicycles to their various occupations'.

The cycling telegraph

Residents corresponded with friends, the press reported the fortunes of the fields, and large-scale mining investment and development depended upon information exchange. The rapid growth of the goldfields and the ephemeral nature of many mining communities made it hard to rationally allocate the available postal and telegraphic staff and services. Amidst this erratic and unsatisfactory situation, many bicycle delivery services were started in 1893. They ranged from major networks to individual riders taking casual orders. Some services pedalled mail, newspapers and parcels on specific, scheduled routes. Some were partially subsidised by mining companies to assure regular service to their district. In addition, 'special' messages could be contracted at any time.

The forte of the cycle messengers was rapid delivery throughout an immense area. David Carnegie noted that the cyclists could travel 160 kilometres in a day (Carnegie, 1898, p. 119), and WB Kimberley observed that cyclists were preferred over horses and camels for delivering urgent messages (Kimberly, 1897, p. 322). The speed and endurance of the cycle riders was marvelled at in the circumstances. The 190-kilometre ride over the notoriously sandy route from Coolgardie to Southern Cross (the inland terminus of the telegraph line for some time) was completed in 12 hours, in contrast to the record camel ride of 21 hours. Percy Armstrong established a Special Bicycle Express service in the goldfields in 1893, and on one occasion rode 550 kilometres in three days. A writer who examined the company's books concluded that Armstrong's cyclists covered a total of 400 000 kilometres during his network's existence. Such efforts to maintain quick links with the rest of the world earned great respect and contributed to an almost legendary status for the special riders.[7]

Most cycle messenger services were closed down by mid-1897 as telegraph lines and regular mail services were established. But special cyclists continued operating where they were quicker, where the regular services were too infrequent, and in isolated areas. Elderly goldfield residents recalled that remote mining

---

[7] For more information about the facts summarised in this paragraph, see Fitzpatrick, 1978b, pp. 226-237.

A glimpse at Australia's cycling history

operations continued to use occasional cycle messengers up to about 1920.

Bicycle and camel pads

Given the machine's ubiquitous use, bicycle paths quickly appeared throughout the goldfields. Cycle paths — acknowledged as such — often were no more than the informal marking of a frequented route. However, the most fascinating aspect is the relationship between cyclists and camels. Scores of Western Australian gold towns depended on Afghans' pack camels for water and supplies.

> The strings of pack camels formed smooth tracks which delighted people on bicycles ... They spoke very highly of camel pads for bicycle tracks ... On stony country, pack camels in single file very soon ... swept loose stones away, or if the ground was damp and the camels were heavily loaded their broad feet pressed the stones into the soil. On sandy country their feet tamped the sand, making it firm enough for a bicycle. (Barker, 1964, pp. 96-97)

Jack Costello, a Kalgoorlie reporter who cycled around the district in the 1930s, found that the passage of a single string of only 12 camels notably improved a riding surface. Where broad wagon tyres had been used in conjunction with camels, the resultant tracks, even on hard, stony roads, were often 'so smooth that you could walk barefooted along them' (Barker, 1964, p. 200), and they remained firm even when covered with water (see Figure 2.3).

Riders extolled the virtues of the camel pads and went out of their way to use them. A Coolgardie resident stated that for a ride, nothing surpasses a 'good camel pad'. Another described them as 'a wheelman's

Figure 2.3: Remnant of the extensive West Australian cycle network from the 1890s, still in use in the Kalgoorlie district in the 1930s. (Photographer: Jack Costello.)

riding luxury'. Shearers along the Strzelecki Track (from South Australia to Queensland) made use of them; and in New South Wales, Albert Ford found camel team tracks 'a pleasure' (as cited in Fitzpatrick, 1978b, pp. 154-157). Because the pad was so smooth, subsequent camel drivers and cyclists tended to use the same narrow path — and, unlike roads and tracks for wider carts and wagons, camel pads frequently resembled narrow alleys through the bush. As late as the 1930s, there were still a few cycle pads in use about the Western Australian goldfields. By the mid-1970s a few routes could still be detected, vestiges of the most extensive cycle path network in the world in the 1890s.

The importance of, and problems associated with, goldfields cyclists' pads led to the formation of the Goldfields Bicycle Pad Protection League, unquestionably one of the more unusual bicycle action groups ever seen — if not in its objectives, at least in its circumstances. It had its origins in a letter from CHA Stone, published in the *Broad Arrow Standard* on 30 June 1897 (p. 3):

> What cyclist has not bitterly felt cruel and unjust destruction of our pads, and longed for the time when they should be protected from general traffic … [O]ur pad from Broad Arrow to Kalgoorlie was made by ourselves, is in nobody's way, yet has been cruelly cut up from end to end … I think, for a start, we might get a bill introduced into Parliament, reserving a strip of, say, three yards on each side of all telegraph lines outside Coolgardie for cyclists alone, and making it punishable by heavy penalty for any horseman or driver of horses found within that area (except of course crossing it) … [T]he trouble I write of has rankled in our bosoms quite long enough. A monster petition to Parliament, or even perhaps to the Government, backed up by the various Road Boards, and certainly backed up by the League of West Australian Wheelmen, might be successful. Concerted action is necessary …

The *Kalgoorlie Miner*, on 31 July 1897, noted that cycling was

> the principal means of inter-communication between centres where the railway has not penetrated. As a matter of fact, on the fields it has come to be regarded as essential, and of course under the conditions just mentioned it forms the one and only mode of rapid transit … [T]he army of cyclists in respect of their numbers, if nothing else, should command respect when they give utterance to grievance, suggestion or request. (As cited in Fitzpatrick, 1980a, p. 114)

Appeals were made to a member of Parliament, and the matter was reported in

A glimpse at Australia's cycling history

Perth newspapers, but goldfields cycle clubs were only interested in obtaining cycle racing facilities and assigning racing dates; the broader interests of the cycling contingent were of no apparent concern. The short-lived Bicycle Pad Protection League died aborning.

The humble tool

By 1900, the novelty of the bicycle had worn off, but it did not become obsolete, nor did it disappear from the scene. The next two decades saw its greatest use throughout Australia, either from necessity or choice. It was adopted by many private and government organisations, as thousands of shearers, commercial travellers, workers, clergymen and boundary riders went about their business. It was the heyday of rural cycling. If not spectacular, it was pervasive.

The bicycle was widely adopted by Australian shearers from the late 1890s and became integral to their work migration pattern (see Figure 2.4). In not requiring food, water or maintenance the bicycle was superbly suited to the shearers' regime. They might work for a period of a few days on a smaller property up to several weeks at a large sheep station, then have to travel sometimes great distances in often sparsely settled country to reach the next property. Shearers were extremely fit and, when completing work at a property, were capable of immediately pedalling off on a one-day trip of 100 kilometres or more. Several thousand kilometres of travel would have been routine for them during a season.

Figure 2.4: Shearers in Coonamble, New South Wales 1902.
(Photographer: Banjo Paterson. Source: *The Sydney Mail*, 6 September 1902, p. 602.)

Interviews with former wool industry workers noted bicycles 'galore' being pedalled through western New South Wales from 1914-24, and sheds employing over 100 men (including shed hands) in which nearly all rode bicycles (Fitzpatrick, 1978b, p. 300).

In his book *On the wool track*, CEW Bean noted that as shearers came across New South Wales each year, the evidence of them was their bicycles which 'had spread through the country as fast as the rabbit ... [I]t is extraordinary in what unlikely places one finds those tyre-tracks' (1910, pp. 81-83). At wool sidings, numerous shearers would

> climb down from the mail train and lift down their swags and their bicycles. As the train pulled out, they would already be stringing off through the white gate, the hubs and spokes of their machines twinkling across the paddock. (p. 31)

The use was so important that the Shed Hands' Agreement in New South Wales eventually required, in addition to food, bunk and other amenities, that 'the employer provide a suitable room or other place, outside the kitchen and sleeping accommodation, for the housing of the ... cycles of the employees' (The Pastoralists' Union of New South Wales, 1916).[8] It was but an early facet of a still-continuing battle by cyclists for adequate facilities for their machines.

The gradual decline in cycling in rural Australia began around the end of World War I and is related to the increasing availability, reliability, affordability and comfort of motor vehicles. For Australians, the use of the motor vehicle was quickly and solidly established. In 1910, there were only about 5000 in the country, but by 1923 Australia ranked sixth in the world in terms of absolute numbers, with some 169 000 motor cars, commercial vehicles and motorcycles. In the next six years, that number increased nearly fourfold, and on a per capita basis Australian car ownership was exceeded only in the United States and New Zealand in 1930 (Forster, 1964, p. 30). An Englishman who visited Australia in 1928 commented upon the number of 'rough homes' that had motor cars parked outside (Thompson, 1932, p. 246). As an identifiable group, shearers were among the first rural workers to abandon bicycles. Their work pattern — they typically worked in teams for long

---

[8] The Shed Hands' Agreement was viewed by the author during an interview with a former shearer in the 1970s. Further source details are no longer available.

periods at one location, punctuated by group travel to another point established well ahead of time by contracts — put them in an excellent position to take advantage of shared motor transport costs.

Nonetheless, the bicycle long remained a popular device for commuting between urban and rural areas or between communities, such as Newcastle-Maitland, Boulder-Kalgoorlie, the smelter works of Port Pirie, and the coal mines around Collie, Western Australia.

There was a resurgence in the use of bicycles for work and travel during the harsh economic conditions of the 1930s Great Depression. During the Second World War, the severe

Figure 2.5: Melbourne, World War II. (Source: Malvern Star Bicycles.)

restrictions on petrol, spare parts and tyres for motor vehicles resulted in the deregistration of many motor vehicles, accompanied by a radical increase in bicycle riding (see Figure 2.5). After the war, use of the bicycle for commuting and general daily travel declined markedly. As towns and cities began sprawling outwards — a situation made possible by, and indeed requiring, increased motorised travel — the bicycle became a less viable, safe, attractive and socially acceptable form of transport. Legendary Australian cycle manufacturers Malvern Star and Speedwell succumbed to a downturn in sales after World War II, economic readjustments and a rationalisation of the industry, and were bought out. By 1970, Australian cycling had probably reached its nadir.[9]

---

[9] The lack of research on the decline of cycle use after World War II is a gap in Australian transport history which merits a significant research effort.

The cycling renaissance

During the latter half of the twentieth century, there was a resurgence in cycling interest. Added to the continuing market for children's bicycles (which account for about a third of annual sales), there was an increase in recreational types of riding such as BMX, off-road and mountain biking. The renewed interest was helped by Australia becoming a powerhouse on the present-day world cycle racing scene after 1990, with the broadcaster SBS's Cycling Central television program now carrying events such as the Tour de France live (Fitzpatrick, 2013, pp. 149-158). As well, more sophisticated machines, increasing environmental concerns and the growth of cycling organisations led to an increased popularity and use of bicycles. The popularity of the bicycle has shown no signs of abating, and from 2002 through to 2013 some 15 million machines were bought — more than the number of motor cars sold during that period (Fitzpatrick, 2013, pp. 171). However, it has been suggested that a million more people would be riding today if Australians now cycled at the same rate as they did in the mid-1980s (Rissel, 2012). Many of those 15 million bicycles (plus an unknown number of still operable pre-2002 machines) may be collecting dust in the garage.

A notable recent development in cycle technology is the electric assisted bicycle, or e-bike. These bikes became practical with the advent of modern high-capacity batteries and the development of controls and torque sensors in the 1990s. Their adoption was explosive in China and they now represent a significant and rapidly increasing percentage of bikes in many cities around the world. In 2011, Australia Post purchased 1000 electric bicycles. They cost less than motorbikes to buy, and their maintenance and running costs are lower. A single charge of the battery can comfortably handle a heavy load and rider on an average daily delivery route of three to five hours, and the batteries last well over a year before requiring replacement. Two further important factors in Australia Post's decision are that it has been difficult to recruit adequate numbers of staff with motorbike licences (which are not required for electric bikes), and e-bikes do not require registration (Fitzpatrick, 2013, pp. 167-168).[10]

---

[10] Bicycles were employed by the mid-1890s for telegram delivery; and in Melbourne they were used from July 1898 for collecting mail from pillar boxes throughout the city. It required only one cyclist to do what it had formerly taken a team of horses, wagon, teamster and box clearer to do (*Austral Wheel*, 1898, p. 191). The Postmaster-General introduced bicycles throughout Australia on a large scale at the end of the First World War.

In the 1890s, bikes were essentially the same basic diamond frame design (along with women's step-through models). Today's bike shop sports a range of models — BMX, cargo, mountain, cruisers, cyclocross, folding, hybrid, recumbent, road, track — with such technological advancements as disc brakes, shock absorption systems, sophisticated gearing, electronic shifting and lightweight frames. But the bicycle is still basically two wheels and a crank, with a saddle and handlebars. With the exception of the e-bike, the power source is still the same. What has changed is the role of the bicycle in Australian society. The bicycle will not go away, but it is not clear as to what will happen next. Much of the rest of this book is devoted substantially to exploring that issue.

References

Barker, H. (1964). *Camels and the outback.* Melbourne: Sir Isaac Pitman & Sons, Ltd.

Bean, CEW. (1910). *On the wool track.* Sydney: Angus and Robertson.

Bijker, W. (1997). *Of bicycles, bakelites and bulbs: Toward a theory of sociotechnical change.* Cambridge, MA: The MIT Press.

Burston, GW, & Stokes, HR. (1890). *Round about the world on bicycles.* Melbourne: George Robertson and Company.

Carnegie, DW. (1898). *Spinifex and sand.* London: C Arthur Pearson Limited.

Fitzpatrick, J. (1978a). Cycling up, down Australia's Alps. *Canberra Historical Journal*, New Series, 2, 15-19.

Fitzpatrick, J. (1978b). *The bicycle in rural Australia: A study of man, machine and milieu* (Doctoral Thesis, The Australian National University).

Fitzpatrick, J. (1979a). The spectrum of Australian bicycle racing: 1890-1900. In R Cashman & M McKernan (Eds.), *Sport in history* (pp. 326-342). St. Lucia: Queensland University Press.

Fitzpatrick, J. (1979b). The bicyclist as a plant dispersal mechanism in rural Australia. *Search*, 10(7-8), 61.

Fitzpatrick, J. (1980a). *The bicycle and the bush: Man and machine in rural Australia.* Melbourne: Oxford University Press.

Fitzpatrick, J. (1980b). The early development of Australian road maps. *The Globe*, 13, 13-29.

Fitzpatrick, J. (1980c). Australian cyclistes in the Victorian era. *Hemisphere*, 24(1), 12-17.

Fitzpatrick, J. (1981). The bicycle and Australian English. *Overland*, 86, 65-69.

Fitzpatrick, J. (1982). Some further notes on the development of early Australian road maps. *The Globe*, 17, 51-55.

Fitzpatrick, J. (1988). Joseph Pearson. In *Australian dictionary of biography* (Vol. 2, p. 187). Melbourne: Melbourne University Press.

Fitzpatrick, J. (1992). Cycling. In W Vamplew & Australian Sports Commission & Australian Society for Sports History, *The Oxford companion to Australian sport* (pp. 111-112). Melbourne: Oxford University Press.

Fitzpatrick, J. (1998). *The bicycle in wartime: An illustrated history*. London: Batsford Brassey's Inc.

Fitzpatrick, J. (2011). *'Major' Taylor in Australia*. Kilcoy: Star Hill Studio.

Fitzpatrick, J. (2013). *Wheeling Matilda: The story of Australian cycling*. Kilcoy: Star Hill Studio.

Forster, C. (1964). *Industrial development in Australia*. Canberra: ANU Press.

Kimberly, WB. (1897). *History of West Australia: A narrative of her past*. Melbourne: FB Niven & Co.

New South Wales Cyclists' Touring Union. (1898). *Cyclists' handbook and guide to the roads of New South Wales*. Sydney: WE Smith.

Oddy, N. (2007). The flaneur on wheels? In D Horton, P Rosen, & P Cox (Eds.), *Cycling and society* (pp. 97-112). Aldershot: Ashgate.

The Pastoralists' Union of New South Wales. (1916, 4 November). *No. 3. Shed hands' agreement. Adults.* Based upon the award of the Commonwealth Court of conciliation and arbitration, 27 October 1911.

Pearson, J. (1925). *Reminiscences including cycling experiences*. Sydney: Vale and Pearson.

Rissel, C. (2012). Australian cycling boom? Nope — it's a myth. Retrieved 10 July 2014 from http://theconversation.com/australian-cycling-boom-nope-its-a-myth-8020.

Simpson, C. (2007). Capitalising on curiosity: Women's professional cycle racing in the late Nineteenth Century. In D Horton, P Rosen, & P Cox (Eds.), *Cycling and society* (pp. 47-65). Aldershot: Ashgate.

Smith, R. (1972). *A social history of the bicycle, its early life and times in America*. New York: American Heritage Press.

Stone, C. (1897, 30 June). Letter. *Broad Arrow Standard*, p. 3.

Thompson, P. (1932). *Down under: An Australian odyssey*. London: Duckworth Press.

3 Health benefits of cycling

Chris Rissel

Introduction

Australia and New Zealand, like other developed countries, face serious health problems due to increasing levels of chronic disease such as type 2 diabetes, obesity and heart disease. The Organisation of Economic Co-operation and Development [OECD] recently reported that chronic non-communicable diseases are now the main cause of both disability and death worldwide (OECD, 2010). Globally, chronic diseases have overtaken communicable diseases and injuries as the leading burden of disease (Nugent, 2008). Of the 58 million deaths that occurred globally in 2005, approximately 35 million, or 60%, were due to chronic causes, and most of them were due to cardiovascular disorders and diabetes (32%), cancers (13%) and chronic respiratory diseases (7%) (Abegunde, Mathers, Taghreed, Ortegon, & Strong, 2007). Global projections are that levels of chronic disease will only worsen in coming years (Nugent, 2008; Lopez, 2006). This chapter describes the chronic disease challenges facing developed countries such as Australia and New Zealand and critically examines the evidence that cycling can assist in addressing these challenges. It provides an overview of the international literature on the health benefits of cycling, including relevant Australian studies. It discusses how Australian health promotion agencies approach health aspects of cycling.

Health challenges

In Australia, the leading underlying cause of death in 2011 was coronary heart disease, followed by lung cancer and cerebrovascular disease among men, and cerebrovascular disease and dementia and Alzheimer's disease among women (Australian Institute of Health and Welfare, 2014). Currently, 9 in 10 deaths have chronic disease as an underlying cause (AIHW, 2014). Data from the 2007-08 National Health Survey indicates that one-third of the Australian population (35%, or 7 million people) reported having at least one of the following chronic conditions: asthma, type 2 diabetes, coronary heart disease, cerebrovascular disease (mainly stroke), arthritis, osteoporosis, chronic obstructive pulmonary disease [COPD], depression or high blood pressure. In Australia and New Zealand, chronic diseases together cause 85% of the total burden of disease (Institute for Health Metrics and Evaluation [IHME], 2013). There are an estimated 1 million people with diagnosed diabetes in Australia, and the incidence of new cases is increasing rapidly, including among young people (AIHW, 2014). The rate of self-reported diabetes more than doubled between 1989-90 and 2011-12, from 1.5% to 4.2% of Australians. The cost of diabetes to the health system is substantial, with the number of hospitalisations for dialysis (a consequence of diabetes) having doubled over the past decade.

Similarly, in the last 25 years there has been a dramatic global increase in overweight and obesity, among both adults and children (OECD, 2010; Lopez, 2006). Being overweight or obese are risk factors for many chronic health conditions such as heart disease, diabetes and some cancers. In 2011-12, according to the AIHW (2014), more than 3 in 5 Australian adults (63%) were overweight or obese (70% of men and 56% of women). In 2011-12, of children aged 5-14 who had their measurements taken for the ABS Australian Health Survey, an estimated 26% were either overweight (19%) or obese (7%) (AIHW, 2012). Being obese as a child increases both the risk of being obese as an adult and the risk of developing chronic diseases (Guo, Wu, Chumlea, & Roche, 2002).

Reducing the prevalence of obesity will lead to substantial population health benefits through the prevention of morbidity and mortality from chronic diseases, in particular diabetes, cardiovascular disease and some cancers (Wilson, D'Agostino, Sullivan, Parise, & Kannel, 2002). If obesity and overweight were eliminated, it is likely that nearly half of all new cases of diabetes would not occur, and a fifth of heart disease and a third of hypertension could also be prevented (Dal Grande et al., 2009). In addition, up to a sixth of some cancers (colon cancer, post-menopausal breast cancer and endometrial cancer), and a sizeable proportion of osteoarthritis, would also be prevented if obesity was eliminated (Dal Grande et al., 2009).

Prevention of chronic disease is strategically important for many reasons, including budgetary ones. As a nation, Australia's health expenditure has grown faster than inflation and the economy as a whole for many years. Mostly as a function of cost of treatment and an ageing population, the ratio of health expenditure to gross domestic product [GDP] increased from 6.8% in 1986-87 to 9.5% in 2011-12 (AIHW, 2014), and it is expected to continue to increase. Investments in programs which support evidence-based programs to prevent overweight and obesity, such as the National Partnership Agreement on Preventive Health[1], will be essential to prevent continued health expenditure costs.

The role of physical activity and cycling in preventing chronic disease

Insufficient exercise is a risk factor for chronic disease. New physical activity guidelines were introduced in Australia in 2013, increasing the minimum levels of physical activity needed to maintain health. Adults are recommended now to accumulate 150 to 300 minutes of moderate-intensity physical activity or 75 to 150 minutes of vigorous-intensity physical activity each week (Australian Department of Health, 2014). The guidelines also note that doing any physical activity is better than doing none, and that people should try to be active on most, preferably all, days of the week.

Population surveys have yet to apply these new standards, however. About 2 in 5 adults (43% — that is, 45% of males and 42% of females) were sufficiently active to meet the previous guidelines, which recommended a minimum level of activity of 150 minutes per week of walking or other moderate or vigorous activity over at least 5 sessions (AIHW, 2014). The proportion of the population considered sufficiently physically active will be lower when the new guidelines are applied.

---

[1] The funding for this program (from 2009 to June 2014) has now ceased.

Chronic diseases can be prevented through better nutrition and more physical activity. Australian diabetes prevention trials (Colagiuri et al., 2010) have demonstrated similar results to international studies (Tuomilehto, 2001) — that is, that weight loss from eating 2 pieces of fruit and 5 vegetables a day and practising moderate calorie restriction, plus accumulating about 60 minutes of physical activity a day, leads to clinically significant health improvement. Given the low levels of physical activity among Australian adults, it is obvious that whatever is being done now to promote more physical activity is not enough. If exercise groups and gyms were the whole answer, a greater proportion of the population would be sufficiently active. A paradigm shift is needed, and it is possible that active travel — for example, walking and cycling — could provide the opportunity for regular daily physical activity for a large extent of the population (Shephard, 2008). Regular physical activity is most sustainable if incorporated into everyday activity.

Activities such as walking or cycling (rather than driving) to destinations of interest have the potential to support people in achieving recommended levels of physical activity (Sahlqvist, Song, & Ogilvie, 2012). In one study of Western Sydney residents, 40% of people cycling in the previous week achieved the (prior) recommended minimum physical activity level just by cycling (Rissel et al., 2010). Use of public transport can also add to additional minutes of physical activity by walking or cycling to and from bus stops or train stations (Rissel et al., 2012). Garrard, Rissel and Bauman (2012) modelled the impact on population levels of sufficient physical activity if 20% of Australians cycled for 20 minutes once, twice and three times per week, and found that the prevalence of adequately active people would increase to 59%, 60.5% and 64.5% respectively.

Defining health benefits

In the past 20 years there have been numerous reports and reviews summarising the health benefits of cycling (British Medical Association, 1992, 2012; Cavill & Davis, 2007; Bauman et al., 2008; Hamer & Chida, 2008; de Silva-Sanigorski et al., 2010; Oja et al., 2011; Garrard, Rissel, & Bauman, 2012). These health benefits are physical, social, psychological, environmental and financial (see Table 3.1).

All of these publications have overwhelmingly concluded that there are multiple health benefits from cycling — benefits consistent with those of physical

Table 3.1: Reports/reviews assessing health benefits of cycling.

Authors	Title	Year	Country
British Medical Association	*Cycling towards health and safety*	1992	United Kingdom
Roberts I, Owen H, Lumb P, McDougall C	*Pedalling health — Health benefits of a modal transport shift*	1996	Australia
Cavill N, Davis A	*Cycling and health: What's the evidence?*	2007	United Kingdom
Bauman A, Rissel C, Garrard J, Kerr I, Speidel R, Fishman E	*Cycling: Getting Australia moving — Barriers, facilitators and interventions to get more Australians physically active through cycling*	2008	Australia
Hamer M, Chida Y	*Active commuting and cardiovascular risk: A meta-analytic review*	2008	Global
Oja P, et al.	*Health benefits of cycling: A systematic review*	2011	Global
British Medical Association	*Healthy transport – Healthy lives*	2012	British Medical Association
Garrard J, Rissel C, Bauman A	*Health benefits of cycling*	2012	Global

activity generally. However, a number of studies have specifically examined the health benefits of cycling. Those research studies demonstrating physiological benefits of cycling in clinical settings, with special populations, and usually on stationary bicycles, are not considered here.

The most common research papers are those cross-section studies that show inverse associations between active commuting and health outcomes such as body mass index, lipid levels and blood pressure (Hu, Pekkarinen, Hänninen, Yu, Guo, & Tian, 2002; Ohta, Mizoue, Mishima, & Ikeda, 2007; von Huth Smith, Borch-Johnsen, & Jørgensen, 2007; Huy, Becker, Gomolinsky, Klein, & Thiel, 2008; Wen & Rissel, 2008). Ecological associations across countries have noted that obesity rates are inversely related to cycling rates (Bassett, Pucher, Buehler, Thompson, & Crouter, 2008; Pucher, Buehler, Bassett, & Dannenberg, 2010). Such data does not demonstrate a causal relationship, but indicates the potential for healthy differences in active cycling populations.

Longitudinal cohort study designs have made important contributions to assessing the health benefits of cycling. A landmark study, the Copenhagen cohort with 15-year follow-up data, identified that cycling to work reduced the risk of all-cause mortality by 28%, independent of other types of physical activity (Andersen, Schnohr, Schroll, & Hein, 2000). Further work in Copenhagen found that relative intensity, rather than the duration of cycling, was of more importance in relation to all-cause and coronary heart disease mortality (Schnohr, Marott, Jensen, & Jensen, 2012). Many studies have identified active commuting as protective against all-cause or cardiovascular deaths (Hu, Tuomilehto, Borodulin, & Jousilahti, 2007; Hamer & Chida, 2008), but most of these studies asked about walking or cycling to work in the same question, and their relative effects cannot be distinguished. In the Zutphen study of elderly Dutch men, physical activity reduced risk and improved metabolic health; but because the most frequent physical activity was cycling, the study provides stronger evidence of a cycling-specific effect (Caspersen, Bloemberg, Saris, Merritt, & Kromhout, 1991). A recent British study showed that cycling for at least 60 minutes per week in total was associated with a 9% reduced risk of all-cause mortality, but when more precise measures of cycling were used (based on a physical activity questionnaire; four specific cycling measures; and the associated measure of metabolic equivalent energy expenditure [METS]), there was little evidence of an association between cycling and mortality (Sahlqvist et al., 2013). This lack of effect was attributed to low cycling frequency and insufficient respondents with a high 'dose' of cycling.

More work is needed to explore whether a minimum dose of cycling is needed before mortality outcomes are affected. At this time there is no agreement on what a 'dose' of cycling consists of: whether it is a minimum time period of specific intensity, or whether this minimum-energy expenditure needs to be repeated over a set time. It is likely that for a fully sedentary person, any cycling at any intensity would have beneficial health effects, but that for a very active person low-intensity cycling would do little beyond maintaining good health.

Psychosocial health benefits

There is increasing evidence that physical activity is important for mental health (Penedo & Dahn, 2005). The specific contribution of cycling to psychosocial health is less well documented. Many qualitative studies have documented the joy and pleasure that people experience from cycling (Whitaker, 2005; Daley, Rissel, & Lloyd, 2007; Zander, Passmore, Mason, & Rissel, 2013), and this contributes to wellbeing as well as providing a motivation to continue cycling. Research is currently underway exploring the relationship between cycling and quality of life using the Australian version of the World Health Organization Quality of Life measure (Murphy, Herrman, Hawthorne, Pinzone, & Evert, 2000; Crane & Rissel, 2014).

Travel mode may also be associated with psychosocial health. Recent research has directly linked driving with adverse health effects, and has noted a dose-response relationship, so that more driving was associated with worse outcomes (Ding, Gebel, Phongsavan, Bauman, & Merom, 2014). There is a small but growing amount of literature on the relative stress associated with different travel (The New York Bicycling Coalition, 2013; O'Regan & Buckley, 2003; Stutzer & Frey, 2008). Several dimensions of the commuting situation, such as impedance (caused, for example, by traffic congestion), along with control over, and predictability of, commuting, influence perceived stress (Gottholmseder, Nowotny, Pruckner, & Theurl, 2009). Predictability is particularly important, especially for women, who may have additional family responsibilities (Roberts, Hodgson, & Dolan, 2011). For some people the work commute induces stress or is associated with episodes of negative feelings during the day (Olsson, Garling, Ettema, Friman & Fujii, 2013). One study in Western Sydney found that active travel to work was perceived to be less stressful than car commuting relative to the stress of a work day (Rissel, Petrunoff, Wen, & Crane, 2013).

Health benefits of cycling versus the risks of injury

While there is convincing evidence that cycling has many health benefits, it needs to be acknowledged that there are also injury risks associated with cycling (see Hatfield, Boufous, & Poulos, Chapter Four, this volume). As Kingham and Tranter (Chapter Seven, this volume) point out, there is also the possibility that cyclists are exposed to more air pollution than other road users, or that, because of increased respiratory action, cyclists inhale more pollutants. However, Table 3.2 shows that

Table 3.2: Studies comparing the health benefits of cycling with injury/pollution costs.

Authors (date)	Location(s)	Basis for comparison	Main findings	Ratio of health benefit to cost
Hillman, 1992	Great Britain	Ratio of life-years gained through health benefits of cycling compared with life-years lost to cycling injuries.	Health-related life-years gained outweigh injury-related life-years lost by 20:1.	20:1
Woodcock et al., 2009	London/ Delhi	Various sustainable travel scenarios considered. Weighs up both mortality effects and 'disability-adjusted life-years' (DALY) effects per million of population due to increased physical activity, injuries and pollution; also the societal benefits of reduced pollution and CO_2 emissions.	Impacts per million population annually: • Physical activity benefits: 528 deaths averted, saving 5496 life-years; plus a reduction of 2245 life-years impaired by disability, a saving of 7742 DALYs. Air pollution net benefits (note: societal benefits of reduced air pollution outweigh the pollution disbenefits for individuals who switch from car to active travel): 21 deaths averted, saving 200 life-years, plus 200 DALYs. • Traffic crashes: net loss of 11 lives and 418 life-years, plus an increase of 101 life-years impaired by disability, a cost of 519 DALYs.	Ratio for mortality: (5496:418) = 13:1 Ratio for DALYs: (7742:519) = 15:1

Authors (date)	Location(s)	Basis for comparison	Main findings	Ratio of health benefit to cost
de Hartog, Boogaard, Nijland, & Hoek, 2010	Netherlands	Gains and losses per person per annum for adults aged 18-64 who switch from a regular car commute to cycling. Weighs up life-years gained per year through health benefits of cycling versus life-years lost to cycling injuries and pollution.	Average mortality gains/losses: • Physical activity benefits: range 3-14 months (mean = 8 months or 245 days). • Injury costs: range 5-9 days (mean = 7 days). • Pollution costs: range 0.8-40 days (mean = 21 days).	9:1
Rabl & de Nazelle, 2012	Data from several EU cities	Considers annual value of mortality benefits and disbenefits for each individual who switches a regular short (5 km one-way) car commute to cycling. Weighs up life-years gained per year through health benefits of cycling, versus life-years lost to cycling injuries and pollution, and also societal benefits of reduced pollution.	Average annual value of benefits per person switching from car to cycle: • Physical activity benefits = $1310. • Public health benefits from reduced pollution = $33. • Individual disbenefits from increased pollution = $19. • Individual disbenefits from injuries = $53.	1310:53 = 24:1 Including pollution effects on individuals and society = 19:1.
Rojas-Rueda, de Nazelle, Tainio, & Nieuwenhuijsen, 2011	Barcelona	Calculates the overall mortality-related impacts of Barcelona's 'BICING' cycle hire scheme in terms of life-years gained through health benefits of scheme-users	Life-years gained and lost annually by BICING scheme users: • Deaths averted due to physical activity: 12.46.	Including pollution effects to individuals = 77:1*

Authors (date)	Location(s)	Basis for comparison	Main findings	Ratio of health benefit to cost
		switching from car travel to cycling, versus life-years lost to cycling injuries and pollution. Also considers CO_2 savings.	• Deaths due to pollution: 0.13. • Deaths due to injury: 0.03.	
Holm, Glumer, & Diderichsen, 2012	Copenhagen	Modelled the health impact assessment using DALYs of policy proposals to increase cycling.	• Burden of disease from physical inactivity reduced by 76.0 DALYs. • Burden of disease from air pollution (5.4) and traffic accidents (51.2) increased by 56.5 DALYs.	Net benefit of DALYs = 19.5 DALYS
Woodcock, Tainio, Cheshire, O'Brien, & Goodman, 2014	London	For London cycle hire scheme uses, assesses change in lifelong DALYs modelled through medium-term changes in physical activity, road traffic injuries and exposure to air pollution.	• Men: all non-injury diseases averted = -83 DALYS. • Men: Observed cycle high-injury rate = 10 DALYS. • Women: all non-injury diseases averted = -22 DALYS. • Women: Observed cycle high-injury rate = 6 DALYS.	Total DALYs[a] = -88 DALYS** [a] negative DALYs represent a health benefit.

*The Rojas-Reuda estimate of 77:1 overstates the benefits, because of incorrect assumptions that most bike trips replaced car trips (Fishman, 2011).

**A more conservative analysis modelled with background cycling injury rates found a still positive net impact of -50 DALYS, and also found that the results were clearer for men than women.

(Source: Adapted from table found at http://www.cyclehelmets.org/1015.html. For more information, see Bicycle Helmet Research Foundation [n.d.].)

all known comparisons of the risks and benefits of cycling have concluded that the benefits outweigh the risks.

The lowest estimate of the ratio of health benefits to injury/pollution costs is 9:1, which is still substantial. This ratio could be improved by making the conditions for cycling safer, or by reducing pollution.

Mandatory bicycle helmet legislation

In an effort to reduce cycling head injuries, Australia introduced mandatory helmet legislation in 1991-92 (and New Zealand followed suit in 1994). This legislation has been consistently contested since its introduction (Curnow, 2005; Robinson, 2006; Clarke, 2012), and the rest of the world has not embraced this policy because of the perceived negative effects on cycling participation. The main objections about laws requiring bicycle helmets to be worn by all people at all times when cycling are that the efficacy of bicycle helmets in protecting cyclists has been exaggerated (Elvik, 2011); the legislation has had an extremely negative effect on cycling participation (Land Transport New Zealand, 2006; Sandblom, 2015); and the evidence that such legislation has achieved any meaningful reductions in rates of brain or head injuries is weak and does not acknowledge the long-term downward trends that are evident (Dennis, Ramsay, Turgeon, & Zarychanski, 2013).

In terms of cycling safety, a drop in cycling participation leads to a decrease in safety because of the effects of the 'safety in numbers', where the more people that walk or cycle, the safer it becomes to walk or cycle (Jacobsen, 2003). Thus the introduction of mandatory helmet legislation had a negative impact on overall cycling safety (Komanoff, 2001). This 'safety in numbers' effect has been demonstrated prospectively in a review of 10 public bike-share programs in the United States (Graves, Pless, Moore, & Nathens, 2013). The results showed that compared to the 24 months before implementation, in the 12 months post-implementation, head injuries in public bike-share cities fell by 14%, despite the increase in cycling from using public bikes and no requirement to wear helmets.

Bicycle helmet legislation has made minimal improvement to cycling safety, and most cycling promotion advocates would say that an investment in cycling infrastructure would achieve much greater improvements in cycling safety (Goldacre & Spiegelhalter, 2013). The compulsion to wear a helmet has consistently been identified as one of the barriers to more people cycling in Australia. A survey of 600 Sydney residents found that 1 in 5 (22.6%) of all respondents said that they would ride more if they did not have to wear a helmet (Rissel & Wen, 2011). If this were translated to the Sydney population of 4.5 million, this could represent a substantial increase in cycling levels, along with the associated health benefits.

Cycling promotion versus risk protection

The vast majority of the human and technical resources of the health system in most developed countries is focused on the clinical treatment of patients. This means identifying and treating illness. In Australia and New Zealand, there is a small public health and health promotion workforce that is concerned about the prevention of disease, but this prevention-oriented sector is traditionally very poorly resourced. Investment in all public health (which includes infectious diseases) is approximately 2% of the total recurrent health expenditure (AIHW, 2011). The National Partnership Agreement on Preventive Health had seen a significant increase in Australian funding for the prevention of chronic disease, but this funding was stopped in the 2014 federal budget.

Within the relatively small part of the health sector which public health inhabits, physical activity has long been accepted as a basic function of health promotion work, but must compete for resources alongside of programs addressing nutrition, tobacco control, falls prevention and HIV/AIDS prevention, among others. Expertise in physical activity program development at a population level (that is, developing programs for communities) remains limited. The recent increase in the training of Exercise Physiologists as a professional discipline has expanded the capacity of the health promotion workforce to address physical activity, but it is unclear how much attention cycling receives in this training, or indeed, in any health professional's training.

Cycling, as part of the active travel agenda, is making slow inroads into the work of health promotion agencies (Bauman & Rissel, 2009; Bauman, Titze, Rissel, & Oja, 2011). There is some recognition within health promotion circles that active travel programs have the potential to achieve population-level increases in physical activity, but there are relatively few well-evaluated exemplar programs

(Ogilvie, Egan, Hamilton, & Petticrew, 2004). Given its treatment culture, the health system has traditionally considered cycling from a trauma and treatment perspective, rather than from the perspective that cycling is an activity to be promoted and encouraged. Therefore, much health sector investment in cycling has been for injury prevention. Excessive concern for safety has inadvertently contributed to creating a culture of fear around cycling, which acts as a significant barrier to people considering cycling, especially for transport (Horton, 2007).

Further, despite cycling being a sport, and a healthy recreation, responsibility for cycling infrastructure and promotion in Australia and New Zealand has generally fallen under the jurisdiction of government transport and road agencies, where it is a poor cousin to motorised transport. Many government agencies stand to benefit from increases in cycling (such as those which work in the area of health, transport, environment and recreation), yet they generally do not work together to maximise their efforts. Unfortunately, within most of the government agencies with potential to support cycling, cycling still represents a small part of their primary roles despite the efforts of individuals within the agencies.

Conclusion and agenda for further research

The benefits of cycling are many, and outweigh the risk of injury. More co-ordinated efforts across government are needed to improve the environment for cycling. While it is clear that cycling is 'healthy', there are still many things not known about how much and how intense everyday cycling needs to be to attain health benefits. Additional effort is likely to be needed for weight loss, but how much is not known, nor how it might vary for individuals. Also, there is no agreed methodology for quantifying the monetary value of the benefits of cycling. This is an important area for future research, so that the needed investment in cycling infrastructure can be legitimately offset by the positive health gains. Related to this is also the relative increase in health associated with new cycling infrastructure. There are promising indications of health gains two years after new infrastructure is in place for those residents living within 1 kilometre of the infrastructure (Goodman, Sahlqvist, Ogilvie, & iConnect Consortium, 2014), but more work is needed in this area (Rissel, Greaves, Wen, Capon, Crane, & Standen, 2013).

Acknowledgements

Thanks to Jan Garrard for the work she did for our book chapter 'Health benefits of cycling', in J Pucher & R Buehler (Eds.), *City cycling*, which I have drawn on here.

References

Abegunde, DO, Mathers, C, Taghreed, A, Ortegon, M, & Strong, K. (2007). The burden and costs of chronic diseases in low-income and middle-income countries. *Lancet*, 370(9603), 1929-1938.

Andersen, LB, Schnohr, P, Schroll, M, & Hein, HO. (2000). All-cause mortality associated with physical activity during leisure time, work, sports, and cycling to work. *Archives of Internal Medicine*, 160(11), 1621-1628.

Australian Department of Health. (2014). *Australia's physical activity and sedentary behaviour guidelines*. Retrieved 12 July 2014 from http://www.health.gov.au/internet/main/publishing.nsf/content/health-pubhlthstrateg-phys-act-guidelines.

Australian Institute of Health and Welfare [AIHW]. (2011). *Public health expenditure in Australia, 2008-09. Health and welfare expenditure*. Cat. no. HWE 52. Canberra: AIHW. Retrieved 31 July 2015 from http://www.aihw.gov.au/publication-detail/?id=10737418329.

Australian Institute of Health and Welfare [AIHW]. (2012). *A picture of Australia's children 2012*. Cat. no. PHE 167. Canberra: AIHW. Retrieved 21 July 2014 from http://www.aihw.gov.au/WorkArea/DownloadAsset.aspx?id=10737423340.

Australian Institute of Health and Welfare [AIHW]. (2014). *Australia's Health 2014*. Canberra: AIHW. Retrieved 21 July 2014 from http://www.aihw.gov.au/workarea/downloadasset.aspx?id=60129548150.

Bassett, DR, Pucher, J, Buehler, R, Thompson, DL, & Crouter, SE. (2008). Walking, cycling, and obesity rates in Europe, North America, and Australia. *Journal of Physical Activity and Health*, 5(6), 795-814.

Bauman, AE, & Rissel, C. (2009). Cycling and health: An opportunity for positive change? *Medical Journal of Australia*, 190(7), 347-348.

Bauman, A, Rissel, C, Garrard, J, Ker, I, Speidel, R, & Fishman, E. (2008). *Cycling: Getting Australia moving — Barriers, facilitators and interventions to get more Australians physically active through cycling.* Melbourne: Cycling Promotion Fund.

Bauman, A, Titze, S, Rissel, C, & Oja, P. (2011). Changing gears: Bicycling as the panacea for physical inactivity? *British Journal of Sports Medicine,* 45(10), 761-762.

Bicycle Helmet Research Foundation. (n.d.) The health benefits of cycling. Retrieved 31 July 2014 from http://www.cyclehelmets.org/1015.html.

British Medical Association. (1992). *Cycling towards health and safety.* London: British Medical Association.

British Medical Association. (2012). Healthy transport = Healthy lives. London: British Medical Association. Retrieved 6 December 2014 from http://bma.org.uk/transport.

Caspersen, CJ, Bloemberg, BP, Saris, WH, Merritt, R.K, & Kromhout, D. (1991). The prevalence of selected physical activities and their relation with coronary heart disease risk factors in elderly men: The Zutphen Study, 1985. *American Journal of Epidemiology,* 133(11), 1078-1092.

Cavill, N, & Davis, A. (2007). *Cycling and health: What's the evidence?* London: Cycling England.

Clarke, CF. (2012). Evaluation of New Zealand's bicycle helmet law. *New Zealand Medical Journal,* 125(1349), 60-69.

Colagiuri, S, Vita, P, Cardona-Morrell, M, Fiatarone Singh, M, Farrell, L, Milat, A … Bauman, A. (2010). The Sydney Diabetes Prevention Program: A community-based translational study. *BMC Public Health,* 10, 328. doi: 10.1186/1471-2458-10-328.

Crane, M, & Rissel, C. (2014, May 27-30). The association between cycling and quality of life. *Velo-City Global Conference,* Adelaide.

Curnow, WJ. (2005). The Cochrane Collaboration and bicycle helmets. *Accident Analysis & Prevention,* 35, 287-292.

Dal Grande, E, Gill, T, Wyatt, L, Chittleborough, CR, Phillips, PJ, & Taylor, AW. (2009). Population attributable risk (PAR) of overweight and obesity on chronic diseases: South Australian representative, cross-sectional data, 2004-2006. *Obesity Research & Clinical Practice,* 3(3), 159-168.

Daley, M, Rissel, C, & Lloyd, B. (2007). All dressed up and no-where to go? A qualitative research study of the barriers and enablers to cycling in inner Sydney. *Road and Transport Research,* 16(4), 42-52.

de Hartog, JJ, Boogaard, H, Nijland, H, & Hoek, G. (2010). Do the health benefits of cycling outweigh the risks? *Environmental Health Perspectives*, 118(8), 1109-1116.

Dennis, J, Ramsay, T, Turgeon, AF, & Zarychanski, R. (2013). Helmet legislation and admissions to hospital for cycling related head injuries in Canadian provinces and territories: Interrupted time series analysis. *British Medical Journal*, 346, f2674.

de Silva-Sanigorski, AM, Bell, AC, Kremer, P, Nichols, M, Crellin, M, Smith, M … Swinburn, B. A. (2010). Reducing obesity in early childhood: Results from Romp & Chomp, an Australian community-wide intervention program. *American Journal of Clinical Nutrition*, 91(4), 831-840.

Ding, D, Gebel, K, Phongsavan, P, Bauman, AE, & Merom, D. (2014). Driving: A road to unhealthy lifestyles and poor health outcomes. *PLoS One*, 9(6), e94602.

Elvik, R. (2011). Publication bias and time-trend bias in meta-analysis of bicycle helmet efficacy: A re-analysis of Attewell, Glase and McFadden, 2001. *Accident Analysis & Prevention*, 43(3), 1245-1251.

Fishman, E. (2011). Evaluating the benefits of public bicycle schemes needs to be undertaken carefully. *British Medical Journal*, 343, d4521.

Garrard, J, Rissel, C, & Bauman, A. (2012). Health benefits of cycling. In J Pucher & R Buehler (Eds.), *City cycling* (pp. 31-55). Cambridge, MA: The MIT Press.

Goldacre, B, & Spiegelhalter, D. (2013). Bicycle helmets and the law. *British Medical Journal*, 346, f3817.

Goodman, A, Sahlqvist, S, Ogilvie, D & iConnect Consortium. (2014). New walking and cycling routes and increased physical activity: One- and 2-year findings from the UK iConnect study. *American Journal of Public Health*, 104(9), e38-46.

Gottholmseder, G, Nowotny, K, Pruckner, GJ, & Theurl, E. (2009). Stress perception and commuting. *Health Economics*, 18, 559-576.

Graves, JM, Pless, B, Moore, L, & Nathens, AB. (2014). Public bicycle share programs and head injuries. *American Journal of Public Health*, e1-6.

Guo, SS, Wu, W, Chumlea, WC, & Roche, AF. (2002). Predicting overweight and obesity in adulthood from body mass index values in childhood and adolescence. *American Journal of Clinical Nutrition*, 76, 653-658.

Hamer, M, & Chida, Y. (2008). Active commuting and cardiovascular risk: A meta-analytic review. *Preventive Medicine*, 46(1), 9-13.

Hillman, MC. (1992). *Cycling: Towards health and safety*. London: British Medical Association.

Holm, AL, Glumer, C, & Diderichsen, F. (2012). Health impact assessment of increased cycling to place of work or education in Copenhagen. *BMJ Open*, 2(4) e001135.

Horton, D. (2007). Fear of cycling. In D Horton, P Rosen, & P Cox (Eds.), *Cycling and society* (pp. 133-152). Aldershot, UK: Ashgate.

Hu, G, Pekkarinen, H, Hänninen, O, Yu, Z, Guo, Z, & Tian, H. (2002). Commuting, leisure-time physical activity, and cardiovascular risk factors in China. *Medicine & Science in Sports & Exercise*, 34(2), 234-238.

Hu, G, Tuomilehto, J, Borodulin, K, & Jousilahti, P. (2007). The joint associations of occupational, commuting, and leisure-time physical activity, and the Framingham risk score on the 10-year risk of coronary heart disease. *European Heart Journal*, 28(4), 492-498.

Huy, C, Becker, S, Gomolinsky, U, Klein, T, & Thiel, A. (2008). Health, medical risk factors, and bicycle use in everyday life in the over-50 population. *Journal of Aging and Physical Activity*, 16(4), 454-464.

Institute for Health Metrics and Evaluation [IHME]. (2013). DALY estimates for Australasia. Retrieved 11 July 2014 from www.healthmetricsandevaluation.org.

Jacobsen, PL. (2003). Safety in numbers: More walkers and bicyclists, safer walking and bicycling. *Injury Prevention*, 9, 205-209.

Komanoff, C. (2001). Safety in numbers? A new dimension to the bicycle helmet controversy. *Injury Prevention*, 7, 343-344.

Land Transport New Zealand. (2006). *Sustainable and safe land transport — Trends and indicators*. Wellington: Land Transport New Zealand. Retrieved 20 May 2010 from http://www.cycle-helmets.com/nz-ltsa-2006.pdf.

Lopez, AD. (2006). *Global burden of disease and risk factors*. New York, NY and Washington, DC: Oxford University Press and World Bank.

Murphy, B, Herrman, H, Hawthorne, G, Pinzone, T & Evert, H. (2000). *Australian WHOQOL instruments: Users' manual and interpretation guide*. Melbourne: Australian WHO Field Study Centre.

Nugent, R. (2008). Chronic diseases in developing countries health and economic burdens. *Annals of the New York Academy of Science*, 1136, 70-79.

Ogilvie, D, Egan, M, Hamilton, V, & Petticrew, M. (2004). Promoting walking and cycling as an alternative to using cars: Systematic review. *British Medical Journal*, 329(7469), 763.

Ohta, M, Mizoue, T, Mishima, N, & Ikeda, M. (2007). Effect of the physical activities in leisure time and commuting to work on mental health. *Journal of Occupational Health*, 47, 46-52.

Oja, P, Titze, S, Bauman, A, de Geus, B, Krenn, P, Reger-Nash, B, & Kohlberger, T. (2011). Health benefits of cycling: A systematic review. *Scandinavian Journal of Medical Science Sports*, 21, 496-509.

Olsson, LE, Garling, T, Ettema, D, Friman, M, & Fujii, S. (2013). Happiness and satisfaction with work commute. *Social Indicators Research*, 111, 255-263.

O'Regan, B, & Buckley, F. (2003). *The psychological effects of commuting in Dublin*. (Centre for Research in Management Learning and Development Working Paper Series 2003, Dublin: Dublin City University Business School).

Organisation of Economic Cooperation and Development [OECD]. (2010, 7-8 October). Healthy choices. Session 2 of the OECD Health Ministerial Meeting, Paris, France.

Penedo, FJ, & Dahn, JR. (2005). Exercise and well-being: A review of mental and physical health benefits associated with physical activity. *Current Opinion in Psychiatry*, 18(2), 189-193.

Pucher, J, Buehler, R, Bassett, DR, & Dannenberg, AL. (2010). Walking and cycling to health: A comparative analysis of city, state, and international data. *American Journal of Public Health*, 100(10), 1986-1992.

Rabl, A, & de Nazelle, A. (2012). Benefits of shift from car to active transport. *Transport Policy*, 19, 121-131.

Rissel, C, Curac, N, Greenaway, M, & Bauman, A. (2012). Physical activity associated with public transport use — A review and modelling of potential benefits. *International Journal of Environmental Research and Public Health*, 9, 2454-2478.

Rissel, C, Greaves, S, Wen, LM, Capon, A, Crane, M, & Standen, C. (2013). Evaluating the transport, health and economic impacts of new urban cycling infrastructure in Sydney, Australia — Protocol paper. *BMC Public Health*, 13, 963.

Rissel, C, New, C, Wen, LM, Merom, D, Bauman, AE, & Garrard, J. (2010). The effectiveness of community-based cycling promotion: Findings from the Cycling Connecting Communities project in Sydney, Australia. *International Journal of Behavioural Nutrition and Physical Activity*, 7(1), 8.

Rissel, C, Petrunoff, N, Wen, LM, & Crane, M. (2013). Travel to work and self-reported stress: Findings from a workplace survey in south west Sydney, Australia. *Journal of Transport and Health,* 1(1), 50-53.

Rissel, C, & Wen, LM. (2011). The possible effect on frequency of cycling if mandatory bicycle helmet legislation was repealed in Sydney, Australia: A cross sectional survey. *Health Promotion Journal of Australia*, 22(3), 178-183.

Roberts, I, Owen, H, Lumb, P, & McDougall, C. (1996). *Pedalling health — Health benefits of a modal transport shift*. Adelaide: The University of Adelaide.

Roberts, JR, Hodgson, R, & Dolan, P. (2011). 'It's driving her mad': Gender differences in the effects of commuting on psychological health. *Journal of Health Economics*, 30(5), 1064-1076.

Robinson, DL. (2006). No clear evidence from countries that have enforced the wearing of helmets. *British Medical Journal*, 332, 722-725.

Rojas-Rueda D, de Nazelle A, Tainio M, & Nieuwenhuijsen MJ. (2011). The health risks and benefits of cycling in urban environments compared with car use: Health impact assessment study. *British Medical Journal*, 343, d4521.

Sahlqvist, S, Goodman, A, Simmons, RK, Khaw, KT, Cavill, N, Foster, C … Ogilvie, D. (2013). The association of cycling with all-cause, cardiovascular and cancer mortality: Findings from the population-based EPIC-Norfolk cohort. *BMJ Open*, 3(11), e003797.

Sahlqvist, S, Song, Y, & Ogilvie, D. (2012). Is active travel associated with greater physical activity? The contribution of commuting and non-commuting active travel to total physical activity in adults. *Preventative Medicine*, 55(3), 206-211.

Sandblom, E. (2015). What happens when you mandate helmet-wearing among young Swedish cyclists? Retrieved 7 April 2014 from http://www.ecf.com/news/what-happens-when-you-mandate-helmet-wearing-among-young-swedish-cyclists.

Schnohr, P, Marott, JL, Jensen, JS, & Jensen, GB. (2012). Intensity versus duration of cycling, impact on all-cause and coronary heart disease mortality: The Copenhagen City Heart Study. *European Journal of Preventive Cardiology*, 19(1), 73-80.

Shephard, RJ. (2008). Is active commuting the answer to population health? *Sports Medicine*, 38(9), 751-758.

Stutzer, A, & Frey, BS. (2008). Stress that doesn't pay: The commuting paradox. *Scandinavian Journal of Economics*, 110(2), 339-366.

Tuomilehto, J, Lindstrom, J, Eriksson, JG, Valle, TT, Hamalainen, H, Ilanne-Parikka, P … Finnish Diabetes Prevention Study Group. (2001). Prevention of type 2 diabetes mellitus by changes in lifestyle among subjects with impaired glucose tolerance. *New England Journal of Medicine*, 344(18), 1343-1350.

von Huth Smith, L, Borch-Johnsen, K, & Jørgensen, T. (2007). Commuting physical activity is favourably associated with biological risk factors for cardiovascular disease. *European Journal of Epidemiology*, 22, 771-779.

Wen, LM & Rissel, C. (2008). Inverse associations between cycling to work, public transport, and overweight and obesity: Findings from a population based study in Australia. *Preventative Medicine*, 46(1), 29-32.

Whitaker, ED. (2005). The bicycle makes the eyes smile: Exercise, aging, and psychophysical well-being in older Italian cyclists. *Medical Anthropology*, 24(1), 1-43.

Wilson, J. (2013, February 3). Study: People who bike or walk to work enjoy their commutes the most [blog post, New York Bicycling Coalition]. Retrieved 15 August 2014 from http://www.nybc.net/study-people-who-bike-or-walk-to-work-enjoy-their-commutes-the-most.

Wilson, PW, D'Agostino, RB, Sullivan, L, Parise, H, & Kannel, WB. (2002). Overweight and obesity as determinants of cardiovascular risk: The Framingham experience. *Archives of Internal Medicine*, 162(16), 1867-1872.

Woodcock, J, Edwards, P, Tonne, C, Armstrong, BG, Ashiru, O, Banister, D, & Roberts, I. (2009). Public health benefits of strategies to reduce greenhouse-gas emissions: Urban land transport. *Lancet*, 374, 1930-1943.

Woodcock, J, Tainio, M, Cheshire, J, O'Brien, O, & Goodman, A. (2014). Health effects of the London bicycle sharing system: Health impact modelling study. *British Medical Journal*, 348, g425.

Zander, A, Passmore, E, Mason, C, & Rissel, C. (2013). Joy, exercise, enjoyment, getting out: A qualitative study of older people's experience of cycling in Sydney, Australia. *Journal of Environmental Public Health*, 547453. doi: org/10.1155/2013/547453.

4 An epidemiological profile of cycling injury in Australia and New Zealand

Julie Hatfield, Soufiane Boufous and Ros Poulos

Introduction

This chapter aims to provide information about cycling crashes and injury patterns in Australia and New Zealand [NZ]. Hopefully, it will soon be outdated! Initiatives to promote cycling, and to improve cycling safety, are already being implemented across Australia and New Zealand. If all goes well, such initiatives could result in more people cycling, and fewer people being injured while cycling (Organisation for Economic Co-operation and Development [OECD]/International Transport Forum [ITF], 2013).

The chapter focuses on cycling on paths and roads because most relevant policy aims to increase cycling for transport, which occurs mostly on paths and roads. Much cycling for recreation and/or fitness also occurs on paths and roads. Cycling on mountain-bike trails, in BMX parks, and in velodromes is not in focus in this chapter. Nonetheless, injuries sustained during such cycling may be included in some data presented. Depending on its source, data may include a range of cycling activities (for example, trekking, travelling to the shops) which may have different risk profiles. There is no administrative data available in which these activities are separated. However, police-reported data, as opposed to hospitalisation data, is more likely to exclude some activities such as riding in off-road settings.

Some cycling advocates shun discussion of cycling crashes and injuries because it may contribute to a perception that cycling is unsafe, and so discourage people from cycling. Indeed, the perceived danger has been shown to be a key deterrent to cycling in Australia (Daley, Rissel, & Lloyd, 2007; Garrard, Crawford, & Hakman, 2006) and New Zealand (Mackie, 2009). However, it is important to understand the patterns and causes of cycling injury so that injury risk can be minimised.

Moreover, as Chris Rissel (Chapter Three, this volume) points out, it is important to recognise that on average people who ride bicycles have been found to have a lower all-cause mortality risk than those who do not, despite any risk of injury associated with cycling (China: Matthews et al., 2007; Denmark: Andersen, Schnohr, Schroll, & Hein, 2000; Finland: Hu et al., 2004). While these results are specific to the cycling environments in which they were observed, which may be more advanced than our own, they suggest that it is possible to create an environment in which cycling is health-enhancing. Increased cycling safety potentially increases the health benefits of cycling.

In the present chapter 'safety' is taken to mean 'a condition of being protected against injury'. It can be defined more broadly in terms of protection from physical, psychological, spiritual, financial, social, political or other types of harm — with very different implications for 'cycling safety' (given the various benefits of this activity; see OECD/ITF, 2013). At an individual level, an understanding of injury risk allows people to make an informed decision about whether to cycle, and where. Importantly, it may arm people with information to maximise the safety of their cycling. This self-efficacy may in turn increase their propensity to cycle (Bandura, 1997; Milligan, McCormack, & Rosenberg, 2007).

With these ideas in mind, we turn to a consideration of the incidence of crashes and injuries that occur when people ride their bicycles on our roads and paths (whether for transport or recreation).

Incidence of cyclist fatality and injury: Trends compared to other road users

Data on road-user fatalities is regularly compiled by the Australian Bureau of Infrastructure, Transport and Regional Economics [BITRE] (2014) and can be

An epidemiological profile of cycling injury

considered fairly complete (see Australian Bureau of Infrastructure [BITRE], 2014, for the most recent statistics). Fifty people died while cycling in road-related areas (including paths) in Australia in 2013 (see Table 4.1). While the overall number of road deaths in Australia decreased by an average of 3.4% per annum over the last decade, cyclist fatalities decreased by only 0.6% per annum (last row, Table 4.1). Had cyclists experienced proportionally the same reduction in fatalities as vehicle occupants since 2004, around 20 fewer cyclists would have been killed. Although cyclists fared similarly to vehicle occupants for 6 of 9 years, they fared much worse in 2010 and 2013 (and marginally better in 2008) — all years in which large reductions were observed for vehicle occupants. The number of fatalities increased by 51.3% from 2012 to 2013 among cyclists, but decreased for all other road-user groups.

Table 4.1: Road crash fatalities by road user, Australia, 2004-13.

Year	Pedal cyclists	Drivers	Passengers	Motorcyclists	Pedestrians	All road users*
2004	43	760	362	195	220	1583
2005	41	775	347	233	226	1627
2006	39	757	336	238	228	1598
2007	41	785	336	237	204	1603
2008	28	670	303	245	189	1437
2009	31	707	333	224	196	1491
2010	38	636	284	224	170	1353
2011	34	568	286	202	186	1277
2012	33	610	260	223	169	1299
2013	50	564	202	213	157	1193
Av. % change p.a.	-0.6	-3.8	-5.0	-0.4	-3.9	-3.4
% change 2012-2013	51.5	-7.5	-22.3	-4.5	-7.1	-8.2

* Includes those with unstated or unknown road-user type.
(Source: This table was compiled using data from BITRE, 2014, pp. 2-3.)

The average percentage change in fatalities (per annum) over the last decade was similar for male and female cyclists, but varied by age and state of residence. Cyclist fatalities decreased (on average) in those aged 16 years and younger (15.5% per annum), but increased among those aged 40-64 years (3.1% per annum) or 65-70 years (7.8% per annum), remaining steady (max. 2.0% per annum) in other age groups. While cyclist fatalities decreased (on average) in New South Wales (2.4% per annum) and Victoria (3.6% per annum), they increased in Queensland (4.5% per annum) and South Australia (2.4% per annum), and remained almost unchanged in other states and territories.

Table 4.2 presents corresponding information about road-user fatalities over the last decade in New Zealand, compiled by the New Zealand Ministry of Transport (2014). Eight cyclists died in New Zealand in 2013. Had cyclists experienced proportionally the same reduction in fatalities as vehicle occupants

Table 4.2: Road crash fatalities by road user, New Zealand, 2004-13.

Year	Pedal cyclists	Drivers	Passengers	Motorcyclists	Pedestrians	All road users*
2004	7	221	133	35	38	435
2005	12	202	123	37	31	405
2006	9	192	107	38	44	393
2007	12	203	119	41	45	421
2008	10	163	104	51	31	366
2009	8	192	103	48	31	384
2010	10	180	98	50	35	375
2011	9	150	61	33	31	284
2012	8	135	82	50	33	308
2013	8	125	49	39	30	253
% change 2012-2013	0.0%	-7.4%	-40.2	-22.0	-9.1	-17.9

* Includes those with unstated or unknown road-user type.

(Source: This table was compiled using data from New Zealand Ministry of Transport, 2014, p. 19.)

since 2004, around 7 fewer cyclists would have been killed. Again, cyclists do not appear to demonstrate the reduced incidence of fatality experienced by the other road-user groups.

It is also important to consider serious injuries when assessing cycling safety. Hospitalisation data arguably provides the most complete records of serious injury, although some serious cycling injuries are known to be excluded (for example, because the injured cyclists are treated in an emergency department — see Sikic, Mikocka-Walus, Gabbe, McDermott, & Cameron, 2009 — or because they are treated by a general practitioner, or even at home; see also Tin Tin, Woodward, & Ameratunga, 2013a). It is also important to acknowledge that for every serious-injury crash there are numerous crashes with only minor, or no, injury outcomes (for example, see Schramm & Rakotonirainy, 2008). Even these relatively minor crashes may negatively impact the people involved in them, as well as having a substantial economic cost (Aertsens et al., 2010).

According to the Australian Institute of Health and Welfare [AIHW], there were 7176 cyclists hospitalised as a result of land transport crashes in 2010-11 in Australia — including 4092 in road-related areas (2013). The AIHW (2012) provides the best recent analysis of trends in hospitalisations due to crashes in road-related areas[1] in Australia. Age-standardised rates of life-threatening injury increased significantly from 2000-01 to 2008-09 for pedal cyclists (6.8%) and motorcyclists (6.8%), while rates did not change for motor vehicle occupants, and decreased for pedestrians (1.8%). Increases occurred among adult cyclists (that is, cyclists aged 25 years and older), particularly those in the age group 45-64 years. (There was an average annual increase of 14.0% for males, and 14.4% for females. See AIHW, 2012.)

In New Zealand, between 2008 and 2012, over 1500 cyclists were hospitalised due to injuries received in crashes involving motor vehicles on public roads, and more would have been hospitalised as a result of crashes that did not involve a motor vehicle (New Zealand Ministry of Transport, 2013). The number of injured cyclists remained fairly s during this period.

Increases in cyclist fatalities and hospitalisations may reflect, at least in part, an increase in cycling participation (in terms of cyclists or bicycle-kilometres).

---

[1] A relatively high proportion of cycling injuries are sustained in non-traffic (that is, off-road) settings (De Rome et al., 2012).

Available cycling participation data is not sufficient to assess this possibility (Sikic et al., 2009). It is worth noting, however, that the number of passenger vehicles registered in Australia has increased by 10.6% between 2009 and 2014 (see Australian Bureau of Statistics [ABS], 2014) — during which time the number of occupant fatalities reduced consistently. It appears that cyclists are not benefiting equally from road safety countermeasures (Garrard, Greaves, & Ellison, 2010).

Moreover, the Safe Systems approach[2] that is used to inform road safety strategy in Australia and New Zealand does not consider safety 'per million kilometres of road use', 'per million hours of road use' or 'per 100 road users'. The approach aims to minimise the number of people killed and seriously injured on our roads, regardless of how many people use the roads, or how much they do so. People who choose to cycle should be treated in the same way. Targeted interventions are required to prevent the death and serious injuries of cyclists.

Rates of crashes and injuries

Rates of injuries and crashes (per population, per kilometre, or per hour) become important when making comparisons between different modes or between different cycling environments, or when investigating causes of crashes and injuries. However, relatively few studies have focused on reporting directly measured, exposure-based rates of crashes and injuries for cyclists, and those conducted overseas may not be particularly relevant to Australian/New Zealand conditions.

In New Zealand, Tin Tin, Woodward, and Ameratunga (2010) investigated pedal cyclist traffic injuries using the Mortality Collection and the National Minimum Dataset (selected admissions to public hospitals for at least 1 day) for the years 2003-07, adjusting for exposure in terms of total time spent cycling computed from National Household Travel Surveys — for which respondents keep a record of the times, places and travel modes for all their trips over a specified two-day period. The observed rate of death or injury was 31 (95% Confidence Interval [CI] 28-33) per million hours — second only to motorcyclists, and similar to the rate reported by the New Zealand Ministry of Transport (2012) for the years 2008-11.

---

[2] The Safe System Approach seeks to minimise fatalities and serious injuries resulting from road crashes by creating a road system (comprising regulations, roads, vehicles and user behaviours) that is forgiving of human error and limiting crash forces (see OECD/ITF, 2008).

For serious injuries (Abbreviatied Injury Scale [AIS] score of 3 or more) the rate was 6.24 (95% CI 5.21-7.28) per million hours.

Tin Tin et al. (2013b) investigated the incidence of recorded bicycle crashes in a cohort of 2590 cyclists (aged 16 and over) recruited when they enrolled for the 2006 or 2008 Lake Taupo Challenge (New Zealand's largest cycling event). Participants were surveyed at recruitment and again in 2009, and gave consent for their data to be linked to records of crashes and injuries in 4 administrative databases (over a median period of 4.6 years). The incidence of recorded crashes was 240 per million hours spent road cycling. The incidence of collisions with a motor vehicle was 38 per million hours spent road cycling. Relatively minor crashes are likely to be under-enumerated in these databases (Sikic et al., 2009; Langley, Dow, Stephenson, & Kypri, 2003).

Koorey (2014) reported that on New Zealand roads, between January 2006 and June 2013, there were 190 million hours spent travelling by bicycle (according to Household Travel Surveys), 94 cyclists were fatally injured, and more than 6200 bicycle-motor vehicle [MV] crashes resulting in a cyclist being injured were reported to police. This amounts to more than 2 million hours of cycling for every cycling death, and more than 30 000 hours of cycling for every reported bicycle-MV injury crash.

In Tasmania, Palmer et al. (2014) surveyed 136 'regular' cyclists (defined as having ridden at least once in the previous month) aged 18 years and over. Participants provided information about their cycling (including hours/kilometres/trips cycled) and crashes (including severity) in the week prior to interview. The incidence of major bicycle crashes (that is, those requiring third-party medical treatment, or resulting in at least 1 day off work) was 16 (95% CI 11-20) per million kilometres, while the incidence of minor bicycle crashes (those interfering with individuals' regular daily activities and/or causing financial costs) was 37 (23-50) per million kilometres.

Based on the New Zealand findings, a cyclist could expect to experience a significant (that is, recorded) crash after around 4000 hours of cycling, and an injury requiring medical treatment after around 33 000 hours of cycling. A person who cycles around 100 kilometres in a week would experience around 1 significant crash a year.

Comparison to other modes of transport

To put these findings in context, it is interesting to consider comparisons with other modes of transport. Cycling appears to be somewhat more dangerous than car travel, although the extent to which this is the case depends on how estimates of risk are calculated and interpreted.

Tin Tin et al. (2010) reported that in New Zealand cycling has around 8 times the rate of serious injury/fatality (per hour travelled) compared to car occupancy (see Table 4.3). Garrard et al. (2010) reported that in Melbourne and Sydney cycling has between 5 and 19 times the rate of fatality per kilometre travelled compared to car occupancy, with relative risk varying as a function of the data source (that is, police or hospital data) and the time period considered. Similarly, the relative risk of injury on a bicycle in Melbourne and Sydney was around 13-19 times higher than in a car (Garrard et al., 2010). Research from other countries also shows higher rates of injury for cycling (see OECD/ITF, 2013, Chapter One). In a meta-analysis of data from Denmark, Great Britain, the Netherlands, Norway and Sweden, Elvik, Høye, Vaa and Sørensen (2009) found that cyclists face 9.4 times the risk of being injured per kilometre as car occupants do.

Research indicates that time-based rates show a less pronounced difference in risk for cycle- versus car-travel. For example, the New Zealand Ministry of Transport (2012) reported that, when calculated per billion *kilometres* travelled, the rate of death or injury for cycling is around 9 times that of driving, but when calculated per billion *hours* travelled, the rate of death of injury for cycling is only around 3 times that of driving (see Table 4.3). Similarly, the UK Department of Transport (2008) reported that in 2007, UK cyclists faced 13 times more fatalities than car occupants per 100 million kilometres of travel but only 4 times more fatalities per 100 million hours of travel, or per 100 million trips. Van Hout (2007) found that the relative risk of death per hour of travel was roughly equal between cyclists and car occupants in Belgium in 1999 (both cited in OECD/ITF, 2013, Chapter One).

Although distance-based injury rates are often considered because travel is typically from point to point, time-based rates may be more appropriate for intermodal comparisons because of the different speeds of different modes (Koorey & Wong, 2013). This is especially so when the duration of cycling and car trips is nearly the same, which may not be uncommon in congested urban areas.

Table 4.3: Rate of death or injury for cyclists and other modes in New Zealand.

Source	Period	Outcome measure	Exposure measure	Mode						
				Cycling	Walking	Moped	Motorcycle	Car driver	Car passenger
NZ MoT (2012)	2008-2011	Killed or hospitalised	100 million km	245	120		540	27	18
NZ MoT (2012)	2008-2011	Killed or hospitalised	million hours	29	5		205	10	7
Tin Tin et al., (2010)	2003-2007	Killed or hospitalised	million hours	31	2		107	2	3

(Source: Authors' own work.)

Moreover, cyclists may 'self-minimise the level of exposure they face' by choosing closer destinations (Koorey & Wong, 2013, p. 5). Koorey and Wong (2013) argue cogently that simple comparisons of per-kilometre rates for cycling versus driving may be misleading because cyclists are more likely than drivers to be children — and so less mature and experienced, with known consequences for risk. These authors observed that the crash rate for cycling is actually slightly lower than for driving for the 15-19 year age bracket, and similar for the 75-79 year age bracket. Different road types also appear to have a different liability for cyclists. For example, Koorey and Wong (2013) found that for rural roads, the rate of death and injury per million hours travelled was very similar for cycling and driving (while urban state highways seem particularly hazardous for cycling).

Some studies have assessed the extent to which the apparent relative safety of car travel results from a relatively large proportion of car travel occurring on motorways, which are typically safer than other roads. One Dutch study (Dekoster & Schollaert, 1999) found that when motorway travel was excluded, cyclists and car occupants have similar rates of fatal crashes (21.0 and 20.8 fatal crashes per million kilometres, respectively). A Belgian study (Hubert & Toint, 2002) found that the relative fatality rate (per billion kilometres) of cyclists was 2.5 times that of car occupants when motorway travel was included, but only 2 times that of car occupants when motorway travel was excluded.

Motorcycle/moped appears to be uniformly the least safe mode of travel (see Table 4.3), while walking may be safer than cycling.

Factors associated with the incidence or rate of crashes and injuries

Personal characteristics

BITRE data on road-user fatalities provides information about the gender and age of cyclists who died in crashes in road-related areas. Over the 5-year period from 2009-13, 85% of cyclists who died in crashes were male (BITRE, 2014). Over the same period, 45.2% of fatally injured cyclists were aged 40-64 years, 17.7% were aged 26-39 years, and 14.5% were aged 65-75 years. Similarly, between 2000-09, of the cyclists admitted to Australian hospitals as a result of an injury with high threat to life, 85% were male, and nearly two-thirds were aged 25-65 years (AIHW, 2012).

The pattern appears to be similar in New Zealand, where males accounted for around three-quarters of all fatally injured cyclists between January 2006 and June 2013 (Koorey, 2014), and also for three-quarters of all cyclists killed or injured in police-reported crashes between 2008 and 2012 (New Zealand Ministry of Transport, 2013). Nearly a quarter of the cyclists killed or injured in police-reported motor vehicle crashes in the same period were aged 10-19 years old (New Zealand Ministry of Transport, 2013).

Much of the difference between males and females is likely to be due to exposure. For instance, while 82% of cyclists killed or injured in a road crash in the UK in 2008 were male, males were only slightly more likely to be involved in a crash than females when the number of kilometres cycled was taken into account (Mindell, Leslie, & Wardlaw, 2012). A study carried out in Tasmania (Palmer et al., 2014) showed that male sex was associated with a significantly *lower* minor accident risk (incidence rate ratio = 0.34, p = 0.01).

While many studies show higher injury *numbers* for middle-aged cyclists, the few studies that have taken exposure into account show a different pattern. In New Zealand, Tin Tin et al. (2010) reported that 5-14 year-olds are most likely to be killed or seriously injured per million hours cycled (but see Koorey, 2014). Similarly in the United Kingdom, young cyclists (aged 10-15 years) were most likely to be killed or seriously injured per million kilometres cycled (Knowles et al., 2009). Risk then declined, rising again after age 70. Elevated injury rates (per distance travelled) have also been reported for older cyclists in New Zealand (Koorey, 2014) and Holland (Oxley, Corben, Fildes, O'Hare, & Rothengatter, 2004).

In a cross-sectional survey of Queensland cyclists, Heesch, Garrard and Sahlqvist (2011) found that respondents who had cycled for at least 10 years as adults were less likely to report a crash resulting in injury during the previous 12 months compared to those who had cycled for 5 years or less (adjusting for variables including age, gender and cycling frequency). This suggests that experience may have a protective role.

Behavioural factors

Analysis of police-reported bicycle-MV crashes in Queensland from 2002-06 (Schramm & Rakotonirainy, 2008) showed that typical crash contributors such as alcohol, speed and fatigue featured in only 3% of all crashes. Among the 44.4% of crashes in which cyclists were deemed to be at fault, the cyclist's negligence (33%) or inexperience (17%) were the most common contributing factors. When drivers were deemed to be at fault, their inattention (18.6%) or their disobedience of traffic lights or signs (16%) or other road rules (14%) were the three most common contributing factors (Schramm & Rakotonirainy, 2008).

A naturalistic cycling study conducted in Melbourne to identify risk factors for collisions and near-collisions between on-road commuter cyclists and motor vehicles found that drivers were at fault in 87% of these events (Johnson, Charlton, Oxley, & Newstead, 2010). More than half of these driver-at-fault events were due to left manoeuvres by the driver, including turning left and turning left across the path of the cyclist. Comparable findings were reported in a similar naturalistic cycling study carried out in Canberra, which shows that the majority of potential conflict events that involved the cyclist and a driver were due to actions by the driver (Johnson et al., 2014).

From a review of 94 crashes in which cyclists were killed on New Zealand roads or pathways between January 2006 and June 2013, Koorey (2014) concluded that approximately half of the bicycle-MV collisions (that fatally injured the cyclist) were deemed the fault of the motorist, with at least another 12 involving partial fault. Nonetheless, 75% of motorists were not at fault when the cyclist was aged either under 15 or 65 and over. The motorist was deemed to be not sufficiently aware of the cyclist in more than half of the bicycle-MV collisions, often due to inadequate checking.

In a cross-sectional survey of Queensland cyclists, Heesch et al. (2011) found that respondents who have cycled for competition, or who had experienced harassment while cycling, were more likely to report a crash resulting in injury during the previous 12 months compared to those who had not (adjusting for variables including age, gender and cycling frequency).

A New Zealand study linked the survey data of 2590 adult cyclists to administrative databases, including crash and hospital data, covering the period from recruitment (in 2006) to 2011. Cox proportional hazards analysis was used to examine the factors influencing the likelihood of experiencing a recorded crash. The risk of being involved in a recorded crash was higher for people who had experienced a prior crash, who ride in a bunch, or who use a road bike (Tin Tin et al., 2013b).

A survey of cyclists who presented to emergency departments in the Australian Capital Territory [ACT] between November 2009 and May 2010 showed that wearing clothing that fully covers a cyclist's body, regardless of the type of the fabric, substantially reduces the risk of injuries, particularly cuts, lacerations and abrasions (De Rome et al., 2014a).

Environmental factors

Two Australian analyses of police-reported crash data indicate that bicycle crashes are most likely to occur at times when the most cycling occurs (with no correction for exposure) — which is consistent with international data (see OECD/ITF, 2013). The vast majority (78.4%) of bicycle crashes reported to the police in Victoria between 2004 and 2008 occurred during weekdays (Boufous, De Rome, Senserrick, & Ivers, 2013). The highest proportion of bicycle crashes occurred on Thursdays, followed by Tuesdays. The lowest occurred on Sundays.

Meanwhile, Boufous et al. (2013) found that in Victoria, around one-third (30.5%) of police-reported bicycle crashes occurred during the morning travel peak (between 6 am and 10 am) and around one-third (32.1%) occurred during the evening travel peak (2 pm to 6 pm). Analysis of road traffic bicycle crashes that were reported to police in Queensland from 2002-06 (Schramm & Rakotonirainy, 2008) also showed the highest incidence of crashes during the morning travel peak (6 am to 9 am: 27.4%) and during the evening travel (3 pm to 6 pm: 31%). A similar pattern was observed in a survey of cyclists who presented to emergency departments in the ACT between November 2009 and May 2010 (De Rome, Boufous, Senserrick, Richardson, & Ivers, 2012).

Overall, 75% of police-reported bicycle crashes in Victoria occurred in daylight. Just over 1 in 10 bicycle crashes occurred during dusk/dawn, and 13.6% occurred in the dark (Boufous et al., 2013). Similar results were shown in Queensland (Schramm & Rakotonirainy, 2008; Schramm, Rakotonirainy, & Haworth, 2010). Consideration of data from Europe and the United States suggests that the lack of visibility of cyclists may contribute to a substantial proportion of fatal crashes around dusk and early nightfall (OECD/ITF, 2013). Nonetheless, in the survey of cyclists who presented to emergency departments in the ACT, the majority of crashes that occurred in poor light conditions were single-vehicle crashes (De Rome et al., 2012) — suggesting that poor visibility of potential hazards (to the cyclist) is also important.

More than half of the bicycle crashes reported to the police in Victoria occurred during the warmer months (October to March). The highest proportion of crashes occurred in March (10.8%), and the lowest in July (7.2%). The weather was clear in 88.7% of police-reported bicycle crashes (Boufous et al., 2013).

Cycling environment

Over 90% of bicycle crashes reported to the police in Victoria between 2004 and 2008 occurred in urban areas, including metropolitan and regional centres (Boufous et al., 2013). Similarly, Koorey (2014) reported that over 90% of all crashes in which a cyclist was fatally injured on New Zealand roads between January 2006 and June 2013 occurred in urban areas. These findings may be owing in part to the fact that urban areas have more cycling, more traffic and more intersections.

Most police-reported bicycle crashes in Victoria (58.7%) occurred at an intersection, with T-intersections and cross-intersections the most common intersection types (Boufous et al., 2013). Similarly, in Queensland from 2002-06 most police-reported bicycle crashes occurred at intersections (54%), with nearly 6 in 10 (or 58.8%) intersection crashes occurring at T-intersections (Schramm & Rakotonirainy, 2008). The survey of cyclists who presented to emergency departments in the ACT between November 2009 and May 2010 (De Rome et al., 2012) also indicated that bicycle-MV crashes are more likely to occur at intersections. In New Zealand urban areas, 58% of bicycle-MV collisions that resulted in a cyclist fatality between January 2006 and June 2013 were at an intersection (Koorey, 2014). Given that intersections comprise well under half of the path- and road-network, this data suggests that intersections pose a crash risk to cyclists.

Infrastructure is likely to have an important influence on crash occurrence and injury outcomes. It should be a focus of prevention strategies, given its potential for widespread, durable influence without major behaviour change (see Reynolds, Harris, Teschke, Cripton, & Winters, 2009). For this reason, the association between crashes and injuries with different infrastructure types and characteristics is taken up by Glen Koorey in this volume (see Chapter Twelve).

Common bicycle crash types

Examination of common bicycle crash types underscores the hazard posed by intersections and transitions between paths and roadways. Motor vehicles turning across the path of cyclists present a particular issue. For cyclists, transitioning between paths and the roadway appears to be a troublesome manoeuvre. A substantial proportion of bicycle crashes are single-vehicle crashes (often falls) — although these seldom appear in police-reported data (Lujic, Finch, Boufous, Hayen, & Dunsmuir, 2008).

Lindsay (2013) explored the circumstances surrounding collisions between a bicycle and a motorised vehicle among a sample of cyclists admitted to hospital in South Australia between 2008 and 2010. Nearly 4 in 10 collisions involved an oncoming motor vehicle (a car or car-derivative in 90% of cases, with the rest being mainly trucks) turning right across the path of a cyclist who was continuing straight (a 'right-through' collision; see Figure 4.1). Other common collision types included a vehicle travelling from the stem of a T-intersection into the path of a cyclist who was travelling straight on the continuing road ('cross-traffic' collisions; see Figure 4.1);

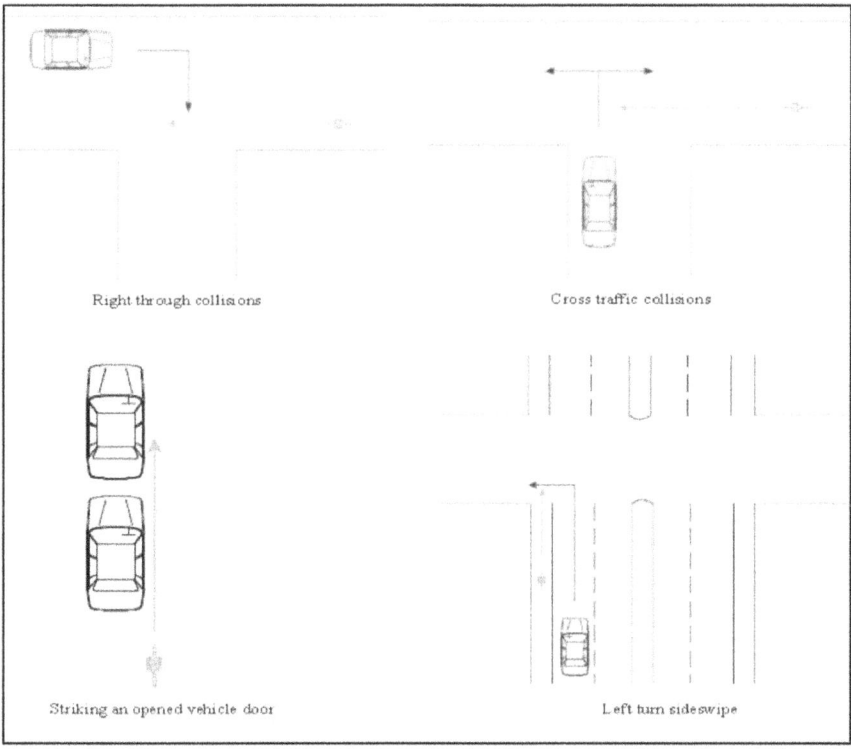

Figure 4.1: Most common cyclist collisions.
(Source: Adapted from several diagrams in Lindsay, 2013.)

a vehicle and a cyclist colliding while travelling in the same direction (in about half of which instances the vehicle was turning left into a side street immediately ahead of the cyclist); and a 'left-turn sideswipe' (see Figure 4.1).

Right-through crashes were also the most common type of casualty crashes reported to the police in Victoria between 2004-08 (Boufous et al., 2010), mostly with a motor vehicle turning right in front of the cyclist. Other common crash types were a motor vehicle and a bicycle colliding after entering a cross-intersection from adjacent arms (cross-traffic crashes: 9.9% of crashes), and cyclists leaving a footpath and colliding with another vehicle (9.3% of crashes). Similarly, among police-reported road traffic bicycle crashes in Queensland from 2002-06 (Schramm & Rakotonirainy, 2008), the cross-traffic collision was the most common crash type (26%). Collisions of bicycles with vehicles leaving driveways (17%) were the next most common type (Schramm & Rakotonirainy, 2008). The most common crash types resulting in cyclist fatalities on New Zealand roads or pathways between January 2006 and June 2013 were sideswipes and right-through crashes (Koorey, 2014).

A naturalistic cycling study using helmet-mounted video cameras to observe near-collisions between cyclists and drivers of motor vehicles (mostly cars) in the ACT found that drivers turning left across the cyclist's path and unexpectedly opened vehicle doors were the most common events (Johnson et al., 2014; see Figure 4.1).

An analysis of bicycle crashes that were reported to police in Victoria between 2004 and 2008 suggests that crash type varies by cyclist age (Boufous, De Rome, Senserrick, & Ivers, 2011). For children and adolescents, the most common scenario was a cyclist riding on a footpath being struck by a motor vehicle emerging from a driveway, followed by a cyclist being struck after entering the roadway from a footpath into the path of a motor vehicle. For adult cyclists, the most common crash types (9.1%) were right-through crashes, cross-traffic crashes, and cyclists colliding with the door of a parked/stationary vehicle (Boufous et al., 2011).

A significant proportion of cyclist crashes resulting in hospitalisation are non-collision crashes. Nearly half (47.5%) of all cyclists hospitalised in Victoria between 2004 and 2008 were injured in single-vehicle non-collision crashes (Boufous et al., 2010). Similarly, in New Zealand 40.4% of hospitalised cyclists hospitalised between 2003 and 2007 were injured in non-collision crashes (Tin Tin et al., 2010).

A survey of cyclists who presented to emergency departments in the ACT between November 2009 and May 2010 showed that around half of the cyclists injured in road-related areas had experienced a crash that did not involve any other road user (De Rome et al., 2012). Almost half of all single-vehicle crashes involved loss-of-control crashes on straight sections. Similarly, most single-vehicle bicycle road crashes in both police records (82.6%) and hospital data (86.7%) in Victoria resulted from non-collision crashes where the cyclist lost control of the bicycle, with the remaining resulting from collisions with fixed or stationary objects (Boufous et al., 2013). European studies based on police data or surveys of injured riders also reported similar findings, and attributed loss of control of the bicycle to poor or defective road surfaces, wet slippery roads, poor lighting, speeding, and alcohol use among cyclists, as well as to bicycle mechanical failures (Knowles et al., 2009; de Geus et al., 2012).

Factors associated with injury severity

Relatively few studies in Australia or New Zealand have investigated factors that are associated with injury severity in the event of a crash. A recent Australian study examined the impact of cyclist, road and crash characteristics on the injury severity for cyclists involved in traffic crashes reported to the police in Victoria between 2004 and 2008 (Boufous, De Rome, Senserrick, & Ivers, 2012). A crash-related severe injury was defined as one that either resulted in the death of the cyclist or in the cyclist being transported to hospital (according to the police report). Factors that increased the risk of severe injury in cyclists involved in traffic crashes were older age (50 years and older), not wearing a helmet, riding in the dark on unlit roads, riding on roads zoned 70 km/h or above, riding on curved road sections of the road, and riding in rural locations. Compared to crashes involving vehicles travelling in the same direction, the following crashes were more likely to result in severe injury: those involving vehicles travelling in opposite directions, those resulting from loss of control of the bicycle, and those involving striking the door of a parked vehicle.

A Queensland study (Heesch et al., 2011) found that respondents who reported a collision with an animal, a pedestrian, another cyclist or a motor vehicle were more likely to report a serious injury (that is, an injury that required a trip to hospital, as compared to one that did not) than were those who reported falling off their bicycle. The same study also reported that respondents who cycled ≤4 days per week were less likely to incur a serious injury compared to those who cycled 5-7 days per week.

Similar findings about the type of cycling crashes that lead to serious injury were reported in studies carried out in the United States (Kim, Kim, Ulfarsson, & Porrello, 2007; Klop & Khattak, 1999) and in Denmark (Kaplan, Vavatsoulas, & Prato, 2013). In addition, these studies found that the risk of severe (versus minor) injury in cyclists involved in road crashes was increased by heavy vehicle involvement, slippery road surface and the lack of cycling paths.

Outcomes of cyclist crashes

Among cyclists involved in crashes reported to the police in Queensland from 2002-06, a small number (1%) died as a result of the crash, 34.3% were hospitalised, 40.2% required medical treatment and 24.4% received minor injury that required no treatment (Schramm & Rakotonirainy, 2008). Similar outcomes, particularly in terms of deaths and hospitalisations, were also found in Victoria (Boufous et al., 2013).

Boufous et al. (2013) found that the most common types of injury in cyclists hospitalised following traffic crashes in Victoria 2004-08 were fractures (46%), followed by open wounds (13.7%), intracranial injuries (including concussion, 9.2%) and superficial wounds (6.7%). The most common body location of injury was upper limbs (37.8%), followed by the head (26.6%) and lower limbs (15.6%). Boufous et al. (2011) found that the proportion of head injuries was higher in children (aged 0-9 years, 37.4%) compared to adolescents (aged 10-19 years, 26.8%) and adults (aged 20 years and over, 23.7%). Further, Boufos et al. (2013) found that while cyclists hospitalised for both single- and multi-vehicle crashes demonstrated similar proportions of head injuries, intracranial injury, including concussion, was slightly more common among casualties of multi-vehicle crashes (10.5%, compared with those in single-vehicle crashes, 8.2%). The mean hospital length of stay was slightly higher for cyclists injured in multi-vehicle crashes (2.6 days) compared with single-vehicle crashes (2.3 days).

Data from South Australia (Lindsay, 2013) and the ACT (De Rome et al., 2012) also showed that the upper and lower extremities, and the head, are the body regions most commonly injured among hospitalised cyclists. In New Zealand during 2003-07, traumatic brain injuries (29.1%), open wounds in the head, face or neck (26.3%) and fractures in upper and lower extremities (25.9% and 24.7% respectively) were the most common injuries for hospitalised cyclists injured in crashes involving a collision with a motor vehicle (Tin Tin et al., 2010). For other hospitalised cycling injuries unrelated to motor vehicle collision, upper extremity fractures (40.3%) were most common, followed by open wounds in the head, and then face or neck and traumatic brain injuries (16.9% and 14.9% respectively). The study also showed that compared to 1988-91, rates of traumatic brain injuries were lower in 1996-99 and 2003-07. In contrast, there was an increasing trend over time in rates of injuries to other body parts (Tin Tin et al., 2010).

A study (Yilmaz et al., 2013) which compared the outcomes of cyclist crashes recorded in trauma registries between Victoria and the south-western region of Holland over a similar period (2001-09) found that Dutch patients had significantly more serious head injuries, with an Abbreviated Injury Scale >= 3 (88.2%), compared to their Australian counterparts (62.4%). However, for other body regions (chest, abdominal and extremities), significantly more serious injuries (AIS >= 3) were observed in the Australian group. The authors partly attributed the difference in serious injury patterns to the higher rate of helmet use in Australia (70-90%) compared to Holland (0.1-5%).

A study carried out in emergency departments in the ACT found few significant differences in types of injury associated with different cycling environments (in traffic, cycle lanes, shared paths and footpaths), although those who crashed while cycling in traffic or on shared paths were more likely to have sustained shoulder, spinal and hip injuries (De Rome et al., 2014b). More importantly, the study found no significant difference, in terms of the severity of injury sustained, between the different cycling environments.

Conclusions

Fifty-eight cyclists died in 2013 in Australia and New Zealand, while thousands more were hospitalised. For each crash that resulted in a cyclist being killed or hospitalised, there were many crashes that did not result in serious injuries but which had a negative effect on the people involved. Casualties among cyclists have not reduced in step with casualties among car occupants. Cycling remains substantially less safe than car travel per kilometre travelled, although the difference is less stark per hour travelled, which may be a more appropriate metric. On average, a cyclist might expect one injury at least requiring medical treatment sometime after 33 000 hours of cycling. Therefore there is a need for a wider rolling out of cycling safety initiatives.

Without adequate data on cycling patterns it is difficult to identify risk factors for crashes and injuries. Available data suggests that elevated risks of crashes or injuries are experienced by children and adolescent cyclists, and by inexperienced cyclists. Although most crashes occur during the day and in pleasant weather (when most cycling occurs), it is probable that cycling at night and in wet weather is more risky. Visibility aids such as bicycle lights and reflective clothing increase visibility and may reduce the likelihood of cyclists being hit by a motorist in such conditions (see Wood et al., 2010). Intersections and transitions from paths to roads feature predominately among police-reported crashes. Careful treatment of intersections, by both designers and users, is likely to improve cycling safety. More generally, the development of cycling infrastructure is likely to play a key role in improving cycling safety and cycling participation (Reynolds et al., 2009). Few rigorous evaluations of cycling safety initiatives have been conducted, and when initiatives are implemented sufficient resources should be allocated to careful evaluation.

On a positive note, there is evidence that the more cyclists there are, the lower each of their individual risks is (in Australia: Turner, Wood, Hughes, & Singh, 2011; Robinson, 2005). Greater cyclist numbers may result in increased cycling safety via several mechanisms. For example, with more cyclists around, drivers may be more aware of cyclists, and so fewer crashes may result from drivers failing to look for cyclists (a common cause of cycle/motor vehicle crashes). In contrast, increased cycling safety (which may result from factors such as improved infrastructure) may promote the uptake of cycling, resulting in increased cyclist numbers. Either way, the 'safety with numbers' phenomenon (Jacobsen, 2003) seems to suggest that initiatives to promote cycling are best pursued in tandem with those that increase cycling safety.

References

Aertsens, J, de Geus, B, Vandenbulcke, G, Degraeuwe, B, Broekx, S, De Nocker, L … Int Panis, L. (2010). Commuting by bike in Belgium — The costs of minor accidents. *Accident Analysis & Prevention, 42*(6), 2149-2157.

Andersen, LB, Schnohr, P, Schroll, M, & Hein, HO. (2000). All-cause mortality associated with physical activity during leisure time, work, sports, and cycling to work. *Archives of Internal Medicine*, 160(11), 1621-1628.

Australian Bureau of Statistics [ABS]. (2014, 31 January). *Motor vehicle census, Australia.* Retrieved 22 July 2015 from http://www.abs.gov.au/AUSSTATS/abs@.nsf/allprimarymainfeatures/EBFEB56F96B02B1FCA257E8A001FD39D?opendocument.

Australian Institute of Health and Welfare [AIHW]. (2012). *Trends in serious injury due to land transport accidents, Australia 2000-01 to 2008-09.* Injury research and statistics series no. 66. Cat. no. INJCAT 142. Canberra: AIHW. Retrieved 12 December 2014 from http://www.aihw.gov.au/WorkArea/DownloadAsset.aspx?id=10737421990.

Australian Institute of Health and Welfare [AIHW]. (2013). *Trends in hospitalised injury, Australia: 1999-00 to 2010-11.* Injury Research and Statistics Series 86. Cat. no. INJCAT 162. AIHW: Canberra. Retrieved 22 July 2015 from http://www.aihw.gov.au/WorkArea/DownloadAsset.aspx?id=60129544396.

Bandura, A. (1997). *Self-efficacy: The exercise of control.* New York: WH Freeman & Company.

Boufous, S, De Rome, L, Senserrick, T, & Ivers, RQ. (2011). Cycling crashes in children, adolescents and adults — A comparative analysis. *Traffic Injury Prevention*, 12(3), 244-250.

Boufous, S, De Rome, L, Senserrick, T, & Ivers, RQ. (2012). Risk factors for severe injury in cyclists involved in traffic crashes in Victoria, Australia. *Accident Analysis & Prevention*, 49, 404-409.

Boufous, S, De Rome, L, Senserrick, T, & Ivers, RQ. (2013). Single-versus multi-vehicle bicycle road crashes in Victoria, Australia. *Injury Prevention*, 19, 358-362.

Boufous, S, De Rome, L, Senserrick, T, Ivers, R, Stevenson, M, Hinchcliff, R, & Ali M. (2010). *Factors in cyclist casualty crashes in Victoria.* Report to Vicroads. Sydney: George Institute for Global Health.

Bureau of Infrastructure, Transport and Regional Economics [BITRE]. (2014). *Road deaths Australia 2013 statistical summary.* Canberra: BITRE.

Daley, M, Rissel, C, & Lloyd, B. (2007). All dressed up and no-where to go? A qualitative research study of the barriers and enablers to cycling in inner Sydney. *Road and Transport Research*, 16(4), 42-52.

de Geus, B, Vandenbulcke, G, Int Panis, L, Thomas, I, Degraeuwe, B, Cumps, E … Meeusen, R. (2012). A prospective cohort study on minor accidents involving commuter cyclists in Belgium. *Accident Analysis & Prevention,* 45, 683-693.

Dekoster, J, & Schollaer, U. (1999). *Cycling: The way ahead for towns and cities.* Bruxelles: European Commission.

De Rome, L, Boufous, S, Senserrick, T, Richardson, D, & Ivers, R. (2012). *The Pedal Study: Factors associated with bicycle crashes and injury severity in the ACT.* Sydney: The George Institute for Global Health, The University of Sydney.

De Rome, L, Boufous, S, Georgeson, T, Senserrick, T, Richardson, D, & Ivers, R. (2014a). Cyclists' clothing and reduced risk of injury in crashes. *Accident Analysis & Prevention,* 73, 392-398.

De Rome, L, Boufous, S, Georgeson, T, Senserrick, T, Richardson, D, & Ivers, R. (2014b). Bicycle crashes in different riding environments in the Australian Capital Territory. *Traffic Injury Prevention,* 15(1), 81-88.

Elvik, R, Høye, A, Vaa, T, & Sørensen, M. (2009). *Handbook of road safety measures.* Bingley: Emerald Group Publishing, Ltd.

Garrard J, Crawford S, & Hakman, N. (2006). *Revolutions for women: Increasing women's participation in cycling for recreation and transport — Final report.* Melbourne: Deakin University.

Garrard, J, Greaves, S, & Ellison, A. (2010). Cycling injuries in Australia: Road safety's blind spot? *Journal of the Australasian College of Road Safety,* 21(3), 37-43.

Heesch, KC, Garrard, J, & Sahlqvist, S. (2011). Incidence, severity and correlates of bicycling injuries in a sample of cyclists in Queensland, Australia. *Accident Analysis & Prevention,* 43, 2085-2092.

Hoffman, MR, Lambert, WE, Peck, EG, & Mayberry, JC. (2010). Bicycle commuter injury prevention: It is time to focus on the environment. *Journal of Trauma, Injury, Infection, and Critical Care,* 69(5), 1112-1119.

Hu, G, Eriksson, J, Barengo, NC, Lakka, TA, Valle, TT, Nissinen, A … Tuomilehto, J. (2004). Occupational, commuting, and leisure-time physical activity in relation to total and cardiovascular mortality among Finnish subjects with type 2 diabetes. *Circulation,* 110(6), 666-673.

Hubert, JP, & Toint, P. (2002). *La Mobilité quotidienne des Belges.* Namur: Presses Universitaires.

Jacobsen, PL. (2003). Safety in numbers: More walkers and bicyclists, safer walking and bicycling. *Injury Prevention, 9*(3), 205-209.

Johnson, M, Charlton, J, Oxley, J, & Newstead, S. (2010). Naturalistic cycling study: Identifying risk factors for on-road commuter cyclists. *Annals of Advances in Automotive Medicine, 54,* 275-283.

Johnson, M, Chong, D, Carroll, J, Katz, R, Oxley, J,& Charlton, J. (2014). *Naturalistic cycling study: Identifying risk factors for cyclists in the Australian Capital Territory.* Melbourne: Monash University Accident Research Centre.

Kaplan, S, Vavatsoulas, K, & Prato, CG. (2013, January 13-17). Cyclist injury severity in a cycling nation: Evidence from Denmark. *Proceedings of the 92nd Annual Meeting of the Transportation Research Board,* Washington DC, USA.

Kim, JK, Kim, S, Ulfarsson, GF, & Porrello, LA. (2007). Bicyclist injury severities in bicycle-motor vehicle accidents. *Accident Analysis and Prevention, 39,* 238-251.

Klop, JR, & Khattak, AJ. (1999). Factors influencing bicycle crash severity on two-lane, undivided roadways in North Carolina. *Transportation Research Record,* 1674(1), 78-85.

Knowles, J, Adams, S, Cuerden, R, Savill, T, Reid, S, & Tight, M. (2009). *Collisions involving cyclists on Britain's roads, Published project reports.* London: TRL Limited.

Koorey, GF. (2014, March 23-26). Investigating common patterns in New Zealand cycling fatalities. Wellington, New Zealand: IPENZ Transportation Group Conference (IPENZTG 2014). Available at http://hdl.handle.net/10092/9718.

Koorey, GF, & Wong, WK. (2013, May 15-17). Is cycling a safe mode? Comparing apples with apples. *Proceedings of the 16th International Conference Road Safety on Four Continents,* Beijing, China.

Langley, JD, Dow, N, Stephenson, S, & Kypri, K. (2003). Missing cyclists. *Injury Prevention, 9*(4), 376-379.

Lindsay, VL. (2013). *Injured cyclist profile: An in-depth study of a sample of cyclists injured in road crashes in South Australia.* Adelaide: Centre for Automotive Safety Research.

Lujic, S, Finch, C, Boufous, S, Hayen, A, & Dunsmuir, W. (2008). How comparable are road traffic crash cases in hospital admissions data and police records? An examination of data linkage rates. *Australian and New Zealand Journal of Public Health*, 32(1), 28-33.

Mackie, H. (2009). *'I want to ride my bike': Overcoming barriers to cycling to intermediate schools.* Wellington: NZ Transport Agency.

Matthews, CE, Jurj, AL, Shu, XO, Li, HL, Yang, G, Li, Q … Zheng, W. (2007). Influence of exercise, walking, cycling, and overall nonexercise physical activity on mortality in Chinese women. *American Journal of Epidemiology*, 165(12), 1343-1350.

Milligan, R, McCormack, GR, & Rosenberg, M. (2007). *Physical activity levels of Western Australian adults 2006 — Results from the Adult Physical Activity Study*. Perth: Western Australian Government. Retrieved 22 July 2015 from http://www.cycle-helmets.com/premiers-health-2006.pdf.

Mindell, JS, Leslie, D, & Wardlaw, M. (2012). Exposure-based, 'like-for-like' assessment of road safety by travel mode using routine health data. *PloS One* 7(12), e50606.

New Zealand Ministry of Transport. (2012). *Risk on the road: Introduction and mode comparison*. Wellington, New Zealand.

New Zealand Ministry of Transport. (2013). Crash fact sheet. Retrieved December 2014 from http://www.transport.govt.nz/assets/Uploads/Research/Documents/cycling-crashfacts-2013.pdf.

New Zealand Ministry of Transport. (2014). *Motor vehicle crashes in NZ 2013*. ISSN: 1176-3949.

Organisation for Economic Co-operation and Development [OECD]/International Transport Forum [ITF]. (2008). *Towards zero: Ambitious targets and the Safe System Approach*. OECD Publishing/ITF. ISBN 978-92-821-0195-7.

Organisation for Economic Co-operation and Development [OECD]/International Transport Forum [ITF]. (2013). *Cycling, health and safety*. OECD Publishing/ITF. doi: org/10.1787/9789282105955-en.

Oxley, J, Corben, B, Fildes, B, O'Hare, M, & Rothengatter, T. (2004). *Older vulnerable road users — Measures to reduce crash and injury risk*. Melbourne: Monash University Accident Research Centre.

Palmer, AJ, Si, L, Gordon, JM, Saul, T, Curry, BA, Otahal, P, & Hitchens, PL. (2014). Accident rates amongst regular bicycle riders in Tasmania, Australia. *Accident Analysis & Prevention*, 72, 376-381.

Reynolds, CC, Harris, MA, Teschke, K, Cripton, PA, & Winters, M. (2009). The impact of transportation infrastructure on bicycling injuries and crashes: A review of the literature. *Environmental Health, 8,* 47.

Robinson, DL. (2005). Safety in numbers in Australia: More walkers and bicyclists, safer walking and bicycling. *Heath Promotion Journal of Australia, 16,* 47-51.

Schramm, AJ, & Rakotonirainy, A. (2008, November 16-20). An analysis of cyclists crashes to identify ITS-based intervention. *15th World Congress On ITS,* Jacob K. Javits Convention Center, New York.

Schramm, AJ, Rakotonirainy, A, & Haworth, NL. (2010). The role of traffic violations in police-reported bicycle crashes in Queensland. *Journal of the Australasian College of Road Safety, 21,* 61-67.

Sikic, M, Mikocka-Walus, AA, Gabbe, BJ, McDermott, FT, & Cameron, PA. (2009). Bicycling injuries and mortality in Victoria, 2001-2006. *Medical Journal of Australia, 190*(7), 353-356.

Tin Tin, S, Woodward, A, & Ameratunga, S. (2010). Injuries to pedal cyclists on New Zealand roads, 1988-2007. *BMC Public Health, 10,* 655.

Tin Tin, S, Woodward, A, & Ameratunga, S. (2013a). Completeness and accuracy of crash outcome data in a cohort of cyclists: A validation study. *BMC Public Health, 13,* 420.

Tin Tin, S, Woodward, A, & Ameratunga, S. (2013b). Incidence, risk, and protective factors of bicycle crashes: Findings from a prospective cohort study in New Zealand. *Preventive Medicine, 57,* 152-161.

Turner, S, Wood, G, Hughes, T, & Singh, R. (2011). Safety performance functions for bicycle crashes in New Zealand and Australia. *Transportation Research Record, Journal of the Transportation Research Board, 2236,* 66-73.

Wood, JM, Tyrrell, RA, Marszalek, RP, Lacherez, PF, Carberry, TP, Chu, BS, & King, MJ. (2010). Cyclist visibility at night: Perceptions of visibility do not necessarily match reality. *Journal of the Australasian College of Road Safety, 21,* 56-60.

Yilmaz, P, Gabbe, BJ, McDermott, FT, Van Lieshout, EM, Rood, PP, Mulligan, TM … Cameron, PA. (2013). Comparison of the serious injury pattern of adult bicyclists, between South-West Netherlands and the State of Victoria, Australia 2001-2009. *Injury, 44,* 848-854.

5 Faster than the speed of bikes

Marilyn Johnson and Derek Chong

Introduction

Speed is a major contributing factor in on-road crashes. Vehicle speed, excessive speed and speed inappropriate for the conditions are known to contribute to road crashes and human trauma (Elvik, Christensen, & Amundsen, 2004; Aarts & Van Schagen, 2006). However, little is known about the speed of cyclists. Cyclists' travel speed, drivers' perceptions of cyclist speed and the potential role of cyclists' speed in relation to safety are poorly understood. It is likely that the travel speed of a cyclist will impact cyclist safety and directly impact how drivers and cyclists interact on the road. For example, if drivers underestimate how fast a cyclist is travelling, they may be more likely to underestimate the distance they needed to turn safely in front of a cyclist, or the time available to open a vehicle door.

For cyclists, speed varies constantly and many factors play a role. The cyclist's wellbeing is a major factor in terms of level of fitness, exertion or fatigue. Terrain directly influences speed; a hill that slows a rider going up provides a free ride down on the return trip. At times cyclists are slowed by headwinds and crosswinds and deterred by rain, and at other times they are helped along by tailwinds and encouraged by warm sunshine (see Kingham and Tranter, Chapter Seven, this volume). Unlike a driver who is cocooned from their environment, the cyclist is exposed to enjoy or combat the elements. The mechanics of the bike, the tyre pressure, bike geometry and the cyclist's position on the bike — upright or tucked over drop handlebars — can also play a part. In addition, the purpose of a trip can increase or decrease the speed a cyclist travels: a daily commute is likely to be travelled at a different speed to a social ride with friends or children on the weekend (van Ingen Schenau, 1988; Hennekam, 1990; Grappe et al., 1999; Thornley, Woodward, Langley, Ameratunga, & Rodgers, 2008).

In countries with high cycling participation rates, cycling is a part of daily life. Streets in many European countries contain people in upright positions on upright bikes, in everyday clothes, pedalling from home to their daily activities (Pucher & Buehler, 2008a; Pucher & Buehler, 2008b; Pucher, Dill, & Handy, 2010). In Denmark and the Netherlands, countries often identified as having aspirationally high levels of cycling participation, bicycles are being used for 18% (DK) and 27% (NL) of *all* trips made (Pucher & Buehler, 2008b). Many of these trips are ridden on separate cycling infrastructure, along cycleways built specifically for cyclists and away from motorised traffic.

Cycling uptake in Australia is yet to reach European rates and few Australians regularly use a bicycle as a transport option. However, the number of people cycling is increasing, up 45% from 2000 to 2010 (Department of Communications, Information Technology and the Arts, 2011), with a reported 17.4% or 4.1 million Australians riding in 2015 (Australian Bicycle Council and Austroads, 2015). There is not yet a connected network of segregated cycleways in any Australian city or town, and cyclists need to travel some portion of their trip on the road, sharing the space with motor vehicles.

Given the sharing of Australian roads, it is essential that cyclists' speed and the perception of cyclist speed is better understood. In this chapter, cyclist speed is explored in four categories:

1. estimates of cyclist speeds
2. actual speed of Australian commuter cyclists
3. drivers' perceptions of cyclist speed
4. role of cyclist speed in cyclist-driver interactions.

Estimates of cyclist speeds

Much research attention on cyclist speed has focused on maximising the performance of elite cyclists to ensure peak speeds during the competitive race season (Pugh, 1974; van Ingen Schenau, 1988; White, 1994; Grappe, Candau, Belli, & Rouillon, 1997; Kun-Feng & Yi-Cheng, 2010). The speeds of professional cyclists are measured with precision and are well known within the sport and by fans of cycling: Anna Meares averaged 66.6 km/h over 500 metres to win gold at the 2012 Olympics, and Mark Cavendish averaged 45.8 km/h over 260 kilometres to win the 2012 International Cycling Union [UCI] men's individual road race. However, much less is known about the speed of non-professional cyclists.

Outside professional cycling, speed has been researched from many different perspectives, often with a focus on vehicle speed, such as in cyclist-vehicle crashes (Summala, Pasanen, Räsänen, & Sievanen, 1996; Hels & Orozova-Bekkevold, 2007; Garrard, Greaves, & Ellison, 2010); posted speed limits (Hoque, 1990; Garrard et al., 2010); the safety benefits to be gained from reduced vehicle speed (Nilsson, 2001; Garrard et al., 2010); and for portions of a cyclist's trip, such as the cyclist travel speed at intersections (Taylor, 1993; Ling & Wu, 2004). Research that has investigated cyclists' speed has used a range of methods and these are discussed below.

Calculations of cyclist speeds

To date, various methods have been used to calculate cyclist speed with wide-ranging results. Studies from the US have used various methods — for example, Thompson, Rebolledo, Thompson, Kaufman, and Rivara (1997) used a radar gun to measure speed on a closed road at a weekend recreational event and reported mean speeds for riders aged 14 years and older. Female mean speed was from 9.04 mph (14.5 km/h) and male mean speed was from 10.5 mph (16.8 km/h). Cyclists' self-reported speeds were likely to be an overestimation when compared to the speed measured by the radar gun (Thompson et al., 1997).

Fajans and Curry (2001) calculated cyclist average speed using an estimation of propulsion. They estimated that an average cyclist was likely to travel at an average speed of 12.5 mph (20 km/h) based on an estimation of 100 watts of propulsion power. However, this was impacted by cyclist exertion (increased average speed) and stopping at stop signs (decreased average speed). An estimation of cyclist speed by Kassim, Pascoe, Ismail, and Abd El Halim (2012) using automatic video analysis and computer vision techniques reported an estimated intersection crossing speed of 18.2 km/h (5.09-41.0 km/h).

In a New Zealand study, Thornley et al. (2008) reported that cyclists' median speed was 23.3 km/h (10-35 km/h). This figure was calculated by using the average time and distance cycled per week over the preceding 12 months (speed = distance/time). Surprisingly, the researchers reported an association between a higher average speed and a reduced rate of injury, which contradicts findings from vehicle crash analysis. The authors suggested that high cyclist speed may be a proxy measurement of skills and may be associated with a more experienced rider with improved bike-handling skills and potentially a more assertive and 'visible' position on the road (Thornley et al., 2008).

A study by Gustafsson and Archer (2013) used GPS and video cameras to record commuter cyclist trips (sample size [n] = 17) in Stockholm, Sweden. The reported average speed of cyclists was 20.4 km/h including stops with a maximum speed of 59.9 km/h.

Estimates and small sample sizes have given an indication of the types of speeds that cyclists ride. The reported average cyclist travel speed ranges from 19.5-23.3 km/h. To understand the travel speed of Australian cyclists, it was necessary to measure cyclist travel speeds empirically across a larger cohort, travelling over a range of different trip distances. This chapter presents a naturalistic cycling study conducted by the authors of this chapter with commuter cyclists in the Australian Capital Territory [ACT] (Johnson et al., 2014). Details of the actual recorded travel speeds are discussed below.

Actual speed of Australian commuter cyclists

To date, prior to this ACT-based naturalistic study, little research has been conducted to determine the travel speeds of bicycle riders in Australia.

Naturalistic methods have been used to better understand the experiences of road users, driver and passenger behaviours and crashes (Neale et al., 2002; Dingus et al., 2006; Charlton, Koppel, Kopinathan, & Taranto, 2010). Helmet-mounted cameras have been used to investigate the experiences of cyclists while mountain bike riding (Brown, Dilley, & Marshall, 2008) and city cycling (Brown & Spinney, 2010), and to investigate cyclist-driver collision and near-collisions (Johnson, Charlton, Oxley, & Newstead, 2010). A recent technological advancement is the addition of integrated GPS data loggers into compact video cameras.

In this study of commuter cyclists in the ACT, compact video cameras with the integrated data logger were used to collect data from October 2011 to April 2012 (that is, during the Daylight Savings period). A camera, Oregon Scientific ATC9K, was mounted to each participant's helmet and used to record their trips to and from work. Participants recorded an average of 12 hours and 57 minutes of video footage over a 4-week period. The GPS data logger recorded participants' location at 1-second intervals. In total, 36 participants (25 males, 11 females) completed the study. A total of 8986 kilometres were cycled, 466 hours and 20 minutes of video footage were recorded, and over 1.5 million GPS data points were generated.

Cyclists in the study travelled the majority of their trips on the road; this on-road travel was a study inclusion criterion. Cyclists also rode on off-road bike paths, shared off-road paths and cycled on the footpath (which is legal for all cyclists in the ACT). Calculations of two speeds were conducted from the GPS data: *average travelling speed* and *maximum speed*.

Average travelling speed

The average travelling speed is the speed that cyclists travelled excluding stops (for example, intersections, the start and end of trips, and so on). The average travelling speed provides a more meaningful speed profile than average speed, as the average travelling speed is more likely to represent the speed cyclists are travelling when they encounter other road users. In contrast, the average speed, complete with stops and delays, will underestimate cyclists' travel speed and therefore their speed when interacting with other road users.

The average travelling speed across the cohort was 22.7 km/h (16.7-29.3 km/h). This average travelling speed was within the range of speeds previously published. It is slightly higher than the speed published in Sweden (which did include stopping times) and slightly lower than the estimated speeds calculated in New Zealand. Male cyclists rode an average travelling speed that was slightly higher — 23.5 km/h (17.2-29.3 km/h) — than female cyclists — 21 km/h (16.9-25.5 km/h). (See Figures 5.1 and 5.2.)

However, care needs to be taken when reducing travel speeds to averages. There were 11 cyclists (9 males, 3 females) whose average speed was on or above 25 km/h, with one cyclist (male) recording an average speed of almost 30 km/h.

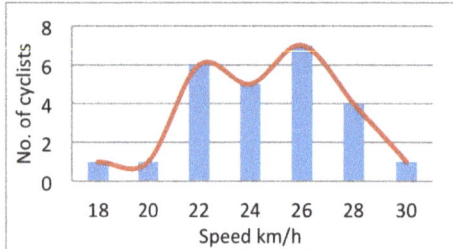
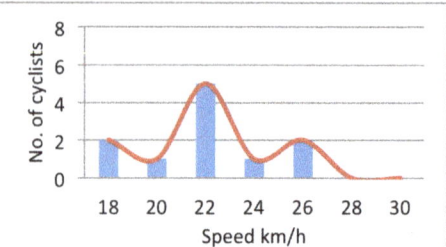

Figure 5.1: Distribution of average travel speed, male cyclists.
(Source: Johnson et al., 2014.)

Figure 5.2: Distribution of average travel speed, female cyclists.
(Source: Johnson et al., 2014.)

Understanding this variability is important when cyclists and drivers are sharing the road, particularly in relation to drivers turning across a cyclist's path.

Maximum speed

The maximum speed across the cohort was 56 km/h (average: 43.6 km/h; 29.5-56.0 km/h). All maximum speeds were recorded when the cyclists were travelling downhill, verified by the elevation profile from the GPS data and a review of the video footage. A further contributing factor to the maximum speed may have been a tailwind; however, it was not possible to determine the presence, absence or direction of wind from the GPS data or video footage.

Again, male cyclist speeds were higher, with a maximum speed of 56 km/h (30.6-56 km/h) compared with female cyclists, who recorded a maximum speed of 49.1 km/h (29.5-49.1 km/h). (See Figures 5.3 and 5.4.)

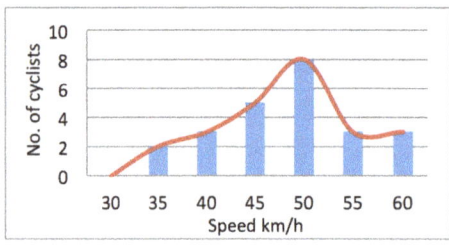
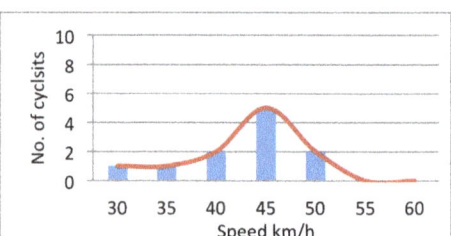

Figure 5.3: Distribution of maximum travel speed, male cyclists.
(Source: Johnson et al., 2014.)

Figure 5.4: Distribution of maximum travel speed, female cyclists.
(Source: Johnson et al., 2014.)

The distribution of the cyclists' maximum speeds is skewed towards slower maximum speed, with a small proportion of cyclists riding at higher speeds. This pattern is the same for both male and female cyclists.

In the ACT naturalistic cycling study, the speed profiles of 36 cyclists were empirically determined over trips measuring almost 9000 kilometres. Using the speeds from this study (average speed: 22.7 km/h; average maximum speed: 43.6 km/h), the next section of this chapter explores how well cyclist speeds were understood by Australians.

Drivers' perceptions of cyclist speed

The number of Australians cycling is increasing; however, the majority of Australian drivers (82%) still do not regularly ride a bike (Department of Communications, Information Technology and the Arts, 2011). Jacobsen's (2003) 'safety in numbers' theory proposes that people who ride a bike themselves are more likely to understand how to interact safely with cyclists. We suggest here that people who ride bicycles will have a better understanding of cyclists' speed compared to people who do not regularly ride a bicycle.

In a national survey, Australians were asked a range of questions about their experiences when interacting on the road, including their estimation of the likely speed of bicycle riders (Johnson, 2011). In this section, these perceptions are compared with the actual speeds recorded in the ACT naturalistic cycling study (Johnson et al., 2014).

All the respondents of the national survey used in this analysis held a valid driver's licence (n = 2607). Respondents were categorised into three groups: those who frequently cycle (n = 2130, 81.7%); those who occasionally cycle (n = 329, 12.6%), and those who do not cycle (n = 148, 5.6%). Respondents were asked how fast they believed cyclists travelled when riding alone or riding in a group of eight or more — both when riding on the flat and when riding downhill. A group of eight cyclists was chosen, as this bunch size offers significant aerodynamic, or drafting, benefits which enable cyclists to travel faster and further with reduced effort compared to a cyclist travelling alone (McCole, Claney, Conte, Anderson, & Hagberg, 1990; Olds, 1998).

Limitation of the calculation due to categories: in the survey, response categories were provided: 5-10 km/h, 11-20 km/h, 21-30 km/h, 31-40 km/h, 41-50 km/h,

Current challenges

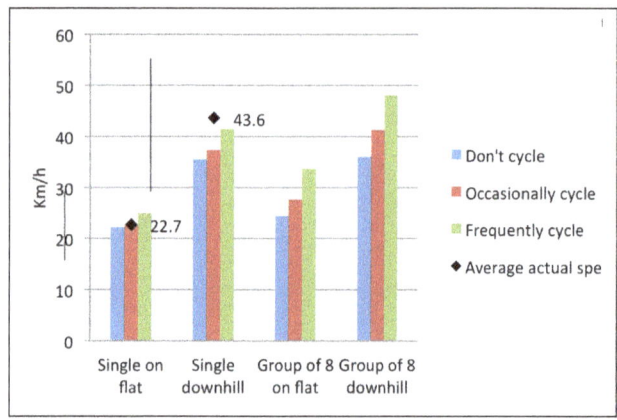

Figure 5.5: Drivers' perceptions of cyclist speed by drivers' cycling frequency.
(Source: Johnson et al., 2014.)

51-60 km/h, 61-70 km/h, over 70 km/h and 'Don't know'. Participants were not offered an option to provide an exact speed. To calculate speed in this analysis, the mid-point values were used for each category to provide a relative comparison of average estimated cyclist speed.

Figure 5.5 shows respondents' perceptions of cyclists' speed by their own cycling frequency. The diamonds indicate the average actual speed recorded by the ACT naturalistic cycling study cohort, and the whiskers indicate the range across the study cohort.

In all cases, respondents who frequently cycled provided the highest estimates of cyclist speed across the four categories, whereas respondents who did not cycle consistently provided the lowest estimates, with occasional cyclists' estimates being in between.

From Figure 5.5, it is clear that people who do not regularly cycle significantly underestimate the travel speed of cyclists. Across all scenarios, people who do not cycle or occasionally cycle consistently reported slower cyclist travel speeds than did regular cyclists.

While it may be argued that in the first category, 'single on the flat' people who do not cycle/occasionally cycle were close to the average in their estimation, it is important to note that 20 participants (55.5%) of the cohort travelled at an average travel speed above 23 km/h. The respondents who do not cycle underestimated the travel speed of a single bike rider by up to 7 km/h below the fastest average travel speed recorded. The discrepancy in perceived speed is even more marked in the 'single downhill' category. All respondents underestimated the actual average speed, although frequent cyclists' estimations were the closest (41.4 km/h).

Travel speeds of groups of cyclists were not recorded in the ACT study; therefore it is not possible to compare the estimated speed of a group of cyclists to the actual speeds. However, again it is clear that people who do not cycle anticipate a slower travel speed for a group of bike riders, both on the flat and downhill, than do occasional cyclist and frequent riders.

People who cycle, both frequently and occasionally, have a higher likelihood of a correct perception of the speed of a single cyclist. This is not surprising, as both groups will have ridden along a flat road and downhill on their own and will be aware of their own experiences in each situation. When interacting on the road, it is likely that people who frequently cycle will provide bicycle riders with a greater buffer as they approach and anticipate their actions. Based on the perceived speeds, it is probable that when people who frequently cycle are driving, they will give greater leeway to bike riders they encounter on the roads. People who do not cycle or only occasionally cycle may be less likely to provide an adequate buffer.

It is clear that Australian drivers who do not cycle underestimate repeatedly the speed of cyclists, both that of a single cyclist and of cyclists in a group, whether riding along a flat road or downhill. Underestimation of the speed of cyclists may be a contributing factor to cyclist-driver near-collisions as well as potentially to crashes. Education about safely interacting with cyclists on the roads is lacking in Australia. In the next section, the role of speed on cyclist interactions with drivers is explored.

Role of cyclist speed in cyclist-driver interactions

In Australia, many cyclists ride on the road. Typically, cyclists and drivers share the road safely, travelling in parallel without incident. However, occasionally, there is deviation from this safe parallel travel, and the interaction between a cyclist and a driver has the potential to lead to a crash.

Concurrent with the increase in cycling participation is an increase in cyclist serious injury crashes (Henley & Harrison, 2011). Of all cyclist crash types, crashes involving a motor vehicle lead to the most serious injury outcomes for cyclists (Bostrom & Nilsson, 2001; Haileyesus, Annest, & Dellinger, 2007; Chong, Poulos, Olivier, Watson, & Grzebieta, 2010). Internationally, cyclists' risk of serious injury has been calculated as 3.6 times greater in a collision with a vehicle compared with all other non-vehicle cyclist crash types (Rivara, Thompson, & Thompson, 1997). In Australia, according to the Australian Transport Safety Bureau (2006), a motor vehicle is involved in the majority of cyclist fatality crashes (86%) and 75.4% of all serious injury crashes (Henley & Harrison, 2009). When compared to drivers, the fatality risk for cyclists was 4.5 times that of a car occupant (Garrard et al., 2010).

Cyclist speed is potentially a factor contributing to unsafe cyclist-driver interactions. Returning to the data generated in the ACT study, all video footage (466 hours and 20 minutes) was manually analysed to identify potentially unsafe interactions between cyclists and other road users. The majority of video footage was uneventful, with cyclists and drivers travelling in parallel without interaction or event. Definitions of three categories of events were used: *collision* is contact between a cyclist and another road user which involved a transfer of kinetic energy; *near-collision* is an event that required rapid, evasive manoeuvring from the cyclist and/or the other road user to avoid a collision (for example, hard braking or swerving); *incident* is an event in which some collision avoidance was required, but was less severe than the near-collision event.

A total of 91 events were identified: 1 near-collision event that required the cyclist to brake heavily to avoid a collision with a vehicle and 90 other incidents. The incidents were defined as interactions that required one or more parties to take some type of evasive action but that were less severe than a near-collision event (Johnson et al., 2014). In the figures below (Figures 5.6 and 5.7), the speed profile of three cyclists is shown with their actual travel speed for 60 seconds before and after the interaction event. Alongside each speed profile is the crash type category from the Vicroads Definitions for Classifying Accidents (DCA).

Cyclist-driver interaction 1

The speed profile shown in Figure 5.6 is for a female cyclist, travelling home from work at 4.08 pm. She was riding in a green bike lane along Commonwealth Avenue, Parkes, and a vehicle cut across her path to turn left into Parkes Way. The cyclist had turned her head to check right, and was beginning to slow in anticipation as evidenced in the graph by her speed at -40 seconds. However, when it became apparent that the vehicle was going to cut across her path, she had to brake heavily. Her speed reduced from 23 km/h to 6 km/h in 20 seconds. From the video footage, the driver only indicated (signalled) once before turning and there was no visible reaction from the driver to indicate that he/she was aware of causing any issue for the cyclist.

Cyclist-driver interaction 2

The speed profile shown in Figure 5.8 is for a male cyclist travelling to work at 8.43 am. He was riding on Langton Crescent, Parkes, with no bike lane on the

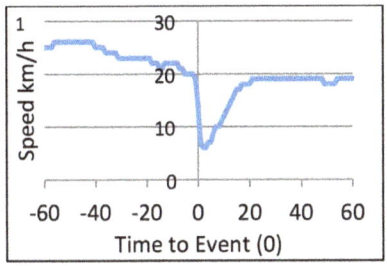

Figure 5.6: Cyclist speed 60 seconds before and after an event. (Source: Johnson et al., 2014.)

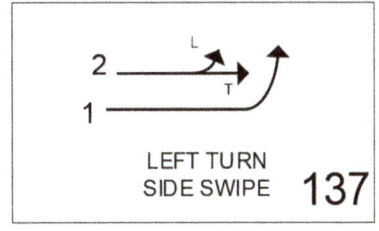

Figure 5.7: Incident type. (Source: Johnson et al., 2014.)

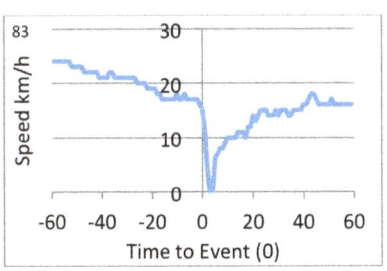

Figure 5.8: Cyclist speed 60 seconds before and after an event. (Source: Johnson et al., 2014.)

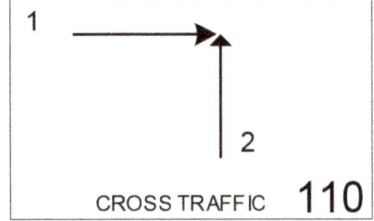

Figure 5.9: Incident type. (Source: Johnson et al., 2014.)

road, when a car cut across his path. The cyclist had to brake hard, his speed reducing from 20 km/h to stationary in 20 seconds. From the video footage, the driver showed no visible reaction to suggest that he/she was aware of causing any issue for the cyclist.

Cyclist-driver interaction 3

The final speed profile is for a male cyclist travelling home from work at 4.53 pm. The incident occurred at the intersection of McCulloch Street and Morgan Crescent, Curtin. Towards the intersection the road narrows and the vehicle overtook the cyclist too closely, causing the cyclist to brake heavily, his speed reducing from 37 km/h to 24 km/h in 6 seconds. From the video footage, there was no visible reaction from the driver to suggest he/she was aware of causing any issue for the cyclist.

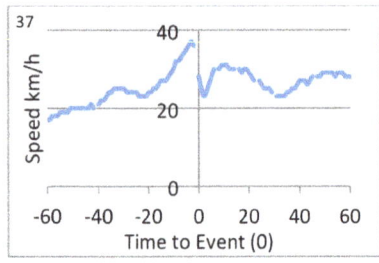 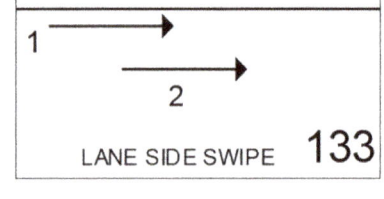

Figure 5.10: Cyclist speed before and after an event. (Source: Johnson et al., 2014.)

Figure 5.11: Incident type. (Source: Johnson et al., 2014.)

Evident from these examples is that a fundamental shift is needed on Australian roads. Drivers must understand the travel speeds of cyclists and afford space appropriately. Substantial change is required to ensure that cyclists are safe on the road, both in relation to drivers' awareness of cyclists on the road and a more accurate understanding amongst drivers of the speed that cyclists can, and do, travel.

Cyclists' skill

On a final note, it is also important that people ride at a speed that is within their level of bike-handling skills. As evidenced by the three scenarios above, it was critical that the cyclist was able to take successful evasive action to avoid a collision. Had the cyclists been travelling at speeds beyond their bike-handling skill level, they may not have been able to slow safely and this may have contributed to a crash event. However, this does not negate the driver's responsibility to understand cyclist speed and interact safely.

Conclusions

The speed profile of Australian cyclists is complex. There is no 'one speed' of cyclists. While commuter cyclists average around 23 km/h, some bicycle riders will travel considerably slower than the average, while others ride much faster.

Currently, almost a fifth of Australians ride a bike. While this is a substantial increase on the number of people who were cycling a decade ago, this is a long way from potential participation levels. Some Australians do not ride a bike and will never ride one, yet they are likely to be drivers. From the data presented in this chapter, Australian drivers underestimate the speed that cyclists travel. However, drivers who are regular cyclists have a better understanding of cyclists' speed than do occasional and non-cycling drivers. These findings extend the 'safety in numbers' theory — that is, people who ride are likely to have a better understanding of how to safely interact with cyclists when they drive than drivers who do not cycle — to include an understanding of cyclist speed. It is important that all drivers are aware of the potential speed of cyclists and that they adapt their driving behaviour accordingly to ensure they give cyclists sufficient space on the road. An education campaign that educates drivers about the speeds of cyclists and the distances needed to interact safely is likely to contribute to a safer cycling environment.

Finally, cyclists typically ride within the posted speed limit, so speed excessive of the posted speed limit is not usually a concern. Yet speed that is excessive for the conditions or an individual's skill level may be a safety issue. Cyclists need to ensure that they travel within their skill level and at a speed suitable for the environment.

Acknowledgements

The authors acknowledge the support of the NRMA-ACT Road Safety Trust, who funded the original naturalistic cycling study. Also, we thank the participants who participated in both the ACT naturalistic cycling study and the national cycling study. We also thank the co-authors of the ACT study report, Justin Carroll, Dr Rod Katz, Dr Jennie Oxley and Associate Professor Jude Charlton.

References

Aarts, L, & Van Schagen, I. (2006). Driving speed and the risk of road crashes: A review. *Accident Analysis & Prevention*, 38(2), 215-224.

Australian Bicycle Council and Austroads. (2015). National Cycling participation Survey 2015. Retrieved 10 November 2015 from https://www.onlinepublications.austroads.com.au/items/AP-C91-15.

Australian Sports Commission. (2011). *Participation in exercise, recreation and sport: Annual report 2010*. Australia: Standing Committee on Recreation and Sport.

Australian Transport Safety Bureau. (2006). *Deaths of cyclists due to road crashes*. ATSB road safety report. Canberra: Australian Government.

Bostrom, L, & Nilsson, B. (2001). A review of serious injuries and deaths from bicycle accidents in Sweden from 1987 to 1994. *Journal of Trauma-Injury Infection & Critical Care*, 50(5), 900-907.

Brown, K, & Spinney, J. (2010). Catching a glimpse: The value of video in evoking, understanding and representing the practice of cycling. In B Fincham, M McGuinness, & L Murray (Eds.), *Mobile methodologies* (pp. 130-151). Hampshire: Palgrave Macmillan.

Brown, KM, Dilley, R, & Marshall, K. (2008). Using a head-mounted video camera to understand social worlds and experiences. *Sociological Research Online*, 13(6). doi: 10.5153/sro.1818.

Charlton, J, Koppel, S, Kopinathan, C, & Taranto, D. (2010). How do children really behave in restraint systems while travelling in cars? *Annals of Advanced Automotive Medicine*. 54th Annual Scientific Conference, Las Vegas.

Chong, S, Poulos, R, Olivier, J, Watson, WL, & Grzebieta, R. (2010). Relative injury severity among vulnerable non-motorised road users: Comparative analysis of injury arising from bicycle-motor vehicle and bicycle-pedestrian collisions. *Accident Analysis & Prevention*, 42(1), 290-296.

Dingus, TA., Klauer, SG, Neale, VL, Petersen, A, Lee, SE, Sudweeks, J … Knipling, RR. (2006). *The 100-Car Naturalistic Driving Study, Phase II — Results of the 100-Car Field Experiment*. Virginia: Virginia Tech Transportation Institute.

Elvik, R, Christensen, P, & Amundsen, A. (2004). *Speed and road accidents: An evaluation of the Power Model*. TØI report 740. Oslo: Institute of Transport Economics [TOI].

Fajans, J, & Curry, M. (2001). Why bicyclists hate stop signs. *ACCESS Magazine*, 1(18), 28-31. Berkeley: University of California Transportation Center. Retrieved 1 June 2015 from http://escholarship.org/uc/item/39h8k0x9.

Garrard, J, Greaves, S, & Ellison, A. (2010). Cycling injuries in Australia: Road safety's blind spot? *Journal of the Australasian College of Road Safety*, 21(3), 37-43.

Grappe, F, Candau, R, Barbier, B, Hoffman, MD, Belli, A, & Rouillon, JD. (1999). Influence of tyre pressure and vertical load on coefficient of rolling resistance and simulated cycling performance. *Ergonomics*, 42(10), 1361-1371.

Grappe, F, Candau, R, Belli, A, & Rouillon, JD. (1997). Aerodynamic drag in field cycling with special reference to the Obree's position. *Ergonomics*, 40(12), 1299-1311.

Gustafsson, L, & Archer, J. (2013). A naturalistic study of commuter cyclists in the greater Stockholm area. *Accident Analysis & Prevention*, 286-98.

Haileyesus, T, Annest, JL, & Dellinger, AM. (2007). Cyclists injured while sharing the road with motor vehicles. *Injury Prevention*, 13(3), 202-206.

Hels, T, & Orozova-Bekkevold, I. (2007). The effect of roundabout design features on cyclist accident rate. *Accident Analysis & Prevention*, 39(2), 300-307.

Henley, G, & Harrison, JE. (2009). *Serious injury due to land transport accidents, Australia, 2006-07.* Injury Research and Statistics Series No 53. Cat. no. INJCAT 129. Canberra: AIHW.

Henley, G, & Harrison, JE. (2011). *Serious injury due to land transport accidents, Australia, 2000-01 to 2007-08.* Injury Research and Statistics Series No 66. Cat. no. INJCAT 142. Canberra: AIHW.

Hennekam, W. (1990). The speed of a cyclist. *Physics Education*, 25(3), 141-146.

Hoque, M. (1990). An analysis of fatal bicycle accidents in Victoria (Australia) with a special reference to nighttime accidents. *Accident Analysis and Prevention*, 22(1), 3-11.

Jacobsen, PL. (2003). Safety in numbers: More walkers and bicyclists, safer walking and bicycling. *Injury Prevention*, 9(3), 205-209.

Johnson, M. (2011). *Cyclist safety: An investigation of how cyclists and drivers interact on the roads* (Doctoral Thesis, Monash University, Melbourne.)

Johnson, M, Charlton, J, Oxley, J, & Newstead, S. (2010). Naturalistic cycling study: Identifying risk factors for on-road commuter cyclists. *Annals Advanced Automotive Medicine*, 54, 275-283.

Johnson, M, Chong, D, Carroll, J, Katz, R, Oxley, J, & Charlton, J. (2014). *Naturalistic cycling study: Identifying crash risk factors for cyclists in the Australian Capital Territory.* Report No. 322. Melbourne: Monash University Accident Research Centre.

Kassim, A, Pascoe, L, Ismail, K, & Abd El Halim, AEH. (2012, January 22-26). Vision-based analysis of cyclists' speed. *Transportaton Research Board 91st Annual Meeting,* Washington DC, USA.

Klauer, SG, Neale, VL, Dingus, TA, Ramsey, D, & Sudweeks, J. (2005). Driver Inattention: A contributing factor to crashes and near-crashes. *Proceedings of the Human Factors and Ergonomics Society Annual Meeting, Surface Transportation* (pp. 1922-1926). Santa Monica, CA.

Kun-Feng, L, & Yi-Cheng, C. (2010, July 1-3). The effects on extremities' muscles while cycling with different speed and gradients. *International Conference on System Science and Engineering (ICSSE)* (pp.142-145). doi: 10.1109/ICSSE.2010.5551753.

Ling, H, & Wu, J. (2004). A study on cyclist behaviour at signalized intersections. *IEEE Transactions on Intelligent Transportation Systems,* 5(4), 293-299.

McCole, SD, Claney, K, Conte, JC, Anderson, R, & Hagberg, JM. (1990). Energy expenditure during bicycling. *Journal of Applied Physiology,* 68(2), 748-753.

Neale, VL, Dingus, TA, Klauer, SG, Sudweeks, J, & Goodman, M. (2005, June 6-9). An overview of the 100-Car Naturalistic Study and findings. *19th International Technical Conference on Enhanced Safety of Vehicles,* Washington DC, USA.

Neale, VL, Klauer, SG, Knipling, RR, Dingus, TA, Holbrook, GT, & Petersen, A. (2002). *The 100-Car Naturalistic Driving Study, Phase 1 — Experimental design.* Blacksburg, Virginia: Virginia Tech Transportation Institute.

Nilsson, A. (2001, September 10-12). Re-allocating road space for motor vehicles to bicycles: Effects on cyclists' opinions and motor vehicle speed. *Proceedings of the AET European Transport Conference,* Homerton College, Cambridge, UK.

Olds, T. (1998). The mathematics of breaking away and chasing in cycling. *European Journal of Applied Physiology,* 77, 492-497.

Pucher, J, & Buehler, R. (2008a). Cycling for everyone: Lessons from Europe. *Transportation Research Record,* 2074, 58-65.

Pucher, J, & Buehler, R. (2008b). Making cycling irresistible: Lessons from the Netherlands, Denmark, and Germany. *Transport Reviews,* 28, 1-57.

Pucher, J, Dill, J, & Handy, S. (2010). Infrastructure, programs, and policies to increase bicycling: An international review. *Preventive Medicine,* 50 (Supplement 1), S106-S125.

Pugh, LGCE. (1974). The relation of oxygen intake and speed in competition cycling and comparative observations on the bicycle ergometer. *The Journal of Physiology*, 241(3), 795-808.

Rivara, FP, Thompson, DC, & Thompson, RS. (1997). Epidemiology of bicycle injuries and risk factors for serious injury. *Injury Prevention*, 3(2), 110-114.

Summala, H, Pasanen, E, Räsänen, M, & Sievanen, J. (1996). Bicycle accidents and drivers' visual search at left and right turns. *Accident Analysis & Prevention*, 28(2), 147-153.

Taylor, D. (1993). Analysis of traffic signal clearance interval requirements for bicycle-automobile mixed traffic. *Transport Research Record*, 1405, 13-20.

Thompson, DC, Rebolledo, V, Thompson, RS, Kaufman, A, & Rivara, FP. (1997). Bike speed measurements in a recreational population: Validity of self reported speed. *Injury Prevention*, 3(1), 43-45.

Thornley, SJ, Woodward, A, Langley, JD, Ameratunga, SN, & Rodgers, A. (2008). Conspicuity and bicycle crashes: Preliminary findings of the Taupo Bicycle Study. *Injury Prevention*, 14(1), 11-18.

van Ingen Schenau, GJ. (1988). Cycle power: A predictive model. *Endeavour*, 12(1), 44-47.

White, AP. (1994). Factors affecting speed in human powered vehicles. *Journal of Sports Sciences*, 12(5), 419-421.

6 Economics of everyday cycling and cycling facilities

Jungho Suh

Introduction

Economics is the study of choice. In narrow terms, economics is concerned with choices in the production or consumption of goods and services traded in the market. In broader terms, economics matters whenever people need to make a choice amongst various options.

People make a choice in travelling amongst various transport modes. The use of bikes as a transport mode varies greatly depending on regional economic and social factors. For example, fossil-fuel-burning transport modes inclusive of motorised bikes and tricycles (also known as rickshaws or tuktuks) are widely used for relatively long-distance travelling in developing countries. Riding pushbikes may not be a desirable option for long-distance travelling in developing countries where the cycling infrastructure is not well established. In contrast, in some developed countries, cycling can be a transport mode even for long-distance travelling for recreation and physical fitness (Börjesson & Eliasson, 2012a; Pattinson & Thomson, 2014).

This chapter discusses the economics of cycling as a choice of transport, based on the neoclassical approach to the economic way of thinking. In the neoclassical economics paradigm, it is assumed that human beings are economic beings (*Homo economicus*) and are responsive to economic (dis)incentives. When some activity is found to become more costly and less beneficial to undertake, a 'rational' economic being is expected to do it less. Conversely, when doing something becomes less costly and more beneficial, the 'rational' person tends to do it more. When decisions are made with respect to transportation, the benefits and costs of each of the available transportation options are weighed up. In doing so, non-market benefits and costs are also taken into account.

The economics of cycling is not just about cycling as a choice of transport mode, but also about cycling facilities as a public choice of road use. In fact, no clear dividing line can be drawn between the benefits of cycling and the benefits of cycling facilities because the two are inextricably linked.

This chapter first develops a taxonomy of the various direct and indirect benefits associated with cycling and cycling facilities. Most of these benefits are not traded in the market and have no market values. The chapter thus introduces a range of non-market valuation methods, which can be employed to estimate the non-market benefits of cycling facilities. The section following this discussion provides a review of existing case studies, although there is very little peer-reviewed research that attempts to estimate the economic benefits of cycling facilities. Finally, the chapter outlines a few conventional techniques of integrating non-market values in the evaluation of cycling infrastructure projects.

The economic benefits of cycling and cycling facilities

Krizek (2007) has classified the benefits of cycling and cycling facilities into *direct benefits* and *indirect benefits*. Direct benefits refer to the benefits to cyclists, whereas indirect benefits refer to the benefits generated to society as itemised in Table 6.1. According to this classification, *direct benefits* include health benefits, recreational benefits and the value of time saved. *Indirect benefits* can be broken down into environmental externalities and industrial benefits. It is notable that there is no concrete boundary between direct and indirect benefits because cyclists are a part of society and can be directly motivated to choose cycling as a mode of transport to reduce traffic congestion and air pollution (see Kingham & Tranter for a discussion of environmental impacts and benefits, Chapter Seven, this volume). Any classificatory system would not be able to account for the multiplicity and interconnectedness of benefits of everyday cycling.

Table 6.1: Classification of the economic benefits of cycling and cycling facilities.

Type		Example
Direct benefits	Health benefits	Physical fitness
	Time saved	Transport cycling
	Recreational benefits	Leisure, tourism
Indirect benefits	Environmental externalities	Reduction in traffic congestion and air pollution
	Industrial benefits	Upstream flow-on benefits (e.g. employment in the bike-manufacturing industries)
		Downstream flow-on benefits (e.g. repair and rental services, eco-tourism industry)

(Source: Adapted from Krizek, 2007.)

Let us turn first to the health benefits of cycling as a form of direct benefit to cyclists. A number of studies (for example, Börjesson & Eliasson, 2012b; Deenihan & Caulfield, 2014; Oja, Vuori, & Paronen, 1998; Oja et al., 2011; Sahlqvist, Song, & Ogilvie, 2012) have documented a myriad of health benefits generated by cycling in terms of reduced risk for cardiovascular diseases, stroke, cancer, and type 2 diabetes, and therefore mortality. Oja et al. (2011) and the World Health Organization [WHO] (2014) meta-analysed the existing literature on the health benefits of cycling and found it evident that there was a strong inverse relationship between all-cause mortality and cycling as a form of physical exercise. This means that more cycling leads to lower all-cause mortality when other variables remain the same. The Department of Infrastructure and Transport (2012) reported that the health cost of inactivity in Australia had been estimated at $13.8 billion per year. Börjesson and Eliasson (2012b) pointed out that an increase in the number of cyclists may not lead to an increase in health benefits because cycling is a substitute for other forms of exercise. However, their point is debatable because active travel is widely promoted as a way for people who do not currently get exercise to incorporate exercise into their daily life (White, Greenland, Hodge, & Bourke, 2014).

Cycling as an active transport mode in lieu of walking gives rise to time saving (Ellison & Greaves, 2011; Heesch, Giles-Cori, & Turrell, 2014). Cycling is time-efficient, particularly in areas of high traffic congestion, and is competitive compared with some forms of public transport such as buses and trams, which frequently stop to pick up and set down passengers. Ellison and Greaves (2011) found that cycling is the most competitive mode of journey for distances of up to 5 kilometres in terms of time spent in travelling. However, short distances are irrelevant if there are barriers to conducting a journey by cycling — for example, traffic, weather and road conditions, or obstacles such as highways, rivers or railways with no safe and convenient crossing. Further, Clement (2008) conducted a pilot study on travel time differences in Adelaide, Australia, and reported that cycling was competitive at distances longer than 5 kilometres during rush hours.

Time has an opportunity cost or scarcity value for each individual, since time is a limited resource. Thus individual time can have a commodity value if the use of time is enjoyable. Traditionally, the monetary value of travel time is thought to depend on the wage rates of individuals. Even though it is doubtful that each and every hour of a day can be counted as available for working, a number of empirical studies have assumed a relationship between time value and income levels (Freeman III, Herriges, & Kling, 2014). However, the traditional theory of the income-influenced time value has been controversial because the value of travel time is influenced by a complex array of cultural and social backgrounds (Boter, Rouwendal, & Wedel, 2005; Freeman III et al., 2014; Garrod & Wills, 1999).

The recreational benefits of cycling capture not only the monetary value of cycling activity as a recreational sport but also any cultural experience occurring during the cycling journey. 'Recreation' is a general word for what people do in their spare time for enjoyment. Interestingly and importantly, Jain and Lyons (2008) pointed out that travel time is wrongly interpreted as a disutility or a burden, which leads transport policy to be driven by the goal of time saving. These authors argued that travel time can generate enjoyable experiences and therefore should be interpreted as a gift rather than a burden.

The indirect benefits of cycling are generally measured in positive environmental externalities and increased economic activities through industrial linkages. Let us first discuss the positive environmental externalities of cycling, which refer to the environmental and ecological benefits generated by cycling —

such as reduction in traffic congestion or air pollution. In other words, the positive environmental externalities of cycling take place by reducing negative environmental externalities including traffic congestion and air pollution generated by fossil-fuel-burning cars (Pattinson & Thompson, 2014).

For example, the Department of Infrastructure and Transport (2013) reported that traffic congestion was a growing issue in Australia's largest cities and was predicted to cost Australians AU$20.4 billion per year by 2020, which does not take into account the cost of cleaning up the emissions. The external benefits of cycling in this example can occur in two different ways. First, existing cyclists implicitly generate external benefits by not shifting to motorised vehicles, given that external costs might accrue if cyclists were to transfer to motor vehicles (Hathway, 1996; Massink, Zuidgeest, Rijnsburger, Sarmiento, & van Maarseveen, 2011; Wang, Fang, & Shi, 2011). Massink et al. (2011) pointed out that one can estimate avoided CO_2 emissions by substituting bicycle trips with their most likely alternative transport modes and by calculating the additional CO_2 emissions resulting from the alternative transport modes. The Department of Infrastructure and Transport (2012) reported that motor vehicles were a major source of air pollution in Australian cities by emitting 302 grams of CO_2 equivalent per passenger per kilometre during peak travel times. This indicates that 1.5 kilograms of CO_2 equivalent emissions are avoided by an Australian urban dweller who travels 5 kilometres by cycling rather than driving a car during rush hours. Second, as Sælensminde (2004) argued, an increase in the number of commuters shifted from motorised cars to bicycles could generate additional external benefits or reduce external costs — for example, air pollution and noise (see Kingham & Tranter, Chapter Seven in this volume, for further discussion of this).

An increase in cycling in any economy can contribute to economic growth as well as pollution reduction (Irish Bicycle Business Association [IBBA], 2011). Upstream industrial benefits include business and employment opportunities in the bicycle production industries. Likewise, an increase in bicycle journeys can generate business and employment opportunities in downstream industries, including retail shops, repair shops and the cycling-related tourism sector (Buis & Wittink, 2000; Flusche, 2012; Litman, 2014). Infrastructure Australia (2009) reported that 10-20% of journeys are made by bicycles in some Western European countries compared to Australia, where less than 2% of journeys are made by bicycle. Blondiau and van Zeebroeck (2014) compiled data on employment in the cycling industries in the European Union countries, reporting that there were about 650 000 full-time-equivalent jobs across upstream and downstream cycling industries in these countries. They predicted that this figure could grow to more than 1 million if the cycling population was doubled. This indicates that there is a high potential for cycling-related industries to grow and contribute to the Australian economy.

Börjesson and Eliasson (2012b) pointed out that cycling promoters and traffic planners tend to place emphasis on indirect benefits, as if the magnitude of direct cycling benefits was not convincingly large enough to support investments in cycling facilities. These authors argued that the misplacement of emphasis results in discriminating against cyclists as if they were not travellers and the direct benefits to them were negligible. Thus it is important for transport planners to be informed of the direct economic benefits of cycling.

Very few studies have been undertaken to comprehend the total benefits of cycling (Cavoli, Christie, Mindell, & Titheridge, in press; Krizek, 2007). This dearth of literature is partly attributed to the fact that the individual benefit components of cycling are not mutually exclusive and therefore not additive to the total benefits of cycling (Wang et al., 2011). For instance, alleviated traffic congestion leads to a reduction in air pollution, which in turn leads to health benefits.

Except for industrial benefits, most types of benefits generated from cycling and cycling infrastructure are not traded in the market. These types of benefits are called non-market benefits. Although it is difficult to estimate the total non-market benefits, various non-market valuation techniques have been developed to measure the individual non-market benefits. The following section gives an overview of the most widely used non-market valuation techniques, and introduces some empirical applications to cycling and cycling facilities.

Valuation of the non-market benefits of cycling and cycling facilities

The direct and indirect benefits that are generated from cycling are not traded in the market and are difficult to estimate due to the lack of market transaction data. This section draws on the broader economic literature to examine how such a valuation might be conducted. The section gives an overview of major non-market valuation techniques and then goes on to review some applications in cycling.

Smith and Krutilla (1982) divided the estimation techniques of non-market benefits into the *physical linkage approach* and the *behavioural linkage approach*. Under the category of physical linkage approach, for example, a researcher can specify a model of the relationship between levels of an air pollutant and some type of observed damage, such as reduced agricultural crop yields or impaired human health. Linked with physical data, the benefit of the reduction in the pollutant can be estimated in dollar terms.

When there is no such physical link to be observed, an alternative is the behavioural linkage approach. The behavioural linkage approach relies on the proposition that non-market benefits can be measured in terms of how much consumers are willing to pay for the benefits. Benefits and *willingness-to-pay* [WTP] are related because, according to Smith and Krutilla (1982), people are willing to pay for something when, and only when, they believe it benefits them. Alternatively, consumers can be asked how much they are willing to accept in compensation for sacrificing the same benefits. In connection with cycling quality, WTP measures benefit estimates for quality-improving changes, whereas *willingness-to-accept* [WTA] compensation measures provide information about welfare decreases resulting from quality-decreasing moves. It is recommended to use WTP in preference to WTA, one of the reasons being that people tend to overstate WTA (Arrow et al., 1993). Table 6.2 presents the types of non-market valuation methods that can be employed for estimating the benefits of cycling or cycling facilities in monetary terms.

Table 6.2: Behavioural linkage approaches to non-market valuation.

Type of valuation approach	Valuation method
Revealed (observed) market behaviour	Travel cost method
	Hedonic price method
Stated (hypothetical) markets	Contingent valuation method
	Choice modelling

(Source: Adapted from de Dios Ortúzar and Rizzi, 2007; Krizek, 2007; and Mitchell & Carson, 1989, p. 75.)

Revealed preference techniques rely on actual consumer choices observed in the real market. With these techniques, the price of a product or service is used as a proxy to infer the WTP for something unpriced but closely related to the product or service (Boyle, 2003). The chief virtue of the revealed preference approach is that it measures the use value of a resource based on actual consumer expenditures. The basic idea of the *travel cost method* [TCM] is to measure the recreational use value of a resource (for example, a national park, a botanical garden or a bike trail) by examining the costs incurred by the visitor to travel to the resource (Clawson & Knetsch, 1966). A demand curve that relates visitation rate to costs per visit indicates demand for the 'whole recreation experience', which includes travel to, and experience, on the site; travel back; and recollection. In practice, there are a number of complexities arising in the application of the TCM:

- The valuation technique cannot be applied to some recreational sites that people do not visit for recreation purposes.
- When people visit multiple sites during a single recreation trip, it is hard to allocate a proportion of their travel cost to a specific site.
- Because recreation demand typically is highly seasonal, and has peak visitation during school and public holidays, it is normally necessary to carry out surveys for peak and off-peak demand periods.
- Where there is a group visit, with members of varying ages, issues arise such as which members to include as recreationists and how to allocate costs between party members.

Another example of a revealed preference technique is the *hedonic price method* [HPM], which utilises variations in property prices so as to estimate the value of the non-market characteristics of property vicinity that may influence the property prices. The data required for HTM applications is collected from the area where specific characteristics are believed to influence property prices. A best-fit multiple regression model is then estimated, property prices being the dependent variable. The independent variables of the model might contain the characteristics of the properties themselves (for example, building type, building space, plot size and number of rooms), neighbourhood characteristics (for example, bike paths, crime rates and proximity to schools or shopping malls), and environmental characteristics of interest (for example, air pollution). In hedonic regression models, bike paths may be controlled as a dummy variable. A differential in property prices is then derived to measure the marginal value of an independent variable of interest when all other variables remained unchanged (Garrod & Wills, 1999). One of the practical problems associated with this valuation technique is that it may not be possible to obtain an adequate sample of property transaction records.

When revealed market data is unavailable or incomplete, economists have used the *stated preference* approach, which relies on hypothetical market situations. One of the main advantages of stated preference techniques is that they can capture values that are not expressed through use or experience and are therefore not revealed in actual markets. The *contingent valuation method* [CVM] has been used to estimate the incremental economic value with respect to a change in the level of environmental service flows of an unpriced natural resource by directly asking people how much they would be willing to pay for a hypothetical change. Mitchell and Carson (1989) provided the full history of the early development of the CVM, which came into use in the early 1960s for the first time. There are two types of methods to elicit WTP amounts from CVM respondents: *continuous* (open-ended) and *discrete* (closed-ended). With the open-ended elicitation method, respondents are asked to state their maximum WTP for the good being valued. The discrete bidding method refers to dichotomous choice questions, where respondents determine whether their WTP is larger or smaller than a set dollar amount.

Choice modelling estimates the amount that people are willing to pay to achieve a greater amount of one or more environmental attribute, given that the dollar cost is treated as one of the characteristics for non-market goods. In fact, the price factor does not represent an inherent attribute of a commodity under consideration. Rather, the price presents dollar costs that are traded off for proposed changes in attribute levels.

The TCM, the HPM and the CVM have been employed to measure the non-market benefits of bicycle facilities (Krizek, 2007; van Leeuwen, Nijkamp, & de Noronha Vaz, 2010). Fix and Loomis (1997) used the TCM to estimate the economic benefits to users of mountain bike trails near Moab, a small town located in south-eastern Utah in the United States. Moab mountain biking trails, including the Slickrock trail, are visited by more than 100 000 mountain bikers per year. According to Fix and Loomis (1997), the estimated consumer surplus per trip per person to Moab biking trails was US$205. This means that the Moab biking trails generate a recreational benefit of US$205 for an individual mountain biker after cancelling out the actual travel costs (transport costs plus on-site costs) per trip to the mountain biking site. Fix and Loomis (1998) then employed the CVM to estimate how much more mountain bikers would be willing to pay for a trip to the Moab biking trails. The mountain bikers were asked whether they would still have come to the Moab area if the travel costs were x dollars higher to visit the area. The hypothetical extra travel cost ranged from $5 to $500, of which one was randomly given to a CVM respondent. The study estimated that the mean WTP per trip per person was $235.

There have been several empirical studies (Jim & Chen, 2010; Krizek, 2006; Lindsey, Man, Payton, & Dickson, 2004; Parent & vom Hofe, 2013; Racca & Dhanju, 2006) which employed the HPM to measure the benefits of cycling trails reflected in the housing markets, and these studies have arrived at conflicting findings. Racca and Dhanju (2006) used the HPM with Geographical Information Systems [GIS] techniques to estimate the impact of proximity to a bike path on the property prices in Delaware, United States. Their study found that the existence of a bike path within the proximity of 50 metres has a significant impact on property prices, other variables (inclusive of the number of bedrooms, and the area size, type and age of buildings) being controlled. Krizek (2006), meanwhile, collected home sales and GIS data for St Paul, Minnesota, in the United States, and measured the effect of bicycle trail proximity on sale prices. The study arrived at a finding that proximity to roadside bike trails actually significantly reduced home value in suburban locations. Krizek (2006) reasoned that bicycle facilities are not always considered an amenity, possibly because suburban residents dislike greater access to their property and neighbourhood by other cyclists. Finally, Parent and vom Hofe (2013) examined the impacts of the Little Miami Scenic Trail on residential property values, using a large sample of housing data in combination with a data set of street network distances. The Little Miami Scenic Trail is located in Hamilton County, the core county of the City of Cincinnati, in the United States. The trail is a public multipurpose trail shared by hikers, runners, skaters, bikers and equestrians. The study found that proximity to trail entrances had a positive effect on property values.

The revealed preference methods (that is, the TCM and the HPM) and the CVM have been employed mostly to estimate the recreational benefits of cycling facilities. There does not appear to be any peer-reviewed research that focuses on the benefits of cycling activity using these non-market valuation techniques. Instead, choice modelling has been widely employed in transport economics in situations where people make a choice in travelling amongst various transport modes (van Dyck, Deforche, Cardon, & de Bourdeaudhuij, 2009; Rabl & Nazelle, 2011). In choice modelling, it is assumed that travellers choose the best option by weighing up the benefits and costs of each and every transportation option available to them.

Choice modelling is grounded on rational choice theory. Like the contingent valuation method [CVM], choice modelling is a stated preference method. Choice modelling begins with establishing a hypothetical market situation in which respondents are expected to state their preferences. Respondents are faced with several choices at a time. It is assumed that rational respondents will weigh up those choices. When the choices are weighed up, it is assumed that rational respondents are aware of their budget constraints as well as the costs and benefits they will experience from each of the choices. Choice modelling relies on the indirect random utility model and on multi-attribute utility theory. Limited dependent variable econometric techniques are preferred to estimate the determinants of the systematic component of the indirect utility function. A regressor's influence on a limited dependent variable can be evaluated using multinomial logit models.

Two types of multinomial logit models are often employed in transportation studies. These models are *conditional logit* models and *polytomous logit* models. Conditional logit models can be employed to forecast the change in transport share as a result of changes in utility caused by alterations in a set of travel attributes such as travel time, transport cost and carbon emissions.[1] Some useful case studies include de Dios Ortúzar and Rizzi (2007), Massink et al. (2011), and Yi, Feeney, Adams, Garcia, and Chandra (2011). A key advantage of using conditional logit models is that one can predict a change in transport mode shares in correspondence to a hypothetical change in any travel attributes. Yi et al. (2011) conducted a choice experiment in Sydney and found that the choice of cycling as a transport mode can be increased three times with dedicated off-road bike paths, and two times with on-road bike lanes.

---

[1] For a more detailed explanation and exploration of conditional logit models, see Adamowicz, Louviere, and Williams (1994), and Zhang and Hoffman (1993).

Using polytomous models, one can treat the choices of transport modes as the dependent variable, and the socio-economic and attitudinal characteristics of the respondents as the independent variables, which may include age, income, gender, and environmental attitudes and behavior. Massink et al. (2011) estimated a polytomous logit model for transport mode choices and found that travellers from the lowest socio-economic stratum are most likely to walk to their school or university, whereas travellers from the highest socio-economic stratum are likely to drive their car for shopping. Massink et al. (2011) also found that cars would be the most likely transport mode alternative to cycling in developed cities, whereas walking or public transport would be the most likely alternative mode in developing cities. This finding indicates that the potential ecological value of cycling will be higher in developed cities than in developing cities. To the knowledge of the author of this chapter, no choice modelling study has been published to date that looks into how the choice of a transport mode is related to its environmental attributes or the environmental attitudes of travellers.

As briefly overviewed, several techniques have been developed to estimate non-market values. Although choice of valuation technique becomes complex in reality, simple statements can be made as a rough guide. When the task is to value the recreation benefits of cycling trails, the TCM is likely to be appropriate. Nevertheless, it is doubtful whether the TCM is appropriate for capturing the value of a specific characteristic of the cycling trails. The CVM can be considered when social welfare changes in relation to a hypothetical change in cycling facilities need to be estimated.

While the importance of non-market values is increasingly being recognised, the accuracy of valuation methods reviewed in this chapter remains a lingering problem. Reliability of value estimates might be the top criterion, from the viewpoint of policy makers, to judge whether to include them in project appraisal. Thus valuation researchers must continue to strive to refine existing valuation methods, or to develop new ones, as a way of enhancing the reliability. However, the ability to estimate non-market values precisely should be treated as a separate issue to the importance of integrating them in project appraisal (Harrison, 1999).

Decision-support systems for transport planning

If there is an increased demand for cycling facilities, policy makers need to evaluate a new investment into cycle facilities. Cycling projects tend to involve various evaluation criteria. Further, decision makers often face the situation where making trade-offs between the multiple decision criteria is unavoidable and a choice needs to be made between competing policy options. Social benefit-cost analysis and multicriteria analysis are widely used tools to aid decision making under these circumstances.

Social benefit-cost analysis

Benefit-cost analysis [BCA] is a discounted cash flow analysis for evaluating the desirability to the community of public sector investments (Callan & Thomas, 2010; Hüging, Glensor, & Lah, 2014). The basic idea of BCA is to determine whether investment projects are worthwhile from a social or taxpayer viewpoint, taking into account all the financial costs and revenues, and positive and negative externalities resulting from the project. Because environmental and social externalities are translated into monetary terms and incorporated into the analysis, BCA is sometimes referred to as *social* or *extended* BCA. BCA is different from 'financial analysis' in that the latter deals with only costs and revenues for the purpose of private investment project appraisal.

The BCA approach is to calculate the difference between project benefits and project costs. To give a green light to a public project, the present value of the project benefits minus the project costs must be positive. The underlying philosophy of BCA is the Kaldor-Hicks compensation principle. According to the Pareto optimum principle, a change in resource allocation in an economy is acceptable only if the change makes at least one person better off without making anyone worse off. In practice, it would be difficult to imagine any change in resource allocation that does not harm anyone. Relaxing the Pareto optimum principle, the Kaldor-Hicks compensation principle states that a 'potential Pareto improvement' can be said to have occurred if the gainers could compensate the losers and still gain a net benefit from a change (Hanley & Spash, 1993). This principle relies on the ethical ground of no interpersonal comparison, and justifies the welfare position that the gains outweigh the losses, even when the compensation is only hypothetical (Campbell & Brown, 2003).

Suppose there is a development project of a new section of bicycle path and a BCA needs to be untertaken. For the project benefits, the BCA of the cycling project can take into account the benefit identified in Table 6.1. The items of the project costs may include land acquisition costs as well as demolition and construction costs and maintenance costs (de Hartog, Boogaard, Nijland, & Hoek, 2010; Hathway, 1996; Sælensminde, 2004). These costs are itemised with the assumption that an off-road cycling path is built especially for cyclists. In the case of conducting a BCA of on-road cycling infrastructure, additional items of costs such as traffic accidents may need to be considered. Table 6.3 attempts to classify the potential project costs of developing cycling facilities. As a side note, the underlying assumption in this case is that roads do not have to be built for all road users. If a road must be built to safely accommodate all road users, one can argue that it would be unthinkable to do a BCA for the cycling component of the road. Thus a BCA of on-road cycling infrastructure is inherently biased, as it regards cycling as an 'option' rather than an integral part of the transport system (Mullen, Tight, Whiteing, & Jopson, 2014).

A major problem in undertaking benefit-cost analyses of developing cycling facilities lies in estimating the non-market benefits and costs of the development project (Wang et al., 2011). Although non-market valuation techniques can be employed to estimate these non-market values, it is not always possible to produce reliable estimates as discussed in the previous section. Multicriteria analysis [MCA] is an alternative to overcome this fundamental problem associated with BCA.

Multicriteria analysis

MCA is a structured framework for the evaluation of several distinct policy options across multiple objectives. In this technique, performance scores are assigned to

Table 6.3: Economic costs of cycling and cycling facilities.

Type		Example
Direct costs	Financial costs to cyclists	Purchase and maintenance of bikes
		Traffic accidents
Indirect costs	Requirement of human-made capital	Acquisition costs
		Demolition costs
		Construction costs including parking facilities
	Industrial costs	Negative impacts on businesses

(Source: Authors' own work.)

each of the policy options on each of various criteria that reflect the multiple objectives (for example, financial, environmental and social objectives) under consideration (Hüging et al., 2014). The performance matrix is called an *effects table* (Janssen, van Herwijnen, & Beinat, 2003; Janssen & van Herwijnen, 2006). The best-performed option is determined by computing the sum of the scores for each of the policy options.

In comparison to BCA, MCA does not have to involve the conversion of all costs and benefits associated with a policy option into monetary terms (Hüging et al., 2014). MCA thus has the advantage of avoiding the risk of spurious quantification of non-market values — that is, the difficulties of converting to dollar value can be avoided by leaving the results of qualitative assessments of environmental values in a qualitative form (Gurocak & Whittlesey, 1998; Hajkowicz, McDonald, & Smith, 2000). Another important aspect of MCA is that this decision-support technique enables diverse groups of stakeholders to play a key role (Hüging et al., 2014). They articulate their views of policy options and participate in identifying evaluation criteria and assigning performance scores to the options being evaluated (Bennett, 2000).

MCA is an integrated computing framework. *DEFINITE* — which stands for *Decisions on a finite set of alternatives* (Janssen et al., 2003; Janssen & van Herwijnen, 2006) — is a widely used MCA software package, the user interface of which is relatively complicated to use. One of the strengths of *DEFINITE* is that it has been designed to run on the Microsoft Windows operating system and allow Microsoft Office programs to be used for exporting *DEFINITE* analysis reports. The software is commercially licensed and therefore must be purchased from the developer.

MCA is applicable to assessing urban mobility projects (Hüging et al., 2014). There are several steps to be followed in the MCA process. The steps described below are adapted from the MCA procedures established in *DEFINITE* (Janssen et al., 2003; Janssen and van Herwijnen, 2006) as well as numerous other similar guidelines (for example, see Department for Communities and Local Government [DCLG], 2009; Hajkowicz et al., 2000; Keeney & Raifa, 1993; Munda, Nijkamp, & Rietvelt, 1994). It should be noted that the order of these steps is not written in stone. Each of the steps can be further divided. The actual working procedure may become more complex, involving interaction between analysts, decision makers and stakeholders.

Current challenges

1. *Identification of alternatives.* Stakeholders, whom MCA modellers need to identify beforehand, define the alternatives to be considered. The MCA modellers should give careful thought to finalising the set of alternatives. The alternatives should represent the current and hypothetical situations of the given issue and should be clearly defined and differentiated. Suppose a local government is considering multiple road-use scenarios in urban areas and needs to choose the best option by evaluating the multiple road-use options. In this scenario, we might suppose there are three alternatives identified — namely, roads without bike lanes, roads with bike lanes, and off-road bike paths.

2. *Identification of objectives and criteria for evaluation.* The stakeholders next identify decision-making criteria. These include the items of benefits and costs listed in Tables 6.1 and Table 6.3, respectively.

3. *Assignment of scores to the identified alternatives on each of the criteria.* The basis of the effects table has been constructed using the identification of policy alternatives and decision criteria. Scores are now assigned to each of the alternatives in relation to each criterion. At this stage, the analysts should consider the relevance of the criteria and the ability of the criteria to help decision makers discern differences in the alternatives. If a criterion gives the same score for each alternative and thus provides no additional information to the analysis, the analysts should consider removing the criterion. Table 6.4 illustrates what an effects table looks like. In this example, the three alternatives are evaluated against eight criteria.

4. *Standardisation of measurement scales into units that are commensurable.* In the effects table, some criteria are expressed in a ratio, whereas others are expressed in an interval scale. For instance, the criterion 'traffic accidents' is measured in a $---/+++$ scale, while the criterion 'time saving' is measured in hours. In MCA, the problem of inconsistent measurement scales is handled through the standardisation of each of the criterion scales. After scoring, criterion scales need to be converted into commensurable units.

5. *Assignment of weights to the criteria to reflect their relative importance.* The next step in the MCA process is to allocate relative weights to

Table 6.4: An effects table for demonstration with three road-use options.

Criteria	Unit	Without bike lanes	With bike lanes	Off-road bike paths
Health	- - -/+ + +	- -	+	+ + +
Time saving	hour	0	1	2
Recreational benefits	$/person	0	3	4
Reduction in traffic congestion	hour	1	3	9
Reduction in air pollution	$ ('000)	5	25	40
Traffic accidents	- - -/+ + +	- - -	+ +	+ + +
Construction costs	$ (M)	1	2	5
Employment	person	100	150	250

(Source: Authors' own work.)

the decision criteria. The process of assigning different weights to the criteria is required in order to make it clear that some of the criteria are more important than others, and therefore should receive greater weights in the analysis. Thus, the weights of the criteria in MCA are usually derived from the stakeholders. Along with scoring the alternatives, giving relative importance to the criteria is one of the major judgmental components in the MCA process. Several methods have been devised for deriving weights information. They include rating and pairwise comparison, fixed point scoring and ordinal ranking.

6. *Aggregating and ranking the alternatives.* Once the effects table has been developed, the phase of ranking alternatives commences. The scores are combined to create an overall score for each option. The aggregated scores are generated by various mathematical methods described below. The type of method that is selected for ranking will depend on whether quantitative data is available in the effects table and which method of weighting was used.

One of the advantages of taking the MCA approach in project appraisal is that the modellers are able to incorporate a relatively large number of criteria from diverse disciplines in order to evaluate various choice possibilities, and are not restricted to using only numerical values. This does not mean, however, that estimates of non-market values are not useful.

The common disadvantage of MCA is that this assessment method relies on inputs from the subjectivity of stakeholders because it requires the stakeholders to identify preference weights for the decision criteria. Subjectivity itself is not necessarily undesirable but may cause an inconsistent framework in making the unavoidable hard choices, diminishing the effectiveness of MCA. In this context, Robinson (2000) emphasised that MCA is a decision-aid process suitable in limited circumstances, and should be used to complement rather than substitute other multi-objective decision-support methods such as BCA, especially to estimate the economic efficiency of a project. The use of qualitative measures in MCA could introduce a high degree of subjectivity and reduce the reliability of the outcomes. Therefore, estimating a monetary value for environmental impacts could remove some degree of the subjectivity surrounding the evaluation and improve the validity of the findings (Robinson, 2001).

Concluding comments

Both cycling and cycling facilities provide a range of socio-economic and environmental benefits beyond cycling activity, including recreation opportunities, reduction in traffic congestion and air pollution. These greatly add to the value of cycling as a time-saving transport mode. When attempting to maximise the sum of the direct and indirect benefits of cycling, one of the key questions is how the benefits can be quantified given there is no common measuring unit. Health benefits, recreational benefits, time saving, reduction in traffic congestion and reduction in air pollution are all measured in different measurement scales.

Most people travel on a daily basis. It is inevitable that they will face a situation where they have to choose a mode of transport for travelling. To make a decision, they take into account not only the financial benefits and costs of each of the modes, but also a range of non-market benefits and costs such as time saving and pollution reduction. Various non-market economic valuation techniques have been devised to translate non-market services into dollar values. While it is debatable whether these values could or should be estimated, such estimates are highly useful, particularly for decision making at a social level.

Transport planners can incorporate the estimates of the non-market values of cycling and cycling facilities into cycling-related project appraisals. Cycling facilities generate multiple classes of benefits and any investment decisions tend to affect a wide range of stakeholder groups. The BCA approach is based on the Kaldor-Hicks compensation principle, in which it does not matter which parties are made better off, or worse off, by a decision. In contrast, MCA takes a participatory decision-support approach, where stakeholders participate in the analysis process and strive to reach a consensus on decision criteria and the prioritisation of the criteria.

References

Adamowicz, W, Louviere, J, & Williams, M. (1994). Combining revealed and stated preference methods for valuing environmental amenities. *Journal of Environmental Economics and Management*, 26(3), 271-292.

Arrow, K, Solow, R, Portney, P, Learner, E, Radner, R, & Schuman, H. (1993). Report of the NOAA Panel on contingent valuation. *Federal Register*, 58(10), 4602-4614.

Bennett, J. (2000). On values and their estimation. *International Journal of Social Economics*, 27, 989-993.

Blondiau, T, & van Zeebroeck, B. (2014). *Cycling works: Jobs and job creation in the cycling economy*. Brussels: European Cyclists' Federation.

Börjesson, M, & Eliasson, J. (2012a). The benefits of cycling: Viewing cyclists as travellers rather than non-motorists. In J Parkin (Ed.), *Cycling and sustainability* (pp. 247-268). Bingley, UK: Emerald Group Publishing.

Börjesson, M, & Eliasson, J. (2012b). The value of time and external benefits in bicycle appraisal. *Transportation Research Part A*, 46(4), 673-683.

Boter, J, Rouwendal, J, & Wedel, M. (2005). Employing travel time to compare the value of competing cultural organizations. *Journal of Cultural Economics*, 29(1), 19-33.

Boyle, KJ. (2003). Introduction to revealed preference methods. In PA Champ, K Boyle, & TC Brown (Eds.), *A primer on nonmarket valuation* (pp. 259-267). Dordrecht: Kluwer Academic Publishers.

Buis, J, & Wittink, R. (2000). *The economic significance of cycling: A study to illustrate the costs and benefits of cycling policy*. Hague: VNG Uitgeverij.

Callan, SJ, & Thomas, JM. (2010). *Environmental economics & management: Theory, policy, and application.* Mason, OH: South-Western Cengage Learning.

Campbell, HF, & Brown, RPC. (2003). *Benefit-cost analysis: Financial and economic appraisal using spreadsheets.* Cambridge: Cambridge University Press.

Cavoli, C, Christie, N, Mindell, J, & Titheridge, H. (In press). Linking transport, health and sustainability: Better data sets for better policy-making. *Journal of Transport & Health.* doi:10.1016/j.jth.2014.08.001.

Clawson, M, & Knetsch, JL. (1966). *Economics of outdoor recreation.* Baltimore: The Johns Hopkins University Press.

Clement, SJ. (2008). An environmental cost model for travel time differences between bicycle and cars. In SJ Clement (Ed.), *Papers of the thinking on two wheels cycling conferences 2005-2007* [CD-ROM]. Transport Systems Centre: The University of South Australia.

de Dios Ortúzar, J, & Rizzi, LI. (2007). Valuation of transport externalities by stated choice methods. In P Coto-Millán, & V Inglada (Eds.), *Essays on transport economics* (pp. 249-272). Heidelberg: Physica-Verlag.

Deenihan, G, & Caulfield, B. (2014). Estimating the health economic benefits of cycling. *Journal of Transport & Health,* 1(2), 141-149.

Department for Communities and Local Government (DCLG). (2009). *Multi-criteria analysis: A manual.* London: Department for Communities and Local Government.Department of Infrastructure and Transport, Australia. (2012). *Walking, riding and access to public transport: Draft report for discussion.* Canberra: Department of Infrastructure and Transport.

Department of Infrastructure and Transport, Australia. (2013). *State of Australian cities 2013.* Canberra: Department of Infrastructure and Transport.

van Dyck, D, Deforche, B, Cardon, G, & de Bourdeaudhuij, I. (2009). Neighbourhood walkability and its particular importance for adults with a preference for passive transport. *Health & Place,* 15(2), 496-504.

Ellison, R, & Greaves, S. (2011). Travel time competitiveness of cycling in Sydney, Australia. *Transportation Research Record: Journal of the Transportation Research Board,* 2247, 99-108.

Fix, P, & Loomis, J. (1997). The economic benefits of mountain biking at one of its meccas: An application of the travel cost method to mountain biking in Moab, Utah. *Journal of Leisure Research,* 29(3), 342-352.

Fix, P, & Loomis, J. (1998). Comparing the economic value of mountain biking estimated using revealed and stated preference. *Journal of Environmental Planning and Management, 41*(2), 227-236.

Flusche, D. (2012). Bicycling means business: The economic benefits of bicycle infrastructure. Retrieved 15 November 2014 from www.advocacyadvance.org/site_images/content/Final_Econ_Update(small).pdf.

Freeman III, AM, Herriges, JA, & Kling, CL. (2014). *The measurement of environmental and resource values: Theory and methods.* New York: Resources for the Future Press.

Garrod, G, & Wills, KG. (1999). *Economic valuation of the environment: Methods and case studies.* Cheltenham: Edward Elgar.

Gurocak, ER, & Whittlesey, NK. (1998). Multiple criteria decision making: A case study of the Columbia River salmon recovery plan. *Environmental and Resource Economics, 12*(4), 479-495.

Hajkowicz, SA., McDonald, GT, & Smith, PN. (2000). An evaluation of multiple objective decision support weighting techniques in natural resource management. *Journal of Environmental Planning and Management, 43*(4), 505-518.

Hanley, N., & Spash, CL. (1993). *Cost-benefit analysis and the environment.* Cheltenham: Edward Elgar.

Harrison, SR. (1999). Progress in estimation of intractable non-market values. In SB Dahiya (Ed.), *The current state of economic science, Vol. 5* (pp. 2719-2737). Model Town, Rohtak, India: Spellbound Publications.

de Hartog, JJ, Boogaard, H, Nijland, H, & Hoek, G. (2010). Do the health benefits of cycling outweigh the risks? *Environmental Health Perspectives, 118*(8), 1109-1116.

Hathway, T. (1996). Assessing the costs and benefits of cycle networks. *World Transport Policy & Practice, 2*(3), 34-41.

Heesch, KC, Giles-Cori, B, & Turrell, G. (2014). Cycling for transport and recreation: Associations with socio-economic position, environmental perceptions, and psychological disposition. *Preventive Medicine, 63*(1), 29-35.

Hüging, H., Glensor, K., & Lah, O. (2014, May 19-20). Need for a holistic assessment of urban mobility measures — Review of existing methods and design of a simplified approach. *International Scientific Conference on Mobility and Transport Sustainable Mobility in Metropolitan Regions,*

Technical University of Munich, Germany. Retrieved 21 August 2014 from <http://www.mobil-tum.vt.bgu.tum.de/fileadmin/w00bqi/www/Session_1/Hueging_et_al.pdf.

Infrastructure Australia. (2009). *Cycling infrastructure for Australian cities*. Sydney: Infrastructure Australia.

Irish Bicycle Business Association [IBBA]. (2011). *Report on the Cycle to Work Scheme tax incentive*. Dublin: IBBA.

Jain, J, & Lyons, G. (2008). The gift of travel time. *The Journal of Transport Geography*, 16(2), 81-89.

Janssen, R, & van Herwijnen, M. (2006). A toolbox for multicriteria decision-making. *International Journal of Environmental Technology and Management*, 6(1/2), 20-39.

Janssen, R, van Herwijnen, M, & Beinat, E. (2003). *DEFINITE 3.0: Case study and user manual*. Amsterdam: Institute for Environmental Studies, Vrije Universiteit.

Jim, CY, & Chen, WY. (2010). External effects of neighbourhood parks and landscape elements on high-rise residential value. *Land Use Policy*, 27(2), 662-670.

Keeney, R, & Raffia, H. (1993). *Decisions with multiple objectives: Preferences and value tradeoffs*. London: Cambridge University Press.

Krizek, KJ. (2006). Two approaches to valuing some of bicycle facilities' presumed benefits. *Journal of the American Planning Association*, 72(3), 309-320.

Krizek, KJ. (2007). Estimating the economic benefits of bicycling and bicycle facilities: An interpretive review and proposed methods. In P Coto-Millán, & V Inglada (Eds.), *Essays on transport economics* (pp. 219-248). Heidelberg: Physica-Verlag.

Van Leeuwen, E, Nijkamp, P, & de Noronha Vaz, T. (2010). The multifunctional use of urban greenspace. *International Journal of Agricultural Sustainability*, 8(1/2), 20-25.

Lindsey, G, Man, J, Payton, S, & Dickson, K. (2004). Property values, recreation values, and urban greenways. *Journal of Park and Recreation Administration*, 22(3), 69-90.

Litman, T. (2014). *Evaluating active transport benefits and costs: Guide to valuing walking and cycling improvements and encouragement programs*. Victoria, BC, Canada: Victoria Transport Policy Institute.

Massink, R, Zuidgeest, M, Rijnsburger, J, Sarmiento, OL, & van Maarseveen, M. (2011). The climate value of cycling. *Natural Resources Forum, 35*(2), 100-111.

Mitchell, RC, & Carson, RT. (1989). *Using surveys to value public goods: The contingent valuation method.* Washington, DC: Resources for the Future Press.

Mullen, C, Tight, M, Whiteing, A, & Jopson, A. (2014). Knowing their place on the roads: What would equality mean for walking and cycling? *Transportation Research Part A, 61,* 238-248.

Munda, G, Nijkamp, P, & Rietvelt, P. (1994). Multicriteria evaluation in environmental management: Why and how? In M Paruccini (Ed.), *Applying multiple criteria and for decision to environmental management* (pp. 1-22). Brussels: Kluwer Academic Publishers.

Oja, P, Titze, S, Bauman, A, de Geus, B, Krenn, P, Reger-Nash, B, & Kohlberger, T. (2011). Health benefits of cycling: A systematic review. *Scandinavian Journal of Medicine and Science in Sports, 21,* 496-509.

Oja, P, Vuori, I, & Paronen, O. (1998). Daily walking and cycling to work: Their utility as health-enhancing physical activity. *Patient Education and Counseling, 33,* S87-S94.

Parent, O, & vom Hofe, R. (2013). Understanding the impact of trails on residential property values in the presence of spatial dependence. *The Annals of Regional Science, 51*(2), 355-375.

Pattinson, W, & Thomson, RG. (2014). Trucks and bikes: Sharing the roads. *Procedia — Social and Behavioral Sciences, 125,* 251-261.

Rabl, A, & Nazelle, A. (2011). Benefits of shift from car to active transport. *Transport Policy, 19*(1), 121-131.

Racca, DP, & Dhanju, A. (2006). *Property value/desirability effects of bike paths adjacent to residential areas.* Project report prepared for the State of Delaware Department of Transportation. Delaware: Delaware Center for Transportation, University of Delaware.

Robinson, J. (2000). Does MODSS offer an alternative to traditional approaches to natural resource management decision making? *Australian Journal of Environmental Management, 7*(3), 170-180.

Robinson, J. (2001). *A review of techniques to value environmental resources in coastal zones.* Brisbane: Coastal Research Centre for Coastal Zone Estuary and Waterway Management, The University of Queensland.

Sælensminde, K. (2004). Cost-benefit analyses of walking and cycling track networks taking into account insecurity, health effects and external costs of motorized traffic. *Transportation Research Part A, 38*(8), 593-606.

Sahlqvist, S, Song, Y, & Ogilvie, D. (2012). Is active travel associated with greater physical activity? The contribution of commuting and non-commuting active travel to total physical activity in adults. *Preventive Medicine, 55*(3), 206-211.

Smith, VK, & Krutilla, JV. (1982). Toward reformulating the role of natural resources in economic model. In VK Smith, & JV Krutilla (Eds.), *Explorations in natural resource economics* (pp. 3-43). Baltimore: The Johns Hopkins University Press.

Wang, H, Fang, K, & Shi, Y. (2011). Benefit-cost analysis with local residents' stated preference information: A study of non-motorized transport investments in Pune, India. *Journal of Benefit-Cost Analysis, 2*(3), 1-37.

White, K, Greenland, R, Hodge, S, & Bourke, P. (2014). *Move it: Australia's healthy transport options*. Canberra: National Heart Foundation of Australia.

World Health Organization [WHO]. (2014). *Development of the Health Economic Assessment Tools (HEAT) for walking and cycling*. Copenhagen: WHO Regional Office for Europe.

Yi, M, Feeney, K, Adams, D, Garcia, C, & Chandra, P. (2011). Valuing cycling — Evaluating the economic benefits of providing dedicated cycle ways at a strategic network level. *Proceedings of Australasian Transport Research Forum 2011*, Adelaide, South Australia. Retrieved 12 October 2014 from http://www.atrf.info/papers/2011.

Zhang, J, & Hoffman, SD. (1993). Discrete-choice logit models: Testing the IIA property. *Sociological Methods and Research, 22*(2), 193-213.

7 Cycling and sustainable transport

Simon Kingham and Paul Tranter

Introduction

One of the most obvious benefits of more people choosing more sustainable transport options is the reduction in pollution emissions — and one such mode is the bicycle. However, the environmental benefits of more people walking or using the bicycle as their form of transport are far greater than just this. These environmental benefits of cycling have long been known, even in nations with extremely low levels of cycling participation. For example, a US study from the 1990s presented a convincing case for the superiority of cycling (and walking) in environmental terms. This study argued that 'by far the greatest environmental benefit of bicycling and walking … is that they bypass the fossil fuel system to which the American economy has become addicted' (Komanoff, Roelofs, Orcutt, & Ketcham 1993, p. 1).

This chapter reiterates many of the arguments about the environmental benefits of cycling, using recent data to support the case. In addition, the chapter introduces a discussion about happiness and personal connections with both the natural environment and with other people, which is often overlooked in discussions about 'the environment', yet can be seen as a vital part of a sustainable environment. In this chapter, using scale as the basis of division, we consider the broader environmental impacts of increasing bicycle use, starting with impacts on the individual, moving through to local communities and nations (specifically Australia and New Zealand), and ending with global impacts.

Personal impacts

There are a number of ways that cycling affects the personal environment of the individual. The most obvious is the health benefits that cycling provides through an increase in levels of physical activity and the increased levels of connectedness that come when people switch from cars to active modes of travel. These health benefits are covered by Rissel (Chapter Three, this volume) and do not need to be repeated in detail here. However, it should be noted that many of these health benefits are the direct result of physical exercise which can take place in a poor-quality environment where people using the bicycle can often be exposed to high volumes of traffic and associated pollution, as is often the case in our towns and cities. In addition, in rural areas, where traffic volumes may be lower, traffic speeds can make the environment uninviting, unpleasant and dangerous. If cycling and walking are to become major modes of transport, the negative impacts of motorised transport must be addressed, by reducing either traffic volumes or speed, or preferably by reducing both. There are also a number of health-related benefits that relate overtly to the quality of the environment, rather than the act of cycling per se.

Infrastructure, speed limits and cycle use

High-quality, physically separated cycle infrastructure has been shown to be a key incentive that attracts individuals to cycling, according to some research in New Zealand (Kingham, Koorey, & Taylor, 2011). This study included questionnaires that asked what would encourage people to cycle (or cycle more frequently), focusing primarily on the journey to work.[1] Follow-up focus groups found that

> the solutions that were most likely to effect a significant change in cycle numbers … [were] … a comprehensive, consistent network of cycle-only paths with separation from motor vehicles, and with dedicated intersection facilities such as hook turns and cycle signals. (p. 11)

---

[1] The questionnaires included tick-box options that included things like speed, traffic volumes, courtesy of drivers and cycle infrastructure.

Koorey (Chapter Twelve, this volume) elaborates on the preferences of different groups of cyclists, but — as Pucher, Dill and Handy (2010) argue — when new high-quality infrastructure is built, more people choose to cycle. This finding has led to the use of the mantra 'build it and they will come' (Geller, 2011). This mantra is partly a result of people feeling safer when cycling — a fact that is demonstrated when data on accident rates is analysed and it is found that in areas where the physical cycling environment is improved, accident rates decrease alongside increases in cycling use. This includes some research conducted in Australia (Harris et al., 2013). Not only does high-quality, physically separated cycling infrastructure make cycling safer, it also makes areas more liveable. This is highlighted by research carried out in North American cities which found that 'nearly three times as many residents felt that the protected bike lanes had led to an increase in the desirability of living in their neighbourhood' (Monsere et al., 2014, p. 13). For a fuller discussion of some of the economic impacts of improving communities through making them more cyclable, see Suh (Chapter Six, this volume).

Despite the clear benefits of separated cycle infrastructure, this separation is unlikely to be achievable (at least in the short to medium term) across large areas of cities, particularly in residential areas. Consequently, another strategy that can make cycling safer in large areas of cities is the reduction of motorised vehicle speeds. Speed limits of 30 km/h (or 20 mph) or lower can significantly improve the sustainability of urban transport systems.

Reducing speed limits, particularly in residential areas, is arguably the most cost-effective strategy for increasing levels of walking and cycling across cities, particularly amongst children. 30 km/h speed limits are now commonplace in European cities, with a city-wide 30 km/h limit planned to be introduced into Paris by the recently elected mayor (Britton, 2014). Under this plan, the speed limit of nearly all streets in Paris would be 30 km/h, apart from a small number of major axes (50 km/h) and the city ring road (70 km/h). The first city to introduce a city-wide 30 km/h limit was Graz, Austria, where a 30 km/h limit was trialled in 1992, on all except some major roads with a 50 km/h limit. After a two-year trial, the lower speeds were maintained, due to majority support from citizens (including motorists) who valued the improved liveability of the city (Hoenig, 2000). There was a 24% reduction in accidents, as well as a significant increase in walking and cycling (Woolsgrove, 2013).

When speeds are reduced to 30 km/h, walking and cycling become more appealing due to the massively decreased traffic danger from motorised vehicles travelling slower. This relates mainly to the laws of physics: in lower-speed streets, cars stop more quickly (and hence avoid crashes altogether), and if pedestrians and cyclists are hit by cars, they have a much greater chance of surviving. For a fuller discussion of factors involved in cyclist injuries, see Hatfield, Boufos and Poulos (Chapter Four, this volume). More important is the fact that when cars are travelling more slowly, there is a change in the psychological feel of the streets: the streets 'feel' safer. When this occurs, more pedestrians (adults and children) are likely to make use of the streets, contributing to a 'safety in numbers' effect (Jacobsen, 2003). Parents are more likely to allow children to play in (or beside) the street, due both to the decreased traffic danger from lower speeds, and to greater passive surveillance provided by more people on the street.

An important feature of the introduction of 30 km/h (or 20 mph) zones is that they are often introduced across large areas of cities, if not an entire city. 'Area-wide' traffic calming is now standard practice, at least in many cities in Europe, where needs of non-motorists are given precedence (Koorey, Chapter Twelve, this volume). Consequently, the culture of the city transforms to a state where pedestrians and cyclists have priority over motorised transport, and streets become places where walking, cycling, social interaction and playing become legitimate uses. The demand for lower residential speed limits is growing, especially across Europe, where there are now significant public campaigns including the European Citizen´s Initiative, *30kmh — making streets liveable!*[2]

Mental health and wellbeing

Recent transport research has demonstrated the beneficial impacts of walking and cycling on mental health. While these impacts can be partly attributed to the benefits of physical exercise, they have also been linked to the 'transport environment'. Though some research has found no relationship between active travel and wellbeing (Humphreys, Goodman, & Ogilvie, 2013), there is a growing body of research that has reported such a relationship. For example, research

---

[2] For more information about this initiative, see http://en.30kmh.eu and the United Kingdom's *20's Plenty for us* (http://www.20splentyforus.org.uk).

in the United Kingdom (Martin, Goryakin, & Suhrcke, 2014) found significant associations between overall psychological wellbeing and active travel and public transport when compared to car travel; it also found similar associations when people switched their mode of transport from car to active modes. Active travel was also associated with reductions in the odds of experiencing two symptoms — being 'constantly under strain' or 'unable to concentrate' — compared to car travel. These relationships remained significant after controlling for a number of potential confounding variables. Martin et al. (2014) suggest that the benefits relate primarily to the disbenefits of driving (for example, boredom) and the physical exercise gained through active transport.

A third mechanism could relate to the quality of the environment. In another study of the relationship between transport modes and wellbeing, Ramanathan, O'Brien, Faulkner, and Stone (2014) examined the impacts of active school travel, and found that parents and children who used active school travel reported more positive emotions versus those of passive travellers, along with stronger connections to dimensions of wellbeing. Specifically, they found that

> parents and children who walk or cycle reported a significantly greater proportion of positive emotions like feeling happy, excited, or relaxed compared with those who use passive, motorized transport. (p. 520)

Citing the earlier work of Fusco, Moola, Faulkner, Buliung, and Richichi (2012), they suggested that a causal mechanism for this was that there was more time for the 'environment' to cognitively register with children. They also suggested that emotional bonds between children and the natural environment were developed through active travel (Brown, Mackett, Gong, Kitazawa, & Paskins, 2008). Together, these findings suggest that a transport environment designed for active travellers can directly and positively improve mental health and wellbeing.

Another recent study examines how the speed of daily travel can displace the 'natural connections between our senses and the world we travel through' (Hoelting, 2010, p. 30) when motorised transport becomes the norm (Tranter, 2014). Not only has the speed of motorised traffic led to the negative impacts of increased risk of death and injury from road crashes, increased pollution and lower levels of active travel, it is also linked with reduced connectedness in local communities. In contrast, the promotion of walking and cycling has benefits for individuals in terms of allowing them to experience and appreciate the natural connections between themselves and the world they inhabit. An inspiring example of a switch to active modes of transport is provided by Kurt Hoelting, who conducted an experiment where he lived an entire year within a 100-kilometre radius from his home in Puget Sound, abandoning his car and air travel and switching to walking, cycling and kayaking (2010).

> The self-enforced practice of active living provided Hoelting with a level of connection and intimacy with place that is not achievable when ensconced in a sealed metal container moving at high speed. (Tranter, 2014, p. 73)

While Hoelting's year of walking, cycling and kayaking may appear to be an extreme example of a switch to active modes of transport, there is now a growing global movement based on the rationale that slower modes of being 'allow individuals to collectively experience life as occupational beings with meaning' (Tranter, 2014, p. 73). Researchers in the fields of occupational science and occupational therapy have identified both increased time pressure and the negative impacts of speed on our lives (Clark, 1997; Farnworth, 2003; Matuska & Christiansen, 2008; Persson & Erlandsson, 2002; Zuzanek, 1998). As Clark (1997) explains, 'when life is rushed as it is in the fast lane of modernity, the result can be the forgetting-of-being, or stated otherwise, doing without being' (p. 86). Walking and cycling are an integral aspect of 'Slow Cities', which allow individuals to experience meaningful connections to local places while living in more ecologically responsible ways (Knox, 2005; Pink & Lewis, 2014).

Liveability and happiness

St-Louisa, Manaugh, van Lieropc, and El-Geneidy (2014) looked at 'commuter satisfaction' and found that pedestrians, train commuters and cyclists are significantly more satisfied than drivers, metro travellers and bus users. An extension of this is that choice of mode of travel can affect personal happiness. This is borne out by research that has shown that people who travel by bicycle are 'happier' than users of other transport modes (Morris & Guerra, 2015). This research also found that

> there are people on the margin of choosing to bike who would be enjoying this activity if society made it somewhat more easy to undertake, for example through the provision of more bike lanes. In all, our findings suggest that promoting or facilitating bicycle use may have additional benefits beyond

public health, transportation and the environment. This will be partly attributable to the exercise but also to the quality of the environment. (p. 39)

Pollution exposure

As previously indicated, the most obvious way in which cycling can positively affect the environment is through a reduction in traffic emissions, and this will be discussed further later. However, research also shows us that how an individual chooses to travel affects the quality of air they will be exposed to. Since the 1990s, an increasing body of research has consistently — and, to many, surprisingly — shown that car drivers are exposed to poorer-quality air than users of other travel modes, including those travelling by bicycle (Kingham, Meaton, Sheard, & Lawrenson, 1998). For example, despite the widespread belief that cycling in traffic is unhealthy due to exposure to pollutants such as benzene, toluene and xylene, as well as dust, a Copenhagen study found that even taking into account the increased respiration rate for cyclists, car drivers are more exposed to airborne pollution than cyclists (Rank, Folke, & Jespersen, 2001).

Over the years, the majority of research has continued to find that cyclists' exposure is lower than that of car drivers (for example, see Karanasioua, Vianaa, Querola, Morenoa, & de Leeuw, 2014). The first Australasian research that included cyclists' exposure was by Farrar, Dingle and Tan (2001) in Perth, who compared cycle commuters and couriers to bus and taxi passengers and found that the cyclists were exposed to lower levels than the bus passengers. Further Australian work by Chertok, Voukelatos, Sheppeard, and Rissel (2004) also found that those travelling by bicycle were exposed to cleaner air than car passengers. More recently, some research in New Zealand with an overt focus on cyclist exposure concluded that cyclists are exposed to significantly cleaner air than users of other modes (Kingham, Longley, Salmond, Pattinson, & Shrestha, 2013). This research also found that off-road cycle paths result in significant additional reductions in personal exposure.

A growing body of research has examined the relative exposure of cyclists in relation to specific route choice and proximity to traffic. Pattinson, Kingham, Longley, and Salmond (2011) found that cyclists travelling on a parallel route just a short distance from traffic — in this case, on the pavement with parking space for cars providing the separation from traffic — significantly reduced exposure to fine particles and carbon monoxide. Further reductions in exposure were achieved for cyclists travelling on a parallel path in a park at an increased distance from traffic. In Australia, Cole-Hunter et al. (2013) found similar findings with exposure to particles.

However, these studies were based on pollution exposure, not dose. *Exposure* is the quality of the air in the vicinity of the individual, while *dose* is the amount absorbed by the body. *Dose* accounts for breathing rates, which are likely to be higher for a cyclist, and can also include length of journey, which in free-flowing traffic can also increase a cyclist's exposure. Accounting for the increased respiration rates of typical commuter cyclists, Dirks, Sharma, Salmond, and Costello (2012), in a study in Auckland, found that when this and commuting time are taken into account, the dose of carbon monoxide was found to be higher for active travellers than for those travelling by motorised modes. Meanwhile, Grange, Dirks, Costello, and Salmond (2014) found that to receive a similar pollution dose to that of motorists, cyclists and pedestrians needed to be located at least 5 metres from the road's centre-line.

Overall, while the impacts of travelling by bicycle on pollution dose are ambiguous and contested, it is clear that even limited separation from traffic significantly improves pollution exposure and dose. As Rissel (Chapter Three, this volume) suggests, it is worth noting that in general the health benefits of cycling far outweigh these potential disbenefits (de Hartog, Boogaard, Nijland, & Hoek, 2010; Lindsay, Macmillan, & Woodward, 2011; Oja et al., 2011).

Community impacts

There are a number of impacts that transport and choice of travel mode have on communities. So how does cycling affect the 'environment' of the communities and places in which we live?

Ambient air pollution concentrations

Travelling by bicycle produces no pollution, and this is obviously better for the environment and health than motorised modes. Due to the relatively small numbers of people changing mode, the time over which modal change might take place, and the potential confounders, measuring the impact of modal shift from motorised modes to bicycle on community levels of pollution has not been specifically researched.

As an indicator of likely impact, however, it is useful to examine situations where motor vehicle use has been dramatically reduced over a short period of time. Recently studied examples are cities where holding the Olympic Games has resulted in planned dramatic reductions in motor vehicle use, largely to aid the movement of large volumes of people, usually through increasing public transport use. While the modal shift was more to public transport than bicycle, the changes in pollution levels are still worth examining. Research looking at the 1996 Atlanta Olympic Games found that decreased traffic density was associated with a prolonged reduction in ozone pollution and significantly lower rates of childhood asthma events (Friedman, Powell, Hutwagner, Graham, & Teague, 2001).

Similar findings were identified for the 2000 Sydney Olympics (Lewis & Ker, 2005): counts of asthma admissions in the Sydney basin dropped dramatically during the time the Olympics were operating, returning to higher levels in the period after the Olympics. During the 2008 Olympic Games in China, where car use was dramatically curtailed partly to improve air quality, pollution levels for volatile organic compounds, carbon monoxide, nitrogen oxides and PM_{10} all reduced by over 50% (Zhou, 2010). A further interesting example relates to the dramatic changes in traffic volumes following the introduction of the congestion charge in London. Tonne, Beevers, Armstrong, Kelly, and Wilkinson (2008) found that reductions in pollution concentrations after its introduction were greater among areas where the congestion charge applied than in local communities. In addition they found that the areas that were more socially deprived, which had higher air pollution concentrations, experienced the greatest improvements in air quality.

It is not feasible to research the impact of increasing bicycles' modal share on local community air quality. However, studies that have looked at the impact of dramatic reductions in motor vehicle use have in essence done the same thing, and found that measurable improvements in local air quality can be found.

Land use

Transport infrastructure uses space. In New Zealand, it has been estimated that 25-30% of the land in New Zealand's towns and cities is given over to transport through roads, car parks, driveways and so on. A similar situation can be seen in Australian cities. Using transport data from Kenworthy and Laube's (1999) study of 44 cities, Melbourne and Adelaide ranked second and third for parking

Current challenges

coverage in the CBD, with over 70% of the CBD land area taken by parking space (Manville & Shoup, 2005). Admittedly, this data is well over a decade old now and these cities have made significant efforts in recent years to improve the situation. Clearly, different modes have different land use needs, with car travel requiring substantially more space than other modes. (This is perhaps most easily visualised in Figure 7.1.) Any road space used for transport is rarely used for other public activities such as parks or other types of communal open space.

National impacts

So far, we have demonstrated that cycling can affect the personal and local environment, with a number of related positive impacts. At a national scale, when more people travel by bicycle there are further additional impacts.

Air pollution

Passenger cars are the largest producers of many health-damaging pollutants in Australian cities (such as carbon monoxide, oxides of nitrogen, sulphur dioxides, ozone-forming substances, hydrocarbons and fine particles). In addition to

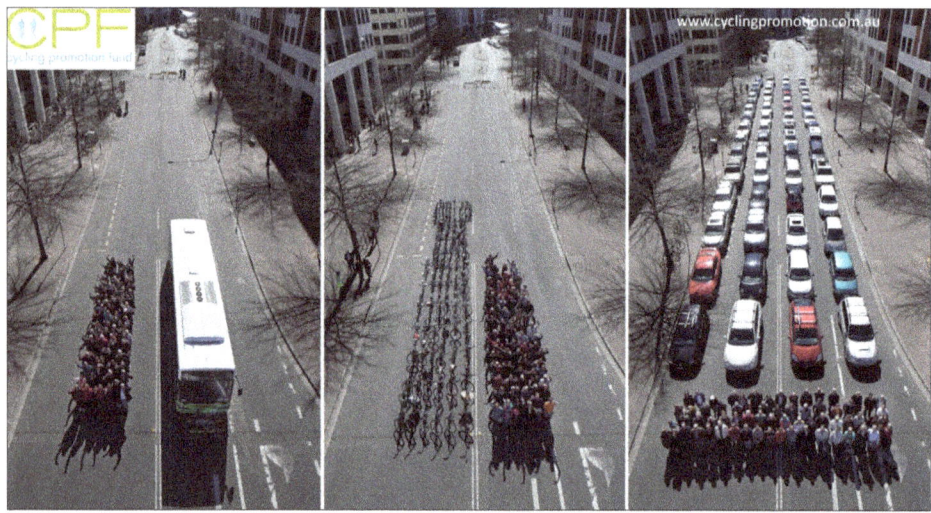

Figure 7.1: Road space required to transport 69 people.
(Source: Cycling Promotion Fund, Australia, http://www.bikehub.co.uk/news/sustainability/iconic-waste-of-space-photo-keeps-on-giving.)

pollution from car exhausts, the interiors of cars (particularly new cars) exude formaldehyde and other dangerous pollutants. In Australia, air pollution from motorised vehicles causes between 900 and 2000 early deaths, and up to 4500 cases of bronchitis, cardiovascular disease and respiratory disease, costing between AU$1.6 and AU$3.8 billion p.a. (Bureau of Transport and Regional Economics, 2005). In New Zealand, where wood-burning for home heating is a significant source of air pollution, vehicle pollution is still responsible for 255 early deaths, and costs around NZ$940 million p.a. (Kuschel et al., 2012). Motor vehicles can also create water pollution, when pollutants such as oil and petrol residues enter stormwater systems. Walking and cycling virtually eliminate these issues.

Research in New Zealand (Lindsay et al., 2011) has attempted to quantify the impact on national levels of pollution using the World Health Organization's [WHO] Health Economic Assessment Tool for Cycling [HEAT]. Rutter et al. (2007) developed this tool to estimate the reductions in mortality and resulting economic savings from increases in the prevalence of cycle commuting, and it in part assesses air pollution impacts. Lindsay et al. used the tool to identify significant annual savings in a range of pollutants from moving journeys of 7 kilometres or less to the bicycle (Table 7.1). They assessed the savings for a range of modal shifts from 1% through to 30%. For a 5% modal shift they estimated a reduction of 1449 tonnes of carbon monoxide, 161 tonnes of nitrogen oxides and 9.3 tonnes of PM_{10}. Not only will this lead to improvements in population health, but it will also increase the chances of governments meeting relevant environmental air quality standards.

Embodied energy

The above figures relate to the emissions from cars as they are being used. However, another important consideration in terms of the environmental impact of motor vehicles involves the indirect greenhouse gas creation and other pollution created as part of the embodied energy involved in the manufacture, delivery and disposal of products. Typically, cars use 50 times the amount of energy in terms of their embodied energy — and 50 times the amount of water — that bicycles use (Bicycle Federation of Australia, 2007). The impact of motor vehicles also extends to the extra energy required for infrastructure and services such as car parks and roads, as well as the energy required for emergency services and hospitals to serve the needs of people injured by traffic crashes or affected by pollution (Bicycle Federation of Australia, 2007).

Table 7.1: Fuel and vehicle emission annual savings from moving short urban car trips (≤7 km) to cycling: from 1% to 30% of vehicle km.

Modal shift to cycle	1%	5%	10%	30%
Fuel savings (litres)[a]	4 413 000	22 065 000	44 129 000	132 388 000
Fuel savings ($NZ)[b]	$7 413 000	$37 069 000	$74 137 000	$222 412 000
CO_2 (tonnes)[c]	10 033	50 167	100 334	301 001
Carbon monoxide (tonnes)[a]	290	1449	2898	8695
NOx (tonnes)[a]	32	161	321	964
PM10 exhaust (tonnes)[a]	1.9	9.3	18.7	56
Volatile organic compounds (tonnes)[a]	19	95	189	568
Methane (tonnes)[d]	2.8	13.9	27.9	83.6

Notes:

a) VEPM 2.3 model light vehicle data used to calculate fuel, CO_2, CO, Nox, PM_{10} and volatile organic compound emissions.

b) Based on average price of petrol (91 octane, NZ$1.75/L) and diesel (NZ$1.12/L) for quarter 1, 2010, and proportion of light vehicles that were petrol and diesel.

c) CO_2eq = Carbon dioxide equivalents. Calculated using the IPCC 2007 100-year Global Warming Potential factors (methane has 25, nitrous oxide 298, and carbon monoxide 1.9 times the warming compared with CO_2).

d) Methane and nitrous oxide calculations based on fuel emission factors for these gases.

(Adapted from Lindsay, Macmillan, & Woodward, 2011, p. 57.)

Walking and cycling are associated with minimal embodied energy, as Komanoff et al. (1993) explain:

> Aside from the modest additional food intake which fuels the bicyclist's or walker's incremental expenditure of muscular energy (and the associated energy requirements to grow and deliver those rations, and to manufacture bicycles as well), bicycle-riding and walking do not contribute to the environmental damage inherent in extracting, transporting, processing, and burning petroleum or other fossil fuels. (p. 1)

Climate change

Transport is a major source of Australasia's greenhouse gas emissions, accounting for 16.6% of total greenhouse gas emissions in Australia (Commonwealth of Australia, 2014) and 18% in New Zealand (Ministry for the Environment, 2014). Cyclists emit negligible greenhouse gases and pollutants. Thus for each kilometre that driving a car can be replaced by cycling or walking, 0.22 kg of CO_2 is not produced (Dunlap, 2013). Switching to walking or cycling is particularly effective for short trips in terms of reducing emissions, as engines do not burn fuel efficiently when they are cold. In Australian capital cities, most trips involve either stop-start driving or short trips, and more than 50% of car trips are a distance of less than 5 kilometres (Fishman, Washington, & Haworth, 2012). These trips could easily be made by bicycle (or even by walking), assuming that the environment was such that the trips could be made safely using that mode of transport.

In both Australia and New Zealand, the vast majority of transport-related greenhouse gas is created from road transport. Any shift away from motorised modes will reduce greenhouse gas emissions. Lindsay, Macmillan, and Woodward (2011) also examined reductions in greenhouse gas emissions of modal shifts to cycling (Table 7.1) and estimated that a 5% modal shift would result in a reduction of carbon dioxide equivalents of 53 676 tonnes.

Climate change and health

The topic of obesity as it relates to transport is covered in other chapters. However, the work of Roberts and Edwards (2010) suggests that the global obesity epidemic and global climate change should not be considered as separate concerns. They argue that they are both caused by the same underlying factor — our use of fossil fuels:

> If you think that obesity and climate change are unrelated, you are wrong. The human race is getting fatter and the planet is getting hotter, and fossil fuels are the cause of both. (p. 3)

They present a convincing argument that the cheap energy provided by fossil fuels (particularly oil) has led to an overabundance of high-energy food, and the replacement of physical activity with movement created by machines. Discounted petrol and large supermarkets mean that people are encouraged to buy more processed food that is easier to produce and easy to transport home (by car). The use of fossil fuels to allow these things to occur has increased Body Mass Index [BMI] levels in most nations, while at the same time leading to unprecedented growth in greenhouse gases. Roberts and Edwards observe that the amount of food humans require to balance our current reduced energy expenditure is at an all-time low. Importantly for this chapter, Roberts and Edwards see one solution to these problems as exchanging the car for a bicycle.

Infrastructure costs

The potential benefits of a modal shift to people using the bicycle are significant, but have to be offset against the infrastructure costs required to achieve such a modal shift. Research has attempted to quantify the ratio of infrastructure costs relative to the benefits that such costs will reap. The benefit cost ratio [BCR] is a standard approach to assessing the value of transport infrastructure projects, and a BCR of 1.5 is seen as good (see also Suh, Chapter Six, this volume). A number of studies have attempted to do the same for cycle infrastructure (Community and Public Health, 2012). In the United Kingdom in the early 2000s, a three-year intervention in six cycling demonstration towns found £2.59 benefit for every £1 invested in decreased mortality alone (Sloman, Cavill, Cope, Muller, & Kennedy, 2009), while a review of 16 economic evaluations of the health effects of transport interventions that increased walking and cycling found a mean benefit-cost ratio of 5:1 (Cavill, Kahlmeier, Rutter, Racioppi, & Oja, 2008).

More recently, research in New Zealand using a more wide-ranging and sophisticated methodology found that

> transforming urban roads over the next 40 years, using best practice physical separation on main roads and bicycle-friendly speed reduction on local streets, would yield benefits 10-25 times greater than costs. (Macmillan et al., 2014, p. 335)

To put this into context, the New Zealand government is currently investing billions of dollars in new state highways, Roads of National Significance [RoNS — also known as motorways] and celebrating the 'substantial economic benefits' that such roads bring, which have an average 'BCR of approximately 1.8' (New Zealand Transport Agency, 2010). Interestingly, one of the RoNS has a BCR of 0.2 (Campbell, 2012; Board of Enquiry, 2012), indicating that there is no economic justification for its construction. Overall, it can be seen that investing in cycling produces significant economic benefits that are substantially higher than many contemporary road-building projects.

Global impacts

As well as providing environmental benefits for individuals, communities and cities, an increase in levels of walking and cycling provides an effective response to increasingly urgent major global challenges. Among the most significant of these challenges are energy stress, particularly the phenomenon known as peak oil (Miller & Sorrell, 2014; Newman, Beatley, & Boyer, 2009), as well as climate change, which climate scientists demonstrate is currently accelerating and having measurable impacts on human health (McMichael, Montgomery, & Costello, 2012) and obesity (UN News Centre, 2014).

Replacing private motor vehicles with more sustainable transport is becoming increasingly important, as the peak of conventional oil production has already passed (Murray & King, 2012). Some may argue that electric cars will enable a seamless switch to new sources of energy. However, this simplistic view ignores the fact that electric cars have only a limited effect on the reduction of oil use, or on pollution, particularly if the electricity comes from coal-fired power stations. For electric and hybrid cars, the whole-of-life costs — in terms of the energy required for their production, the waste they create and pollution — are still significant.

Even assuming that electric cars may reduce total energy use significantly, the Jevons Paradox will likely operate: when new technologies increase efficiencies, the typical behavioural response is to use the technology more, hence counteracting savings from higher efficiency. If a switch to electric cars means that we use them more, this is particularly bad news for the environment and for health. In addition, electric cars have many of the same negative impacts of internal combustion cars: traffic dangers to pedestrians and cyclists; undermining the viability of local shops, schools and services; cutting local communities with road building; and contributing to problems related to physical inactivity such as obesity. Electric vehicles would thus impede changes in occupational habits which are needed to improve environmental and human health.

> As people change their occupational habits, use their cars less, walk, cycle and use public transport more, and spend more time in their gardens, the

energy demands of cities lessen. This increases the resilience of cities to reductions in oil supplies. Active travel also strengthens local communities as a consequence of increased connections between people. Stronger local communities are important not only for health, but also for developing local responses to global challenges, including food security. (Tranter, 2014, p. 74)

While it is easy to be overwhelmed by the challenges of responding to these global challenges, the response becomes easier with a positive vision of a better future. Such a vision can be linked to the goal of a city transport system based largely on the active modes — walking, cycling and public transport. This would not only reduce reliance on increasingly expensive energy, and reduce greenhouse gases, but would also allow closer connections between people and nature, and between people and other human beings. A switch to these (supposedly) slower modes of transport is also likely to change the mindset of the traveller to produce a greater awareness of the world around us — a greater environmental awareness.

Conclusions

There is a growing body of evidence that increased bicycle use results in significant environmental benefits and that these benefits can be seen at a variety of spatial scales — for the individual, local communities, nations and globally. These include benefits in terms of air pollution, climate change, landscape, physical activity, wellbeing and happiness, connection with place and people, and economic wellbeing. The switch from motorised vehicles to walking and cycling is positive from all perspectives. Despite being aware of these advantages for several decades, we are not making the switch to cycling to a significant degree in most nations. This is probably due to the vested interests of those involved in maintaining the dominance of motorised transport — the oil and car companies in particular (Woodcock & Aldred, 2008). Overcoming the current marginalisation of human-powered transport is likely to produce significant environmental benefits for all citizens, both now and in the future.

References

A very expensive stretch of road [television broadcast]. (2012). In *Campbell Live*. New Zealand: 3news. Retrieved 21 November 2014 from http://www.3news.co.nz/tvshows/campbelllive/a-very-expensive-stretch-of-road-2012103016.

Bicycle Federation of Australia. (2007). Environmental benefits of cycling. Retrieved July 17 2015 from http://www.cyclingpromotion.com.au/images/stories/factsheets/02_TheEnvironmentalBenefitsOfCycling.pdf.

Bidwell, S. (2012). *Quantifying the economic benefit of increasing physical activity*. Report prepared for Canterbury District Health Board. Canterbury, New Zealand: Community and Public Health. Retrieved 19 July 2015 from www.cph.co.nz/Files/QuantEconBenefitPhysicalActive.pdf.

Board of Enquiry. (2012, November 21). MacKays to Peka Peka Expressway Proposal. *Board of Enquiry: Hearing at Kapiti Coast — Transcript of Proceedings*. Retrieved July 17 2015 from http://www.epa.govt.nz/Publications/Hearing%20Transcript%20Day%206%20-%2021%20November%202012.pdf.

Britton, E. (2014). Paris to limit speeds to 30 km/hr over entire city. Retrieved 28 October 2014 from http://worldstreets.wordpress.com/2014/05/21/paris-to-limit-speeds-to-30-kmhr-over-entire-city.

Brown, B, Mackett, R, Gong, Y, Kitazawa, K, & Paskins, J. (2008). Gender differences in children's pathways to independent mobility. *Children's Geographies*, 6(4), 385-401.

Bureau of Transport and Regional Economics. (2005). *Health impacts of transport emissions in Australia: Economic costs*. Canberra: Department of Transport and Regional Services.

Cavill, N, Kahlmeier, S, Rutter, H, Racioppi, F, & Oja, P. (2008). Economic analyses of transport infrastructure and policies including health effects related to cycling and walking: A systematic review. *Transport Policy*, 15, 291-304.

Chertok, M, Voukelatos, A, Sheppeard, V, & Rissel, C., (2004). Comparison of air pollution exposure for five commuting modes in Sydney — Car, train, bus, bicycle and walking. *Health Promotion Journal of Australia*, 15(1), 63-67.

Clark, F. (1997). Reflections on the human as an occupational being: Biological need, tempo and temporality. *Journal of Occupational Science*, 4(3), 86-92.

Cole-Hunter, T, Jayaratne, R, Stewart, I, Hadaway, M, Morawska, L, & Solomon, C. (2013). Utility of an alternative bicycle commute route of lower proximity to motorised traffic in decreasing exposure to ultra-fine particles, respiratory symptoms and airway inflammation — A structured exposure experiment. *Environmental Health*, 12, 29-41.

Commonwealth of Australia. (2014). *National Inventory Report 2012: Vol. 1. The Australian Government submission to the United Nations Framework Convention on Climate Change.* Canberra: Commonwealth of Australia.

de Hartog, J, Boogaard, H, Nijland, H, & Hoek, G. (2010). Do the health benefits of cycling outweigh the risks? *Environmental Health Perspectives,* 118(8), 1109-1116.

Dirks, K, Sharma, P, Salmond, J, & Costello, S. (2012). Personal exposure to air pollution for various modes of transport in Auckland, New Zealand. *The Open Atmospheric Science Journal*, 6, 84-92.

Dunlap, R. (2013). A simple and objective carbon footprint analysis for alternative transportation technologies. *Energy and Environment Research*, 3(1), 33-39.

Farnworth, L. (2003). Time use, tempo and temporality: Occupational therapy's core business or someone else's business. *Australian Occupational Therapy Journal*, 50(3), 116-126.

Farrar, D, Dingle, P, & Tan, R. (2001). Exposure to nitrogen dioxide in buses, taxis, and bicycles in Perth, Western Australia. *Bulletin of Environmental Contamination and Toxicology*, 66(4), 433-438.

Fishman, E, Washington, S, & Haworth, N. (2012). Understanding the fear of bicycle riding in Australia. *Journal of the Australasian College of Road Safety*, 23(3), 19-27.

Friedman, M, Powell, K, Hutwagner, L, Graham, L, & Teague, G. (2001). Impact of changes in transportation and commuting behaviors during the 1996 Summer Olympic Games in Atlanta on air quality and childhood asthma. *Journal of the American Medical Association*, 285(7), 897-905.

Fusco, C, Moola, F, Faulkner, G, Buliung, R, & Richichi, V. (2012). Toward an understanding of children's perceptions of their transport geographies: (Non)active school travel and visual representations of the built environment. *Journal of Transport Geography,* 20(1), 62-70.

Geller, R. (2011). *Build it and they will come: Portland Oregon's experience with modest investments in bicycle transportation.* Portland, Oregon: City of Portland. Retrieved 17 July 2015 from https://www. portlandoregon.gov/transportation/article/370893.

Grange, S, Dirks, K, Costello, S, & Salmond, J. (2014). Cycleways and footpaths: What separation is needed for equivalent air pollution dose between travel modes? *Transportation Research Part D, 32,* 111-119.

Harris, A, Reynolds, C, Winters, M, Cripton, P, Shen, H, Chipman, M … Teschke, K. (2013). Comparing the effects of infrastructure on bicycling injury at intersections and non-intersections using a case-crossover design. *Injury Prevention, 19,* 303-310.

Hoelting, K. (2010). *The circumference of home: One man's yearlong quest for a radically local life.* Cambridge, MA: Da Capo Press.

Hoenig, M. (2000). The Graz traffic calming model and its consequences for cyclists. Retrieved 15 August 2014 from www.velomondial.net/velomondiall2000/PDF/ HONIG.PDF.

Humphreys, D, Goodman, A, & Ogilvie, D. (2013). Associations between active commuting and physical and mental wellbeing. *Preventive Medicine, 57(2),* 135-139.

Jacobsen, P. (2003). Safety in numbers: More walkers and bicyclists, safer walking and bicycling. *Injury Prevention, 9(3),* 205-209.

Karanasioua, K, Vianaa, M, Querola, X, Morenoa, T, & de Leeuw, F. (2014). Assessment of personal exposure to particulate air pollution during commuting in European cities — Recommendations and policy implications. *Science of The Total Environment, 490,* 785-797.

Kenworthy, J, & Laube, F. (1999). *An international sourcebook of automobile dependence in cities, 1960-1990.* Boulder, CO: University Press of Colorado.

Kingham, S, Koorey, G, & Taylor, K. (2011). *Assessment of the type of cycle infrastructure required to attract new cyclists.* NZTA Report 449. Wellington, NZ: New Zealand Transport Agency.

Kingham, S, Longley, I, Salmond, J, Pattinson, W, & Shrestha, K. (2013). Variations in exposure to traffic pollution while travelling by different modes in a low density, less congested city. *Environmental Pollution, 181,* 211-218.

Kingham, S, Meaton, J, Sheard, A, & Lawrenson, O. (1998). Assessment of exposure to traffic related fumes during the journey to work. *Transportation Research D: Transport and Environment, 3(4),* 271-274.

Knox, P. (2005). Creating ordinary places: Slow cities in a fast world. *Journal of Urban Design, 10(1),* 1-11.

Komanoff, C, Roelofs, C, Orcutt, J, & Ketcham, B. (1993). *The environmental benefits of bicycling and walking*. Case study no. 15 for the National Bicycling and Walking Study, Publication no. FHWA-PD-93-015. Washington, DC: US Department of Transportation, Federal Highway Administration.

Kuschel, G, Metcalfe, J, Wilton, E, Guria, J, Hales, S, Rolfe, K, & Woodward, A. (2012). *Updated Health and Air Pollution in New Zealand Study. Vol. 1.* Summary report prepared for Health Research Council of New Zealand, Ministry of Transport, Ministry for the Environment and New Zealand Transport Agency. Retrieved 13 April 2015 from www.hapinz.org.nz.

Lewis, P, & Ker, S. (2005, September 28-30). The relationship between Australian transport systems and public health. *28th Australasian Transport Research Forum*, Sydney, Australia.

Lindsay, G, Macmillan, A, & Woodward, A. (2011). Moving urban trips from cars to bicycles: Impact on health and emissions. *Australian and New Zealand Journal of Public Health, 35*, 54-60.

Macmillan, A, Connor, J, Witten, W, Kearns, R, Rees, D, & Woodward, A. (2014). The societal costs and benefits of commuter bicycling: Simulating the effects of specific policies using system dynamics modelling. *Environmental Health Perspectives, 122*(4), 335-344.

McMichael, T, Montgomery, H, & Costello, A. (2012). Health risks, present and future, from global climate change. *British Medical Journal, 344*, e1359.

Manville, M, & Shoup, D. (2005). Parking, people, and cities. *Journal of Urban Planning and Development, 131*(4), 233-245.

Martin, A, Goryakin, Y, & Suhrcke, M. (2014). Does active commuting improve psychological wellbeing? Longitudinal evidence from eighteen waves of the British Household Panel Survey. *Preventive Medicine, 69*, 296-303. doi: 10.1016/j.ypmed.2014.08.023.

Matuska, KM, & Christiansen, CH. (2008). A proposed model of lifestyle balance. *Journal of Occupation Science, 15*(1), 9-19.

Miller, RG, & Sorrell, SR. (2014). The future of oil supply. *Philosophical Transactions of the Royal Society A: Mathematical, Physical and Engineering Sciences, 372*, 1-27.

Ministry for the Environment. (2014). *New Zealand's Greenhouse Gas Inventory 1990-2010*. ME 1148. Wellington, New Zealand: Ministry for the Environment.

Monsere, C, Dill, J, McNeil, N, Clifton, K, Foster, N, Goddard, T … Parks, J. (2014). *Lessons from the green lanes: Evaluating protected bike lanes in the US.* Final report, NITC-RR-583. Retrieved 13 April 2015 from http://works.bepress.com/christopher_monsere/34.

Morris, EA & Guerra, E. (2015). Mood and mode: Does how we travel affect how we feel? *Transportation,* 42(1), 25-43.

Murray, J, & King, D. (2012). Climate policy: Oil's tipping point has passed. *Nature,* 481(7382), 433-435.

New Zealand Transport Agency. (2010). *Roads of national significance — Economic Assessments 2.* Report prepared by Saha International Limited (SAHA) for the NZTA. Wellington: New Zealand Transport Agency.

Newman, P, Beatley, T, & Boyer, H. (2009). *Resilient cities: Responding to peak oil and climate change.* Washington, DC: Island Press.

Oja, P, Titze, S, Bauman, A, de Geus, B, Krenn, P, Reger-Nash, B, & Kohlberger, T. (2011). Health benefits of cycling: A systematic review. *Scandinavian Journal of Medicine & Science in Sports,* 21, 496-509.

Pattinson, W, Kingham, S, Longley, I, & Salmond, J. (2011, July 31-August 3). Cyclist exposure to traffic pollution: Microscale variance, the impact of route choice and comparisons to other modal choices in two New Zealand cities. *20th International Clean Air and Environment Conference,* Auckland, New Zealand.

Persson, D, & Erlandsson, L-K. (2002). Time to reevaluate the machine society: Post-industrial ethics from an occupational perspective. *Journal of Occupational Science,* 9(2), 93-99.

Pink, S, & Lewis, T. (2014). Making resilience: Everyday affect and global affiliation in Australian Slow Cities. *Cultural Geographies,* 21(4), 695-710.

Pucher, K, Dill, J, & Handy, S. (2010). Infrastructure, programs, and policies to increase bicycling: An international review. *Preventive Medicine,* 50, S106-S125.

Ramanathan, S, O'Brien, C, Faulkner, G, & Stone, M. (2014). Happiness in motion: Emotions, well-being, and active school travel. *Journal of School Health,* 84(8), 516-523.

Rank, J, Folke, J, & Jespersen, PH. (2001). Differences in cyclists' and car drivers' exposure to air pollution from traffic in the city of Copenhagen. *The Science of the Total Environment,* 279, 131-136.

Roberts, I, & Edwards, P. (2010). *The energy glut: The politics of fatness in an overheating world.* London: Zed Books.

Rutter, H, Cavill, N, Kahlmeier, S, Dinsdale, H, Racioppi, F, & Oja, P. (2007). *Health Economic Assessment Tool for Cycling (HEAT for Cycling).* Copenhagen: WHO Regional Office for Europe.

Sloman, L, Cavill, N, Cope, A, Muller, L, & Kennedy, A. (2009). *Analysis and synthesis of evidence on the effects of investment in six Cycling Demonstration Towns.* Report for Department of Transport and Cycling England. London: Department for Transport.

St-Louisa, E, Manaugh, K, van Lieropc, D, & El-Geneidy, A. (2014). The happy commuter: A comparison of commuter satisfaction across modes. *Transportation Research Part F: Traffic Psychology and Behaviour, 26,* 160-170.

Tonne, C, Beevers, S, Armstrong, B, Kelly, F, & Wilkinson, P. (2008). Air pollution and mortality benefits of the London Congestion Charge: Spatial and socioeconomic inequalities. *Occupational and Environmental Medicine, 65,* 620-627.

Tranter, P. (2014). Active travel: A cure for the hurry virus. *Journal of Occupational Science, 21*(1), 65-76.

UN News Centre. (2014, November 26). Obesity-related cancers on the rise, especially in developed countries. *UN News Centre.* Retrieved 9 June 2015 from http://www.un.org/apps/news/story.asp?NewsID=49453Woodcock, J, & Aldred, R. (2008). Cars, corporations, and commodities: Consequences for the social determinants of health. *Emerging Themes in Epidemiology, 5*(1), 4. doi: 10.1186/1742-7622-5-4.

Woolsgrove, C. (2013). The power of 30K speed limit: 30k Analysis. Retrieved 28 October 2014 from http://www.ecf.com/?post_type=news&p=20043&preview=true.

Zhou, Y, Wua, Y, Yang, L, Fu, L. He, L, Wang, S … Li, C. (2010). The impact of transportation control measures on emission reductions during the 2008 Olympic Games in Beijing, China. *Atmospheric Environment, 44,* 285-293.

Zuzanek, J. (1998). Time use, time pressure, personal stress, mental health, and life satisfaction from a life cycle perspective. *Journal of Occupational Science, 5*(1), 26-39.

8 Cycle touring

Matthew Lamont

Introduction

The bicycle was an early facilitator of tourist mobility prior to popularisation of motorised transport in the early 1900s. Before widespread adoption of motor vehicle transportation, tourists' mobility was largely achieved on foot, by horseback or by rail (Tobin, 1974). From an engineering perspective, bicycles evolved iteratively from inefficient and cumbersome contraptions in the 1700s to become sleek, functional means of personal transport by the late 1800s (Watson & Gray, 1978). As Fitzpatrick demonstrates (Chapter Two, this volume), the advent of functional bicycles opened up the countryside to independent tourism, freeing people from the confines of limited transportation options: 'The individual who rode the two-wheeler could travel routes beyond corridors of the railroad and also experienced the joys of motion' (Tobin, 1974, p. 841).

However, the growing proliferation of motor vehicles in the early 1920s contributed to a decline in cycling. Associations such as the League of American Wheelmen and the Cyclists' Touring Club in the United Kingdom sought to keep the tradition of cycle touring alive (Tobin, 1974). The nexus between cycling and tourism is long established and is therefore worthy of consideration today, especially given the recent resurgence in recreational cycling and because of challenges faced by society in the form of unsustainable, carbon-intensive modes of tourism transportation.

Current challenges

This chapter explores the contemporary nexus between cycling and tourism as it emphasises the significance of the bicycle beyond being simply a means of transportation. A further purpose of this chapter is to summarise the existing scholarly research examining cycling and tourism. Given this volume's focus on the Australian and New Zealand cycling context, attention is also given to discussing the manifestation of cycle tourism in Australia, with particular attention paid to conditions that may be impeding the potential of cycle tourism from being realised in Australia.

Understanding the cycle tourism market

Definitions of cycle tourism

Defining cycle tourism is a contentious issue. Whilst numerous definitions of cycle tourism have been proposed (for example, see Lumsdon, 1996; Ritchie, 1998; Simonsen & Jorgenson, 1998; South Australian Tourism Commission, 2005; Sustrans, 1999), issues such as trip purpose, motivation, trip characteristics, and the extent to which a bicycle serves as tourism transport have hampered acceptance of a universal definition. It is clear that although cycle tourism is a niche segment within the broader milieu of tourism, it is a broad, multidimensional segment. Lamont (2009b) critiqued existing definitions of cycle tourism in order to highlight common themes and ambiguities. He proposed the following technical definition, aimed at facilitating measurement of cycle tourism impacts (for example, economic and social):

> Trips involving a minimum distance of 40 kilometres from a person's home and an overnight stay (for overnight trips), or trips involving a minimum non-cycling round trip component of 50 kilometres and a minimum four hour period away from home (for day trips) of which cycling, involving active participation or passive observation, for holiday, recreation, leisure and/or competition, is the main purpose for that trip. Participation in cycling may include attendance at events organised for commercial gain and/or charity (competitive and non-competitive), as well as independently organised cycling. (p. 20)

Other authors advocate a broader, more inclusive definition. For example, Weed and Bull (2009) note that defining cycle tourism by trip purpose is contentious. They point out that most definitions only include activities in which cycling sports tourism is a fundamental and significant part of the trip and thus exclude spontaneous participation in cycling sports tourism, or participation that has been planned post-trip decision. (p. 275)

Cycle tourism typologies

Numerous typologies of cycle tourism have been proposed (for example, Lumsdon, 1996; Simonsen & Jorgenson, 1998; South Australian Tourism Commission, 2005). However, debate continues within the academic literature and within practitioner writings regarding the nature of activities involving cycling that could constitute cycle tourism. Based on a critical review of cycle tourism definitions and typologies published up to 2009, Lamont (2009b) identified five cycle tourism subsegments. These included independent cycle tourism, recreational cycling, participatory cycling events, competitive cycling events and passive participation (spectating) at cycling events. Each is summarised briefly below.

Independent cycle touring encapsulates holidays more than 24 hours in duration of which participation in cycling is a core trip purpose, and a bicycle is the main mode of transport within the destination region. Utilising a popular theoretical model within tourism studies, *whole tourism systems* (Leiper, 2004), it has been suggested that for independent cycle tourists, mobility at the destination is a key element of the tourism experience (Lamont, 2009a). Mobility is facilitated by embracing the bicycle as a form of tourism transport, enabling experiences in which the tourist becomes kinaesthetically immersed within, and must adapt to, the surrounding landscape and elements (Cox, 2012). According to Lamont's (2009a) adapted whole tourism system model for independent cycle tourism, such tourists will initially select a broad destination area as a backdrop for their travels. That broad area will be divided into segments where cycle tourists travel between *node destinations*, conceptualised as places of overnight rest where some exploration of local attractions may occur. Travel between node destinations occurs along *secondary transit routes* — routes traversed by bicycle in which the cycle tourist experiences a kinaesthetically embodied connection with their surrounds (Cox, 2012), therefore constituting a core source of satisfaction within independent cycle touring experiences.

To provide some brief perspective on the 'why?' of independent cycling holidays, Coghlan's (2012) qualitative auto-ethnographic study explores the motives and emotions experienced by cycle tourists. Although Coghlan's study focused on an event-based cycle tourism experience, her findings constitute rare interpretive insights into the subjective experiences of cycle tourists — insights that are likely to transcend multiple modes of cycle touring. Notions of escapism, socialising, adventure, feelings of achievement, recognition, companionship and a hierarchy of involvement in cycling were identified. For example, Coghlan noted that cycle touring provides an opportunity to temporarily escape from the stresses of everyday life. She recounted:

> I love those moments of monotonous road, when you can get lost in your thoughts and realise that no one is making any demands of you, and your only job to keep pedaling [sic] … You have not a care in the world beyond following the wheel in front of you, keep [sic] pushing those pedals, and staying hydrated. What complete and utter escapism! I wish it could last forever. (p. 114)

Further, Coghlan noted the sense of achievement that cycle tourists can experience when they overcome challenges presented by the elements or terrain. Below, she recounts the sense of achievement she felt upon conquering a gruelling hill climb:

> I still can't get over that [sic] I made it up Desailey Range. Oh what a feeling! All that hard work in training paid off. I am now one of 'them', the ones that I admired last year from the bus, as they stubbornly ground their way up the hill. Next year I will make it all the way up Kuranda, and complete the whole event from start to finish. (p. 115)

Recreational cycling encompasses daytrips for the purpose of going cycling. Despite debate over whether daytrips constitute a valid subsegment of tourism within the broader tourism studies literature (for example, Hall, 2003; Leiper, 2004), cycling daytrips have been advocated by both scholars and practitioners as a significant cycle tourism subsegment worthy of research and policy attention. Whilst a precise definition of recreational cycling is yet to be agreed upon, it has been suggested that time and distance thresholds adopted by statutory tourism agencies in compiling tourism statistics (for instance, Tourism Research Australia) could be used to delineate recreational cycling. For example, Lamont (2009b) suggested that in Australia, utilising Tourism Research Australia parameters, recreational cycling could be characterised as daytrips which incorporate a round-trip, non-cycling component of a minimum of 50 kilometres, are a minimum of 4 hours away from home, and are for the purpose of participating in non-competitive cycling.

Beyond cycle tourism experiences that are organised and undertaken by individual tourists on a largely independent basis, cycle tourism experiences centred around organised cycling events have become increasingly prolific. Three segments are identifiable with regard to cycling events. *Participatory events* are commercially organised, non-competitive events that provide cycling opportunities in a social and somewhat controlled environment. Participatory cycling events may be of single or multi-day duration, emphasise participation over competition, and are often organised in aid of particular charitable or other causes (Faulks, Ritchie, & Fluker, 2006; Lamont & Jenkins, 2013). Furthermore, Bull's (2006) research into racing cyclists in Great Britain found that amateur cyclists undertake frequent trips to pursue their sport, hence establishing a clear link between cycle racing events and tourism. Travel to participate in competitive cycling events has therefore gained some acceptance as a further subsegment of cycle tourism.

Moreover, travel to engage in *passive participation* is becoming an increasingly prevalent cycle tourism subsegment. This subsegment relates to travelling to spectate at major professional cycle races. Drawing upon Standeven and DeKnop's (1999) sport tourism typology, it has been argued that this cycle tourism subsegment comprises mostly *connoisseur observers* — that is, persons with a specific interest in cycling who are knowledgeable about the sport's intricacies and history (Lamont, 2009b). Although passive participation by way of spectating can be a dominant travel motive, research has identified that such tourists will often integrate active participation by taking or hiring a bicycle to participate in active cycling when not spectating. Two recent studies have explored how cycle tourists at the Tour de France combine active and passive participation to facilitate rich, authentic experiences at that global sporting mega-event (Lamont, 2014a; Lamont & McKay, 2012).

Scholarly research into cycle tourism: Scope and status

A stream of scholarly research into the cycling-tourism nexus has been evident since the late 1990s. Despite failing to gain traction when empirical studies first appeared in peer-reviewed journals, research into cycle tourism has experienced a renaissance in recent years. Indeed, a recent issue of the peer-reviewed journal *Tourism Review International* constituted the first dedicated scholarly collection of empirical research papers addressing the cycling-tourism nexus. Below, the

Co-ordinating Editor of this themed issue (and also the author of this chapter) speculates on why cycle tourism research has experienced such reinvigoration:

> [R]esearch addressing the cycling-tourism nexus has increased markedly since 2010. This may be attributable to a number of factors, including increased governmental interest in cycle tourism due to favorable economic and social outcomes for host communities; intensification of climate change research as it pertains to tourism, particularly themes around low-carbon transport modes; and a realization amongst researchers that cycle tourism lends itself to multidisciplinary inquiry, particularly approaches focusing inward on the cyclist. Theoretical and methodological approaches to studying cycle tourism have expanded significantly, and promisingly, have shown signs of moving away from description and towards explanation. (Lamont, 2014b, p. 4)

Disciplinary and methodological approaches to the study of cycle tourism have broadened in recent times. Early research tended to be applied in nature; however, researchers today seem more open to deploying theoretical concepts from related disciplines. Three broad streams dominate the cycle tourism research landscape: economic impacts; planning, management and policy issues; and more recently, the experiences of cycle tourists, as explored by social science researchers.

Economic impact research

Existing literature suggests that cycle tourism generates mostly favourable economic impacts. Although valuations of the cycle tourism market at national levels are scant, the economic value of cycling-related tourism in the United Kingdom was once estimated at £635 million (approximately AU$1.69 billion[1]) per annum and was projected to increase in value to £14 billion (approximately AU$37.3 billion[1]) per annum across European nations by 2020 (Sustrans, 1999). The cycle tourism research literature is, however, characterised by numerous case studies investigating the economic impacts of cycle tourism on specific regions (for example, Cope, Doxford, & Hill, 1998; Insall, 1999; Pendleton, 1999; Ritchie & Hall, 1999). Cope et al. (1998) report that in 1996, the Coast to Coast Cycle Route, a 220-kilometre cycle path in the north of England, attracted between 12 000 and 15 000 users, who spent between £1.07 and £1.85 million

---

[1] Currency conversion based on year of publication, using web-based currency converter www.xe.com.

(approximately AU$2.23 million and AU$3.86 million[2]). This study also found that 23% of cyclists surveyed were accompanied by a friend or relative driving a support vehicle. Thus Cope et al. suggest that provision of cycling infrastructure can also attract substantial numbers of cyclists' entourages to the area, thereby enhancing the economic contributions of such infrastructure. Further, research conducted on the Murray to the Mountains Rail Trail in Victoria's Alpine region (Beeton, 2003; 2006) indicated an average spend per person per day on the trail of AU$258. Cyclists' expenditure was distributed across accommodation, food and beverage, transport, and cycling-associated expenses.

Numerous authors have acknowledged that businesses in rural areas benefit significantly from cycle tourists visiting their region. The accommodation sector has been singled out as the largest beneficiary from visiting cycle tourists — for example, up to 80% of hotel beds along the Danube Cycle Route in Austria are occupied by cyclists each year (Insall, 1999). Similarly, Lumsdon (2000) reports that 'several towns on the [Danube] route now depend on cycle tourism with bed-nights from cycling visitors accounting for between 60% and 80% of all stays' (p. 366). Ritchie and Hall (1999) identified seven business sectors in which bicycle tourists in New Zealand spent money. These included accommodation; cafes, restaurants and pubs; bicycle hire and equipment stores; entertainment; tourist attractions/activities; supplementary transport services (such as rail and coach transport); and miscellaneous expenditure.

Favourable economic benefits associated with cycle tourism have stimulated interest amongst governments at local, state and national level in Australia and abroad in pursuing cycle tourism initiatives (Lamont & Buultjens, 2011; Lumsdon, Downward, & Cope, 2004). In particular, such interest has stemmed from the potential for cycle tourism to contribute towards economic diversification in non-metropolitan areas. Beyond the development of specific jurisdictional strategic plans for developing cycle tourism (for example, South Australian Tourism Commission, 2005; Tourism Victoria, 2011), governmental interest has sustained a research stream addressing planning, management and policy issues surrounding cycle tourism. Of specific research interest has been the identification

---

[2] Currency conversion based on year research was conducted, using web-based currency converter www.xe.com.

of cycle tourists' infrastructure and support service requirements (for example, Bil, Bilova, & Kubecek, 2012; Cope et al., 2003; Downward & Lumsdon, 2001; Mason & Leberman, 2000). Often, infrastructure studies take the form of case study performance/importance analyses for particular jurisdictions (for example, Fang, Chang, & Huang, 2011; Lee & Huang, 2012; Ritchie, 1998). Bonham, Bacchi and Wanner explore gender and cycling in Australia (Chapter Nine, this volume).

Policy, planning and management research

Furthermore, a small number of studies have addressed policy issues such as competing policy agendas between adjacent jurisdictions seeking to develop cycle tourism (for example, Cox, 2012). However, an important stream of research has considered the role of cycle tourism in reducing the environmental impacts associated with tourism. Tourism is largely reliant on carbon-intensive transportation (Robbins & Dickinson, 2007), hence various authors have suggested that cycle tourism could play a role in a new tourism paradigm embracing less carbon-intensive tourism transport modes (for example, Lumsdon, 2000). Recent research has suggested that cycle tourists may inherently possess a heightened awareness of environmental sustainability which influences their tourism transport modal choice (Meschik, 2012).

However, whilst cycle touring may appear less damaging to the natural environment than other tourism transport modes, recent research has shown that cycle touring is often integrated with carbon-intensive transport prior to, and following, the cycling component of that journey (Dickinson, Lumsdon, & Robbins, 2011). Consequently, Dickinson et al. (2011) argue that although 'slow' travel, including cycle tourism, could contribute towards reducing the negative environmental impacts of tourism, further research is needed around how tourists' mindsets might be shifted towards embracing models of tourism that result in genuine low-carbon outcomes.

Social science research: Understanding cycle tourists' experiences

Whilst policy, planning and management research has tended to dominate the literature, this research stream appears to be giving way to social science research aimed at interpreting and understanding cycle tourists' experiences. It is through this emerging research stream that research into cycle tourism has shifted towards more theoretically informed inquiry. Scholars have begun applying theoretical concepts from sociology and social psychology to interpret cycle tourists' kinaesthetically embodied experiences with their surrounds. Cycle tourism seems suited to sociological inquiry. Indeed, Weed and Bull (2009) point out, it 'clearly involves the interaction of people, activity and place' (p. 273), whilst Cox adds that cycle tourists become 'embedded in and sensitive to the landscape and elements' (2012, p. 28).

As an example of such research, Coghlan's (2012) auto-ethnographic study of cycle tourists participating in an organised multi-day, charity-oriented cycle tour event recounted experiences of fear and anxiety associated with tackling inhospitable terrain and such a significant physical challenge. In a similar context, Fullagar (2012) adopted a feminist perspective to examine female cyclists' motives for participating in an organised, multi-day, non-competitive cycle tour. She contrasted her research with the masculine stance which dominated the cycle tourism research literature hitherto, revealing themes of hedonism and identity creation/celebration as dominant motives.

Furthermore, sociological concepts including postmodernism, authenticity and authentication, mediation and embodiment were recently deployed to interpret the experiences of cycle tourists attending the Tour de France as active spectators (Lamont, 2014a; Lamont & McKay, 2012). In a similar vein, Fox, Humberstone, and Dubnewick (2014) adopt an innovative epistemological stance — that of 'sensuous scholarship' — to interpret the lead author's (Fox's) own self-supported cycle tour of the Hawaiian island of Oahu. It is through this approach that rich insights were obtained around cycle tourists' immersion in an embodied, sensory world punctuated by intense exertion and physical and mental battles with the elements.

Cycle tourism in Australia

Cycle tourism in Australia can be observed in numerous forms. Indeed, there is evidence of cycle tourism across all the five subsegments discussed previously. This section discusses examples of how the five cycle tourism subsegments manifest in Australia, and also summarises research examining potential barriers to cycle tourism in this country.

Current challenges

Extent and focus of cycle tourism in Australia

Many Australian states and territories, along with some local government jurisdictions, have compiled strategic plans for developing cycle tourism. Depending on available infrastructure and other resources (such as natural scenery, tourist attractions and so on), jurisdictions have tended to tailor strategic plans around one or more cycle tourism subsegments. For example, the *Victorian Cycle Tourism Action Plan 2011-2015* (Tourism Victoria, 2011) emphasises nature-based cycling experiences on Victoria's rail trails; mountain biking on established trails such as in national parks; and organised, non-competitive road cycling events in Victoria's High Country. In contrast, South Australia's *Cycle Tourism Strategy 2005-2009* (South Australian Tourism Commission, 2005) primarily sought to leverage tourism benefits from a showcase event, the Tour Down Under — an international professional cycling event that attracts significant tourist numbers to Adelaide each January. A more local-level strategic plan example is the *Southern Flinders Ranges Cycle Tourism Master Plan* (Southern Flinders Ranges Development Board, 2008). Although a range of cycling experiences are identified as possible target segments, the plan primarily seeks to capitalise on the region's extensive trail network and target mountain biking enthusiasts visiting the Southern Flinders Ranges.

However, a lack of unified research has hampered understanding of the size, scope and value of cycle tourism in Australia. At present, knowledge is scant and fragmented. In the *Victorian Cycle Tourism Action Plan 2011-2015*, it is lamented that '[o]ne of the challenges facing Victoria's cycle tourism sector is the lack of economic analysis and research' (Tourism Victoria, 2011, p. 3). An earlier report published by the former Cooperative Research Centre for Sustainable Tourism (Faulks et al., 2006) also pointed out that a co-ordinated research effort into measuring the size and scope of cycle tourism in Australia has been impeded by a lack of consistency in definitions applied. Faulks et al. further note that some national-level measurement has been achieved in other countries such as the United Kingdom, where a consistent definition of cycle tourism has long been applied. Below, examples of each cycle tourism subsegment from the Australian context are discussed.

Independent and commercial cycle touring

Attributes such as a suitable year-round climate, an abundant variety of scenic backdrops, and small towns linked by quiet roads within manageable cycling distances have been identified as strengths for Australia as a cycle tourism destination (EcoGIS Consultants, 2000; Solly, 2003). Independent cycle touring was identified in the Howard Government's national tourism strategic plan as a niche market capable of enhancing competitive advantage for Australian tourism (Department of Communications, Information Technology, and the Arts, 2003). However, as previously discussed, data quantifying the size and value of independent cycle touring in Australia is not readily available (Faulks et al., 2006).

A recent development in providing safe cycling routes away from roads is the conversion of disused railway corridors into multi-use trails known as *rail trails* (Oxer, 2001). Creating a rail trail involves the removal of railway lines from a disused corridor and configuring the railroad bed into a trail capable of accommodating a range of recreational activities (Siderelis & Moore, 1995). The development of rail trails has been observed in countries such as Australia (Oxer, 2001), New Zealand (Ritchie, 1998), and the United States (Siderelis & Moore, 1995). Rail trails can be used not only for cycling, but also for hiking, horse riding, and, in colder climates, cross-country skiing (Pendleton, 1999).

Victoria boasts nearly 30 operational rail trails (Oxer, 2001). They not only provide recreational opportunities for local residents, but also serve as tourism infrastructure. The Murray to the Mountains Rail Trail is perhaps the most significant rail trail in Victoria. Stretching 94 kilometres between Wangaratta and Bright, it is one of the longest trails in Australia, with cyclists usually taking two to three days to cover the entire distance (Murphy, 2002). The lengthy nature of rail trails such as the Murray to the Mountains is conducive to multi-day touring experiences because the trail can be cycled in segments, with small towns serving as overnight stopover points.

Whilst Victoria has invested heavily in rail trail infrastructure, other states such as New South Wales are realising the potential economic, social and environmental benefits that can accrue through investing in rail trails. For example, at the time of writing, the New South Wales Government had approved funding for the development of a rail trail on a 130-kilometre disused rail corridor between Casino and Murwillumbah in Northern New South Wales. The corridor passes through world-heritage-listed areas and takes in the popular tourist destination of Byron Bay. A feasibility study commissioned by the New South Wales Government noted:

> The Northern Rivers region is a key tourism destination, with the second highest level of international tourists in NSW. The region contains

spectacular national parks such as Mount Warning, as well as long stretches of unspoilt coastlines and significant World Heritage rainforest reserves. The development of a rail trail along the Casino-Murwillumbah rail corridor presents an opportunity to leverage off the high visitation levels and further develop the region as a tourist destination as well as providing a facility for those residing in the region. (Arup Consultants, 2014, p. 1)

Beyond independently organised cycling tours, commercially organised multi-day cycling holidays seem quite prevalent. Whilst there is no data quantifying the extent nor value of commercially organised cycling tours in Australia, the number of companies offering such tours has been previously used as a proxy measure (Faulks et al., 2006). Product offerings range from all-inclusive packages including cycling tour guides, accommodation, meals, luggage transfers, en-route mechanical support and cycling equipment, through to self-guided cycling tours utilising predetermined routes and stopover points. Tour products also vary from on-road to off-road, requiring the use of mountain bikes.

Recreational cycling

As discussed earlier, recreational cycling encompasses trips in which cycling is a core purpose, where the trip is less than 24 hours in duration and involves a significant non-cycling component to escape the individual's home region (Lamont, 2009b). As with independent and commercial cycling tours, data regarding recreational cycling participation in Australia is sparse. Australian Bureau of Statistics [ABS] data indicates that approximately 10% of the Australian population participated in cycling for recreation during 2011/2012 (Australian Bureau of Statistics, 2013), a figure which has increased markedly since the mid-1990s when participation was around 0.6% (ABS, 1998). However, the ABS data does not distinguish between participation at home or away from the home region. Thus utilising such measures in a tourism context to estimate the extent of recreational cycling away from the home region is a somewhat spurious effort.

Although difficult to measure, the potential scope for recreational cycling participation in Australia is broad. Opportunities exist for cyclists to travel by car to participate in cycling away from busy metropolitan roads. For example, the Great Ocean Road is within daytrip-distance of Melbourne, and cycling on that picturesque road is actively promoted on the 'Visit Victoria' tourism website:

> While the coastal road and its breathtaking views (best enjoyed mid-week during non-peak periods) will dominate your ride, be prepared to be blown away as you round bends and turns into lush inland pastures, dramatic rainforests, magnificent lakes, volcanic craters and steep sand dunes. (Visit Victoria, n.d.)

Daytrips to Australia's growing number of rail trails are also a potentially significant catalyst for recreational cycling. Indeed, Beeton's (2006) survey of 625 cyclists on Victoria's Murray to the Mountains Rail Trail found that 38% spent one day or less cycling on the trail. Further, daytrips to participate in mountain biking on the ever-increasing specialist trails, mountain bike parks or designated cycling trails within national parks are also potentially significant. The Australian arm of the International Mountain Bicycling Association provides a comprehensive list of mountain bike trail options within each state and territory on its website (International Mountain Bicycling Association, n.d.), such as in Mt Buller in Victoria, Thredbo in New South Wales, and Mt Coot-tha in Queensland.

Participatory cycling events

With their emphasis on participation over competition, participatory cycling events provide a socially constructed space for cyclists to interact, often in a relatively controlled environment (Lamont & Jenkins, 2013). In some instances, participatory events occur under closed-road conditions, and thereby allow cyclists a rare opportunity to cycle without the stresses of interacting with vehicular traffic. Such events are becoming increasingly popular in Australia. Participatory events take place in most Australian states and territories each year and can vary according to distance; duration (single-day versus multi-day events); challenge of terrain; and setting (urban versus rural). Although many participatory cycling events are commercially organised and thus profit oriented, they are increasingly being held in aid of charitable causes, and participants are sometimes obligated to meet minimum fundraising thresholds.

For example, the Sydney to the Gong ride is an annual event of 90 kilometres attracting around 10 000 cyclists. Each participant must raise a minimum of $250 towards research into Multiple Sclerosis. Similarly, the Tour de Cure is an annual multi-day event in Australia raising funds for cancer research. This event is exclusive: cyclists must apply to join the tour, commit to meeting substantial fundraising targets (up to AU$12 000), and also be physically prepared for the event's gruelling daily distances (Tour de Cure, 2014). Other examples of participatory cycling events in Australia include the Great Victorian Bike Ride and Cycle Queensland. Both events take a different route in their respective Australian states each year and attract thousands of participants (Faulks et al., 2006). Moreover, there are participatory cycling events aimed at facilitating broader social causes. For example, the Cycling for Culture event held in Kaurna Country, South Australia, seeks, according to its website, to 'enable a better understanding between Aboriginal and non-Aboriginal people and a greater appreciation for culture, country and history' (Cycling for Culture, 2014).

Competitive cycling events

Whilst there is no data quantifying travel to competitive cycling events in Australia, participation in competitive cycling is growing. Participation in sanctioned competitive cycling events requires purchase of a license from the sport's governing body, Cycling Australia. In 2013 there were 24 642 members of Cycling Australia, up from 22 005 in 2011 (Cycling Australia, 2013). Further, research conducted in the United Kingdom (Bull, 2006) found that competitive cyclists often travel away from their home region to participate in competitive cycling events, hence establishing a link with tourism. In Australia there is an extensive calendar of events catering for cyclists of all ages and abilities, as well as different disciplines of cycling (that is, road, track, mountain bike and BMX).

Passive participation: Spectating at cycling events

Within some definitions of cycle tourism (for example, Lamont, 2009b; South Australian Tourism Commission, 2005), travel to spectate at cycling events is recognised. In Australia, this passive form of cycle tourism is arguably centred around a small number of high-profile events, notably the Tour Down Under, and the National Road Cycling Championships.

First staged in 1999, the Tour Down Under is a multi-day racing event for professional cyclists at the upper echelons of the sport. Held in Adelaide and its surrounds each January, the Tour Down Under is today part of the prestigious World Tour series of international cycling events held by the Union Cycliste

Internationale [the UCI, cycling's global governing body]. According to the event's organisers, in 2013 approximately 760 000 people lined the 810-kilometre route across seven days to watch the Tour Down Under peloton pass by. The event also reportedly attracted approximately 40 000 interstate and international visitors (Tour Down Under, 2014). Further, participatory cycling events integrated into the overall festival program allow amateur cyclists to cycle some sections of the official Tour Down Under route prior to the professional race, and under closed-road conditions. Thus opportunities exist for visitors to the Tour Down Under to combine active and passive participation in cycle tourism.

Meanwhile, the Australian National Road Cycling Championships are a precursor to the Tour Down Under each year. This multi-day festival of cycling showcases elite Australian cycling talent as the cyclists pursue the honour of wearing a national champion's jersey in their respective category and discipline for the coming season. Now established in the town of Buninyong, near Ballarat in Victoria, the event continues to grow in popularity with spectators. Accurate data regarding spectator numbers is not published; however, anecdotal reports estimated 25 000 spectators in 2014 (Culbert, 2014). The event is also identified in the *Victorian Cycle Tourism Action Plan 2011-2015* as being worthy of strategic investment for developing cycle tourism in that state:

> Major regional cycling events such as the Bendigo International Madison, the Jayco Herald Sun Tour and the Australian Open Road Cycling Championships provide invaluable opportunities to showcase Victoria's quaint villages, local food and wine and stunning nature-based experiences.
> (Tourism Victoria, 2011, p. 18)

Now that a basic understanding of the extent and focus of cycle tourism in Australia has been established, the next section goes on to identify and discuss barriers to further developing cycle tourism in Australia.

Barriers to developing cycle tourism in Australia

A detailed discussion of barriers to the development of all forms of cycle tourism in Australia is beyond the scope of this chapter. Here, attention is paid to identifying barriers to developing independent cycle touring and recreational (daytrip) cycling. Numerous authors have written about such barriers, but few pieces of writing are backed by empirical evidence. One published study to date (Lamont & Buultjens,

2011) reports empirical evidence regarding factors that cycle tourists perceive as impeding the development of independent cycle tourism in Australia. Data was collected from 389 subscribers to a nation-wide magazine with a cycle-touring focus in 2007; however, representativeness of the study's findings was limited by the convenience sampling approach. Lamont and Buultjens's (2011) study paid particular attention to cyclists' road safety, infrastructure provisioning, and carriage of bicycles on various modes of mass transportation in Australia. These issues had been identified in previous literature as probable barriers to developing independent cycle touring in Australia (for example, EcoGIS Consultants, 2000; Harland, 1999; Stone, 1999), though the authors could only provide anecdotal evidence for their claims.

Data indicated that respondents held concerns about the safety of cyclists on Australian roads and also believed that governments were not doing enough to improve safety for cyclists. Qualitative data revealed perceptions among respondents that there is a power imbalance between motorists and cyclists with resultant tensions between the two groups; that some motorists treat cyclists with contempt; and that many motorists hold erroneous beliefs that bicycles do not belong on roads. Indeed, the negative attitude of some motorists toward cyclists has been identified in the *Australian National Cycling Strategy 2005-2010* as a barrier to cycling participation generally (Austroads, 2005). Consequently, publicity campaigns designed to educate motorists about the vulnerability of cyclists may assist in ameliorating such tensions. However, a limitation of the Lamont and Buultjens study was its nationwide focus. Policy relating to cycling and cycling infrastructure varies between jurisdictions, as does the extent and quality of cycling infrastructure. More targeted research is needed in order to guide jurisdictions in prudent policy decisions around the strategic promotion of cycle tourism.

Further, respondents called for initiatives aimed at fostering a societal culture in which cycling is accepted as a legitimate mode of transport, and relations between motorists and cyclists are harmonious. Indeed, many respondents drew comparisons with European countries, where cycling is culturally embraced as an integrated transportation mode and where there is respect between motorists and cyclists. However, as Grant (Chapter Seventeen, this volume) argues, governments are beginning to act upon public concerns regarding the safety of cyclists on public roads. In 2014, the Queensland Government set a significant precedent by mandating minimum distances that motor vehicles must afford cyclists when overtaking. Further, acknowledging that harmony between the two groups is dependent on mutual respect, Queensland also introduced cyclist fines equal to motorist ones for breaking road rules (Bicycle Queensland, 2014).

Physical infrastructure for cycling was also identified as a barrier to developing independent cycle touring. Whilst the quality and extent of cycling infrastructure varies considerably between jurisdictions, respondents in the Lamont and Buultjens (2011) study were concerned about roadways that impede separation buffers between cyclists and vehicular traffic. This was particularly the case for non-metropolitan roads, where speed limits tend to be higher than on metropolitan roads, and road shoulders are often inconsistent, narrow or in some cases non-existent. A possible solution may be to encourage more public investment in infrastructure that segregates cyclists from vehicular traffic — such as rail trails. Indeed, rail trails provide considerably safer environments for cycling because interaction with motor vehicles is largely eliminated.

The final development barrier examined by Lamont and Buultjens (2011) was the carriage of bicycles on mass transportation modes in Australia. Due to Australia's large land mass and wide geographic dispersal, modes of mass transportation are a crucial element of tourism systems, particularly air transport. Further, it had previously been suggested that transporting bicycles within Australia can be problematic (EcoGIS Consultants, 2000; Harland, 1999; Stone, 1999). Respondents generally believed that transporting bicycles on air, coach and rail services in Australia was difficult. Airlines' policies pertaining to excess baggage charges and carriage of sports equipment, as well as the potential for damage to bicycles, were seen as deterrents to travelling with a bicycle by air. Coach transport services were criticised because carriage of bicycles is often at the discretion of the driver and subject to available luggage space, meaning that cycle tourists can experience uncertainty as to whether their bicycle will be carried or not. Rail services were criticised by respondents for similar reasons, with discretionary carriage policies rendering rail transport somewhat unreliable.

In summary, barriers to developing cycle tourism in Australia are not well understood, and constitute an avenue for future research. Whilst some work has been done in understanding barriers to Australia's realising its potential for independent cycle touring, that work is limited to exploring road safety, cycling infrastructure provisioning and carriage of bicycles on mass modes of transportation. Additional research is needed to explore latent development barriers, whilst jurisdiction-specific research would be useful in generating more in-depth insights that policy makers can draw upon to inform strategic planning initiatives.

Conclusion

This chapter has discussed the nexus between cycling and tourism, with particular emphasis on the Australian context. In summary, cycle tourism constitutes an array of cycling participation modes away from an individual's home region. It is evident that scholarly enquiry into cycle tourism emerged in the late 1990s, with publications appearing sporadically in peer-reviewed journals addressing tourism and leisure management, sustainable tourism, and transport policy. Early research themes tended to centre primarily on economic valuations of cycle tourism in certain jurisdictions, along with applied research seeking to understand necessary infrastructure and other requirements necessary to support and attract cycle tourists. However, scholarly cycle tourism research has experienced somewhat of a renaissance since around 2010, as researchers have begun to deploy more sophisticated theoretical and methodological approaches to this research context. Researchers have only scratched the surface when unpacking the experiences of cycle tourists: significant scope exists for developing theoretical understandings of interactions and experiences of their surroundings.

Cycle tourism in Australia is quite prolific, as we have seen, and occurs in multiple modes. Australia is reasonably well equipped to facilitate independent and commercially organised holidays by bicycle, and opportunities to participate in cycling on a recreational (daytrip) basis are abundant. Event-based cycle tourism is also increasing across Australia, with the number of participatory and competitive cycling events increasing in line with demand. Passive participation in cycle tourism — by way of spectating at major cycling events — is a growing subsegment. However, several conditions potentially impede the further development of cycle tourism in Australia. These include road safety issues for cyclists; infrastructure provisioning issues; and carriage of bicycles on mass transportation modes within Australia. Whilst cycle tourism has the potential to develop as a valuable tourism subsegment in Australia, much work is needed around research and policy to better understand and cater for this market.

References

Arup Consultants. (2014). *Casino to Murwillumbah Rail Trail study: Final report*. New South Wales, Australia: NSW Government Premier & Cabinet. Retrieved 1 August 2014 from http://www.nsw.gov.au/sites/default/files/regions/casino_to_ murwillumbah_rail_trail_study_final_report.pdf.

Australian Bureau of Statistics [ABS]. (1998). *Participation in sport and physical activities Australia*. Cat. No. 4177.0. Canberra: ABS.

Australian Bureau of Statistics [ABS]. (2013). *Participation in sport and physical recreation, Australia, 2011-12*. Cat. No. 4177.0. Retrieved 1 August 2014 from http://www.abs.gov.au /ausstats/abs@.nsf/Products/4177.0~201112~Main+Features~Characteristics+of+participation?OpenDocument.

Austroads. (2005). *The Australian National Cycling Strategy 2005-2010*. Retrieved 9 August 2006 from http://www.abc.dotars.gov.au/downloads/TheAustralianNationalCycling Strategy2005-2010.pdf.

Beeton, S. (2003). *An economic analysis of rail trails in Victoria, Australia*. Melbourne: La Trobe University. Retrieved 5 August 2006 from http://www.latrobe.edu.au/bus/Rail%20Trails%20Report.pdf.

Beeton, S. (2006). *Regional communities and cycling: The case of the Murray to the Mountains Rail Trail, Victoria, Australia*. Melbourne: La Trobe University.

Bicycle Queensland. (2014). *New cycling rules*. Retrieved 1 August 2014 from https://www.qld.gov.au/transport/safety/rules/other/cyclists/index.html.

Bil, M, Bilova, M, & Kubecek, J. (2012). Unified GIS database on cycle tourism infrastructure. *Tourism Management, 33*, 1554-1561.

Bull, C. (2006). Racing cyclists as sport tourists: The experiences and behaviours of a case study group of cyclists in East Kent, England. *Journal of Sport & Tourism, 11*(3/4), 259-274.

Coghlan, A. (2012). An autoethnographic account of a cycling charity challenge event: Exploring manifest and latent aspects of the experience. *Journal of Sport & Tourism, 17*(2), 105-124.

Cope, A, Cairns, S, Fox, K, Lawlor, D, Lockie, M, Lumsdon, L … Rosen, P. (2003). The UK National Cycle Network: An assessment of the benefits of a sustainable transport infrastructure. *World Transport Policy and Practice, 9*(1), 6-17.

Cope, A, Doxford, D, & Hill, T. (1998). Monitoring tourism on the UK's first long-distance cycle route. *Journal of Sustainable Tourism*, 6(3), 210-223.

Cox, P. (2012). Strategies promoting cycle tourism in Belgium: Practices and implications. *Tourism Planning and Development*, 9(1), 25-39.

Culbert, D. (2014, July 10). Tour de France 'an investment not a cost' for Yorkshire. *Sports Business Insider*. Retrieved 1 August 2014 from http://sportsbusinessinsider.com.au/blogs-features/tour-de-france-an-investment-not-a-cost-for-yorkshire.

Cycling Australia. (2013). *Cycling Australia Annual Report 2013*. Retrieved 1 August 2014 from http://www.slideshare.net/Bengodkin/1310-162-cycling-aus-text-v8#.

Cycling for Culture. (2014). About Cycling for Culture. Retrieved 22 January 2015 from http://www.cyclingforculture.com.au/about.

Department of Communications, Information Technology, and the Arts. (2003). *Tourism White Paper: A medium to long term strategy for tourism*. Canberra: Department of Industry, Tourism and Resources. Retrieved 10 June 2015 from http://www.industry.gov.au/content/itrinternet/cmscontent.cfm?objectID=D2FD7EF3-F58D-9BD8-5BB7212011F07B12.

Dickinson, J, Lumsdon, L, & Robbins, D. (2011). Slow travel: Issues for tourism and climate change. *Journal of Sustainable Tourism*, 19(3), 281-300.

Downward, P, & Lumsdon, L. (2001). The development of recreational cycle routes: An evaluation of user needs. *Managing Leisure*, 6(1), 50-60.

EcoGIS Consultants. (2000). *Submission on cycle tourism to the Tourism Strategy Group*. A report commissioned by the Cycling Promotion Fund of Australia and the Bicycle Federation of Australia.

Fang, W, Chang, H, & Huang, Y. (2011). Cycling recreation experiences and facilities: A case study of the Danshui Riverside bike path, Taiwan. *International Journal of Agricultural Travel and Tourism*, 2(1), 7-19.

Faulks, P, Ritchie, BW, & Fluker, M. (2006). *Cycle tourism in Australia: An investigation into its size and scope*. Australia: Cooperative Research Centre for Sustainable Tourism. Retrieved 10 June 2015 from http://atfiles.org/files/pdf/Faulks-Austraila-Cycle-Tourism.pdf.

Fox, K, Humberstone, B, & Dubnewick, M. (2014). Cycling into sensoria: Embodiment, leisure, and tourism. *Tourism Review International*, 18(1/2), 71-85.

Fullagar, S. (2012). Gendered cultures of slow travel: Women's cycle touring as an alternative hedonism. In S Fullagar, K Markwell, & E Wilson (Eds.), *Slow tourism: Experiences and mobilities* (pp. 99-112). Bristol: Channel View.

Hall, CM. (2003). *Introduction to tourism: Dimensions and issues* (4th ed.). Frenchs Forest, Australia: Pearson.

Harland, J. (1999). *Infrastructural support for bicycle tourism: Submission to the Standing Committee on Primary Industries and Regional Services*. Adelaide: Bicycle Federation of Australia. Retrieved 29 June 2006 from http://www.aph.gov.au/house/committee/Primind/rdinq/sub162-e.pdf.

Insall, P. (1999, 13-16 April). Eurovelo: Getting Europe cycling. *Velo City '99: The 11th international bicycle planning conference*, Graz, Austria, and Maribor, Slovenia.

International Mountain Bicycling Association. (n.d.). Where to ride. Retrieved 1 August 2014 from http://www.imba-au.com/where-to-ride.

Lamont, M. (2009a). Independent bicycle tourism: A whole tourism systems perspective. *Tourism Analysis*, 14(5), 605-620.

Lamont, M. (2009b). Reinventing the wheel: A definitional discussion of bicycle tourism. *Journal of Sport & Tourism*, 14(1), 5-23.

Lamont, M. (2014a). Authentication in sports tourism. *Annals of Tourism Research*, 45, 1-17.

Lamont, M. (2014b). Introduction: Cycling and tourism. *Tourism Review International*, 18(1/2), 1-7.

Lamont, M, & Buultjens, J. (2011). Putting the brakes on: Impediments to the development of independent bicycle tourism in Australia. *Current Issues in Tourism*, 14(1), 57-78.

Lamont, M, & Jenkins, J. (2013). Segmentation of cycling event participants: A two-step cluster method utilizing recreation specialization. *Event Management*, 17(4), 391-407.

Lamont, M, & McKay, J. (2012). Intimations of postmodernity in sports tourism at the Tour de France. *Journal of Sport & Tourism*. 17(4), 313-331.

Lee, C, & Huang, H. (2012). The attractiveness of Taiwan as a bicycle tourism destination: A supply-side approach. *Asia Pacific Journal of Tourism Research*. doi: 10.1080/10941665.2012.739190.

Leiper, N. (2004). *Tourism management* (3rd ed.). Frenchs Forest, Australia: Pearson Education.

Lumsdon, L. (1996). Cycle tourism in Britain. *Insights* (March), 27-32. UK: English Tourist Board.

Lumsdon, L. (2000). Transport and tourism: Cycle tourism — A model for sustainable development? *Journal of Sustainable Tourism*, 8(5), 361-377.

Lumsdon, L, Downward, P, & Cope, A. (2004). Monitoring of cycle tourism on long distance trails: The North Sea cycle route. *Journal of Transport Geography*, 12(1), 13-22.

Mason, P, & Leberman, S. (2000). Local planning for recreation and tourism: A case study of mountain biking from New Zealand's Manawatu region. *Journal of Sustainable Tourism*, 8(2), 97-115.

Meschik, M. (2012). Sustainable cycle tourism along the Danube Cycle Route in Austria. *Tourism Planning and Development*, 9(1), 41-56.

Murphy, D. (2002). *Murray to the Mountains Rail Trail media kit and visiting journalist program*. Victoria: Rail Trails Australia.

Oxer, M. (2001, 21-22 September). Rail trails in Australia: Developing our green corridors. *New Zealand Cycling Conference 2001: Transport for Living*, Christchurch, New Zealand. Retrieved 4 November 2005 from http://archived.ccc.govt.nz/ recreation/cycling/conference/2001/proceedings.asp.

Pendleton, T. (1999, 13-16 April). Bicycle touring in America. *Velo City '99: The 11th international bicycle planning conference*, Graz, Austria, and Maribor, Slovenia.

Robbins, DK, & Dickinson, JE. (2007). Can domestic tourism growth and reduced car dependency be achieved simultaneously in the UK? In P Peeters (Ed.), *Tourism and climate change and mitigation: Methods, greenhouse gas reductions and policies* (pp. 169-187). Breda, NL: Stichting.

Ritchie, BW. (1998). Bicycle tourism in the South Island of New Zealand: Planning and management issues. *Tourism Management*, 19(6), 567-582.

Ritchie, BW, & Hall, CM. (1999). Bicycle tourism and regional development: A New Zealand case study. *Anatolia: An International Journal of Tourism and Hospitality Research*, 10(2), 89-112.

Siderelis, C, & Moore, R. (1995). Outdoor recreation net benefits of rail-trails. *Journal of Leisure Research*, 27(4), 344-359.

Simonsen, P, & Jorgenson, B. (1998). *Cycle tourism: An economic and environmental sustainable form of tourism?* Bornholm, Denmark: Unit of Tourism Research, Research Centre of Bornholm. Retrieved 3 December 2006 from http://brugerforum.crt.dk/media/Cycling_tourism.pdf.

Solly, P. (2003). *Cycle tourism: The perfect niche market for Australia. Submission to the Tourism Green Paper*.

South Australian Tourism Commission. (2005). *Cycle Tourism Strategy 2005-2009*. Retrieved 9 August 2006 from http://www.tourism.sa.gov.au/tourism/plan /cycley_tourism_strategy.pdf.

Southern Flinders Rangers Development Board. (2008). *Southern Flinders Ranges Cycle Tourism Master Plan*. Retrieved 10 June 2015 from http://www.yorkeandmidnorth.com.au/uploads/files/Resources/MASTERPLANFINAL.pdf.

Standeven, J, & DeKnop, P. (1999). *Sport tourism*. Champaign, Il: Human Kinetics.

Stone, D. (1999). *Cycling and cycle tourism opportunities in the Hunter region of NSW: Submission to the inquiry into infrastructure and the development of Australia's regional areas*. Newcastle: Newcastle Cycleways Movement Inc.

Sustrans. (1999). Cycle tourism information pack. Retrieved 16 November 2005 from http://www.sustrans.org.uk/webfiles/Info%20sheets/ff28.pdf.

Tobin, G. (1974). The bicycle boom of the 1890s: The development of private transportation and the birth of the modern tourist. *Journal of Popular Culture*, 8(Spring), 838-849.

Tour de Cure. (2014). Join a tour. Retrieved 1 August 2014 from http://www.tourdecure. com.au/pages/get-involved/join-a-tour.

Tour Down Under. (2014). Student Information. Retrieved 1 August 2014 from http://www. tourdownunder.com.au.

Tourism Victoria. (2011). *Victoria's Cycle Tourism Action Plan 2011-2015*. Retrieved August 1 2014 from http://www.tourism.vic.gov.au/component/edocman/?task= document.download&id=150.

Visit Victoria. (n.d.). Great Ocean Road: Cycling. Retrieved 1 August 2014 from http://www.visitvictoria.com/Regions/Great-Ocean-Road/Activities-and-attractions/ Outdoor-activities/Cycling.

Watson, R, & Gray, M. (1978). *The penguin book of the bicycle*. Middlesex, England: Penguin.

Weed, M, & Bull, C. (2009). *Sports tourism: Participants, policy and providers* (2nd ed.). Oxford: Butterworth Heinemann.

Part II

Strategies for change

9 Gender and cycling: Gendering cycling subjects and *forming* bikes, practices and spaces as gendered objects

Jennifer Bonham, Carol Bacchi and Thomas Wanner

Introduction

The landmark decision by the New South Wales Court of Appeal in the case of *Norrie v NSW*[1] to recognise the right of Norrie to register as sex 'non-specific' on a birth certificate serves as a caution to researchers, policy makers, planners — in fact the entire community — to remain sceptical of sex as an essential biological fact, and of gender as the culturally produced meanings which proceed from that fact. *Both* biological sex and gender are social productions (Gatens, 1983; Butler, 1990). Differentiating bodies by reference to anatomical (hormonal, physiological) features is not a self-evident or necessary way of ordering existence. As Bacchi notes:

> if indeed 'boys' were boys and 'girls' were girls, there would not be the amount of disquiet generated by attempts to challenge gender-specific hairstyling (long hair for boys and short hair for girls), or attempts to challenge dress codes. (1996, p. 4)

---

[1] *Registrar of Births, Deaths and Marriages* [2013] NSWCA 145.

'Women' and 'men' are political, rather than natural, categories which have significant consequences for those who do not fit such categories (Bacchi, 1996, p. 4).

So what does this have to do with cycling? It provides an important opportunity to question assumptions about the relation between gender categories and cycling. This questioning has two aspects. First, thinking about 'women' and 'men' as socially produced categories allows us to challenge the content of those categories and, more importantly, explore the processes by which they are formed. In this chapter we have used the term 'gendering' to refer to these processes of gender formation. As Bacchi puts it:

> [g]endering describes an ongoing and always incomplete process that *constitutes* (makes come into existence) (Jones, 1997, p. 265) 'women' and 'men' as specific kinds of unequal political subjects. (2012, p. 1, emphasis in the original)

The second aspect of this questioning concerns the formation of some 'entity' — in this instance, cycling (bikes, practices, spaces) by reference to 'attributes' differentiated as belonging to 'woman' or 'man' (Bacchi, 2012, p. 5). For example, cycling jerseys are formed as women's or men's jerseys by reference to physical 'attributes' differentiated as belonging to 'women' and 'men'. As particular associations stick, such as women's jerseys and men's jerseys, they operate to reinforce the categories of 'woman' and 'man' (see also Faulkner, 2001, pp. 82-84). We refer to the second aspect of our inquiry as the 'formation of gendered objects' or 'gendered formations'.

Our particular interest in this chapter is in the way in which gender is brought into the *ongoing-formation* of bikes, practices and spaces. The type of questioning we pursue interrogates these formations as it foregrounds the instability of 'gender' and the ongoing possibilities for change. This chapter uses interviews conducted for a research project on 'Women returning to cycling' to examine how researchers and the researched participate in both gendering — that is, constituting 'women' and 'men' — and forming bikes, bicycling practices and cycling spaces as gendered 'objects'. Further, we are interested in how researchers and the researched unsettle gendering and gendered formations to produce alternative lives. The first section of the chapter explains the theoretical underpinnings of our analysis before elaborating our analytic approach. The final section reports on our analysis of gendering, the formation of gendered objects, and the unsettling of each of these processes.

Theoretical underpinnings

In line with recent theoretical developments across the humanities and social sciences, we suggest that the things we often presume to be fixed and durable — objects such as bicycles, traffic lights, roads and pedal actions; and subjects such as cyclists, motorists, women, men — are in a continual process of becoming (Bardon & Josserand, 2010). In other words, as Bonham and Bacchi (2013) put it, they are in *ongoing-formation*. This point is important, as it draws attention both to how 'things' continue to be formed in taken-for-granted ways and to the ever-present possibilities for transformation. It also forces us to consider how individuals are located in these processes. Our interview analysis is informed by three key theoretical propositions outlined below.

We use Michel Foucault's (1972) concept of *discursive practice* as a starting point to understand the *ongoing-formation* of objects and subjects of 'cycling'. In its simplest terms, a discursive practice[2] can be understood as a historically specific set of routines through which social knowledges are continually formed (Bacchi & Bonham, 2014). This set of routines produces sites dispersed throughout society. For example, departments of transport, parliamentary select committees, households in which household travel surveys are implemented, university planning and engineering schools, local government traffic departments, transport consultants, planning and transport journals, motor accident commissions and insurers, and motor vehicle, cycling, public transport and pedestrian lobby groups are sites formed through spatio-temporal routines. It is in these sites and through the routines which form them that transport knowledges with varying degrees of authority are produced. These sites are also connected through routines — such as the state department of transport sending licence or vehicle registration forms to individual householders on an annual basis; or federal, state and local

---

[2] It is important to note that discursive practice does not refer to the use of language or logical propositions; rather, it refers to knowledge making. For a detailed explanation of the concept of discursive practice, see Bacchi and Bonham (2014). We use the term *discursive practice* interchangeably with Foucault's recently popularised term *dispositif*, which he defines (1980, p. 194) as ' … a thoroughly heterogeneous ensemble consisting of discourses, institutions, architectural forms, regulatory decisions, laws, administrative measures, scientific statements, philosophical, moral and philanthropic propositions — in short, the said as much as the unsaid. Such are the elements of the apparatus. The apparatus itself is the system of relations that can be established between these elements'.

Strategies for change

governments conducting traffic counts on the road network; or hospitals, police departments and insurers creating statistics on road crashes and disseminating these to parliamentary select committees and departments of transport (see Figure 9.1).

It is through these routine relations involving materials, movements, documents, words, symbols and so forth that objects (bicycles, trips), subjects (cyclists, travellers), concepts (derived demand, transport) and strategies (interactions between agencies, procedures for creating policy documents) are formed, re-formed and transformed (see also Schwanen, 2013). Interviews — whether conducted under the auspices of a government department or research institution — are also part of these routines of relations, so that researchers and the researched participate in the formation, re-formation and transformation of objects, subjects, concepts and strategies (Bonham & Bacchi, 2013). In this chapter, we are concerned with gendering — the production of categories of boy/

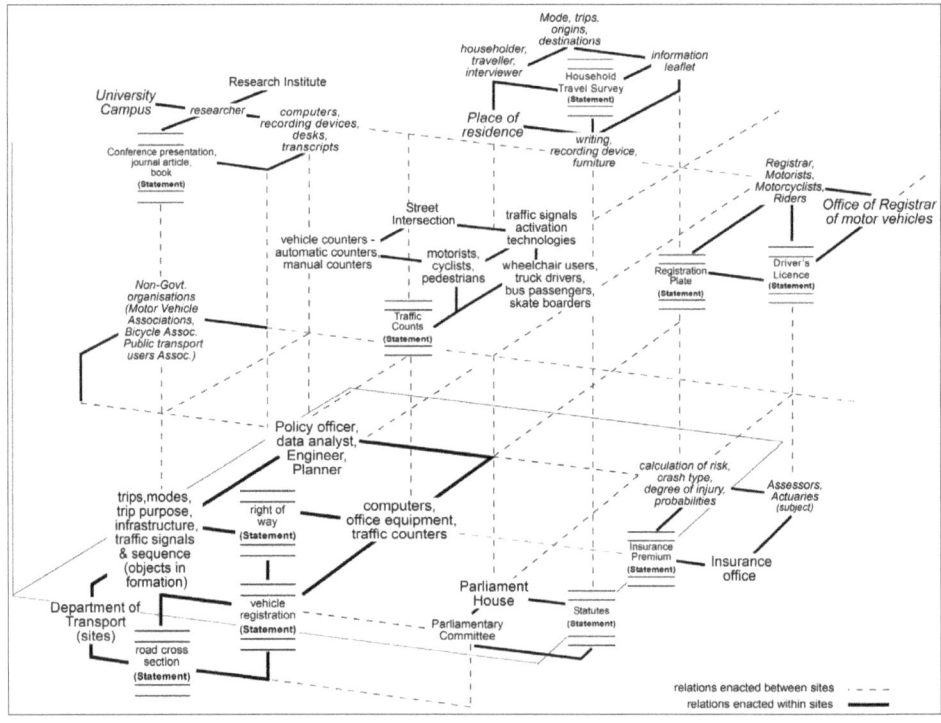

Figure 9.1: Discursive practice of transport.
(Source: Diagram created by Chris Crothers for the authors.)

man/masculine and girl/woman/feminine — and the formation of bikes, cycling practices and cycling spaces as gendered objects (that is, gendered formations).

Our second theoretical point relates to the individuals who participate in interviews. The ontological status (Mol, 1999) of the 'individual' is rarely interrogated within transport or cycling literatures (Bonham & Cox, 2010). Rather the 'individual' is widely accepted as a self-evident, pre-discursive[3] fact (Butler, 1990, pp. 20-21). The 'individual' of liberal thought is at the centre of transport and cycling literatures. This 'individual' is assumed to be a coherent being that possesses an array of characteristics and capabilities, such as autonomy and rationality, in common with other human beings. This 'individual' is also assumed to be a 'unique' being with an interiority (subjectivity) which shapes her/his particular perceptions, desires and preferences (for example, Murtagh, Gatersleben, & Uzzell, 2012).[4]

We take a very different view of the individual and suggest that the very possibility of thinking ourselves as individuals, and particular kinds of individuals at that (Heyes, 2007, pp. 16-17), is an outcome of power/knowledge relations (discursive practices or *dispositifs*). As Miller and Rose put it, the 'idea of the human subject as individuated, choosing, with capacities of self-reflection and a striving for autonomy, is a result of practices of subjectification' (2008, p. 8).

The *interiority*, which is assumed to be a pre-social, self-evident fact, is an effect (Markula & Pringle, 2006, pp. 38-39)[5] of the 'individual' being located within, and required to respond to, a multiplicity of discursive practices. For example, before we are born we are located in discursive practices of biology (classification of species), obstetrics and midwifery. At birth we are located within

---

[3] By *pre-discursive*, we mean that the 'individual' is considered to exist prior to the social practices of ordering existence. We are not denying the materiality of the 'individual'; we are saying simply that its separation from the mass of existence (everything contained in the world) is not a necessary way of ordering life.

[4] Within transport and cycling literatures, this interiority (subjectivity) is assumed to pre-exist society. For example, Murtagh et al. explain the imperfect internalisation of social roles as the result of personal or subjective interpretations of those roles (2012, p. 515).

[5] As Markula and Pringle argue, the individual's 'incessant engagement in self-interpretation' locks the individual into particular subject positions (woman, man, cyclist, motorist), and thoroughly naturalises both that subject position and the effect of interiority produced through 'self-interpretation' (2010, p. 39).

discursive practices of kinship and citizenship. Our attendance at the health clinic locates us in discursive practices of epidemiology, medicine and paediatrics, while our attendance at school locates us in discursive practices of education. Targeted within multiple (and ever-multiplying) discursive practices, we are worked upon, and we work upon ourselves, to respond — to move, to speak, to think, to feel — in relation to those discursive practices. It follows that it is not a 'natural' woman or man that participates in the research interview; it is an individual which is itself the product of discipline (Heyes, 2007, p. 17). Further, when this interviewee speaks s/he says what it is *possible* to say within the given cultural context.[6]

This insight leads to our third theoretical point, which directly addresses the use of the term 'gender' to refer to particular processes (gendering and the formation of gendered objects). Similar to the 'individual', the term 'gender' is frequently deployed, but rarely interrogated within transport and cycling literatures (notable exceptions include Hanson & Pratt, 1995; Law, 1999; Hanson, 2010). 'Gender' is generally discussed as one of a number of characteristics that 'individuals' possess (for example, Sigurdardottir, Kaplan, Møller, & Teasdale, 2013; Spencer, Watts, Vivanco, & Flynn, 2013); and it is used by researchers in creating[7] and explaining 'patterns' in attitudes, behaviours and perceptions.[8] 'Gender patterns' of mobility have been explained as the outcome of either 'natural' differences between 'men' and 'women' (for example, risk aversion reported on by Pucher, Garrard, and Greaves, 2011) or the socialisation of 'sexed' bodies into prevailing gender roles (Emond, Tang, & Handy, 2009). More often, it seems, 'gender patterns' in attitudes, behaviours and perceptions remain a mysterious combination of both 'naturally' endowed and 'culturally' inculcated characteristics. On the one hand, the naturalisation of gender operates to 'fix' women and men in their biology, leaving us to wonder about the many people who do not neatly fit into the categories available. On the other hand, the socialisation thesis implies a culturally constituted set of attributes which can be taken up or shed more or less

---

[6] We do not wish to deny or diminish the attachment of the individual to what they think, feel or do.

[7] We use the term 'create', as the researcher actively engages in differentiating populations into gender categories.

[8] The concepts of 'attitude', behaviour' and 'perception' assume that the individual has an interiority which processes and produces true meanings of the world.

at will (Eveline, 2005, p. 642). Combining these two positions returns us to the intellectual dead end of the 'nature/nurture' debates.

A handful of researchers use a performative approach to gender in their analysis of the relationship between gender and mobility. Drawing on Pierre Bourdieu, for example, Cresswell and Uteng (2008), and Steinbach, Green, Datta, and Edwards (2011), offer important insights. They argue that mobility practices[9] become gendered as specific movements are cultivated by the individual in reference to her/his gender identity, and in turn these practices become a marker of that gender identity. This gender identity is socially produced. Steinbach et al. (2011) locate individuals within social contexts as they examine the culturally specific demands on 'women' and 'men' to conduct their mobility practices (such as cycling) in particular ways. These authors foreground the fluidity of cycling practices in London today and imply that this fluidity will ultimately congeal into specific feminine and masculine performances of cycling, as it has for other mobility practices like catching public transport or walking (Steinbach et al., 2011, p. 1125). However, we are concerned that Steinbach et al. (2011, p. 1125) retain the pre-discursive individual as they focus on the (constrained) *choices* their interviewees make in conforming to or resisting culturally acceptable practices of femininity and masculinity. Further, although practices are inherently unstable, there is no examination of how gendered mobility practices are transformed — for example, the various shifts in the United Kingdom from cycling being acceptable-unacceptable-acceptable for 'women' (Oddy, 2007; Cox, 2014).

Finally, Steinbach et al. (2011) participate both in gendering 'women' and 'men' and in the formation of gendered objects of cycling, such as clothing. It is the researchers, for instance, who create a typology of femininities as they classify some interviewee responses according to 'orthodox' or 'marginal' femininities. And it is the researchers, as much as the researched, who participate in forming cycling 'objects' — wearing particular clothes, thinking about cycling in terms of autonomy and freedom — as 'gendered objects'. For example, Steinbach et al. describe 'jeans and trainers and a jumper' as adherence to a more 'orthodox feminine aesthetic' (2011, p. 1025). Steinbach et al. do not reflect on their own gendering practices or on the processes of forming gendered cycling objects.

---

[9] Mobility practices range from long-distance travel to fine body movements such as hand-eye co-ordination.

Letherby and Reynolds (2009) also examine journeys and emotions with reference to Judith Butler's theorisation of gender as performative. Butler (1990) elaborates on the work of Michel Foucault (1978) as she argues that sexuality — and specifically, the normalisation of heterosexuality — is at the heart of the differentiation and regulation of 'woman' and 'man'. The subject positions 'woman' and 'man' are constituted in the process of excising and assembling 'attributes' according to a heterosexual norm. In turn, these 'attributes' — physical characteristics, ways of feeling, thinking and doing — operate to *regulate* those who are categorised as 'woman' and 'man'.[10] In Western contexts, where mobility is constituted and valued in different ways (for example, 'expeditions' and 'transport' are valued over 'nomadism' and 'wandering'), greater mobility is linked to masculinity, while reduced mobility is linked to femininity.[11] We are interested in *how* such links are made — that is, in the process through which 'man' is constituted as more mobile and 'woman' as less mobile. With Butler, we understand gender as a continual process; hence we use the verb form 'gendering' to describe 'the active shaping of the categories of "woman" and "man"' (Bacchi, 2012, p. 5) or the 'active doing of differentiation' (Bacchi, 2012, p. 9). In this approach, we interrogate how researchers *and* the researched participate in this differentiation.

Gendering occurs within a multiplicity of discursive practices. We suggest that the formation and 'taking up'[12] of subject positions such as 'woman' or 'man' does not have an end point. Rather, these — like all — subject positions are, as

---

[10] We are not denying the materiality of 'bodies'; rather, we are arguing, along with Butler, that bodies are not ontologically prior to gendering. Instead, gendering occurs within the same processes (that is, within the same discursive practices) which differentiate 'bodies' from the mass of existence (see also Subramanian, 2008, p. 39).

[11] This position contrasts markedly with mobility researchers such as Mimi Sheller. Drawing on Pierre Bourdieu, Sheller argues that 'the male body is culturally performed as a more mobile body, while the female body becomes more restricted and spatially circumscribed' (Sheller, 2008, p. 259). Although Sheller draws on Iris Marion Young's concept of performance (as cited in Sheller, 2008, p. 259), she also uses the categories of 'men' and 'women' as if they are unproblematic. For example, she repeats the oft-stated view that 'largely male experts and technicians … may overlook women's experiences, perspectives and needs' (p. 258) as if these 'experiences, perspectives and needs' simply exist, rather than being constituted through gendering practices (including, within the discursive practice of transport).

[12] 'Taking up' does not refer to individuals choosing to adopt a subject position; rather, it refers to them doing something (such as ticking 'female' or 'male' on a census form) which acknowledges them as either female or male.

Chris Weedon puts it, 'precarious, contradictory and in process, constantly being reconstituted in discourse each time we think or speak' (as cited in Jones, 1997, p. 263). At the birth of a child (or in the ultrasound unit), midwives, obstetricians and parents are already employing a discursive practice of anatomy as they compare, differentiate, locate and pronounce, 'It's a girl', or 'It's a boy'.[13] Parents and hospital staff are required to complete forms which attest to the birth of that 'girl' or 'boy' (and now, perhaps, simply 'infant'). This differentiation — made more durable in the naming — is a process of gendering, and it locates the infant within discursive practices of anatomy and demography.

At numerous times throughout life, the individual will be called upon to acknowledge the self as female or male — for example, when completing forms (censuses, household travel surveys), participating in a sport (male and female codes), auditioning for a theatrical performance, or attending a school (all girls, all boys, co-ed). Similarly, the interviews conducted for the 'Women returning to cycling' study required interviewees to acknowledge themselves as women while the interviewers oversaw this process, monitoring who could be included in the research project — not just any 'body' could pronounce itself or be pronounced as 'woman'. As with any research project that differentiates participants in terms of gender (exclusively interviewing women or men or differentiating their interviewees as man or woman), the 'Women returning to cycling' researchers participated in gendering. Our concern in doing this was to acknowledge women who practice cycling and to interrupt the tendency in some studies that explicitly link women to, and consequently risk normalising women as, 'not cycling'.

The second way of thinking about gender as a process refers to the 'formation of gendered objects'. This process refers to the linking of 'attributes' constituted as feminine or masculine to particular objects — such as the formation of 'women's' and 'men's' jerseys by reference to physical attributes constituted as feminine and masculine, referred to above. As these attributes 'stick' (that is, as they come into widespread usage) they operate to (re)form the categories 'women' and 'men' with

---

[13] Today, a number of other responses have been made possible. We might say: 'The dividing practice available does not acknowledge what it is'; or: 'An alternative dividing practice does not create gender categories'; or: 'It's a baby' (which in itself continues to produce the division between 'human' and 'non-human'). We have borrowed the term *dividing practice* from Foucault, who adopts the term when discussing the mechanisms used in contemporary Western societies to differentiate populations (1982, p. 208).

these attributes, and this has consequences for the everyday lives of those categorised as 'women' and 'men'. Bruno Latour (1991) argues that technologies are social relations made durable. We would like to borrow this argument to suggest that the formation of bikes, practices and spaces as 'feminine' or 'masculine' assists in making particular formations of 'women' and 'men' durable. However, as feminist technology theorist Wendy Faulkner points out, these formations are never straightforward or stable (2001, pp. 82-83). We demonstrate this point with reference to the 'Women returning to cycling' project as we examine how bikes, practices and spaces are in *ongoing-formation* and, consequently, always open to change.

The 'Women returning to cycling' research participants were required to reflect on their own thinking, feeling, characterising and doing in relation to 'cycling', and, in doing this, to acknowledge themselves as cycling subjects (or not), thereby binding themselves to the subject positions available. 'Cycling' is also an object in *ongoing-formation* within discursive practices of transport, sport, health and urban planning. It is not possible to say just 'anything' about cycling or to link any movement whatsoever to cycling, just as it is not possible to say 'anything' about 'women'. We can only say 'what it is culturally possible' to say about cycling and gender. However, because gendering and the formation of gendered objects of cycling are ongoing processes, it is possible to interrupt attributions of gender and cycling. In the process of forming categories such as 'woman' and 'man' or relating gender to particular bicycles or riding practices we simultaneously form, re-form and transform both gender and cycling.

We are not claiming that the interruption of gender in a single interview automatically leads to change, but we are interested in analysing interviews for the change they might enable. Further, we are concerned that how we analyse interviews and distribute our 'findings' has political implications. If we fail to reflect on our own gendering practices and assume, first, the pre-discursive existence of 'women' and 'men', and second, the possibility of identifying norms amongst these 'women' and 'men', then we participate in making particular formations durable. These formations have consequences for all people, but especially for those who live their lives outside the range of socially constituted norms. This chapter examines the processes of gendering and the formation of gendered objects in relation to 'cycling' in order to open up new possibilities for gender and cycling practice.

Methodology: Analysing interviews

The 'Women returning to cycling' study, conducted in 2009, used in-depth interviews to gather information about women's engagement in cycling. Forty-nine women participated in the study. Women who had returned to cycling more than a year before the study were interviewed once, while those who had more recently returned to cycling were interviewed on two or more occasions, in order to track the process of becoming a 'cyclist'. The interview transcripts were initially analysed using a conventional analytic technique — specifically, a thematic approach (Bonham & Wilson, 2012a; 2012b). However, we were concerned that this technique risked essentialising and normalising women who cycled as particular *kinds* of women (for example, sporty, 'outdoors-ish', tough, unconventional), thereby making cycling a difficult option for women in general. In addressing this issue, Bonham and Bacchi (2013) developed a new approach to analysing interviews, 'poststructural interview analysis', and used it to examine how cycling and cyclists were formed and transformed in the interview process. In this chapter, we report on the use of this analytic technique to examine the gendering of 'women' and 'men' and the formation of gendered objects of cycling.

Poststructural interview analysis focuses on '*what* is said' in the interview process rather than on the people who say it (Stainton-Rogers & Stainton-Rogers, 1990). Following Bonham and Bacchi, we have analysed '*what* is said' in the interview material by looking for moments of 'excision and attribution', 'measurement' and 'self-formation' (2013, pp. 15-16). Moments of 'excision and attribution' refer to points in the interview where particular ways of thinking, feeling, characterising and doing are differentiated from the mass of existence as an attribute of 'women' or 'men' and related to 'cycling'. 'Measurement' refers to those moments where some form of quantification is used (such as 'more', 'less', 'many', 'few', 'old', 'young') in the process of relating 'attributes' of gender to cycling — that is, in the process of forming cycling as a gendered object. Finally, 'self-formation' refers to those moments when the interviewee self-genders — that is, when the interviewee speaks of the self in the subject position of 'woman', 'girl', 'lady' or 'female', thereby binding the self to that position.

Our analysis has been concerned with those instances in which specific 'attributes' are generalised to all men or all women. Partners, relatives and friends were frequently gendered through the use of terms such as 'husband', 'wife', 'fiancée', 'fiancé', 'girlfriend', 'boyfriend', 'aunt', 'uncle' and so forth. However, we have confined our analysis to those moments when particular 'attributes' of that individual ('husband', 'boyfriend' and so on) were extrapolated to the category of 'men' or 'women' — thereby gendering 'women' and 'men'. We raise questions about whether this is a pervasive formation; how it has become possible to relate a particular 'attribute' to a particular gender; and how the respondent unsettles or reaffirms that formation.

Drawing on Bonham and Bacchi (2013), we are interested in precisely *what* interviewees say and how this forms, re-forms or has the potential to transform what is possible in terms of women, men and cyclists. Where relevant, we have drawn on historical texts to demonstrate formations at different historical moments and to foreground sites and moments of transformation. We have ordered the discussion around the 'objects' of bikes, practices and spaces, and we consider both their gendered formation and their gendering effects. We are specifically interested in the discursive practices in which these objects are gendered, and whether the 'Women returning to cycling' interviews continue or disrupt, and propose alternatives to, pervasive gendered formations. It is important to tease out these interruptions and bring them into play, as they open possibilities for multiple cycling existences.

Transforming bikes, practices and spaces

Transforming bicycles

Bicycles are not quite the sturdy, stable objects we assume them to be. The taken-for-granted 'materiality' of the bicycle is in continual or *ongoing-formation*[14] within discursive practices of engineering, biomechanics, science, technology, transport, health and recreation. In the following section, we demonstrate the continual transformation of the bicycle as we contrast the gendered formation of the bicycle in the late nineteenth century with its gendered formation in the 'Women returning to cycling' interviews.

At various moments 'Women returning to cycling' interviewees spoke of the bicycles they owned as a 'lady's', 'man's', 'girl's' or 'boy's' bike. The gendered formation

---

[14] This includes forming in the same and in different ways.

of the bicycle has been apparent almost since the emergence of bicycle technologies themselves (Oddy, 1996; Mackintosh & Norcliffe, 2007). Designers and engineers have been especially engaged in this process, as they have integrated particular knowledges of women and men with knowledges of materials and mechanics. For example, in his 1890s treatise on *Bicycles and tricycles*, the British instructor in civil engineering Archibald Sharp generally spoke of the diamond frame bike in generic terms as a 'safety bike', 'safety' or 'bike'.[15] However, at particular points in his treatise he differentiates safety bikes according to the presence or absence of a top-tube, and it is at this point that he genders the safety bike. Bikes with top-tubes become a 'man's safety', while bikes without top-tubes become 'ladies' safeties' (1896, p. 287).[16] The 'ladies' safety' was recommended 'if the lady rider wears skirts' (p. 287). *What* Sharp says brings together discursive practices of engineering, design, clothing, class and gender. It also foregrounds the possibility that lady riders might *not* wear skirts. The 'rational clothing' debates of the day made it possible for the lady to wear knickerbockers (Bijker, 1995, p. 95; Furness, 2010, pp. 19-23), pantaloons or some variant of the 'bifurcated costume' used by women in France (Oddy, 1996, p. 64) and by lady racing cyclists (Simpson, 2007, pp. 59-60). If the 'ladies' safety' provided for ladies who wore skirts, it is possible to ask whether the 'safety' — a bike with a top-tube — catered for all other ladies as well as men. Differentiating safety bikes into the 'ladies' safety' and 'men's safety' — rather than into the 'safety with'/'safety without' a top-tube or the 'skirt-wearing ladies' safety'/'safety' — formed bicycles as gendered objects. Thus formed, the 'ladies' safety' operates to gender its user as 'woman' or 'lady'. The formation of the bicycle as a gendered object was taken up more than 100 years later — and no doubt at many points in between (Cox, 2014) — in the 'Women returning to cycling' study.

In the following exchange, both Interviewee One and the Interviewer participate in, and unsettle, the gendered formation of the 'ladies' bicycle'.

Interviewee One: Yes. I'm not mad about my bike because it's a male bike. It's a hybrid, whatever they call them, generic bike. It's got the bar across the top and I don't like that ... I would rather have one without the bar. It would be a lot easier.

---

[15] The 'safety bicycle' is the basic diamond frame design still used today.

[16] An alternative to the bike frame without a top-tube was a bike frame with two down tubes — one set above the other on a different angle (Sharp, 1896, p. 288).

Interviewer: Right, so a step-through?

Interviewee One: Yes, a step-through one.

Interviewer: Like the old [kind of] women's bikes that we used to have and then they took them away from us?

Interviewee One: Yes, and then they took them away. They all seem to be the same.[17]

'*What* is said' in this exchange is a moment of potential transformation. First, the 'male bike', 'generic bike 'and 'hybrid' have been conflated, opening up an array of possibilities. But our interest at this point is the differentiation of the bikes according to the presence or absence of the top-tube — the 'one without the bar'. The Interviewer and Interviewee One agree that this bike is a 'step-through'. It is *not* a ladies' or a women's bike, but it is *like* the old 'women's bikes'. Speaking about bikes 'without the bar' as a 'step-through' de-genders this particular bike; and whether or not it continues to be de-gendered will depend on how this exchange is reported by the analyst, how bikes without top-tubes are spoken of in other forums and whether those who use such bikes go undifferentiated.[18] 'Taking them away' — presumably the withdrawal of bikes without top-tubes from the market by retailers — may have made the de-gendering of these bikes possible, as their reintroduction as 'step-throughs' forms them simply as variants of the 'bike'.

At the same time that the step-through is being re-formed as 'not' gender-specific, in other interviews bikes with top-tubes are in the process of being re-gendered. The following excerpts from Interviewees Two and Three demonstrate respondents binding themselves to the category 'woman', but they also demonstrate the differentiation and formation of bikes with top-tubes as gendered objects in new ways.

---

[17] The comment 'then they took them away from us' raises the possibility that women were either expected to ride (bikes in *formation* as) 'men's bikes' or that they were not to ride at all. This line of inquiry opens myriad questions about changing practices of cycling — from cycling mainly for everyday journeys to cycling mainly as a form of sport or exercise — through the second half of the twentieth century. 'Men's bikes' — which could be made lighter because of the additional strength afforded by the top-tube — were used for racing (Simpson, 2007, p. 60). If 'men's bikes' and 'sport cycling' — sport being linked to masculinity — became prevalent, then it is clear that 'women' would be considerably less likely to cycle.

[18] Peter Cox notes that some insurance companies use this differentiation in their insurance processes (2014, p. 1).

> *Interviewee Two:* I was looking at a Giant originally but a female version.
>
> *Interviewee Three:* Well, first of all it was really hard to find female road bikes.

The formation of the bikes as a gendered object shifts from the presence or absence of the top-tube to the specifications of a range of attributes not previously gendered. Interviewees Four and Five elaborate on these attributes.

> *Interviewee Four:* I ended up with a women's specific bike, which I wasn't going to do because I don't [pause] — a bike's a bike, isn't it? But he explained the handlebars were narrower which probably suited me. I have problems with my shoulder because the other bike was too far forward. So I thought, 'Well, okay, maybe that's important'.
>
> *Interviewee Five:* I got a SUBzero … It's a women's range named after [pause] — the athlete has had a hand in designing it. So it's actually [pause] — yes, the women's range, which up until that point I was like, 'I don't need a women's range bicycle'. But then they explained it to me … It had a compact chain ring rather than a triple chain ring … It had blocks on the gear levers. So your hand can reach around the hoods … Whereas on a man's bike [pause] they've got these *big fat* things. And [it has] *smaller* hoods, *closer* together. A women's specific seat. There was just all these things that I didn't think were relevant. But once I felt them, I was like that's amazing. (Emphasis added)

This re-formation of bikes (with top-tubes) is made possible as discursive practices of anatomy and physiology and biomechanics are distributed into sites of design, manufacture, retail, marketing and research interviews. In both excerpts, there is resistance to 'differentiation' — not fitting the bicycle norm. In the first excerpt, this resistance is overcome as a discursive practice of physiology — shoulder function — displaces the discursive practice of anatomy.[19] In the second excerpt, the interviewee compares the fit of a bike to her own body with that of a 'man's' body. In this comparison, she excises, forms and measures an attribute (reach) and binds herself to the subject position of 'woman' through a particular anatomical difference (hand size) from men. But this differentiation may not 'stick' (become widespread), as Interviewee Five says:

> *Interviewee Five:* So there's some arguments over whether there is such a thing as a women's specific bike.

---

[19] Anatomical attributes are themselves in *ongoing-formation*.

This alternative possibility is invoked by Interviewee Six:

Interviewee Six: The only thing is, we changed to a female-designed seat — which my husband finds very comfortable as well.

The issue in discussing these excerpts is not to explain 'why' interviewees bind themselves to the category of 'woman' or not. Rather, it is to foreground the techniques involved in individuals positioning themselves as 'women' — or not — by reference to 'attributes' of bikes that are specified as 'women's bikes'. It is also to indicate the range of potential effects of this process in the *re-formation* of the materiality of bikes. It is possible to consider how the formation of bikes as gendered objects might differentially value bikes and bodies bound to femininity and masculinity. This gendered formation is itself gendering, as it shapes the categories of 'woman' and 'man' and makes it possible to call into question those individuals specified as 'women' and 'men' who do not conform to the norms made durable in gendered bikes and bike accessories.

Forming practices

Risk

The 'Women returning to cycling' interviews provide a site to examine the gendered formation of cycling practices. At various moments, specific ways of moving and manoeuvring were related to men or women. However, as responses from Interviewee Seven demonstrate, this attribution was always provisional, since other discursive practices could be deployed to challenge any certainties.

Interviewee Seven: My husband takes more risks and I get cross with him the way he encourages my son sometimes *just to pull out*. I'm fairly cautious.
I think women tend to be more cautious anyway … (Emphasis added)

Interviewee Seven excises the sequence of movements involved in '*just to pull out*' as a risky way of moving.[20] In this process Interviewee Seven genders herself as a woman by speaking of her own way of moving as 'cautious' and relating this caution to women in general. But in this instance, Interviewee Seven unsettles any straightforward formation of 'risky ways of moving' as masculine. Although

---

[20] Another chapter could be written on the mechanisms which have made it possible to speak of some ways of moving as 'risky' and others as 'cautious'.

her partner 'takes more risks' and encourages her son to take more risks, '*what Interviewee Seven says*' later in the interview calls into question the formation of risk taking as a gendered manoeuvre. Risk is potentially de- or re-gendered as Interviewee Seven relates cycling to driving.

> *Interviewee Seven:* I'm wondering if the way you drive is the way you cycle. Various women say, 'I'm taking the female option. I'm not turning right here — I'm turning left and then right because it's a hard turn'. And my husband does the same thing; he'll take the 'risk turning' right. There is a difference between the way women and men drive. I don't know if the *alpha women* drive like the men but I think [pause] — I'm sure that's reflected in the way they cycle [pause]. (Emphasis added)

Interviewee Seven makes apparent the ever-finer differentiations within gender categories. 'Alpha women' are not normal women; rather, they are a subcategory of women who are more like men. But, again, any certainty is called into question when Interviewee Seven says:

> *Interviewee Seven:* I am sure we have a [pause] — women [pause] — girls, we are a bit more reserved [pauses] — although as kids we did cycle around with no hands [pause] but I haven't had any major bike spills.

And later:

> [Y]ou have to put yourself in some situations … You have to keep pushing the edge a little. The same as when I was saying before about cycling home [pause] — you're still taking a calculated risk … I'll try to counter that risk in some way but I'll still take that risk and acknowledge that it might be a very slight risk. If you don't do it then I think you lose something as well … I think [pause] you need to be exposed [pause] —you need to keep exposing yourself too [pauses] otherwise you do become a bit closed.

Concepts of childhood development in *formation* in psychology and pedagogy — such as risk taking and learning-through-experience — interrupt any straightforward linking of 'risky manoeuvres' to men and 'cautious manoeuvres' to women. This interruption coalesces with concepts of 'use it or lose it' in *formation* in the health sciences and 'calculated risk' in *formation* across the health sciences and economics, to name but a few disciplines. These excerpts demonstrate the unstable process of relating particular cycling practices to 'women' and 'men'. They also force us to examine the political consequences of 'fixing' cycling practices as arising from attributes of 'women' and 'men'.

Speed and effort

Describing her cycle journey to and from work, Interviewee Eight compares her body and bicycling practices to the bodies and practices of others, and in doing so she rejects the subject position of cyclist.

> *Interviewee Eight:* When I ride home I feel like one of those middle-aged old women you know, kind of [pause] I don't go that slow but I don't race. I'm at the lights and there are these other young guys and off they go and I just puddle along. Well, I don't puddle along — I get a bit of a sweat up because you do it for exercise as well as a means of transport. But, you know, I don't go that fast. So that's why I don't really see myself as a cyclist.

In making the comparison, Interviewee Eight excises aspects of physical appearance and binds herself to 'middle-aged woman' in relation to 'young guys'. She also excises particular ways of moving and differentiates herself from 'cyclists' according to these ways of moving: 'off they go', 'I just puddle along', 'I don't go that fast'. Speed differentiates 'cyclist' from 'not cyclist', and in this differentiation there is a tentative formation of 'cyclists' as of a particular age and gender — 'young guys'.

However, the excerpt from Interviewee Eight is particularly instructive as she says, 'I get a bit of a sweat up'. A detailed examination of this excerpt is beyond the scope of this chapter, but it does foreground the association of certain amounts of physical exertion with 'women' and 'men'. Interviewee Eight forms herself as a middle-aged woman but one that gets a 'bit of a sweat up', as she cycles 'for exercise as well as a means of transport'. This excerpt allows us to explore the formation of 'exercise' and 'sport' as masculine and the suspicions this makes possible about women who participate in 'exercise' and 'sport' (and men who do not). Further, we could investigate how, in the Australian context, cycling has been assembled together with sport and masculinity, thereby making both 'cycling' (other than for sport) problematic and 'women-cycling' particularly suspect. We could also analyse whether '*what* Interviewee Eight' says operates to de-gender 'exercise' and the mechanisms that enable 'exercise' to be de-gendered — for example, through a discursive practice of public health.

Forming spaces

At no point did interviewees gender spaces of cycling. They spoke of the spaces in which they cycled in terms of 'rights', 'stress', 'danger', 'concentration', 'relaxation' and more. Several contrasted the spaces they used for cycling (on-road spaces, cycle paths, footpaths) with the spaces used by their partners, but they did not associate particular cycling spaces with gender. We suggest that the formation of cycling spaces as gendered spaces is taking place within academic literature as researchers employ gendering practices (scrutinising physical appearance) to differentiate cycling bodies and link particular bodies to particular spaces (for example, Garrard, Rose & Lo, 2008). One of the effects of this gendering is to link women to 'special' spaces — such as off-road cycle paths — which makes it possible to raise questions about the normality of women who do not use such spaces, as well as about the men who do use these spaces. It also leaves aside the more important issue that the public spaces of the road are not designed, constructed or regulated to meet the needs of all road users. Even if we narrow that need to movement[21], the formation of Australian roads continues to foster a particular set of social relations — the convenience, speed and safety of some road users (particularly motor vehicle operators) over others. The formation of cycling spaces as gendered spaces does not advance the possibility of re-forming road spaces to secure the convenience, safety and comfort of a multiplicity of road users.[22]

Conclusion

Through focusing on the *ongoing-formation* of bikes, practices and spaces it is possible to observe both the creation of gendered objects and the role they play in gendering 'women' and 'men'. Rather than taking objects as fixed, durable and internally coherent we have sought to demonstrate the processes through which they are continually formed — that is, the processes by which materials, words, movements, feelings and so forth are continually brought into relation as particular kinds of things.

In particular, our analysis has demonstrated how the interrelations between discursive practices operate to produce new objects (and subjects). For example, the discursive practices of engineering, clothing manufacture, class and anatomy

---

[21] Movement, that is, as opposed to the multiplicity of uses that a road has at different times and places — such as a political space, festive space, gathering space and so forth.

[22] For example, there is no allowance made for the re-formation of road spaces to meet the requirements of cyclists as well as other slow- and medium-paced travellers (those who use wheelchairs or devices to assist walking, skateboarders, roller-bladers and scooter riders).

(and also, perhaps, physiology and endocrinology) produced the 'ladies' safety' and the 'feminine' subject who should ride that bike. Despite the seemingly self-evident and fixed nature of the 'ladies" and 'men's' 'safety', the recent use of the term 'step-through' demonstrates the instability of these objects and points to their continual formation. By interrupting this formation it is possible to challenge the gendered formation of objects and to constitute 'women' and 'men' otherwise.

This study has implications for research, policy making and cycle planning. It brings to attention the contingency in taken-for-granted 'objects' such as bikes, cycleways, traffic and so forth. It also highlights the part played by researchers in gendering practices — for example, differentiating women and men in advertising and conducting interviews, or in counting cyclists using cycle paths and roads. We need to remain critical of these processes of differentiation and their political effects.

References

Bacchi, C. (1996). *The politics of affirmative action: 'Women', equality and category politics*. London: Sage.

Bacchi, C. (2009). *Analysing policy: What's the problem represented to be?* French's Forest: Pearson.

Bacchi, C. (2012, December 4-6). Policies as gendering practices: Moving past categorical distinctions. *Fay Gale Conference*, The University of Adelaide, Australia.

Bacchi, C, & Bonham, J. (2014). Reclaiming discursive practices as an analytic focus: Political implications. *Foucault Studies*, 17, 179-192.

Bardon, T, & Josserand, E. (2010). A Nietzschean reading of Foucauldian thinking: Constructing a project of the self within an ontology of becoming. *Organization*, 18(4), 497-515.

Bijker, W. (1995). *Of bicycles, bakelite and bulbs: Toward a theory of sociotechnical change*. Cambridge, Mass: The MIT Press.

Bonham, J, & Bacchi, C. (2013, January 6-7). Cycling subjectivities in on-going-formation: Interviews as political interventions. *Foucault and Mobilities Symposium*, University of Lucerne, Switzerland.

Bonham, J, & Cox, P. (2010). The disruptive traveller: A Foucauldian analysis of cycleways. *Road & Transport Research*, 19(2), 43-54.

Bonham, J, & Suh, J. (2008). Pedalling the city: Intra-urban differences in cycling for the journey-to-work. *Road and Transport Research*, 17(4), 25-40.

Bonham, J, & Wilson, A. (2012a). Women cycling through the life course: An Australian case-study. In J Parkin (Ed.), *Cycling and sustainability* (pp. 59-82). Bingley: Emerald.

Bonham, J, & Wilson, A. (2012b). Bicycling through the life course: The start-stop-start experiences of women cycling. *International Journal of Sustainable Transportation*, 6(4), 195-213.

Butler, J. (1990). *Gender trouble: Feminism and the subversion of identity*. New York, NY: Routledge.

Cox, P. (Ed.). (2014). *Cycling cultures*. Chester: University of Chester Press.

Cresswell, T, & Uteng, TP. (2008). Gendered mobilities: Towards an holistic understanding. In TP Uteng, & T Cresswell (Eds.), *Gendered mobilities* (pp. 1-12). Burlington, VT: Ashgate.

Emond, C, Tang, W, & Handy, S. (2009). Explaining gender difference in bicycling behaviour. *Transportation Research Record*, 2125, 16-25.

Eveline, J. (2005). Woman in the ivory tower: Gendering feminised and masculinised identities. *Journal of Organisational Change Management*, 18(6), 641-658.

Faulkner, W. (2001). The technology question in feminism: A view from feminist technology studies. *Women's Studies International Forum*, 24(1), 79-95.

Foucault, M. (1972). *The archaeology of knowledge*. London: Tavistock Publications Ltd.

Foucault, M. (1978). *The history of sexuality*. London: Penguin.

Foucault, M. (1980). The confession of the flesh. In C Gordon (Ed.), *Power/Knowledge: Selected interviews and other writings 1972-1977* (pp. 194-228). London: Harvester Press.

Foucault, M. (1982). The subject and power. In H Dreyfus, & P Rabinow (Eds.), *Michel Foucault: Beyond structuralism and hermeneutics* (pp. 208-226). Hemel Hempstead: Harvester Wheatsheaf.

Furness, Z. (2010). *One less car: Bicycling and the politics of automobility*. Philadelphia, PA: Temple University Press.

Garrard, G, Rose, G, & Lo, SK. (2008). Promoting transport cycling for women: The role of bicycle infrastructure. *Preventive Medicine*, 46(1), 55-9.

Gatens, M. (1983). A critique of the sex/gender distinction. In J Allen, & P Patton (Eds.), *Beyond Marxism: Interventions after Marx* (pp. 143-162). Leichardt: Intervention Publications.

Hanson, S. (2010). Gender and mobility: New approaches for informing sustainability. *Gender, Place and Culture*, 17(1), 5-23.

Hanson, S, & Pratt, G. (1995). *Gender, work and space*. London: Routledge.

Heyes, C. (2007). *Self-Transformations: Foucault, ethics, and normalized bodies*. Oxford: Oxford University Press.

Jones, A. (1997). Teaching post-structuralist feminist theory in education: Student resistances. *Gender and Education*, 9(3), 261-269.

Latour, B. (1991). Technology is society made durable. In J Law (Ed.), *A sociology of monsters: Essay on power, technology and domination* (pp. 103-131). London: Routledge.

Law, R. (1999). Beyond 'women and transport': Towards new geographies of gender and daily mobility. *Progress in Human Geography*, 23(4), 567-88.

Letherby, G, & Reynolds, G. (2009). Emotion, gender, and travel: Moving On. In G Letherby, & G Reynolds (Eds.), *Gendered journeys, mobile emotions* (pp. 19-32). Farnham: Ashgate.

Mackintosh, PG, & Norcliffe, G. (2007). Men, women and the bicycle: Gender and social geography of cycling in the late-nineteenth century. In D Horton, P Rosen, & P Cox (Eds.), *Cycling and society* (pp. 153-177). Aldershot: Ashgate.

Markula, P, & Pringle, R. (2006). *Foucault, sport and exercise: Power, knowledge and transformation of the self*. Abingdon: Routledge.

Miller, P, & Rose, N. (2008). *Governing the present: Administering economic, social and personal life*. Cambridge: Polity Press.

Mol, A. (1999). Ontological politics: A word and some questions. In J Law, & J Hassard (Eds.), *Actor network theory and after* (pp. 74-89). Oxford: Blackwell Publishers.

Murtagh, N, Gatersleben, B, & Uzzell, D. (2012). Multiple identities and travel mode choice for regular journeys. *Transportation Research Part F*, 15(5), 514-524.

New South Wales Court of Appeal. (2013). *Norrie v NSW Registrar of Births, Deaths and Marriages* [2013] NSWCA 145. Sydney, Australia: Government of New South Wales. Retrieved 24 July 2015 from https://

www.caselaw.nsw.gov.au/decision/54a63a723004de94513dab59
http://www.caselaw.nsw.gov.au/action/pjudg?jgmtid=165088.

Oddy, N. (1996). Bicycles. In P Kirkham (Ed.), *The gendered object* (pp. 60-69). Manchester: Manchester University Press.

Oddy, N. (2007). The flaneur on wheels? In D Horton, P Rosen, & P Cox (Eds.), *Cycling and society* (pp. 97-112). Aldershot: Ashgate.

Pucher, J, Garrard, J, & Greaves, S. (2011). Cycling down under: A comparative analysis of bicycling trends and policies in Sydney and Melbourne. *Journal of Transport Geography*, 19(2), 332-345.

Schwanen, T. (2013, January 6-7). Passenger transport as object of knowledge: Shifts in nature and implications for government. *Foucault and Mobilities Research Symposium*, Luzern, Switzerland.

Sharp, A. (1896). *Bicycles and tricycles: A treatise on their design and construction.* London, UK: Longmans, Green and Co. Retrieved 11 June 2015 http://archive.org/stream/bicycles.

Sheller, M. (2008). Gendered mobilities: Epilogue. In TP Uteng, & T Cresswell (Eds.), *Gendered mobilities* (pp. 257-265). Burlington, VT: Ashgate.

Sigurdardottir, S, Kaplan, S, Møller, M, & Teasdale, T. (2013). Understanding adolescents' intentions to commute by car or bicycle as adults. *Transportation Research Part D*, 24, 1-9.

Simpson, C. (2007). Capitalising on curiosity: Women's professional cycle racing in the late nineteenth century. In D Horton, P Rosen, & P Cox (Eds.), *Cycling and society* (pp. 47-65). Aldershot: Ashgate.

Spencer, P, Watts, R, Vivanco, L, & Flynn, B. (2013). The effect of environmental factors on bicycle commuters in Vermont: Influences of a northern climate. *Journal of Transport Geography*, 31, 11-17.

Stainton-Rogers, R, & Stainton-Rogers, W. (1990). What the Brits got out of the Q: And why their work may not line up with the American way of getting into it! *The Electronic Journal of Communication*, 1(1). Retrieved 24 July 2015 from http://www.cios.org/EJCPUBLIC/001/1/00113.html.

Steinbach, R, Green, J, Datta, J, & Edwards, P. (2011). Cycling and the city: A case study of how gendered, ethnic and class identities can shape healthy transport choices. *Social Science & Medicine*, 72(7), 1123-1130.

Subramanian, S. (2008). Embodying the space between: Unmapping writing about racialised and gendered mobilities. In TP Uteng, & T Cresswell (Eds.), *Gendered mobilities* (pp. 35-45). Burlington, VT: Ashgate.

10 Making (up) the child cyclist: Bike Ed in South Australia

Anne Wilson

Introduction

Today we have two issues which often intersect: first, widespread concern among health professionals about childhood obesity, and its causes and effects on children's general health status; and second, concern among geographers and sociologists about children's active, independent mobility and their diminishing use of public space. This chapter undertakes an analysis of a South Australian program, Bike Ed, which aims to address such concerns through cycling skills development and safety education, encouraging increased physical activity through active travel and greater access to public space.

While such programs appear to have multiple benefits, evaluations are few. This chapter examines a 2012 Bike Ed program in Adelaide, South Australia, through a Foucauldian lens, thereby raising questions about the ways in which the program and its practices shape 'the child' as a particular kind of subject — a child subject with arguably sole responsibility for its own safety. The paradoxical result is that a program designed to encourage cycling acts to reinforce the norms of automobile culture — whilst, however, retaining spaces for contestation.

The chapter proceeds in three steps. First, it will explain the analytic strategy applied. Next, the chapter briefly introduces the Bike Ed program. Third, the chapter will duly interrogate and describe the texts of Bike Ed and their effects.

Strategies for change

Theory and analytic strategy

The chapter takes as its point of departure the position identified in Chapter One of this volume (Bonham & Johnson) and further developed in Bonham, Bacchi and Wanner (Chapter Nine, this volume) and Nielsen and Bonham (Chapter Eleven, this volume) that subjects have to be understood, not as sovereign and pre-social, but as formed through ongoing practices. The target in this chapter is 'the child' and specifically 'the cycling child'.

As historical accounts of children show, 'the child' and 'childhood' are culturally constituted categories; children's worlds and lives have been shaped by adult concepts of childhood and its significance in different times and places. Though children were once regarded as small adults, taken for granted as part of adult life and not seen as needing special treatment (Ariès, 1962; Holloway & Valentine, 2000; Cunningham, 2005), their lives and bodies have now been politicised: they carry unrecognised social burdens (Colls & Hörschelmann, 2010; Ruddick, 2010), becoming both 'an idea and a target', with childhood 'the most intensively governed sector of personal existence' (Rose, 1999, p. 123).

Nowadays bound materially and socially to the adult social body from gestation, children are 'positioned as "human futures"' (Lee & Motzkau, 2011, p. 10), monitored from conception, and regularly subjected to interventions on many fronts to detect aberrations and deviations from norms (Cole, 2007; Department of Health, Government of Western Australia, 2006; National Health and Medical Research Council [NHMRC], 2007; 2014; Australian Paediatric Surveillance Unit [APSU], 2015). It is therefore unsurprising to find concern about children's inactivity and health (Australian Institute of Health and Welfare [AIHW], 2014; Department of Health, 2014a, 2014b; Schoeppe, Duncan, Badland, Oliver, & Browne, 2014) and their lack of independent and active travel (Hillman, Adams, & Whitelegg, 1990; Garrard, 2009; Tranter & Pawson, 2001; Malone & Rudner, 2011; Mackett, 2012), as well as fears for their safety (Valentine, 1997; Brockman, Jago, & Fox, 2011; Kimbro & Schachter, 2011; Niehues, Bundy, Broom, & Tranter, 2015). These adult conceptions shape children, making them subjects of adult cultural production, categorised as 'good', 'bad', 'at risk', 'risky' (Jenks, 1996; Valentine, 2010; Colls & Hörschelmann, 2010; Holloway &Valentine, 2000), 'unpredictable', 'undisciplined' (Maley, 2014; Myttas, 2001), 'inactive', 'obese' (Bastian, 2011;

Wake, Hardy, Canterford, Sawyer, & Carlin, 2007), 'technology-obsessed' (Rowan, 2010; see Valentine & Holloway, 2003), 'educable' and 'trainable' (Dekker, Koot, van der Ende, & Verhulst, 2002; Rynders & Horrobin, 1990).

In line with these perspectives, this chapter sees the child as an unstable category — malleable, able to be formed by adult social norms which, in this instance, are found in those practices which shape 'the cycling child': practices which, broadly speaking, are 'governmental practices'. Foucault's primary interest was in how governing takes place. His view of governing practices included state practices alongside the practices of numerous agencies and individuals involved in societal management or the 'conduct of conduct'. Foucault's particular concern was how we are produced as 'governable' subjects: that is, how governing discourses (knowledges)[1], associated with experts and professionals, for example, frame issues in ways that elicit certain forms of subjectivity — forms that are amenable to 'rule'. Dean and Hindess (1998, p. 9), for example, suggest that, in a neoliberal 'mentality of rule' (or governmentality), individuals are created as responsible for their own health, welfare and economic success, facilitating forms of rule that limit government services. The shaping of subjects as governable is captured in the concept 'subjectification' (Bacchi, 2009, p. 214).

To identify governmental practices and their subjectification effects, Foucault targeted what he called 'practical texts':

> The domain I will be analyzing is made up of texts written for the purpose of offering rules, opinions, and advice on how to behave as one should: 'practical' texts, which are themselves objects of a 'practice' in that they were designed to be read, learned, reflected upon and tested out, and they were intended to constitute the eventual framework of everyday conduct. (1986/1984, pp. 12-13)

This chapter treats Bike Ed and some associated texts as 'practical texts', teasing out assumptions and presuppositions, and considering how they impact on the creation and governing of 'child cyclists'. The program, as this chapter will describe, is 'designed to be read, learned, reflected upon and tested out', and is 'intended to constitute the eventual framework of everyday conduct' (Foucault, 1986/1984, pp. 12-13). Hence the program provides an ideal starting place for discerning

---

[1] A poststructuralist perspective highlights the ambiguity and contested nature of knowledge, pluralising the term as 'knowledges', thus adding a political dimension to the construction of 'truth'.

the manner in which 'the child cyclist' is produced. From this perspective, the task becomes identifying the discourses and practices (knowledges and programs) through which educators seek to shape 'child cyclists', making them governable. Through this analysis, space is opened up to reflect on the implications of particular subjectification practices. This chapter asks specifically: What kind of 'child subject' is produced in the Bike Ed program? To what extent does this 'child subject' support a normative automobile culture? Are there spaces for contestation?

Children's bicycle education programs appear to be worthwhile initiatives, but their effectiveness is debated and difficult to assess. Programs vary in design; ages and numbers of participants; perspectives; aims and methods of studies; and diverse methods of data collection and assessment. Evaluations range from effective to ineffective, with possible negative effects. Two prominent evaluations — Imberger, Styles, Hughes, & Di Pietro (2006) in Australia, and IpsosMORI (2010) in the United Kingdom — show positive results. However, these programs differ — the former concerned with skills and safety, the latter with attitudes and behaviour.

The Australian evaluation is of two programs in the Australian Capital Territory [ACT] — one held at an off-road traffic centre (two sessions with police instructors, one classroom session with a school teacher), the other a bicycle education program within school grounds (taught by Pedal Power ACT Incorporated, a cycling promotion body). While the school-based program was deemed worthwhile, lack of on-road training was seen as a shortcoming in both programs, with traffic-centre training of little benefit and possibly encouraging over-confidence (Imberger et al., 2006).

The United Kingdom government's 'Bikeability' program evaluation was to determine whether the program had influenced perceptions of, and attitudes to, cycling, and whether there was an increase in cycling appeal and frequency among children. Specific objectives with regard to cycling attitudes and behaviours were assessed, with input from both parents and children. The aims of the program were found to be met, with positive perceptions of cycling by both parents and children: parents showed awareness of health and environmental benefits, and children cycled more frequently, and to different destinations, with enjoyment and increased confidence. Both parents and children reported an improvement in children's risk assessment and skills, although parents maintained concern about traffic speed, levels of traffic and road users in general (Ipsos MORI, 2010).

These evaluations use conventional frameworks and methods. The current research takes an alternative perspective to Bike Ed analysis by scrutinising the program to identify the practices and the discourses — the informing bodies of knowledge — which the program enacts, and in this way constitutes 'the cycling child'. The intention of this work is not to offer criticism of Bike Ed programs per se, but to use a method which offers the opportunity to examine the productive effects of such programs. Accordingly, rather than taking the category of 'cyclist' as self-evident, the interest here is in the qualities, characteristics, abilities and other like attributes assembled together as 'cyclist' in the Bike Ed program.

The analysis contains three sections: the first section introduces the background and rationale for Bike Ed in South Australia; the second analyses the practical instructional sessions in tandem with the Learning Journal (a workbook provided as a testing and revisionary accompaniment to six of the seven sessions); and the third comments on the pervasive safety discourse underpinning the program. It thus becomes possible to reflect on whether, and how, the 'child cyclist' is shaped to conform (or not) to conventional views of road space and the norms of automobile culture. The responsibilisation of the 'child cyclist' is emphasised, with contrast drawn to the motorist's relative 'freedom' from scrutiny.

Bike Ed SA

Background and rationale

Bike Ed is part of the Department of Planning, Transport and Infrastructure's Way2Go initiative. It is

> a statewide holistic program geared to promoting safer, greener and more active travel for primary school students and their communities … built on a partnership between local councils, school communities and the Department of Planning, Transport and Infrastructure. (Department of Planning, Transport and Infrastructure [DPTI], 2015a)

The Way2Go project states on its website that it

- promotes the development of safe, people friendly local streets near schools to support independent student travel
- encourages children and the community to safely walk, ride bikes or scooters, and use public transport for school travel

- supports students to be safe walkers, bike riders and passengers
- relies on sound evidence and models of leading practice for decision making, planning and classroom teaching. (DPTI, 2015a)

Way2Go Bike Ed, part of the above initiative, aims 'to develop students' confidence and competence as a safe bike rider for travel to and from school'. It is estimated that '[m]ore than 5000 students in 60 schools across South Australia will participate in the program in 2015' (DPTI, 2015b). It has both in-school and on-road components, and is taught by Bike-SA-trained and accredited personnel, assisted by school teachers.

Bike SA describes Way2Go Bike Ed as an initiative which

> encourages personal cycling safety, and the development of responsible behaviours when travelling … Through a considered decision-making process … [children] develop awareness of road safety and the consequences of their behaviour … [and] learn the skills and attitudes required for safe cycling in low to medium traffic environments. (Bike SA, 2015a)

In this rationale, child cyclists are produced as subjects that are capable of being trained to conduct themselves in a rational and responsible manner as near-citizens. The focus on competence in travelling to and from school by bike in traffic environments locates Bike Ed within a discursive practice of transport (see Bonham, Bacchi and Wanner, Chapter Nine, this volume).

The Bike Ed program is currently under revision, so the following discussion is based on the program in place in 2012.[2] Bike Ed is designed to teach children to ride bicycles on the road, conforming to required safety norms, through a series of seven sessions — the first three off-road (instructor/student ratio 1:10), the remaining four on-road (instructor/student ratio 1:6). Sessions are 1.5 hours, with a maximum of 30 children — a total of 10.5 hours, held either on a weekly basis or on consecutive days. Children's own bicycles and helmets are used, with a number of bicycles and helmets provided, as wearing helmets is mandatory in Australia (Bike SA, n.d.-c; see also Bike SA, n.d.-a, b.). Each child is given a Learning Journal, to be completed after each session as a retrospective, revisionary and

---

[2] The material used in the current analysis demonstrates the application of a Foucault-informed discourse analysis. This type of analysis can be applied to the updated Bike Ed program once it is has been developed.

self-correcting exercise. This Journal, in tandem with the program content, provides the focus for the following analysis — one which examines the program for how it constitutes both child subject and cycling subject.

The program and the Learning Journal in 2012

The first exercise for the child begins four weeks prior to the program. DPTI (2015d) provides information pamphlets and an 'optional Bike Ed quiz' on cycling and the law. This can be completed at home in conjunction with parents, and is the first positioning of the child as a cycling subject in relation to road rules, safety procedures and self-responsibility. It is also the first strategy to include parents (DTEI, 2011a, b, c; Bike SA, 2011; see also Bike SA, n.d.-a).

Before the teaching program begins, participating children are required to sign a stricture of both obligation and commitment, a 'Code of Conduct Agreement' — a contract — between themselves, Bike SA and its instructors and teachers. Consisting of 11 pledges, the contract lists in detail children's responsibility for safety practices and behaviours. The Code of Conduct document, the commitment it requires, and its placement at the beginning of the first session, are significant. The child is encouraged to recognise her/himself as being responsible for her/his own safety, and for that of others (Bike SA, 2012).

The asymmetries of power in this exercise make it possible to interpret the signing of the contract as indirectly coercive. The initial decision to adopt the program is made by the school, which is obliged to meet criteria set by DPTI and Bike Ed. Parent involvement is sought from the beginning and throughout. The program is designed to mesh with the school curriculum. The combination of school policy, curriculum, teacher involvement, parent involvement, and Bike Ed promotion and instruction is ultimately targeted at the child, with the weight of status and consequent authority positions conferred on the adult participants — thus highlighting binaries of inequity: adult/child, teacher/student, instructor/learner, parent/child.

Moreover, contract signing in itself indicates a significant shift in how the child is traditionally thought about, reaching far beyond the child as a safe or mobile subject. The child has little choice but to sign, but is then identified as fully responsible for both the decision to sign and for the expectations which follow, as set out in the contract. This is in tension with discourses of the child as less-than-adult — less competent and less responsible for its actions, as in questions of legal responsibility for contract signing (Cockburn, 2013) and criminal responsibility (Urbas, 2000). Therefore, where the child stands with regard to ability to comprehend or take responsibility for its actions in this particular instance deserves further investigation.

Furthermore, the location of the Bike Ed program within the school — a site of education knowledge with inbuilt assumptions and practices of educational authority — is significant to the mode of delivery. Education scholars are using Foucault to examine such current pedagogical practices as the responsibilisation of children in contemporary education systems through learning contracts, which 'transfer the responsibility of overseeing learning from the teacher to the learner' (Brookfield, 2007, p. 332). Allied mechanisms — LSIs [learning style inventories], ILPs [individual learning plans], SRL [self-regulated learning], learning action plans and learning agreements have similar goals. These practices are shaping subjects which enable new ways of governing to conform with neoliberal forms of rule: self-governing, self-responsible, entrepreneurial, flexible subjects, accepting of such concepts as lifelong learning and employment mobility in a 'knowledge society' (see Vassallo, 2013a, b, c; 2011; Peters, 2001).

After the child has signed the contract, the first three sessions on the bicycle are in the schoolyard. Each is followed by a classroom exercise with the Learning Journal, which is used in tandem with the teaching program for six of the seven sessions. This Journal is designed as a revisionary and retrospective exercise in an examination format — it is a means of reinforcing the self-production of the child cycling subject with each session as the child reflexively reiterates its own knowledge and obedience (see Gros, 2005).

The first session, which has both bike handling and Journal components, is dedicated to safety and continues the theme of responsibility, where the child '[t]akes responsibility for checking their bike and helmet for safety' (Bike SA, n.d.-b, p. 1) and is instructed through the Journal that '*You are responsible for your own safety!! Need a head, need a HELMET!!*' The Journal page ends with the statement: '*Remember if something is not working YOU are responsible for telling an adult about the problem*' (Bike SA, 2012b, p. 2, emphasis in the original).

Journal instructions to check the bike and the helmet, to ensure one's safety, produce cycling as risky and cyclists as vulnerable. Further, these instructions constitute the child cyclist as responsible for her/his own safety which might ultimately translate to all cyclists being responsible for their own safety. There is silence about the responsibility of the motorist. Further to this, placing responsibility with the child to ensure that an adult fixes any mechanical problem with the bicycle is an inequitable responsibility. This responsibilisation of the child risks diminishing the responsibility of adults and other authorities who have traditionally been required to ensure children's safety, and constitutes the cyclist from the beginning as one who is responsible for her/his own safety — a matter which this chapter will return to later.

Moreover, the reference to 'an adult' signals the enlistment of the family in governing. This practice is not new. The governing of the child and the family has been intense, with 'a panoply of programmes that have tried to conserve and shape children by moulding the petty details of the domestic, conjugal and sexual lives of their parents' (Rose, 1999, p. 123). Families have a history of being co-opted into governing roles, regulated through images of normality and 'the activation of individual guilt, personal anxiety, and private disappointment' (Rose, 1999, p. 132). Parents are encouraged to participate through evaluation surveys, calls for assistance, co-operation with attending to equipment, home information kits, assistance in delivering the program and extension activities (DTEI, 2011a, b).

This session, the first, also introduces the child to the components and mechanics of the bicycle, seeking identification of 18 points on the bicycle for which the child is responsible for checking. This task is taken further in Session 2 with some detailed instruction on gear components and function. Session 3 places responsibility for the bike's security with the child, with instruction on locks, placement of locks, and places to secure the bike and lock. The child cyclist, therefore, is produced as someone who has some competency in mechanical knowledge of the bicycle. This raises questions about the need for mechanical knowledge being part of other, different forms of mobility. How much mechanical knowledge, for example, does a motorist need? Differentiating the cyclist in this way is tricky, particularly in a society which continues to gender mechanical knowledge as masculine. Constituting the cyclist as someone with mechanical knowledge may undermine girls' participation in cycling but it might also assist in 'de-gendering' mechanical knowledge. These disruptive possibilities require careful management.

Along with the Journal practices, instruction on bike handling skills, as per the separate content delivery guide, is practised and assessed in the second and third sessions. Instruction on 'personal safety, in relation to helmets, bicycles and observing road rules', 'the road laws and rules for cycle safety', and 'an understanding of his/her responsibility to follow road rules and laws', while 'understanding their responsibility to keep themselves and others safe in typical traffic settings (e.g. roundabouts)' is taught throughout (see Bike SA, n.d.-b, p. 2; see also Bike SA, n.d.-a). Such skills as starting, braking, slow riding, double- and single-file riding, signalling and scanning, slalom, figure 8, straight line riding, turning, passing cars, and driveway procedures are practised within the confines of the school (Bike SA, n.d.-a, b, pp. 1-3). In this way the child, through habituation of these movements and manoeuvres, is in the process of becoming a cyclist — self-responsible, with mechanical knowledge and specialised handling skills.

Thus far, among bike handling skills, the child has been made responsible for its own safety, the safety of others, the good condition of the bicycle and helmet, the need to ensure that parents maintain the bicycle and helmet in good condition, appropriate and safe use of the bicycle and helmet, and bicycle security, along with road rules and legal obligations. The child can no longer just 'pick up a bicycle and go for a ride' — this cyclist in-the-making bears a considerable weight of responsibility for cycling in public spaces. Cycling has become complex for the child: not only through responsibilisation but also because the context in which it takes place has been normalised, if not naturalised — from the design, construction and regulation (via posted speeds, traffic signal timing and sequencing) of roads through to educating and training motorists — as a space for motorised vehicles.

It is during the fourth session that children enter the road space, habituating the movements and practices that 'make' the cyclist, beginning to meet Bike Ed's aims. Here, and in the following three sessions, '[s]tudents are prepared for on road cycling and learn the skills and attitudes required for safe cycling in low to medium traffic environments' (Bike SA, n.d.-c). Students are ultimately expected to ' … demonstrate an understanding [of] their responsibility to keep themselves and others safe in typical traffic settings (e.g. roundabouts)'. This responsibility includes acquiring, among other skills, the ability to 'anticipate potential hazards' and to 'communicate how their actions promote personal safety', while obeying road rules and choosing 'appropriate action for traffic conditions' (Bike

S.A., n.d.-b, pp. 1-2). Through these practices, children are taught to manage their presence and movement among cars and other vehicles, recognising and assessing risk as they engage with motor vehicle traffic in an increasingly complex interaction within a motor vehicle environment. It is important to note that in Australia motorists, as yet, are not required to learn how to manage their presence and movement among cyclists: although mandatory testing on questions related to cyclists is being introduced into South Australia other states are yet to follow, and there is no practical testing of skills when engaging with cyclists.

In Session 5 the program instructs on the negotiation of right-hand turns. This complex series of movements is carefully and sequentially choreographed, and demands vigilance. Here the child leaves the customary left-side position of deferring to motorists, and takes the centre of the lane — a position usually reserved for motorists.

> SCAN BACK FIRST and check for anything coming behind you. Do this at least 30 metres from the intersection to give yourself enough time to let any cars past.
>
> When it is safe, make a clear RIGHT SIGNAL holding arm out for at least 5 seconds then move across towards the centre of the road. Make sure you stay on your side of the line! If there is no line use the seam in the road to keep you on the correct side. Put your hand back on the handlebars to cover both brakes as you approach the intersection.
>
> SCAN in all directions and GIVE WAY OR STOP depending on the signs and if any traffic is coming. Make EYE CONTACT with all drivers around you if possible.
>
> When it is safe to go, travel straight across without cutting corners.
>
> (Bike SA, 2012, emphasis in the original)

Positioning the child cyclist in the centre of the lane challenges current road hierarchy norms. Although legally entitled to this space, the child cyclist is now, for the first time in the program, accorded the space of a car — a position which is maintained in the session on roundabouts. Roundabout manoeuvres are more complicated. The child is taught to maximise its safety by 'claiming the lane' — the cyclist's legal road space — to encourage lane-sharing, maintain visibility and force motorists to either change lanes or remain behind. As in the right-turn manoeuvre, considerable assertiveness is required. However, the road is a space largely available to, and claimed by, adults and motorists: children and cyclists have no authority in these spaces. While negotiating this space and engaging with adult motorists the child needs to maintain awareness of responsibility for its own safety and that of others, while simultaneously seeking eye contact with motorists and effectively performing manoeuvres. This creates a dilemma for the child, particularly when engaging with larger and faster vehicles. Roundabouts are relatively safer for motorists than signalised intersections but incur a higher rate of crashes for cyclists (Austroads, 2014).

There is further ambivalence in the program as to whether cyclists ought to take up the position of pedestrians or motorists. At busy intersections, the child is encouraged to walk the bike across or use a pedestrian crossing with lights, in the manner of a pedestrian. When travelling straight along the road, the child cyclist is taught to maintain a subordinate position to the left, allowing motorists to pass on the right side. Passing parked cars requires a temporary movement further into the road space, as do the right-hand turn and roundabout manoeuvres, which ultimately require a position near the centre of the road (unless the hook turn is chosen). This position (a motorist position), while necessary for the cyclist to be visible to motorists, requires both skill and assertiveness, something even adult cyclists frequently find difficult.

The sessions culminate in the Presentation, where the program is finalised. A certificate-presentation ceremony by Bike Ed instructors is held at the school, in 'a regular school assembly or at a special Way2Go Bike Ed ceremony', where Council and media participation is encouraged (Bike SA, 2010b). The certificate and the public nature of the ceremony mark the culmination of the making of 'the child cyclist'. The child is now acknowledged, and therefore can acknowledge itself, as a cyclist.

To attain this certificate, the child has been worked upon to become a particular kind of cyclist — one trained, disciplined and examined to obey road rules and traffic norms. The contract signing marked the child's first public act of self-recognition as a member of a road-using group by relating to the rules of the contract and recognising an obligation to obey attitudinal, behavioural, and above all road rules — an ethical position — throughout the training. Journal practices, through practice, revision and reiteration, have promoted and reinforced both obedience and self-responsibilisation. In this way the child cyclist has been coached to handle the challenges of road sharing through contradictory instructions to give way or assert a claim to space. These contradictions are managed through the pervasiveness of the message that the child is responsible for safety: its own and that of others.

It might seem perverse to suggest that we would *not* want our children to be trained to keep themselves safe or to be concerned about others' safety. However, a discourse of safety, much analysed in the social sciences, raises some challenging questions. The question of making children responsible for their own and others' safety in dangerous environments is problematic. As the safety discourse (discourses here being seen as knowledges) is taken for granted, and discourses have effects (Bacchi, 2009), it is useful to examine Bike Ed's safety message.

The safety discourse

Safety is Bike Ed's dominant discourse, and one which holds a prominent place within discourses of transport. Because safety is a human construct, and as an abstract concept is difficult to define, it is generally assumed to be freedom from danger or protection from harm or undesired events. However, it is insufficient to see safety in purely negative or retrospective terms, as 'the absence of accident, the avoidance of error, or even the control of risk' (Rochlin, 1999, p. 1550). Safety is also more than 'rules', 'procedures' and 'training skills' (Rochlin, 1999, p. 1558). It often relies on 'technical expert knowledges, popular truths, and differing assumptions about the value of lives of different populations' (Packer, 2003, p. 151).

Safety can be used by governments for various purposes. In one instance, Packer (2003, p. 151) directs attention to how a safety discourse can legitimate diverse practices by tolerating different levels of death and injury for different activities. Within the motoring area, for example, actuarial practices create and target groups through categorisation, where dividing practices are arbitrarily used and altered to both 'limit and redirect' mobilities of groups (Packer, 2003, p. 151). In another instance, Bonham (2002) shows how road safety campaigns are aimed at producing 'safety-conscious', 'self-responsible' subjects. Her account of a safety campaign aimed at South Australian children in the 1930s shows the extent of its penetration into the lives of citizens, an example of the previously noted practice of enlisting family in the production of children to conform to governmental norms. It has earlier been noted that neoliberal governments encourage the self-responsibility of citizens, using such means as the dividing practices and normalisation techniques seen above. The 'child cyclist' in Bike Ed is an emergent neoliberal subject, instructed that if it learns and obeys the rules, takes responsibility for the maintenance of equipment, and has the appropriate attitudes while taking responsibility for itself and others, it will be safe.

A focus on safety highlights danger, its concomitant binary. Transport discourses recognise cyclist vulnerability (DPTI, 2015c). As Simmons (2003, pp. 78-80) emphasises, safety education, by its very nature, normalises danger. In this way, safety *serves* technology (Packer, 2003), reinforcing existing situations: the danger or hazard of traffic is normalised (Parusel &McLaren, 2010; McLaren & Parusel 2011; 2012; 2014), with acceptable levels defined by an economic discourse of efficiency (Packer, 2003). Nevertheless, the dangers are not removed: rather, the child is expected to integrate itself into a dangerous environment, protected by its own resources of knowledge and confidence, a sustained co-ordination of physical and cognitive abilities, and the ability to maintain these in dangerous and stressful situations.

Producing the 'child cyclist' as responsible for its own safety and the safety of others silences the legitimacy accorded to the causes of danger — in this instance, automobiles. The 'child cyclist' is taught to maintain a primarily passive presence, negotiating carefully around parked cars, and dismounting to navigate busy intersections. An ambivalent note is struck when the child is called upon to assertively claim road space at roundabouts, where danger is momentarily de-privileged.

Spaces for contestation/Places for disruption

Absences/silences

In the Bike Ed program, responsibility is transferred from motorist to child. The role of the motorist, and motorist responsibility for the child cyclist, is absent. The emphasis is on the child, with responsibility for her/his own safety: '*You are responsible for your own safety!!*' (Bike SA, 2012, emphasis in the original).

The 'green' and 'active' components of 'safer, greener and more active travel' objectives (Department of Transport, Energy and Infrastructure [DTEI — later DPTI], 2011a) do not appear to be met. Bike Ed acknowledges health and environmental goals under 'other great benefits of riding to school' in its promotional literature (Bike SA, 2010a), yet the Content Delivery Guide and Learning Journal lack both 'green' and 'active' components. It would appear that any content related to environment, health and active travel is left to the classroom teacher's discretion, supplemented with 'Home Info' leaflets on 'active travel' and 'greener travel' available from DTEI. Of DTEI's provision of 33 home information leaflets, available for school order, most were concerned with safety, with 6 addressing active travel, 4 environment and 1 health (DTEI, 2011b). The current DPTI (2015e) series of 40 leaflets for schools is likewise most heavily weighted toward safety, but has an increased 'active travel' component.

The child may well be constituted differently in the program being currently developed by DPTI. For example, equal emphasis might be put on constituting the cyclist as a subject with journey planning skills, with knowledges about the environmental and health aspects of different mobility practices, and with a wider range of bike handling skills.

Contradictions/tensions

The ambivalence of the child cyclist's place on roads has been identified. The mobile child at times takes a pedestrian position, keeps to the left, avoids and makes space for cars as a cyclist, but 'claims the lane' for right-hand turns and at roundabouts as a motorist. This ambivalence creates a hybrid mobility of some inconsistency — defensiveness, yet assertiveness and confidence when called upon for complex manoeuvres in dangerous situations. These manoeuvres can be difficult for some adults to master, requiring considerable physical and cognitive abilities, yet the child is expected to assert a claim to space. As the program teaches the child that s/he will be safe if retaining and obeying the road rules and practices, the child may expect to be free from harm. This assumes that road rules have equal impacts on all road users and does not address the (automobile) norms which road rules are based upon.

In this way, Bike Ed simultaneously conforms to, and challenges, mobility norms by embedding a safety norm in a behavioural challenge: the safety content conforms to an existing automobile norm, while cycling behaviour challenges it. This incongruity places the responsibilised child cyclist in an ambiguous position — subordinate, yet required to defy existing mobility norms.

The inherent contradictions here open a space to query existing road rules. They show that, in some places, road sharing is unavoidable. The question could then be raised — if in some situations, why not in others?

Assumptions

Contract signing by children has become taken for granted in education environments. The ethics of whether this readily translates from adult to child, particularly given that education pedagogy is itself based on a developmental model, deserves questioning.

Considering the inequities of the child cyclist and adult motorist brings into question the concept of safety itself, and the need to examine what is considered an acceptable rate of accidental death and injury to cyclists. We are attuned to the term 'road toll' — an economic euphemism for death and injury on the roads. This is a taken-for-granted part of transport and safety discourses and seems to be accepted as the price citizens must pay for road use. The ready acceptance of an economic terminology with regard to human life brings into question the weight of an economic discourse within the transport discourse itself. Consideration of these assumptions could lead to de-privileging an economic discourse, having the advantage of initiating different, more effective means of targeting road users.

This attempt to disrupt dominant and assumed transport relations could be encouraged through some additional interventions.

Interventions

Hillman's (2006, p. 64) observation that 'withdrawing danger' from the streets has not been addressed, and that parents have instead taken the step of 'withdrawing children', shows the need for such considerations. Parusel & McLaren (2010, p. 131) draw attention to a society that 'entitles cars to dominate roads and constructs parents and children as responsible for their traffic safety': a responsibilising of the individual, serving modern governmental ends. The category of 'slow transport', used in the Netherlands, may enable different ways of thinking and valuing different mobility practices. Following from this, it may be possible to produce different knowledges and interventions in all aspects of road use — from road user education and training through to road design.

An improved distribution of responsibility in areas of road safety obligations and accountability is another initiative deserving of consideration. Responsibilising the motorist, rather than the child, would place the onus for change on the group largely involved in producing danger. For example, motorists (and particularly learner-drivers) could be obliged to sign a contract such as that expected of children but including specific reference to cyclists — a fairer expectation, given that motorists are seen as adult and a car is capable of far greater damage than a bicycle.

Driver education and training, therefore, is primary, with a need for motorists to be as aware of cyclists as cyclists are (assumed and taught to be) aware of motorists. Practical training for motorists with regard to behaviour toward cyclists could be incorporated in driver education programs. In most accidents involving cars and cyclists, the cyclist is rarely deemed to be at fault (DPTI, 2014): Lindsay (2013) reported that in car/cyclist crashes where cyclists were injured, the driver was at fault in 80% of these.

Conclusion

This chapter asks specifically: What kind of 'child subject' is produced in the Bike Ed program? To what extent does this 'child subject' support a normative automobile culture? Are there spaces for contestation?

Bike Ed is a means of encouraging children to exercise by making them responsible for their health, combating the childhood 'obesity epidemic', with 'obesity' being determined by an arbitrary measurement of body fatness, the BMI (Coveney, 2008). This fits with government neoliberal rationalities of self-responsibilisation for body weight (Share & Strain, 2008), exercise (Jette, Bhagat, & Andrews, 2014) and private sector and multi-party involvements (Powell & Gard, 2014). In addition, schools are 'positioned as a key cause of *and* solution to childhood obesity' (Powell & Gard, 2014, p. 1, emphasis in the original), and are assumed to be an appropriate space for intervention.

The 'child cyclist' produced in Bike Ed is one who conforms to established norms of motor transport. The child is instructed in taking responsibility for its own safety and that of others. The program's overriding focus on safety with regard to bike function, helmet use and self-responsibilisation constructs cycling as dangerous, possibly adding to an already established fear of cycling — highlighting the danger of cycling and the cyclist's vulnerability, whereas the distribution of responsibility goes unquestioned (Horton, 2007).

Bike Ed, in encouraging cycling, challenges the automobile norm. Its initiatives are firmly in the activity arena: 'more people cycling more often'; and the statement that 'all we want is more people on bikes, more children on bikes' is indicative of Bike SA's commitment to increased cycling participation (Bike SA, 2015b). Nevertheless, because its overriding safety component is based on, and reinforces, the established norms of motor vehicle transport, the Bike Ed objective of increasing participation in cycling as a form of active travel is undermined. There is no visible content of DPTI's emphasis on the benefits of active travel on health and environment. There are no materials, written exercises or Journal entries focused on the relationship between cycling and health (for example, the relationship between cycling and aerobic fitness and muscle strength) or on journey planning, where a child becomes engaged in identifying journeys where s/he and her/his family might swap the car for a bike. These practices of relating cycling to health and active travel may be left to individual classroom teachers, but they do not form a fundamental component of Bike Ed despite the program's objectives.

Hillman (2006, p. 64) says consideration of 'withdrawing danger' from the streets has not been addressed, and that parents have instead taken the step of 'withdrawing children'. Bike Ed's intent is to reintroduce children on bicycles to the streets, thereby appearing to challenge an automobile cultural norm. Through self-responsibilisation within a safety discourse, the child produced in Bike Ed learns the deferential attitudes and hypervigilance necessary for cyclists in an automobile culture. This allows the dangers to persist unchanged and unchallenged, with the child 'at risk', while recognising, accepting and being prepared for an automobile future. The question of how this message translates — in terms of both current and future motorists' attitudes to the cyclist's subordinate position — is one which deserves consideration.

The individual child is charged with road safety in an environment where inbuilt inequities create a dangerous competition for space among road users. As the Bike Ed program illustrates, cyclists cannot be accommodated entirely on separated infrastructures — they need the use of roads. Children need to learn to ride bicycles safely — both on and off the road. Nevertheless, the declared objective of increasing cycling requires more than training children to negotiate the hazards of traffic.

Acknowledgements

The author would like to acknowledge the invaluable comments and suggestions of both Jennifer Bonham and Carol Bacchi on this and earlier versions of the chapter.

References

Ariès, P. (1962). *Centuries of childhood*. London: Jonathan Cape.

Australian Institute of Health and Welfare [AIHW]. (2014). *Childhood overweight and obesity*. Information Leaflet 6.6. Canberra: AIHW. Retrieved 5 April 2010 from http://www.aihw.gov.au/WorkArea/DownloadAsset.aspx? id=60129547761.

Australian Paediatric Surveillance Unit [APSU]. (2015). Other surveillance systems. Retrieved 19 August 2015 from http://www.apsu.org.au/surveillance-systems.

Austroads. (2014). *Assessment of the effectiveness of on-road bicycle lanes at roundabouts in Australia and New Zealand*. Research Report AP-R461-14. Sydney: Austroads.

Bacchi, C. (2009). *Analysing policy: What's the problem represented to be?* Frenchs Forest: Pearson Australia.

Bastian, A. (2011). Representations of childhood obesity in Australian newsprint media and academic literature. *Australian and New Zealand Journal of Public Health, 35*(2), 135-139.

Bonham, J. (2002). *The conduct of travel: Beginning a genealogy of the travelling subject* (Doctoral thesis, The University of Adelaide, Australia).

Brockman, R, Jago, R, & Fox, K. (2011). Children's active play: Self-reported motivators, barriers and facilitators. *BMC Public Health*, 11, 461. doi: 10.1186/1471-2458-11-461.

Brookfield, S. (2007). Ideological formation and oppositional possibilities of self-directed learning. In J Kincheloe, & R Horn (Eds.), *The Praeger handbook of education and psychology: Vol. 2* (pp. 331-340). Westport, Connecticut & London: Praeger.

Bike SA. (2010a). *Way2Go Bike Ed.: 1.5 Why participate in Way2Go Bike Ed?* South Australia: Bike SA.

Bike SA. (2010b). *Way2Go Bike Ed.: 5.1 Certificate presentations introduction.* South Australia: Bike SA.

Bike SA. (2011). Teacher resources 3.1-3.5. Retrieved 2011 from http://www.bikesa.asn.auRiderInfo_Programs_BikeEd_Resource.

Bike SA. (2012). Way2Go Bike Ed Student resources 4.2. Student learning journal. Retrieved 16 November 2012 from http://yooyahcloud.com/BICYCLESA/gQ0im/4.2_Student_learning_journal_please_print_1_for_each_student.pdf.

Bike SA. (n.d.-a). The way2go Bike Ed program: Preparation, content, evaluation. Retrieved 27 August 2015 from http://www.yooyahcloud.com/BIKESA/aNX9Wb/2.3_Program_outline.pdf.

Bike SA. (n.d-b). The Way2Go Bike Ed program: Content delivery guide. Retrieved 27 August 2015 from http://www.yooyahcloud.com/BICYCLESA/vUTlvb/Content_delivery_Way2Go_Bike_Ed.pdf.

Bike SA. (n.d.-c). The Way2Go Bike Ed program. Retrieved 19 August 2015 from http://www.bikesa.asn.au/servlet/Web?s=2060570&action=displayRawContent&pageID=734330313.

Bike SA. (2015). Bike education for schools: Way2 Go Bike Ed. Retrieved 13 August 2015 from http://www.bikesa.asn.au/forschools.

Cockburn, T. (2013). Authors of their own lives? Children, contracts, their responsibilities, rights and citizenship. *International Journal of Children's Rights, 21,* 372-384.

Cole, TJ. (2007). Early causes of child obesity and implications for prevention. *Acta Paediatrica,* 96 (Supplement S454), 2-4.

Colls, R, & Hörschelmann, K. (2010). Introduction: Contested bodies of childhood and youth. In K Hörschelmann, & R Colls (Eds.), *Contested bodies of childhood and youth* (pp. 1-21). Houndmills, Hampshire: Palgrave Macmillan.

Coveney, J. (2008). The government of girth. *Health Sociology Review, 17,* 199-213.

Cunningham, H. (2005). *Children and childhood in Western society since 1500* (2nd ed.). Harlow, UK: Pearson Education.

Dean, M, & Hindess, B. (1998). *Governing Australia: Studies in contemporary rationalities of government.* Cambridge: Cambridge University Press.

Dekker, MC, Koot, HM, van der Ende, J, & Verhulst, FC. (2002). Emotional and behavioural problems in children and adolescents with and without intellectual disability. *Journal of Child Psychology and Psychiatry, 43*(8), 1087-1098.

Department of Health. (2014a). *National monitoring in public health nutrition.* Canberra: Department of Health. Retrieved 20 August 2015 from http://www.health.gov.au/nutritionmonitoring.

Department of Health. (2014b). *Australia's physical activity and sedentary behaviour guidelines.* Canberra: Department of Health. Retrieved 20 August 2015 from http://www.health.gov.au/internet/main/publishing.nsf/content/health-pubhlth-strateg-active-evidence.htm.

Department of Health, Government of Western Australia. (2006). *Child health services, birth to school entry: Universal contact schedule.* Western Australia: Department of Health. Retrieved 20 August 2015 from http://www.health.wa.gov.au/circularsnew/attachments/267.pdf.

Department of Planning, Transport and Infrastructure [DPTI]. (2014). *Fact sheet: Cyclists involved in road crashes in South Australia.* Retrieved 27 August 2015 from http://dpti.sa.gov.au/__data/assets/pdf_file/0003/85395/Cyclists.pdf.

Department of Planning, Transport and Infrastructure [DPTI]. (2015a). Welcome to Way2Go. Retrieved 27 August 2015 from http://www.dpti.sa.gov.au/way2go.

Department of Planning, Transport and Infrastructure [DPTI]. (2015b). Welcome to Way2Go Bike Ed. Retrieved 27 August 2015 from http://www.dpti.sa.gov.au/way2go/bike_ed.

Department of Planning, Transport and Infrastructure [DPTI]. (2015c). Towards Zero together, bicycle paths and lanes. Retrieved 27 August 2015 from http://www.dpti.sa.gov.au/towardszerotogether/safer_roads/safer_roads_for_cyclists.

Department of Planning, Transport and Infrastructure [DPTI]. (2015d). Cycling and the law. Retrieved 29 August 2015 from https://www.sa.gov.au/__data/assets/pdf_file/0020/23438/DPTI-Cycling-the-Law-Booklet.pdf.

Department of Planning, Transport and Infrastructure [DPTI]. (2015e). *Way2Go: Order form*. Retrieved 20 August 2015 from http://www.dpti.sa.gov.au/way2go/resources/home_info_brochures_order_form.

Department of Transport Energy and Infrastructure [DTEI]. (2011a). *About Way2Go*. Retrieved 5 May 2011 from http://www.dtei.sa.gov.au/way2go/about_way2go.

Department of Transport Energy and Infrastructure [DTEI]. (2011b). *Way2Go home order form*. Retrieved 5 May 2011 from http://www.dtei.sa.gov.au/way2go/way2go_home_info_order_form.

Foucault, M. (1986/1984). *The use of pleasure: The history of sexuality, Vol.2* (R Hurley, Trans.). London: Viking Press.

Garrard, J. (2009). *Active transport: Children and young people*. Melbourne: VicHealth. Retrieved 16 August 2015 from http://trove.nla.gov.au/version/50809739.

Gros, F. (2005). Course context: The 1982 course in Foucault's work. In M Foucault, *The hermeneutics of the subject: Lectures at the Collège de France 1981-1982* (F Gros, Ed., G Burchell, Trans., pp. 507-550). New York: Picador.

Hillman, M. (2006). Children's rights and adults' wrongs. *Children's Geographies*, 4(1), 61-67.

Hillman, M, Adams, J, & Whitelegg, J. (1990). *One false move … A study of children's independent mobility*. London: Policy Studies Institute.

Holloway, S, & Valentine, G. (2000). Spatiality and the new social studies of childhood. *Sociology*, 34(4), 763-783.

Horton, D. (2007). Fear of cycling. In P Rosen, P Cox, & D Horton (Eds.), *Cycling and society* (pp. 133-152). Aldershot, UK: Ashgate.

Imberger, K, Styles, T, Hughes, I, & Di Pietro, G. (2006). *Contract report: Evaluation of Bike Ed and the Traffic Centre Road Safety package*. ARRB Research. Retrieved 5 April 2015 from http://www.arrb.com.au/admin/file/content13/c6/18Evaluation%20of%20two%20bicycle%20programs%20for%20primary%20school%20children%20in%20the%20ACT.pdf.

Ipsos MORI. (2010, December). *Research to explore perceptions and experiences of Bikeability training amongst parents and children*. Retrieved 14 August 2015 from https://bikeability.org.uk/publications.

Jette, S, Bhagat, K, & Andrews, DL. (2014). Governing the child-citizen: 'Let's Move!' as national biopedagogy. *Sport, Education and Society*. doi: 10.1080/13573322.2014.993961.

Kimbro, RT, & Schachter, A. (2011). Neighborhood poverty and maternal fears of children's outdoor play. *Family Relations*, 60, 461-475. doi: 10.1111/j.1741-3729.2011.00660.x.

Lee, N, & Motzkau, J. (2011). Navigating the bio-politics of childhood. *Childhood*, 18(1), 7-19.

Lindsay, VL. (2013, January). *Injured cyclist profile: An in-depth study of a sample of cyclists injured in road crashes in South Australia*. CASR report series, CASR 112. The University of Adelaide: Centre for Automotive Safety Research. Retrieved 21 August 2015 from http://www.abc.net.au/mediawatch/transcripts/1424_adelaideuni.pdf.

Mackett, R. (2012). Children's travel behaviour and its health implications. *Transport Policy*, 26, 66-72.

Maley, J. (2014). Undisciplined children in public places are a result of parental guilt. *The Sydney Morning Herald*. Retrieved 21 August 2015 from http://www.smh.com.au/comment/undisciplined-children-in-public-places-are-a-result-of-parental-guilt-20141024-11as12.html.

Malone, K, & Rudner, J. (2011). Global perspectives on children's independent mobility: A socio-cultural comparison and theoretical discussion of children's lives in four countries in Asia and Africa. *Global Studies of Childhood*, 1(3), 243-259.

McLaren, AT, & Parusel, S. (2011). Parental traffic safeguarding at school sites: Unequal risks and responsibilities. *Canadian Journal of Sociology*, 36(2), 161-183. Retrieved 21 August 2015 from https://ejournals.library.ualberta.ca/index.php/CJS/article/.../8025/8109.

McLaren, AT, & Parusel, S. (2012). Under the radar: Parental traffic safeguarding and automobility. *Mobilities*, 7(2), 211-232. doi: 10.1080/17450101.2012.659465.

McLaren, AT, & Parusel, S. (2014). 'Watching like a hawk': Gendered parenting in automobilized urban spaces. *Gender, Place and Culture: A Journal of Feminist Geography*. doi: 10.1080/0966369X.2014.970141.

Myttas, N. (2001). Understanding and recognizing ADHD. Retrieved 20 August 2015 from http://www.adders.org/research49.htm.

National Health and Medical Research Council [NHMRC]. (2007). *Genetics in family medicine: The Australian handbook for general practitioners — Testing and pregnancy.* Retrieved 20 August 2015 from https://www.nhmrc.gov.au/_files_nhmrc/file/your_health/egenetics/practioners/gems/sections/03_testing_and_pregnancy.pdf.

National Health and Medical Research Council [NHMRC]. (2013). *Clinical practice guidelines for the management of overweight and obesity in adults, adolescents and children in Australia.* Reference number N57. Retrieved 20 August 2015 from https://www.nhmrc.gov.au/guidelines-publications/n57.

Niehues, AN, Bundy, A, Broom, A, & Tranter, P. (2015). Parents' perceptions of risk and the influence on children's everyday activities. *Journal of Child and Family Studies*, 24(3), 809-820. doi: 10.1007/s10826-013-9891-2.

Packer, J. (2003). Disciplining mobility: Governing and safety. In JZ Bratich, J Packer, & C McCarthy (Eds.), *Foucault, cultural studies and governmentality* (pp.135-161). Albany, NY: State University of New York Press.

Parusel, S, & McLaren, AT. (2010). Cars before kids: Automobility and the illusion of school traffic safety. *Canadian Review of Sociology*, 47(2), 129-147. doi: 10.1111/j.1755-618X.2010.01227.x.

Pedal Power ACT. (n.d.). Retrieved 20 August 2015 from http://www.pedalpower.org.au.

Peters, M. (2001). Education, enterprise culture and the entrepreneurial self: A Foucauldian perspective. *Journal of Educational Enquiry*, 2(2), 58-71.

Powell, D, & Gard, M. (2014). *The governmentality of childhood obesity: Coca-Cola, public health and primary schools — Discourse: Studies in the Cultural Politics of Education.* doi: 10.1080/01596306.2014.905045.

Rochlin, GI. (1999). Safe operation as a social construct. *Ergonomics*, 42(11), 1549-60. doi: 10.1080/001401399184884.

Rose, N. (1999). *Governing the soul: The shaping of the private self* (2nd ed.). London & New York: Free Association Books.

Rowan, C. (2010). Unplug — Don't drug: A critical look at the influence of technology on child behavior with an alternative way of responding other than evaluation and drugging. *Ethical Human Psychology and Psychiatry*, 12(1), 60-68. doi: 10.1891/1559-4343.12.1.60.

Ruddick, S. (2010). Commentary: Imagining bodies. In K Hörschelmann, & R Colls (Eds.), *Contested bodies of childhood and youth* (pp. 97-102).

Houndmills, UK: PalgraveMacmillan.

Rynders, JE, & Horrobin, JM. (1990). Always trainable? Never educable? Updating educational expectations concerning children with Down syndrome. *American Journal of Mental Retardation*, 95(1), 77-83.

Schoeppe, S, Duncan, MJ, Badland, HM, Oliver, M, & Browne, M. (2014). Associations between children's independent mobility and physical activity. *BMC Public Health*, 14(91), 1-18. doi: 10.1186/1471-2458-14-91.

Share, M, & Strain, M. (2008). Making schools and young people responsible: A critical analysis of Ireland's obesity strategy. *Health and Social Care in the Community*, 16(3), 234-243. doi: 10.1111/j.1365-2524.2008.00763.x.

Simmons, P. (2003). Performing safety in faulty environments. *Sociological Review*, 51 (Supplement 2), 78-93. doi: 10.1111/j.1467-954X.2004.00452.x.

Tranter, P, & Pawson, E. (2001). Children's access to local environments: A case study of Christchurch, New Zealand. *Local Environment*, 6(1), 27-48. doi: 10.1080/13549830120024233.

Urbas, G. (2000). The age of criminal responsibility. *Australian Institute of Criminology: Trends and issues in crime and criminal justice*, 181. Retrieved 20 August 2015 from http://www.aic.gov.au/media_library/publications/tandi_pdf/tandi181.pdf.

Valentine, G. (1997). 'Oh Yes I Can', 'Oh No You Can't': Children and parents' understandings of kids' competence to negotiate public space safely. *Antipode*, 29(1), 65-89. doi: 10.1111/1467-8330.00035.

Valentine, G. (2010). Children's bodies: An absent presence. In K Hörschelmann, & R Colls (Eds.), *Contested bodies of childhood and youth* (pp. 23-37). Houndmills, UK: Palgrave Macmillan.

Valentine, G, & Holloway, S. (2003). *Cyberkids: Children in the information age*. London: Routledge Falmer.

Vassallo, S. (2011). Implications of institutionalizing self-regulated learning: An analysis from four sociological perspectives. *Educational Studies*, 47(1), 26-49. doi: 10.1080/00131946.2011.540984.

Vassallo, S. (2013a). Critical pedagogy and neoliberalism: Concerns with teaching self-regulated learning. *Studies in the Philosophy of Education*, 32 (6), 563-580. doi: 10.1007/s11217-012-9337-0.

Vassallo, S. (2013b). Considering class-based values related to guardian involvement and the development of self-regulated learning. *New Ideas in*

Psychology, 31(3), 202-211. doi: 10.1016/j.newideapsych.2011.12.002.

Vassallo, S. (2013c). Resistance to self-regulated learning pedagogy in an urban classroom: A critique of neoliberalism. *Journal for Critical Education Policy Studies,* 11 (2), 240-281. Retrieved 20 August 2015 from http://www.jceps.com/archives/432.

Wake, M, Hardy, P, Canterford, L, Sawyer, M, & Carlin, JB. (2007). Overweight, obesity and girth of Australian preschoolers: Prevalence and socio-economic correlates. *International Journal of Obesity,* 31(7), 1044-1051. doi: 10.1038/sj.ijo.0803503.

11 More than a message: Producing cyclists through public safety advertising campaigns

Rachael Nielsen and Jennifer Bonham

Introduction

Despite the burgeoning field of cycling research and widespread concerns over media representations of cyclists (Horton, 2007; Skinner & Rosen, 2007; Advertising Standards Bureau, 2011) very little academic work has been published on cycling and the media. A few notable exceptions include Zac Furness's (2010) detailed account of cycling in North American popular culture (film, literature and television), Ben Fincham's (2007) discussion of bike messengers in the British press, and the comparative study of representations of cyclists in Australian newspapers by Rissel, Bonfigliolo, Emilsen, and Smith (2010). The limited scrutiny of cycling in the Australian media contrasts with the recent spate of government-sponsored road safety advertising campaigns which feature cyclists (for example, 'Share the road'; 'Be safe be seen'; 'It's a two-way street').[1] Many of these campaigns aim at

---

[1] The Department of Transport and Main Roads [Qld] has implemented the 'Share the road' campaign. For more details, see http://www.tmr.qld.gov.au/Safety/Safety-campaigns/Bicycle-safety.aspx. The Motor Accident Commission [SA] has implemented the 'Be safe be seen' campaign; see https://www.mac.sa.gov.au/besafebeseen/be-aware. The Amy Gillett Foundation has implemented the 'It's a two-way street' campaign; see https://cyclesafe.gofundraise.com.au/cms/2waystreet.

fostering more positive interactions between cyclists and motorists. In this chapter, we are specifically interested in a road safety campaign which features cyclists as a point of contrast in its advice to young drivers.

Young drivers are often targeted in road safety campaigns because of their over-representation in road crash statistics (Bureau of Infrastructure, Transport and Regional Economics [BITRE], 2013a; Wundersitz, 2012; Curry, Hafetz, Kallan, Winston, & Durbin, 2011). In 2012, people aged 17-25 made up just 13% of the Australian population yet accounted for 22% of fatalities on Australian roads (BITRE, 2013b, p. iii). Graduated licensing systems and mass media advertising campaigns are two interventions used by Australian state and territory governments to address high crash rates amongst young people. Although a number of evaluative studies have questioned the efficacy of mass advertising campaigns (for example, Ulleberg, 2001, p. 293; Delaney, Lough, Whelan, & Cameron, 2004; Wundersitz, Hutchinson, & Woolley, 2010), they remain an important part of the road safety tool kit. The current chapter analyses the road safety advertising campaign screened by the South Australian Motor Accident Commission [MAC] from 2010 to 2014. We are specifically interested in the characteristics and behaviours assembled together under the term 'cyclist' in the MAC campaign.

Road safety campaign messaging has started to shift over the past two decades from 'shock' to 'humour' (Wundersitz et al., 2010; Delaney et al., 2004). But messaging is rarely the focus of attention when researchers evaluate these campaigns (exceptions include Delaney et al., 2004). Rather, evaluations are directed at the *uptake* of the message by the target audience, and this is often assessed using interviews or self-reporting studies (Kaye, White, & Lewis, 2013; Walton & McKeown, 2001). Alternatively, message uptake is analysed by correlating crash statistics with the timing and duration of an advertising campaign (Phillips, Ulleberg, & Vaa, 2011; Tay, 2005). In contrast to this evaluative research, our work does not focus on the uptake of the message but on the message itself — the specific advice being given in the MAC's advertising campaign. Along with Fincham (2007), Furness (2010) and Rissel et al. (2010), we are interested in interrogating media representations as part of a greater social commentary (Wimmer & Dominick, 2006, p. 371). We have used Carol Bacchi's 'What's the problem represented to be?' analytic strategy [WPR] to examine the MAC television commercial which features cyclists (2009; 2012). Bacchi's poststructuralist-informed approach is generally used in policy analysis (for example, Goodwin, 2012); however, we suggest it can also be applied to public awareness campaigns, as these campaigns, like policies, provide advice to individuals on how to conduct themselves.

The following section examines existing research into media representations of cycling and contrasts the approaches taken in these analyses with the strategy we have employed in the MAC research. After detailing our analytic approach, we describe the MAC advertisements and then go on to discuss the findings of our analysis. The concluding section considers the lived effects of the MAC advertisements and offers recommendations for future engagement with young travellers.

Analysing media representations

As stated at the outset, only a handful of researchers have analysed representations of cycling in popular culture. Informed by a critical approach, Furness (2010) examines the characteristics attributed to cyclists in North American popular culture throughout the twentieth century. He reports that cyclists in film, television and newspaper reports are usually male and, apart from during a short period of wartime petrol rationing, they are represented as social misfits. This negative representation ranges from the loveable but eccentric, socially incompetent and sexually immature teenager through to the aggressive, public menace of the bicycle messenger. Where women have featured in cycling, it has been in terms of *automobile pedagogy* — learning the road rules in preparation for becoming a driver — or for the purpose of demonstrating the superiority of the automobile (Furness, 2010, pp. 108-139).

Clearly, these representations do not lead to any straightforward rejection of cycling or uptake of the motor vehicle. However, Furness argues that they are located within a specific cultural context and serve an ideological function in producing and reproducing the automobile as the cultural norm:

> Mass media do not obviously invent the dominant norms of mobility … [They do, however,] play a collective role in amplifying, and extending the predispositions constituting dominant culture. (2010, p. 114)

Furness's quote deserves closer attention, as it locates the mass media outside of, yet 'cheering on', the production of mobility norms. We would question this symbolic/material divide, suggesting instead that the media is yet one site of several in which mobile subjects are produced (see below).

Chris Rissel, Catriona Bonfiglioli, Adrian Emilsen and Ben Smith (2010) compare representations of cycling in Melbourne and Sydney newspapers across the decade from 1998 to 2008. The authors report that there has been a shift away from negative, and toward more positive, representations of cyclists through this time (p. 4). They reject any straightforward causal relation between negative media representations and negative public attitudes toward cyclists. Working from a (particular) social constructionist position, the authors argue that as individuals engage with, and seek to make sense of, media representations of cycling, their attitudes will be influenced by those representations. Consequently, broader public opinion will be shaped to some extent by positive and negative messaging. Rissel et al. position the media as playing a central role in the success of public health and safety campaigns relating to tobacco use, firearms, HIV and road crashes (p. 6). However, as Ronnie Lipschutz (2012) demonstrates in relation to tobacco use (using an example that applies elsewhere), a plethora of measures are operationalised in making smoking socially unacceptable — from banning smoking in public places to filling out health insurance or medical forms which require information on smoking habits. Rissel et al. flag the increase in cycling through the 10 years covered in their media analysis, but they sidestep the relation between the media and the broader social context — including government cycling strategies, reconfiguration of some public spaces (streets, paths), production of knowledge about cycling — within which increases in cycling have occurred.

Ben Fincham's (2007) study of bicycle messengers uses a form of content analysis to examine how this group of cyclists is represented in the media. Fincham classifies media reports on bike messengers according to two criteria: firstly, the standpoint of the correspondent, speaking from a position as a bike messenger (inside) or not a bike messenger (outside); and secondly, the content of the report itself — as positive or negative. Fincham argues that standpoints are 'important because of their role in informing the wider population about a particular group', while the content creates a 'set of generalizations and stereotypical characteristics' that compete for dominance in the public domain (p. 182). These arguments are important, as we suggest that inherent in each 'standpoint' (what we would refer to as a *subject position*) is the socially constituted level of authority which attaches to that standpoint. Fincham also foregrounds the formation and contestation of the category and content of the 'bike messenger' (characteristics, ways of thinking, activities, language). It is Fincham's 'productive' approach — that is, that categories are in continuous formation — that resonates with our own interest in media representations.

In the next section we provide an overview of Bacchi's WPR approach to policy analysis and in particular her interrogation of policy problems. We then go on to discuss our application of Bacchi's analytic strategy in relation to the Motor Accident Commission advertising campaign.

WPR as an analytic strategy

In contrast to the evaluative and critical approaches described above, we are proposing to use Carol Bacchi's WPR analytic strategy to analyse the MAC advertising campaign. Bacchi's approach is usually applied to policy documents, but we believe her focus on *practical texts* lends it to a broader range of applications (see below). WPR differs markedly from conventional policy evaluations, which address competing ways of *solving* policy 'problems'. These evaluations do not question *how* a problem is being constituted. That is, they do not question the processes through which particular characteristics or activities are identified as problematic. Rather, they tend to assume that certain activities exist objectively as problems and are waiting to be solved, corrected or addressed through government policies (Goodwin, 2012, p. 27). Instead of accepting 'problems' at face value and governments as merely reacting to these problems, Bacchi argues that governments are active in 'creating' problems (2009, p. 33). This activity is not a matter of manipulation; rather, as government policies 'make proposals for change', they simultaneously — and necessarily — constitute whatever is identified as 'needing to be changed' as the problem (Bacchi, 2009, p. 1; Bacchi, 2012, p. 4). For example, restricting the hours of sale for alcohol constitutes (or creates) alcohol availability as 'the problem' (Bacchi, 2015). The important point is to understand the active role of governments in problematisation.

The WPR approach also takes us beyond the policy maker's *intentions*, as it allows us to interrogate the assumptions which underpin a particular problem representation. For example, for 'alcohol availability' to be the 'problem', we must be assuming that people lack self-discipline (Bacchi, 2015). It is this elaboration of 'the problem' and how this representation has become possible that opens a space for creating new ways of thinking and doing. WPR provides tools to examine *how* a particular phenomenon (behaviour, process) — such as the behaviour of alcohol drinkers — has become an object for thought, including the circumstances and processes which gave specific shape to that object. To take a directly relevant example, in the early to mid-twentieth century a plethora of relations — interactions between people in public space; materials such as road surfaces and hawkers' carts; behaviours like standing about, or alighting from a tram; parliamentary speeches about gambling in the street; engineering discussions regarding the weight of vehicles; regulations relating to loitering and furious driving; newspaper reports on 'hit and run' fatalities; contestations over how to conduct oneself in public — operated to forge 'traffic' as an object for thought out of a multitude of street activities (Bonham, 2006). Each of the sites (community, parliament, law courts, media) in this network of relations participates, albeit with different levels of authority, in the production of 'traffic'. Further, the routinisation of this network of relations (Bacchi & Bonham, 2014) has naturalised 'traffic' as a self-evident object or fact of existence. And it is within the routinisation of these relations that shape is given to the object 'traffic' — what is to be included or excluded as 'traffic' — and knowledge about 'traffic' is socially produced.

It is also within these relations that people are differentiated as pedestrians, cyclists, motorists, tram travellers, loiterers, hawkers (that is, they are differentiated as subjects of knowledge) and governed in line with the knowledge created about the new object of 'traffic'. Consequently, it becomes difficult to think about 'traffic', or indeed any other 'taken-for-granted' object in any other way (Bacchi, 2009, p. 16). Bacchi argues that if we replace the study of the 'object' with the study of 'relations', it is possible to open up new ways of thinking and being (2012, p. 2). This point is politically important for 'cycling'. By rejecting cycling as a self-evident fact and examining the relations through which it is produced, we are making explicit the *activity* of producing cycling. Following from this, we can foreground the mutability of those relations and open a space for cycling to be produced 'otherwise'.

Bacchi developed the WPR approach as she elaborated Michel Foucault's concept of *practical texts* in the field of political science (2009, p. vi). Practical texts, Foucault wrote in 1986, refer to texts 'written for the purpose of offering rules, opinions and advice on how to behave as one should ... to constitute the eventual framework of everyday conduct' (as cited in Bacchi, 2009, p. 34). While policies clearly provide such advice on 'what to do', Nina Marshall (2012) has taken Bacchi's work further, applying it to the World Bank's statements on disability. Marshall argues that these statements are practical texts, as they offer opinions on what organisations should do in relation to disability. Like Marshall, we would argue that public service campaigns qualify as practical texts, as they offer advice on everyday conduct to their target populations.

The WPR analytic strategy asks six questions (see Figure 11.1) of a policy document or practical text (Bacchi, 2012, p. 2) and then recommends that researchers take the additional step of subjecting their own proposals to the six WPR questions. These questions, and the final step, take us beyond the message itself to interrogate not only what we take for granted but also how it has become possible to accept this version of reality. The WPR strategy also foregrounds what is silenced — and whether, making these silences apparent, we can begin to think differently. We can also examine the effects of these problem representations and where and how they are produced and distributed. We have analysed the MAC advertising

---

WPR Questions

1. What is the problem represented to be in a specific policy?
2. What presuppositions or assumptions underlie this representation of the problem?
3. How has this representation of the problem come about?
4. What is left unproblematic in this problem representation? Where are the silences? Can the problem be thought about differently?
5. What effects are produced by this representation of the problem?
6. How/where has this representation of the problem been produced, disseminated and defended? How could it be questioned, disrupted and replaced?

Final step:
Apply the above list to your own problem representation.

Figure 11.1: WPR Questions.
(Source: Adapted from Bacchi, 2012.)

campaign using only the six WPR questions because the final step 'interrogating our own policy recommendations' — would require an entirely new chapter.

In 2011, the South Australian Motor Accident Commission launched an advertising campaign focused on losing a driver's licence. The campaign, not currently active, includes three television and radio advertisements and two posters which are displayed on bus shelters and used as webpage banners. The television commercials include a mother picking up her 20-something year old son from football practice; a couple kissing in the back of a taxi with the meter running up an expensive fare; and two young men riding a tandem bicycle. The posters include a tradesman riding a donkey to work and a young man riding his bicycle to pick up a young woman for a date.

Although all of the commercials enact disturbing gender stereotypes, our research focuses on the television advertisement that features the tandem cyclists. We have not included the MAC's, or the advertising agency's, explanation of the advertisement in our analysis, as this explanation does not accompany the screening of the ads. We are specifically interested in the advice being given to the viewer at the moment of viewing, as this is likely to be the only advice s/he receives on how to conduct her/himself. As Bacchi suggests, we have worked 'backwards' from the 'solution' — that is, what advice the viewer receives on how to conduct her/himself — to determine what the MAC and the advertising agency represent to be the 'problem' (Bacchi, 2009, p. 55). The following section discusses our analysis of the MAC advertisements as it weaves together the findings from each of the WPR questions.

What's the problem for the MAC?

Examining this advertisement frame by frame, we are presented with a view of a young man wearing a bicycle helmet. Clearly constituted as a 'cyclist', he peers through the window of a Sports Utility Vehicle [SUV] at the young woman behind the steering wheel. His conduct is intrusive, but his youthful smile suggests he is socially inept rather than threatening. Nonetheless, the young woman/driver takes precautionary action, rolling up the window to place a physical barrier between herself and the cyclist/young man. A second young man, also wearing a bicycle helmet, is brought into view and appears embarrassed under the scrutiny of the woman in the back seat of the car. His embarrassment contrasts with the broad grin of his companion, suggesting that the companion lacks awareness of the social awkwardness of their situation. As the young women drive off and the young men cycle through the intersection, the tagline 'Lose your licence and you're screwed' explains that they are cycling as a result of losing their driver's licences. The binaries — driver/cyclist, woman/man — are central to this advertisement, as they operate to contrast the appropriate conduct of the women/driver-passengers with the inappropriate conduct of the men/cyclists.

Leaving aside its troubling hetero-sexist and classist stereotypes, this advertisement implicitly provides advice to young women as well as young men. For women, the motor vehicle offers protection against unwanted attention, and the driver demonstrates the correct way to discourage that attention and disengage from undesired (or undesirable?) interactions. She does not tell him what he might do with his ungainly grin, but, like a well-mannered young lady, she withdraws from the situation. The woman-driver's response combined with the campaign tagline, 'Lose your licence and you're screwed', sounds a warning to young men not to ride a bicycle: 'Men who cycle are undesirable'. The cyclist/driver binary described by Zac Furness (see above) clearly resonates in the Australian context. Cyclists are also produced either as children learning road skills in anticipation of becoming motorists or as socially and economically incompetent individuals (usually men) who lack self-awareness and are sexually unappealing.[2] According to Furness, negative representations of cyclists emerge from, and assist in, reproducing 'automobility' — a set of processes intrinsic to capitalist growth through the twentieth century (Urry, 2004). However, this representation of cyclists would not make sense in market economies such as the Netherlands or Denmark. The important question for us is how it has become possible to assemble a series of negative attributes together as 'cyclists', not only in North America or the United Kingdom but also in Australia. Before responding to this question we first need to interrogate the target audience for this commercial — 'youth'.

Bacchi urges us to interrogate what is taken for granted — the necessary but unstated knowledge required — for a particular problem representation to be intelligible (2009, p. 5). The viewer must comprehend 'youth' as a discrete

---

[2] John Doyle's recent (2013) play *Vere (Faith)* features precisely such a character — the cyclist as a physics 'nerd' in his late 20s or early 30s.

population segment that can be targeted by messages. There is a significant literature which demonstrates the socially constructed nature of categories such as 'childhood' (see Anne Wilson, Chapter Ten, this volume) and 'youth' (for example, Hörschelmann & Colls, 2010). These categories have been produced within population studies, psychology and pedagogy, and have been taken up in fields such as transport, law and economics. A key characteristic of the category 'youth' is taking risks (Abbott-Chapman, Denholm, & Wyld, 2008). A number of activities and ways of thinking have been excised out of the mass of human possibilities and assembled together as 'risk taking'. These include particular levels of sexual activity, or drug and alcohol use; specific types of engagement with other people and/or property; and a range of driving behaviours, such as exceeding the speed limit by at least 20 km/h, running red lights, street racing, changing lanes without signalling, overtaking illegally and following too closely (Fergusson, Swain-Campbell, & Horwood, 2003, p. 338).

As Bacchi suggests, 'the category of "youth" functions to facilitate a wide range of governmental objectives around policing, education, population and economic concerns' (2009, p. 58). As a result, legally enforced limits on smoking, drinking, voting and driving are all in place to limit young people from making what are deemed to be risky decisions and from engaging in reckless behaviour (Tymula, Belmaker, Roy, Ruderman, Manson, Glimcher, & Levy, 2012, p. 17135). Education and public awareness campaigns demonstrate 'risk-taking' behaviours and the consequences of 'youth' engaging in those behaviours. There are multiple mechanisms operating within, but certainly not exclusive to, Australian society which require people to acknowledge themselves in terms of age (filling out forms is one of the most obvious) and a particular age group (for example, through school attendance, public immunisation programs, showing proof of identify to enter clubs and bars). There are a number of policies directed at the category of 'youth', such as Work For The Dole or the 'Green Army', in an effort to guide their conduct in a particular direction; and these policies are underpinned by the understanding of 'youths' as 'risk takers' (see Bacchi, 2009, p. 58).

It is thus accepted that young people are not yet *prepared* for adult life, to make what are considered sensible choices, as they are still developing physiologically, emotionally and mentally (Kloep, Güney, Cok, & Simsek, 2009, p. 136). Given this assessment, the representation of the problem of youths losing their licence is a proposition that makes sense to the audience, and the MAC campaign is *able* to target the category of 'youth' according to this deep-seated assumption about the 'natural' qualities and developmental stages of the individual. What distinguishes the MAC campaign from, for example, the New Zealand 'Legend' campaign[3] is that risk-taking behaviours are not made explicit in the MAC advertisement and there is no advice on how to behave otherwise in a non-risky manner.

Thoroughly entangled with the assumption that 'youth' is a discrete subpopulation, located at a particular point on the physiological and psychological development trajectory, is the assumption that driving a car is both necessary and desirable. It is beyond the scope of this chapter to detail the complex power-knowledge relations at work in producing the automobile as a 'necessary' means of mobility (see Bonham, 2002; Paterson, 2007). However, concepts such as 'friction-of-distance' and evolutionary theories of land use/transport interactions (Adams, 1970; Forster, 2004) have functioned in the Australian context to form the motor vehicle as the most, if not the only, efficient means of transport. Identifying, measuring and mapping origins and destinations provides us with a way of thinking about people, facilities, services and employment as thinly dispersed across a wide urban landscape. Coupled with this way of thinking is the incitement to think of our mobility in terms of temporal efficiency (for further discussion, see Jain & Lyons, 2008; Bonham, 2000; 2006). Consequently, the efficient traveller in the dispersed Australian or North American city has no choice but to travel by automobile.

In contrast, European or Asian cities — with their short travel distances, dense settlement patterns and close arrangement of origins and destinations — are often used to demonstrate the inverse case that walking, cycling and public transport are only efficient in compact cities (for a critique of this argument, see Mees, 2010). For example, journeys up to 400 metres or even 1 kilometre can be made on foot; journeys under 5-7 kilometres are suitable for cycling; and anything over 7 kilometres requires a car or public transport (Rybarczyk & Gallagher, 2014). As the young men in the MAC advertisement pedal slowly through the intersection, they activate authoritative knowledge (that is, knowledge produced

---

[3] This advertisement examines the dilemmas faced by a young man trying to decide whether or not to intervene to stop his friend drink driving. It provides advice on how to behave otherwise — that is, stay at a friend's house rather than drink and drive.

in research institutions and government departments) about the inefficiency of the bicycle in the Australian city. The absurdity of cycling relies on assumptions about travel modes and travel distances.

The advertisement is also informed by the assumption that driving is 'desirable'. Driving has become 'desirable' through the multifarious processes of forming ourselves as efficient travellers (Bonham, 2006). Mobility is located within a plethora of discursive practices — transport, road trauma treatment, road safety, economic and national development — but the knowledge produced in physiology and psychology and enacted within the law provides both scientific and juridical acknowledgement of the transition from childhood to adulthood. The observation that obtaining a driver's licence serves as a kind of rite of passage (for example, Daley & Rissel, 2011; Delbosc & Currie, 2014) only becomes interesting when we no longer accept it at face value and instead examine the mechanisms by which obtaining a driver's licence has come to be experienced as a 'rite of passage'. Further, in the Australian context, motor vehicle ownership has long been constituted as an indicator of personal wealth and national economic development; and conversely, lack of car ownership is produced in the transport literature as an indicator of transport disadvantage. It is hardly surprising that driving a car has become more socially acceptable than riding a bicycle.

The effects of the MAC problem representation — advice to young people to drive rather than cycle — is to produce driving, once again, as the more desirable form of conduct. Cycling is a punishment rather than a freely chosen form of transport. Cycling and cyclists are positioned as inferior to driving and drivers (economically and socially), and are thus stigmatised through the dividing practice which sets the driver in opposition to the cyclist. As Bacchi (2009, p. 16) suggests, the stigmatisation of minorities 'serves a useful government purpose, indicating and encouraging desired behaviours among the majority'. The marginalisation of cyclists has significant lived effects.

Within the MAC campaign, two 'transport subjects' are presented in opposition to each other. Firstly, the 'cyclist subject' is that of an unlawful 'bad citizen', one who has lost his licence and must resort to an inferior transport option. Secondly, the 'driver subject' assumes the position of the lawful 'good citizen', one who has maintained her/his licence. We propose that the privileging of the 'driver subject' in the MAC campaign produces driving as the only socially acceptable transport mode. This not only shapes what people are advised to think about as they scrutinise their own travel practices (Bonham & Bacchi, 2013) but also impacts on people's embodied existence. The MAC does not 'reflect' a way of thinking about cyclists which exists 'out there', exogenous to the organisation. The MAC is inextricably networked into society and makes decisions about the movements, materials, symbols and ways of thinking that will be assembled together as 'cyclists' and 'drivers'. Certainly, as demonstrated above, the particular assemblage formed within the MAC advertisements has been produced in many other sites — from the academy to theatre, film and newspaper stories. Nonetheless, within each site, 'elements' are assembled together, and it is essential that decision makers reflect on the effects of these assemblages.

Since this MAC advertisement forms 'not driving' as the problem, it remains silent on speeding and drinking while driving (Department of Planning, Transport and Infrastructure [DPTI], 2014). These ways of conduct are not problematised in this MAC advertising campaign and hence not produced as socially unacceptable.

Further, by positioning cycling within a car/bicycle binary, the advertisement also silences the numerous benefits that cycling offers to individuals, society, urban liveability and the environment. These alternative ways of creating cycling and cyclists are widely documented and circulated both in academia and government strategies (see 'Smart move — The City of Adelaide's transport and movement strategy', 2012). In terms of social, economic and environmental sustainability, cycling is regarded as the best option. Numerous studies are devoted to this research, demonstrating that increasing bicycle use over private car use will lead to the following: reduced greenhouse gas emissions and fuel consumption (Schwanen, Banister, & Anable, 2011; Newman, Kenworthy, & Glazebrook, 2008; Mees, 2010; Lindsay, Macmillan, & Woodward, 2011), reduced deaths and injuries to cyclists due to road crashes (see Jacobsen, 2003, for the 'safety in numbers' theory); and improvements to health due to increased physical activity (Lindsay et al. 2011). Pucher and Buehler (2008) go on to highlight the increased liveability of cities with the increase in cycling, as *people* are given priority in public space over cars. Additionally, the bicycle is deemed to be among the most equitable of transport modes due to the affordability of both the initial and the continuing cost of operating a bicycle.

Following this line of thinking, in silencing the benefits of cycling, the ads also silence the detrimental effects of driving. These include (but are not limited to) the rising economic cost of fuel to operate a car, along with the costly infrastructure needed to support high levels of car use; congestion issues in major cities affecting mobility for all road users; and the environmental issues, as fuel-powered transport is one of the fastest-growing greenhouse gas emitters in many countries, including Australia (Lindsay et al., 2011, p. 54). By limiting consideration of the only viable form of transport as driving, through representing cycling as the problem, all the detrimental issues regarding cars are silenced.

The MAC representation also silences the possibility that young people are not necessarily risk takers. Indeed, contrasting cyclist and driver crash statistics offers an alternative way to think about the pervasive view that young people are risk takers and that cycling is a problem. Crash rates of cyclists who are 16-24 years old are significantly lower than for drivers in the same age cohort. According to 2011 data, cyclists were responsible for 171 crashes but only 22 of these crashes (13%), were attributed to cyclists in the 16-24 age cohort (DPTI, 2012). By contrast, drivers aged 16-24 years old were found responsible for 29% of crashes. Further, cyclists aged 40+ were responsible for 65 crashes (38%) despite these age cohorts having cycling participation rates of less than 10% (Austroads, 2011) (see Table 11.1).[4]

Conclusion

There is no doubt that the MAC did not intend to participate in the devaluing of cycling and the normalisation of motoring. Yet their tandem-cycling advertisement has exactly this effect. Impelled to produce the advertisement by the over-representation of young drivers in crash statistics, the campaign sought to curb young people's engagement with risk-taking driving. Applying the WPR approach to this advertising campaign, it has been possible to make explicit both the advice being given to young people on how to conduct themselves and how it has become possible for such advice to be given. On the basis of our analysis, we suggest that driving is offered as the appropriate way to travel. Further, in this campaign at least, drink-driving, speeding, using a mobile phone while driving or endangering other road users is not constituted as socially unacceptable. Rather, the MAC campaign

---

[4] Further research comparing crash rates by age cohort and mode would be beneficial. See Maring and Schagen (1990) for research on age-dependent attitudes of cyclists.

Table 11.1: Responsibility for crashes by age and mode.

	Driver responsible for crash			Bicyclist responsible for crash		
Age Cohort	Percentage of all Drivers	Number	Percentage	Percentage of age cohort that cycles*	Number	Percentage
0-15	N/A	N/A	N/A	43.1	16	9
16-24	13	5675	29	15.6	22	13
25-39	26	5698	29	15.6	50	29
40+	61	8110	42	8.1	65	38
Unknown	N/A	N/A	N/A	N/A	18	11
TOTAL	100	19483	100	N/A	171	100

*Figures are adapted from the 'Australian cycling participation 2011' report which does not disaggregate cyclist volumes by age cohort but calculates proportion of people within each age cohort that participate in cycling. Cycling participation age cohorts do not match age cohorts used in crash analysis. Figures have been calculated by averaging across age cohorts where necessary — the 16-24 age cohort is likely to be an underestimate of participation in cycling. Percentages of each age cohort that regularly cycled in 2011 are as follows: 0 -9, 57%; 10-17, 29%; 18-39, 15.6%; 40+, 8.1% (Austroads, 2011, p.42.)

forms cycling as socially unacceptable and cyclists as socially undesirable. It is impossible to determine exactly how an advertisement will be interpreted across its entire audience. However, by devaluing cycling and cyclists, the MAC campaign may go beyond deterring young people from cycling to providing tacit support for behaviours that undermine the safety of cyclists.

The Motor Accident Commission does not simply reflect or re-present an existing view of cycling and cyclists. Rather, the MAC, as a site located within the discursive practice of safety, actively participates in producing cycling and cyclists in particular ways — in this instance, as immature, socially inept, physically slow and sexually undesirable. It is possible for the MAC to assemble these characteristics together because of the *ongoing-formation* of cycling and cyclists within a multiplicity of discursive practices — from transport and psychology to law and economics. The formation of the cyclist by the MAC contrasts with the formation of cycling and cyclists in discursive practices such as health and environment. Sites within these discursive practices — such as the Heart Foundation, the Australian Bicycle Council, the Department of Transport, Schools of Public Health — are forming cycling as a valuable way of travelling, and cyclists as responsible subjects of health, environment, and urban economics (for example, in terms of road congestion).

Young people cycling are problematised in the MAC campaign, and yet they are considerably less likely to harm themselves in crashes than young motorists or middle-aged cyclists. Several other approaches to this advertising campaign are possible. They range from post-licence training programs (Fisher, Pollatsek, & Pradhan, 2006; Isler, Starkey & Sheppard, 2011; Raftery & Wundersitz, 2011; Beanland, Goode, Salmon, & Lenne, 2013) through to advertising campaigns that are both humorous and positive (New Zealand Transport Authority, 2011) and do not promote one form of mobility at the expense of another.

The important point for organisations, researchers, policy makers and so forth is to reflect critically on how they produce the objects (such as cycling and driving) and subjects (such as cyclists, motorists, young people) in their policies, programs and research. We do not simply reflect what already exists: we actively participate in constituting what exists.

References

Abbott-Chapman, J, Denholm, C, & Wyld, C. (2008). Gender differences in adolescent risk taking: Are they diminishing? An Australian intergenerational study. *Youth & Society*, 40(1), 131-154.

Adams, J. (1970). Residential structure of mid-western cities. *Annals of the Association of American Geographers*, 60(1), 37-62.

Advertising Standards Bureau [ASB]. (2011, November 14). *Case report: Motor Accident Commission SA*. Case Number: 0335/11. ACT. Retrieved 24 July 2015 from http://ms.adstandards.com.au/cases/0335-11.pdf.

Austroads. (2011). *Australian cycling participation 2011*. Publication no: AP-C91-11. Sydney: Austroads. Retrieved 24 July 2015 from https://www.onlinepublications.austroads.com.au/items/AP-C91-11.

Bacchi, C. (2009). *Analysing policy: What's the problem represented to be?* French's Forest: Pearson Australia.

Bacchi, C. (2012). Why study problematizations? Making politics visible. *Open

Journal of Political Science, 2(1), 1-8.

Bacchi, C. (2015). Problematizations in alcohol policy: WHO's 'alcohol problems'. *Contemporary Drug Problems*, 42(2), 130-147.

Bacchi, C, & Bonham, J. (2014). Reclaiming discursive practices as an analytic focus: Political implications. *Foucault Studies*, 17, 179-192.

Beanland, V, Goode, N, Salmon, PM, & Lenne, MG. (2013). Is there a case for driver training? A review of the efficacy of pre- and post-licence driver training. *Safety Science*, 51(1), 127-137.

Bonham, J. (2000, April 13-15). Safety and speed: Ordering the street of transport. In C Garnaut, & S Hamnett (Eds.), *Fifth Urban History/Planning History Conference — Proceedings* (pp. 54-66). Adelaide: The University of South Australia.

Bonham, J. (2002). *The conduct of travel: Beginning a genealogy of the travelling subject* (Unpublished PhD Thesis, The University of Adelaide, Australia).

Bonham, J. (2006). Transport: Disciplining the body that travels. *Sociological Review*, 54 (Supplement 1), 57-74.

Bonham, J, & Bacchi, C. (2013, January 6-7). Forming cycling 'subjectivities': Interviews as political interventions. *Foucault and Mobilites Symposium*, University of Lucerne, Lucerne, Switzerland.

Bureau of Infrastructure, Transport and Regional Economics [BITRE]. (2013a). *Young adult road safety — A statistical picture*. Information Sheet 51. Canberra, ACT: BITRE. Retrieved 24 July 2015 from https://www.bitre.gov.au/publications/2013/is_051.aspx.

Bureau of Infrastructure, Transport and Regional Economics [BITRE]. (2013b). *Road deaths Australia, 2012 Statistical Summary*. Canberra, ACT: BITRE. Retrieved 24 July 2015 from https://www.bitre.gov.au/publications/ongoing/road_deaths_australia_annual_summaries.aspx.

City of Adelaide. (2012). *Smart move: Transport and movement strategy 2012-2020*. Adelaide: City of Adelaide.

Curry, A, Hafetz, J, Kallan, M, Winston, F, & Durbin, D. (2011). Prevalence of teen driver errors leading to serious motor vehicle crashes. *Accident Analysis & Prevention*, 43(4), 1285-1290.

Daley, M, & Rissel, C. (2011). Perspectives and images of cycling as a barrier or facilitator of cycling. *Transport Policy*, 18(1), 211-216.

Delaney, A, Lough, B, Whelan, M, & Cameron, M. (2004). *A review of mass media campaigns in road safety*. Report No. 220. Monash: Monash University Accident Research Centre.

Delbosc, A, & Currie, G. (2014). Using discussion forums to explore attitudes toward cars and licensing among young Australians. *Transport Policy*, 31, 27-34.

Department of Planning, Transport and Infrastructure [DPTI]. (2012). *Road crashes in South Australia: Statistical summary of road crashes & casualties in 2011*. Statistical report. Adelaide: Government of South Australia.

Department of Planning, Transport and Infrastructure [DPTI]. (2014). My licence — P1 Provisional Licence rules. Retrieved 24 July 2015 from http://mylicence.sa.gov.au/my-car-licence/p1-provisional-licence.

Fergusson, D, Swain-Campbell, N, & Horwood, J. (2003). Risky driving behaviour in young people: Prevalence, personal characteristics and traffic accidents. *Australian and New Zealand Journal of Public Health*, 27, 337-342.

Fincham, B. (2007). Bicycle messengers: Image, identity and community. In D Horton, P Rosen, & P Cox (Eds.), *Cycling and society* (pp. 133-152). Hampshire: Ashgate.

Fisher, DL, Pollatsek, AP, & Pradhan, A. (2006). Can novice drivers be trained to scan for information that will reduce their likelihood of a crash? *Injury Prevention*, 12 (Supplement 1), i25-i29.

Forster, C. (2004). *Australian cities: Continuity and change* (3rd ed.). South Melbourne: Oxford University Press.

Furness, Z. (2010). *One less car: Bicycling and the politics of automobility*. Philadelphia, PA: Temple University Press.

Goodwin, S. (2012). Women, policy and politics: Recasting policy studies. In A Bletsas, & C Beasley (Eds.), *Engaging with Carol Bacchi: Strategic interventions and exchanges* (pp. 25-36). Adelaide: University of Adelaide Press.

Hörschelmann, K, & Colls, R. (2010). *Contested bodies of childhood and youth*. Basingstoke: Palgrave Macmillan.

Horton, D. (2007). Fear of Cycling. In D Horton, P Rosen, & P Cox (Eds.), *Cycling and society* (pp. 133-152). Hampshire: Ashgate.

Isler, RB, Starkey, NJ, & Sheppard, P. (2011). Effects of higher-order driving skill training on young, inexperienced drivers' on-road driving performance.

Accident Analysis & Prevention, 43(5), 1818-1827.

Jacobsen, P. (2003). Safety in numbers: More walkers and bicyclists, safer walking and bicycling. *Injury Prevention*, 9, 205-209.

Jain, J, & Lyons, G. (2008). The gift of travel time. *Journal of Transport Geography*, 16(2), 81-89.

Kaye, SA, White, MJ, & Lewis, IM. (2013). Individual differences in drivers' cognitive processing of road safety messages. *Accident Analysis & Prevention*, 50, 272-281.

Kloep, M, Güney, N, Cok, F, & Simsek, ÖF. (2009). Motives for risk-taking in adolescence: A cross-cultural study. *Journal of Adolescence*, 32(1), 135-151.

Lindsay, G, Macmillan, A, & Woodward, A. (2011). Moving urban trips from cars to bicycles: Impact on health and emissions. *Australian and New Zealand Journal of Public Health*, 35(1), 54-60.

Lipschutz, R. (2012). Getting out of the car: Decarbonisation, climate change and sustainable society. *International Journal of Sustainable Society*, 4(4), 336-356.

Maring, W, & Van Schagen, I. (1990). Age dependence of attitudes and knowledge in cyclists. *Accident Analysis & Prevention*, 22(2), 127-136.

Marshall, N. (2012). Digging deeper: The challenge of problematizing 'inclusive development' and 'disability mainstreaming'. In A Bletsas, & C Beasley (Eds.), *Engaging with Carol Bacchi: Strategic interventions and exchanges* (pp. 53-70). Adelaide: University of Adelaide Press.

Mees, P. (2010). *Transport for suburbia: Beyond the Automobile Age*. London: Earthscan.

Motor Accident Commission [MAC]. (n.d.). Lose your licence and you're screwed. Retrieved 27 May 2014 from http://www.youtube.com/watch?v=J8lZT-L1AR.

Newman, P, Kenworthy, J, & Glazebrook, G. (2008). How to create exponential decline in car use in Australia cities. *Australian Planner*, 45(3), 17-19.

New Zealand Transport Authority. (2011). *'Legend' campaign* [Youtube video]. Retrieved 27 May 2014 from http://www.youtube.com/watch?v=CtWirGxV7Q8.

Paterson, M. (2007). *Automobile politics: Ecology and cultural political economy*. Cambridge: Cambridge University Press.

Phillips, RO, Ulleberg, P, & Vaa, T. (2011). Meta-analysis of the effect of road safety campaigns on accidents. *Accident Analysis & Prevention*, 43(3), 1204-1218.

Pucher, J, & Buehler, R. (2008). Making cycling irresistible: Lessons from the Netherlands, Denmark and Germany. *Transport Reviews*, 28(4), 495-528.

Raftery, SJ, & Wundersitz, LN. (2011). *The efficacy of road safety education in schools: A review of current approaches*. Report No. CASR077. Adelaide: Centre for Automotive Safety Research.

Rissel, C, Bonfigliolo, C, Emilsen, A, & Smith, BJ. (2010). Representations of cycling in Metropolitan newspapers — Changes over time and differences between Sydney and Melbourne, Australia. In J Bonham, & P Lumb (Eds.), *Australian Cycling Conference 2012: Proceedings of the Second Australian Cycling Conference* (pp. 1-10). Adelaide: The University of Adelaide.

Rybarczyk, G, & Gallagher, L. (2014). Measuring the potential for bicycling and walking at a metropolitan commuter university. *Journal of Transport Geography*, 39, 1-10.

Schwanen, T, Banister, D, & Anable, J. (2011). Scientific research about climate change mitigation in transport: A critical review. *Transportation Research Part A*, 45, 993-1006.

Skinner, D, & Rosen, P. (2007). Hell is other cyclists: Rethinking transport and identity. In D Horton, P Rosen, & P Cox (Eds.), *Cycling and society* (pp. 83-96). Hampshire: Ashgate.

Tay, R. (2005). The effectiveness of enforcement and publicity campaigns on serious crashes involving young male drivers: Are drink driving and speeding similar? *Accident Analysis & Prevention*, 37(5), 922-929.

Tymula, A, Belmaker, LAR, Roy, AK, Ruderman, L, Manson, K, Glimcher, PW, & Levy, I. (2012). Adolescents' risk-taking behavior is driven by tolerance to ambiguity. *Proceedings of the National Academy of Sciences*, 109(42), 17135-17140.

Ulleberg, P. (2001). Personality subtypes of young drivers: Relationship to risk-taking preferences, accident involvement, and response to a traffic safety campaign. Transportation Research Part F, 4(4), 279-297.

Urry, J. (2004). The system of automobility. *Theory, Culture and Society*, 21(4-5), 25-39.

Walton, D, & McKeown, PC. (2001). Drivers' biased perceptions of speed and safety campaign messages. *Accident Analysis & Prevention, 33*(5), 629-640.

Wimmer, DR, & Dominick, JR. (2006). *Mass media research: An introduction* (8th ed.). USA: Cengage Learning.

Wundersitz, LN. (2012). *An analysis of young drivers involved in crashes using in-depth crash investigation data.* Report No. CASR101. Adelaide: Centre for Automotive Safety Research.

Wundersitz, LN, Hutchinson, TP, & Woolley, JE. (2010). Best practice in road safety mass media campaigns: A literature review. *Social Psychology, 5,* 119-186.

12 Spaces for cycling

Glen Koorey

Introduction

Across Australasia (and indeed the world) the debate has long continued about how to best provide for cycling. Leaving aside for now issues such as cycling promotions, driver behaviour and relevant legislation, which are covered in other chapters of this volume, the physical infrastructure and spaces provided play a crucial role in ensuring that existing people cycling have adequate levels of service (thus preventing further declines in numbers) whilst also attracting more people to choose to cycle.

High traffic speeds and volumes, as well as poor cycling facilities, are often identified as key deterrents to cycling in areas of relatively low cycling usage like Australasia. There is also some tension between those who want separated (often off-road) cycle facilities and those who prefer 'integrated' (on-road) facilities. The state of the art of professional guidance in this part of the world is still rapidly evolving; even the latest Austroads guidelines (Austroads, 2014) do not reflect some of the most recent developments elsewhere or guidance from countries demonstrating the world's best practice in cycling (for example, Centre for Research & Contract Standardisation in Civil Engineering [CROW], 2007, in the Netherlands).

This chapter provides some reflections on these issues, based on current research and practice in this area. It will focus particularly on on-road spaces for cycling.

Terminology

Before continuing the discussion, it is useful to clarify some of the terminology being used. Cycle facilities are often called by various names, which can lead to confusion by both practitioners and the general public alike about what exactly is being referred to. Lieswyn et al. (2012) provided a useful breakdown of cycling[1] facility types, with the following key points:

- 'Cycleway' is generally an all-encompassing term for describing all types of dedicated cycling facilities.
- 'Cycle lane' describes an on-road cycling facility, often denoted only by road markings. A variation of this is a 'protected' or 'segregated' cycle lane, where cycles and motorised traffic are separated by some form of physical divider.
- 'Cycle path' describes an off-road cycling facility, either behind the roadway kerb or completely away from road alignments. A 'shared path' also allows pedestrians[2] and other non-motorised users to use it.
- 'Cycle track' usually describes a specific cycle path facility (originally of Danish origin) that is separated vertically by kerbs from both the roadway and the footpath (sometimes referred to as 'Copenhagen lanes'). Note that this is different from a (usually recreational and often unsealed) 'cycle trail'.
- 'Separated bicycle facility' [SBF] is sometimes used to denote those treatments (on- or off-road) that are solely for cyclists and that provide some form of physical separation from other road users.

---

[1] It should be noted that the terms 'cycling' and 'cycle' are more inclusive than 'bicycle' or 'bike' when referring to infrastructure, as generally such facilities are also available for other self-propelled vehicles, including three-wheeled cycles (for example, recumbent three-wheelers and cargo trikes).

[2] 'Pedestrian' in this case means any person on foot or using a mobility aid or means of conveyance propelled by human power, *other than* by cycle — for example, a wheelchair, rollerblades, skateboard, mobility scooter, and so on.

- There are also various treatments that do not involve a specific cycling facility, including 'bicycle boulevards', shared-lane markings, wide kerbside lanes and shared spaces.

These terminology conventions will be applied in this chapter.

Options for cycle provision

There are a number of different options that could be considered when providing for cycling[3] (this list being by no means exhaustive):

- Do nothing to an existing street, on the basis that it is already adequate for cycling on.[4]
- Introduce traffic management/calming features on streets to reduce the volume of traffic, slow down the traffic, and/or remove major pinch points for cyclists.
- Provide marked on-road cycle lanes.
- Provide segregated cycle facilities in the road corridor, often behind the kerb line.
- Provide cycle paths completely away from road corridors — for example, through parks or utility corridors.

It is, in fact, likely that an overall network will contain a mixture of all of these options. Questions may well remain, however, about what the relative proportions should be. Certainly, around the world there has been a whole spectrum of responses with regards to how much the pendulum swings towards on- or off-road solutions — for example, contrast the extensive off-road networks of the Netherlands with the historically much larger on-road component of many Anglo-centric countries like the United States, Australia and New Zealand (although this can vary by city).

---

[3] Note that 'providing for cycling' is rather different from 'providing cycle facilities'. In many cases, in the former instance no specific cycle facilities (such as lanes or paths) are actually provided, yet the environment for cycling is improved.

[4] Although this may be true for quiet local streets, a similar line is often put forward for streets in general by proponents of 'vehicular cycling' (for example, Forester, 2001).

Cycling preferences

Various stances are often espoused by cyclists[5] or would-be cyclists. Two quite different viewpoints identified by Koorey (2005), for example, are:

- The regular experienced rider (perhaps also a serious sports cyclist) prefers to stay on-road because of the perceived directness and lack of hazards such as pedestrians and poor path standards. Such cyclists have few concerns with motor traffic, so long as adequate space is provided for them (for example, a road shoulder or cycle lane).
- The current non-cyclist (or parent of a young cyclist) is concerned about the prospect of cycling on roads with motor traffic (especially busy roads, or roads with high posted speed limits). As a result, such cyclists would like to see more pathways provided, whether alongside the road or (even better) along separate 'green corridors'.

For someone trying to provide a network for all (potential) cyclists, it can seem very difficult to reconcile all these conflicting viewpoints. However, as noted by Kingham and Tranter (Chapter Seven, this volume), the latter viewpoint can often be the key to growing cycling numbers. Frustration is also sometimes expressed by various parties (for example, transport planners or politicians), who may feel that people will not use the cycle facilities provided (often with an implied threat of limiting future cycleway funding). Following the death in 2010 of a woman cycling in Auckland who was hit by a truck, an official report suggested that she should have used the adjacent off-road 'cycleway', despite the facility in question being a very narrow and busy shared path (Dearnaley, 2012).

Examination of feedback from existing or would-be cyclists identifies concerns that seem to centre around the perceived quality and level of service that would be afforded by the alternative options. For example:

---

[5] The term 'cyclist' will be used sparingly in this chapter. The aim is to promote and provide for 'cycling', not 'cyclists'. The former term is an activity that virtually anyone can do for transport under the right circumstances, whereas the latter often gives connotations of a relatively small bunch of 'weird' people who only ever cycle, or aggressive lycra-clad sports riders. Therefore, communications like policy advice, strategic planning documents, promotional material and media releases should also be careful not to create 'us and them' situations by referring to 'cyclists'. For more information, refer to Koorey (2007).

- On-road cycling is often associated with lots of motor traffic (often fast and polluting), conflicts with parked vehicles, inconsistent provision for cycling along routes, and sometimes very little space for cycling.
- Off-road cycling is often associated with narrow paths with poor construction/maintenance standards, where conflicts with pedestrians and other users are commonplace, and it is difficult to cross roads and accessways (see Figure 12.1).

Clearly, a lot of this bad reputation is not due to the type of facility per se, but the quality of facility that has been provided to date: a bad experience may leave a strong imprint in a rider's mind. Historically, in many countries where cycling culture is not strong, authorities have often stinted on cycle facilities (widths in particular have been very inadequate) and have probably paid little attention to related issues such as traffic volumes/speeds.

It is useful to remember that some reluctance to use alternative facilities may stem simply from lack of knowledge about what is available. For example, while many adults who also drive may be familiar with the road network in general, they may not know about some path alternatives or where they lead to. Similarly, some pathway proponents may be wary of travelling along a road for fear that

Figure 12.1: Substandard shared pathway next to parking, Auckland, New Zealand. (Source: Author.)

any cycle facilities will end abruptly and leave them in a dangerous position. This is where extensive destination/route signage and cycle maps can be very handy allies. New facilities should also be strongly promoted via the media when they are completed.

Theoretical underpinnings

The 'four types of cyclist'

Geller (2009) expounded a useful way of thinking about the various groups of people who might be attracted (or not) to cycling. Conceived initially for the development of the *Portland bike plan* (City of Portland, 2010), the 'four types of cyclist' concept has subsequently found broad appeal in many other parts of the world that are trying to grow their cycling modal share.

Essentially, the concept is that the general adult population can be placed into one of the four following groups, based on their relationship to cycling for transportation:

- The *strong and fearless* are perhaps 1-2% of the population at most, who will ride regardless of the roadway conditions.
- The *enthused and confident* are 5-10% of the population — that is, those who are comfortable sharing the roadway with motorised traffic, so long as they are provided with their own spaces for cycling, including cycle lanes, shoulders and intersection areas like advanced stop boxes.
- The *interested but concerned* are the largest group, perhaps 50-60% of people — those who would be attracted to cycling if they had cycling facilities separate from traffic, or alternatively streets with very low traffic volumes and speeds.
- The final group, perhaps up to one-third of the population, are called the *no way, no how* group and are simply not interested in cycling for transportation, regardless of the environment provided.

The separation between these four broad groups is not quite as clear-cut as described above. In reality, there is likely to be a continuum of views across the populace, which blurs the lines (for example, certain separated cycle facilities might appeal to some, but not all, *interested but concerned* people). However, this concept has proven to be a reasonable way to understand the existing and potential cyclists within a population.

A common theme in this categorisation is people's relative level of concern or 'fear' about cycling with traffic. This leads to identification of what it would take to get more people cycling. For example, those cities that have provided no more than simple unprotected cycling infrastructure — such as marked cycle lanes — have often typically attracted less than 10% of people regularly cycling for transport. However, those places that have invested in more separated facilities (with many notable examples in the Netherlands and Denmark) have typically had well in excess of 25% of the population regularly cycling.

It should be noted that the level of investment to achieve such cycling provision in Amsterdam, Copenhagen and the like has typically been about AU$30-40/year per capita (Holligan, 2013), whereas Australian states and territories have generally been spending about AU$4-6/year per capita (Australian Bicycle Council, 2014). Similar investment rates have historically been found in New Zealand, too, although recently there have been notable examples of more substantial expenditure, such as the NZ$70 million 'Major Cycleways' program in Christchurch costing about AU$35/year per capita (Transportblog, 2014).

Geller's typology has since been verified by Dill and McNeil (2013), who analysed phone interviews from over 900 Portland residents. The relative proportions of respondents across the Portland region who fell into the four categories appeared to match Geller's original estimates relatively well. They noted that women seemed to be less represented in the *strong* or *enthused* categories, while people over 35 years of age were less prominent in the *strong and fearless* category. Those categorised as *interested but concerned* were also much more comfortable with separated cycle facilities or quiet, low-speed streets than other treatments. Similar research is currently underway in Christchurch, New Zealand.

The effect of speed

A significant challenge for cycle planning at present in most parts of Australasia is the lack of acknowledgment of the role that lower traffic speeds can play in encouraging more cycling and reducing the crash risk. In many other Western countries, particularly in Europe, speed limits less than our conventional 50 km/h

Strategies for change

(urban) and 100 km/h (rural) defaults are commonly used. Away from Australasia, there is also a significant take-up in road treatments that encourage slower speeds (for example, 'self-explaining roads', shared spaces and traffic-calming devices), with or without the presence of supporting speed limits.

Although there have been a few positive localised initiatives in recent times (for example, Charlton et al., 2010; see Figure 12.2), New Zealand has generally been rather slow in adopting these practices, a matter that is of particular concern both when considering the safety of cycling and encouraging a greater use of this mode. This was acknowledged by New Zealand's Cycling Safety Panel (2014), whose final report identified measures to reduce traffic speeds around people cycling as one of the high-priority recommendations. Similar cultural attitudes also exist in Australia, with the general public not seeing the benefit in lower speed limits, especially in urban areas (Lahausse, van Nes, Fildes, Langford, & Keall, 2009).

A number of official publications over the years have quoted the relative effects of motor vehicle impact speed on the 'survivability' of pedestrians and cyclists struck by them (for example, Ministry of Transport [MOT], 2010). Some past studies have suggested that, at impact speeds of 70 km/h and above, the chances of survival are less than 10%. However, more recent research by Rosén,

Figure 12.2: Low-speed street environment in Auckland, New Zealand. (Source: Author.)

Stigson, and Sander (2011) has identified methodological flaws in the earlier work, which resulted in a bias to more severe injuries; also, modern motor vehicle designs and medical care are now somewhat better at minimising the injuries of externally struck people. Nevertheless, it is clear that the relative fatality risk as speeds go up still increases considerably. For example, Rosén and Sander (2009) conclude that the risk of pedestrian fatality if struck at 50 km/h is twice that at 40 km/h and five times that at 30 km/h.

Koorey (2011) undertook a simple study of New Zealand pedestrian and cycle crash severities based on speed limits, and noted a clear distinction between the respective fatality rates (pedestrians being higher). Most overseas studies (such as those identified by Rosén et al., 2011) have focused on pedestrian impacts, and the findings have then been assumed to translate to other similarly vulnerable road users like cyclists. The findings of the New Zealand research suggest that this is not correct, possibly due to the different relative speeds of cyclists, the types of collisions, the ages of the two road user groups, and the mechanics of impacts with bicycles. Further research into this issue would be worthwhile.

Perceptions of quiet streets can also affect the likelihood of people undertaking active modes in the first place. For example, Trumper (2013) investigated a number of pairs of adjacent residential streets in Christchurch, New Zealand, one with a normal 50 km/h street environment and one with a lower-speed 'slow zone' environment. Residents who were interviewed noted that traffic speed and safety had 'some-moderate' influence on average on their own propensity to walk to local destinations. However, when it came to their children, parents were more protective with regards to the speed of traffic and safety of their children, with traffic speed and safety having a 'moderate-large' influence on average. Respondents also felt safer walking down the slow zone street, compared with the untreated street, particularly in terms of crossing it. This is also reflected in the perception that 73% of residents felt that traffic in the slow zone travelled more slowly than traffic in the untreated street. It is reasonable to conclude that similar perceptions would apply when deciding whether to cycle or not. Traffic speed has also been cited by Jacobsen, Racioppi, and Rutter (2009) as a reason for people not walking or cycling as much as desired. Kingham and Tranter discuss the effects of speed further in their earlier chapter (Chapter Seven) in this volume.

Strategies for change

Hierarchy of cycling treatments

Provision for cycling may not require specific cycle facilities *en route*. The following 'five-step hierarchy' of treatments, developed in the United Kingdom (Institution of Highways and Transportation [IHT], Cyclists' Touring Club [CTC], Bicycle Association, & Department of Transport, 1996), has been previously proposed when providing for cycling in the existing transport network. Practitioners considering cycle treatments for a particular route work their way down the hierarchy, testing the feasibility of each step.

1. **Reduce traffic volumes**: Local area traffic management schemes (particularly where cyclists can bypass the closures and restrictions) and off-road shortcuts are some ways of achieving this (see Figure 12.3).
2. **Reduce traffic speeds**: Lower speeds reduce the speed differential between cyclists and motor vehicles and the risk of severe injury (as well as the perceived risk). Some options here include 30-40 km/h

Figure 12.3: Cycle bypass of a street closure, Melbourne, Victoria. (Source: Author.)

(20-25 mph) speed zones, traffic-calming measures, narrowing of very wide carriageways, and deflection at roundabouts.

3. **Intersection treatment and traffic management**: Many of the biggest impediments for cycling are actually relatively small 'pinch points' — for example, no waiting space at intersections, narrow shoulders and bridges, difficult locations for crossing or turning. These should be identified and addressed.
4. **Reallocation of, or additional, carriageway space**: Road corridors often have more than enough room to cater for cycling, particularly if underused or oversized traffic/parking lanes and medians are removed or modified, or if shoulders are extended.
5. **Specific cycle facilities**: If the above approaches are not appropriate, then specific provision of cycle lanes, pathways and underpasses/overbridges may be required.

The first thing to notice about this list is that traditional 'cycle facility' solutions are at the very bottom — that is, they should be the *last* thing to consider. The next thing to notice is that the treatments above this are often barely discussed in some district cycling strategies.

One has to be a bit careful about interpreting this hierarchy. For example, it could be argued that an off-road cycle path helps to meet Objectives 1 and 2 in the hierarchy by shifting cycling away from traffic. This is no good, however, to many riders if the path in question is less direct than the on-road route they would prefer to take, or if it introduces new problems at intersections and road crossings (violating hierarchy Objective 3) or if the path creates problems for cyclists from sharing the space with pedestrians and other non-motorised users (hierarchy Objective 4).

In many respects, the hierarchy is intuitive in terms of why many people say they *do not* cycle. The stock reply is often, 'Cycling is too dangerous' (for example, in Kingham, Taylor & Koorey, 2011). However, if this response is teased out, then more specific answers are likely to be, 'I'm afraid of all that traffic'; 'The traffic is much too fast'; 'I hate the pinch point at location xyz'; or 'I keep getting squeezed by motorists'. Tellingly, these responses are dealt with by the first four steps of the hierarchy. It is far less likely for people to not cycle solely because there are no cycle facilities *en route*.

The hierarchy also reflects the fact that, even with a comprehensive network of cycle facilities, the end points of many cycle trips will be on the conventional street network, and much of the cycling is also likely to be away from specific cycle facilities. This point may not be an issue if the final destination happens to be a quiet residential cul-de-sac; it may be more of a problem if the cyclist is heading for a major shopping centre on an arterial road. These trips also need to be catered for, and using the hierarchy provides a total network approach. Therefore municipal agencies should always take heed of the credo from the famous Geelong Bike Plan of 1977: 'Every street is a cycling street' (State Bicycle Committee, 1977).

Everyone should be able to coherently access all of their desired destinations by cycle. Using the hierarchy allows one to concentrate more on area-wide treatments. As explained by Patterson, Crowther & Solly (2003), this avoids the problem whereby only certain 'routes' are improved for cycling, while other streets do not receive any consideration and often become worse over time for cycling (particularly if traffic conditions continue to get worse). Focusing solely on site- and route-based cycle provision marginalises those who have to cycle via other routes. Therefore, some consideration needs to be given to treatments that ensure adequate cycle provision in non-priority areas. For example, local area traffic management and low-speed residential zones can be used across large areas to make cycling more attractive in those areas, or intersections could be treated to improve cycle crossing ability.

Parkin and Koorey (2012) note that a flaw of the 'five step hierarchy' is that it presumes that the route has already been determined (typically along a road), and that it is now just a matter of identifying the correct treatment. They suggest that spatial planning and demand modelling are important prior steps to considering the broader network first. These steps may include the identification, provision and protection of suitable corridors for cycling (whether along road networks or elsewhere). Otherwise, one may be constrained in terms of optimal treatment options available via the 'five step hierarchy' process.

'Best practice' guidance

Land Transport New Zealand [LTNZ] provides some useful advice about the merits of roads and paths (2004). Some key points highlighted include:

- It is generally only practical to consider a fully segregated (off-road) cycle network when planning new suburbs and townships.
- Where comprehensive off-road networks have been developed with poor standards and little directness or coherence, they have failed to provide a greater modal share for cycling. The experience of Milton Keynes's 'Redways' in the United Kingdom is a salutary lesson in this regard (Franklin, 1999).
- Increased segregation from motor traffic is usually accompanied by increased interference from pedestrians, pets, skateboarders, slower cyclists and so on.
- One choice (path or road) is not inherently safer than another; both can be hazardous and both require high-quality design to achieve safety.
- The needs of commuter and leisure can potentially be met by both road and path solutions: it is incorrect to assume that they require mutually exclusive facilities.
- Along paths, the freedom from traffic danger brings obvious benefits for novice and child cyclists, who can focus on practising basic cycle control skills.

LTNZ (2004) also suggests that dual networks may be pragmatic in some cases to provide a range of options for different cyclists. In Christchurch, New Zealand, for example, an off-road pathway was constructed adjacent to a high school and intermediate school to help pupils cycling to school. The adjacent road is also a popular adult commuter route and so on-road cycle lanes have been provided as well.

Surveying would-be riders

Kingham et al. (2011) investigated the barriers to cycle use in New Zealand, with a specific focus on the infrastructure needed to attract people who do not cycle regularly for utility trip purposes. The researchers surveyed workplaces, recreational cyclists and community groups in Christchurch to identify potential (but not current) regular utility cyclists. Focus groups were then held with them to discuss the motivations for, and barriers to, cycling. In addition, a series of plans and pictures of various types of cycling infrastructure (both mid-block and intersections) were shown. Participants were asked to rate each of the options on a four-point qualitative scale regarding how often they would cycle if the option shown was the standard along their utility cycle routes, and if their other personal barriers had been eliminated.

Common barriers to utility cycling were identified in the focus groups. Safety, particularly traffic behaviour and the perceived safety of cycle lanes, was clearly of most importance. Less crucial, but also mentioned regularly, were workplace showering or changing facilities and the simple enjoyment of the journey. People would cycle when the route was attractive, but also when it was considered safe, so that they did not have to be constantly on their guard for motorists' behaviour.

Cycling infrastructure preferences

Participants in the focus groups were shown examples of a variety of different types of cycle infrastructure for mid-block street sections, signalised intersections (both through-movements and right-hand turns) and roundabouts. These examples (presented in random order) drew on existing New Zealand and international cycle infrastructure and ranged from no specific provision through a variety of on-road and off-road treatments. Brief discussion was also raised with the participants in regard to traffic calming and local area traffic management as means of providing a cycle-friendly environment without cycle facilities. However, there was little understanding and hence enthusiasm displayed for these options, possibly due to the lack of experience of such environments in New Zealand.

The most preferred type of facility for mid-block street sections were kerbed cycle tracks adjacent to the traffic lane, as they were seen to be keeping the rider in the view of vehicles; or, alternatively, a path between parking and the footpath. For signalised intersections where cyclists were performing a straight-ahead manoeuvre, the favoured infrastructure was on-road cycle lanes; and for right-hand turn manoeuvres, the most preferred were hook-turns (where cyclists stay on the kerbside and cross in two phases; see Figure 12.4: A hook turn box to allow two-stage right turns, in Christchurch, New Zealand. (Source: Author.)4). 'Head-start' traffic signals for right-turning cyclists were also liked by participants, but interestingly there were concerns about delaying the general traffic with this type of facility.

Figure 12.4: A hook turn box to allow two-stage right turns, in Christchurch, New Zealand.
(Source: Author.)

Roundabouts continued to be viewed as extremely difficult, with most participants preferring signalised intersections. Although the research attempted to focus participants' attention on low-speed, single-lane roundabouts, clearly their responses were influenced by many of the higher-speed, multi-lane roundabouts prevalent in New Zealand. Underpasses were considered extremely safe in the physical sense, but there were concerns for social safety, particularly after dark. There seemed to be little agreement on other types of roundabout infrastructure, such as cycle lanes or paths; both had benefits and difficulties.

An interesting observation from the focus group discussions was the lack of understanding of how to use some of the treatment options presented, even when they were already reasonably prevalent around Christchurch. Participants were not always clear about when they should use certain facilities, where they should position themselves, or what their rights were in respect to other road/path users (or whether those other users knew what to do). Some participants noted that the facilities generally did not have sufficient explanatory material (for example, advance signs), and that there was virtually no public education on using these facilities. Participants pointed out that if there was more consistency of cycling infrastructure, then *all* road users would be more likely to understand how to use various facilities — and consequently inexperienced people would have more confidence when cycling.

It is important to provide a type of infrastructure that will appeal to current utility cyclists but, perhaps more importantly, will also attract the 'next 10%' of people to regularly cycle for utilitarian reasons. The findings suggest that potential cyclists (in Christchurch, at least) will be attracted to regular cycling through a network of infrastructure that provides separation from other users rather than shared space. The results displayed a common trend of people preferring to have some level of separation from traffic but to be kept within view of drivers. While sharing with pedestrians was also disliked (it was seen as no better than marked cycle lanes), it was preferred to sharing space with motor vehicles.

Some lessons learned

The above discussion leads to some emerging trends in regards to cycling provision in Australasia, which will be explored below.

On-road marked cycle lanes

Cycle lanes help to specify where motor vehicles and riders should position themselves to safely interact. They also have a useful side effect: their mere presence helps to remind motorists of the possibility of people cycling nearby, making them more likely to (even subconsciously) 'look for cyclists'. The relative narrowing of the remaining traffic lane by installation of cycle lanes can also provide a slight speed-calming effect (Fowler & Koorey, 2006). The relatively low cost of cycle lanes has made them a long-time favourite of many Australasian roading authorities (the bigger hurdle often being when their introduction requires the removal of car parking).

However, for many people there is only limited appeal to use them for cycling, and there are even regular claims that cycle lanes are 'dangerous'. Where poorly designed lanes have been created (for example, under-width lanes next to parked vehicles), this response is perhaps justifiable. However, recent evidence would suggest that well-designed cycle lanes have a useful safety benefit.

Parsons and Koorey (2013) investigated the relative effects on cycle count and crash numbers of installing a series of cycle lanes. Twelve routes (approximately 24 kilometres in total) installed in Christchurch during the mid-2000s were analysed, together with three previously installed control sites. Ongoing cycle count data from a series of route locations was used to establish cycling trends before and after installation. These were also compared against cycle crash numbers along these routes during the same periods. Overall, the average reduction in the cycle crash rate (crashes per kilometre cycled) was 43%, with 7 of 12 treated routes experiencing a reduction in crash rates of 40% or greater. Adjusting for the observed control site crash reductions, the expected overall average crash reduction after installing cycle lanes was 23%.

Further improvement of the perception of existing cycle lanes may come from the simple introduction of low-cost separators. A wide variety of physical devices and delineators are now available to provide such separation. Koorey, Wilke, and Aussendorf (2013) investigated on-road trials in Christchurch of low, raised cycle-lane separators and vertical delineator posts. Separators were placed in two locations where motorists were commonly encroaching into cycle lanes, on the inside of curves and approaching intersections. Road-user behaviour was observed before and after installation, and qualitative feedback was also sought from site users.

The results showed a significant effect on reducing motor vehicle encroachments following installation, particularly when the low separators were supplemented by vertical posts. Very positive feedback was also received from existing cyclists, especially women. Further cycle lane separators have subsequently been retrofitted around Christchurch (see Figure 12.5: Cycle lane with separator posts and coloured surfacing in Christchurch, New Zealand. (Source: Author.)). Another useful treatment is the act of colouring conflict points — for example, Koorey and Mangundu (2010) found that motorists were significantly less likely to encroach into cycle lanes and boxes at intersections if they had coloured surfacing.

Separated cycle facilities

The cycle lane separator trials mentioned above highlight a growing interest in Australasia in introducing various forms of separation from at least motor traffic (if not pedestrians, too) as part of cycleways along arterial routes. This mirrors a similar trend in North America over the past five years,

Strategies for change

Figure 12.5: Cycle lane with separator posts and coloured surfacing in Christchurch, New Zealand.
(Source: Author.)

Figure 12.6: A two-way separated cycle path in central Brisbane, Queensland.
(Source: Author.)

which has seen a proliferation of new protected cycle facilities, particularly inspired by new technical guidance there (National Association of City Transportation Officials [NACTO], 2010). In a similar fashion, separated cycle facilities have been trialled in all the main Australian state capitals (see

Figure 12.6: A two-way separated cycle path in central Brisbane, Queensland. (Source: Author.)), as well as New Zealand cities such as Auckland and Christchurch. A plethora of options for separation have appeared (such as kerbs, low islands, delineator posts, longitudinal barriers, planter boxes, and so on); and, other than issues of available width, there seems to be little evidence so far to recommend one treatment over the other.

The catalyst has come from many sources. Geller's (2009) 'four types' typology has certainly had an influence in trying to better target the *interested but concerned* market. Research like that by Kingham et al. (2011) has helped to confirm the support for such facilities from potential riders in this part of the world. There is also an element of official acceptance (finally) to the fact that nothing else to date has been successful in achieving the high levels of cycling common in many parts of Europe.

Separated cycle facilities are often seen by lay-people in particular as the panacea for cycling, based on their use in European countries where cycling is popular, such as the Netherlands and Denmark. There is no doubt that well-designed cycle paths and tracks can be wonderful facilities for cycling. However, it is also important to understand why the European examples cannot always be taken at face value in Australasia.

- In many European countries, the traffic regulations give right of way over side roads to everyone travelling along a road corridor, including cyclists and pedestrians on paths. Here in New Zealand and Australia, the same level of priority is not present (and there is also some uncertainty by New Zealand transport officials about whether an on-road separated cycleway is still considered part of the 'roadway'). People cycling are less likely to use separated cycleways if they continually have to give way when crossing side roads.
- European motorists are more likely to expect riders appearing from a path than their Australasian counterparts would be (especially from their left side when entering the main road), since cycle volumes are generally higher and the concept of pathways off the carriageway has long been established.
- Many European facilities are truly segregated between cyclists and pedestrians; there are separate 'exclusive' paths for each road user and

these are widely respected. In Australasia, a common approach is to provide a shared path (and with few rules for path behaviour). People are less likely to cycle on a path if they feel that the pedestrian volumes and available width do not allow them sufficient unimpeded progress.

One should be particularly wary of taking the 'easy option' to provide separation (for example, by just widening and marking an existing footpath). A well-designed separated cycleway can also require considerable expense to plan and construct (particularly at intersections). Other problems that may be encountered include parking removal, suitable intersection treatments, and general resistance by the public to 'new' facilities. The last problem is particularly important to manage when introducing initial trials, lest it threatens to derail future projects; witness the 'controversy' surrounding the implementation of cycleways on Bourke Street, Sydney (McDougall, 2011), and Frome Street, Adelaide (Templeton, 2015).

Whilst on-road cycle facilities are invariably one-way on each side of the street, many separated cycleways can be provided as two-way cycling facilities. There may be some practical advantages to doing so (for example, less street width required, thereby avoiding problematic side accesses). However, there are also potential complications in terms of relative safety at intersections (if crossing traffic is not expecting riders in the 'opposite' direction) or in the ease with which riders can access the facility from the other side of the street.

Neighbourhood greenways and quiet streets

In Australasia and many other parts of the world, physical provision for cycling often focuses on specific cycle infrastructure, such as cycle lanes and pathways. Yet, as noted by Koorey (2012), some of the best cycling routes in the world have few conventional cycle facilities. Neighbourhood greenways (aka 'bicycle boulevards' or 'local street bikeways') are a form of street treatment where simple measures such as lower speeds, traffic restraints, wayfinding, and crossing treatments are used to create an environment that is friendly for cycling. They are particularly useful for connecting people to community facilities such as schools, parks, shops and other key destinations in a neighbourhood and beyond. Neighbourhood greenways [NGs] are a popular tool in North America, but have yet to catch on in Australasia, despite many similarities in street environment.

NGs historically had their origins in proposals to make certain streets more cycle-friendly and less attractive to motor vehicles. In Europe this included the development of 'bicycle priority streets' (*fietsstraat*) in the Netherlands (Ministerie van Verkeer en Waterstaat [MVW], 2009), but the more benign 'bicycle boulevards' appear to have had their origins on the west coast of North America, where they were first implemented in Palo Alto, California in 1981, on a 3-kilometre length of Bryant Street (City of Palo Alto, 1982).

Other cities followed suit with NGs, including Berkeley (California), Albuquerque (New Mexico), Minneapolis (Minnesota), Vancouver (British Columbia) and Portland (Oregon). The grid nature of many North American cities lends itself to developing suitable quiet cycling routes that are parallel to other busier routes. In Australasia, 'greenways' have been developed in suburban areas of Adelaide; and in New Zealand there are NGs under planning and construction in Auckland, Christchurch and Dunedin.

Unlike separated cycleways, the key to NGs is successful *integration* of road users. Taking its cue from the aforementioned 'five step hierarchy', this integration relies heavily on the removal of unnecessary motor traffic and the slowing down of any remaining traffic. One common tool to reinforce this shared behaviour is the use of shared use arrows or 'sharrows'; they can be found on Adelaide's greenways (see Figure 12.7) and are currently being formally trialled at various locations in New Zealand (Hancock & Patel, 2014). The evidence to date suggests that sharrows can result in a slight calming effect on motorist speeds, and better lateral positioning by both riders and drivers alike.

NGs, if done well, can be a very important and cost-effective part of the cycle network. Research by Dill and McNeil (2013) indicates that the *interested but concerned* are quite comfortable with street environments of this nature. The majority of streets in typical urban networks are relatively low-volume local streets, where a formal cycle facility would often seem unnecessary. NGs allow for rapid expansion of cycling routes, particularly in suburban areas connecting residents to many local community facilities.

Strategies for change

Figure 12.7: A neighbourhood greenway in Adelaide, South Australia, featuring 'sharrow' markings.
(Source: Author.)

Figure 12.8. A separated cycleway with some ambiguity over side-road priority, in Nelson, New Zealand.
(Source: Author.)

Intersection treatments

Although much of the attention of cycling tends to focus on the mid-block cycle facilities, in terms of safety it is the intersections that are more crucial. Typically more than two-thirds of all cycle crashes occur at intersections and driveways

(Cycling Safety Panel, 2014). Intersection treatments also play an important part in providing connections of local cycling routes across arterial roads (for example, as part of NGs). A lack of such treatments can result in isolated 'islands' of cycling comfort, severed by busy roads; in such an environment it would not be surprising to see low levels of cycling.

As more separated cycle facilities are developed in Australasia, a growing problem is how best to continue them across intersections. Cycleways that are set too far back (for example, behind parked vehicles or medians) may be less noticeable to turning traffic, leading to unexpected conflicts. Clarification may also be needed to identify which party has right of way when crossing a side road (see Figure 12.8. A separated cycleway with some ambiguity over side-road priority, in Nelson, New Zealand. (Source: Author.)8). At busy signalised intersections, it may be prudent to separate the signal phases for cyclists and turning traffic, since many serious cycle crashes involving heavy vehicles often feature this type of conflict.

The different problems faced at intersections compared with mid-block locations are highlighted by Danish research (Jensen, 2008), which found that, while off-road cycle tracks were safer in general than their on-carriageway counterparts, they were less safe at intersections. Stichting Wetenschappelijk Onderzoek Verkeersveiligheid [SWOV] (2010) therefore recommended that cycle tracks parallel to roads should either rejoin roads ahead of intersections or be taken further away to cross the side roads.

Rural cycling facilities

Generally less than 10% of all cycling occurs in rural areas, limited mostly to training cyclists, cycle tourists, and cyclists making short inter-town trips. However, the significant difference in motor vehicle speeds means that typically about half of all cycle fatalities occur on rural roads (Koorey, 2014). These ensure that the profile of rural cycling safety is given high prominence by the public and policy makers alike.

As mentioned above, the predominant cycle crash type overall is intersection-related, and 30% of rural cycle crashes occur at intersections. However, rural roads are more likely to feature same-direction crashes, where a motor vehicle has either clipped a cycle while passing or hit the cycle from behind (perhaps going around a blind corner). New Zealand's Cycling Safety Panel (2014) noted that lack of shoulder width is a significant factor; an analysis of rural New Zealand cycle crashes and sealed shoulder widths found that the majority of crashes occur where there is no (or relatively negligible) road shoulder. A program of targeted shoulder widening would therefore have great benefit for cycling, although technically the greatest economic benefits of such widening are generally for others in terms of road safety, traffic efficiency and maintenance costs.

However, long lengths of seal widening are costly, particularly in difficult terrain. A more cost-effective solution in many places may be to concentrate on the areas where sight distance is very limited. A narrow but straight section of road may not pose too many dangers if motorists have enough time to safely move over when passing cyclists. Instead, it may be prudent to focus on providing localised seal widening around horizontal curves, over vertical crests, and at other localised pinch points like narrow culverts. It is important to remember that for many rural roads there are no feasible alternative routes, so any pinch point has to be endured by all cyclists going that way. Bridges and tunnels present some of the most difficult barriers for cycling, through either their narrowness or lack of cycling access. Opportunities to use paths and corridors away from traffic certainly should be encouraged where possible. But in rural areas there are often fewer possibilities to do this. Therefore it is vital that motorists and cyclists can safely coexist on the same road.

If widening is not an option due to topography or cost, then one option is to consider warning signs and markings. A common treatment in North America, particularly ahead of narrow bridges and tunnels, is the use of 'active warning' signs that flash for approaching traffic when triggered by passing riders. Similar treatments have been installed in rural locations in Nelson and Marlborough, New Zealand (Gardener & Kortegast, 2014). Where additional road width cannot be provided on low-volume rural roads, another option is to reconfigure the cross-section to provide two shoulders and a single traffic lane (preferably with a lower speed limit). This '2 minus 1 road' configuration is common in rural roads in Scandinavia and the Netherlands (Erke & Sørensen, 2008) and is being considered for trialling in New Zealand.

Spaces for cycling

Car parking

A discussion about spaces for cycling would not be complete without considering the challenge that on-street car parking presents when providing for cycling in urban environments. On many arterial or commercial roads, considerable controversy is raised when fitting in a proposed cycleway requires the removal of on-street parking (or the removal of a traffic lane if the parking is considered sacrosanct). Retailers and motorists alike often raise concerns about the effect on businesses and accessibility, particularly for what is often seen as 'a few cyclists'.

Fleming (Allatt), Turner, and Tarjomi (2013) investigated the economic impacts of road space allocation in shopping areas located in various New Zealand cities. Retail spending data showed that non-car users accounted for 40% of the total spend in the shopping areas, despite being only 37% of all respondents; typically, they spent less per trip than those who drove, but visited more frequently. The study also identified that retailers generally overestimate the importance of on-street parking outside shops. Shoppers valued high-quality pedestrian and urban design features in shopping areas more than they valued parking, and those who drove were willing to walk to the shops

Figure 12.9: Reallocation of central city street space to bike parking and a cycle lane, Adelaide, South Australia.
(Source: Author.)

from other locally available parking areas. Similarly, Lee and March (2007) investigated the value of on-street parking in Melbourne and identified that bike parking provided better use of space (see Figure 12.9: Reallocation of central city street space to bike parking and a cycle lane, Adelaide, South Australia. (Source: Author.)), in terms of retail expenditure per square metre, than car parking.

Beetham (2014) investigated the feasibility of a proposed cycleway in Wellington, New Zealand, between the southern suburbs and city centre, with a particular focus on the impact that removing some on-street car parks along one section might have on businesses in the area. A survey of around 600 people found that a significant majority of respondents said they would be willing to consider the removal of some on-street parking to provide for safe cycle routes — even those who were not interested in cycling. This was mostly because of their concern for cycle safety or because, as drivers, they found sharing the road with cyclists stressful. An additional survey of shoppers along the street showed that only 6% were using the on-street parking there.

Similar concerns about parking are often expressed in suburban neighbourhoods by residents worried that guests will not be able to easily visit. In most cases, however, there are ample alternatives (not including cycling there instead), such as other nearby streets or off-street locations. Field data in many places typically notes exceptionally low parking occupancy rates on suburban streets and thus inefficient use of what is a valuable resource (for example, providing parking on both sides of a street when occupancy never even reaches 50%).

Conclusion

From the above discussion, a few key points emerge. A lot of the perceived past problems with cycle facilities, both on- and off-road, have been due to inadequate design or maintenance standards rather than the choice of facility. This can (and should) be resolved; and better training and technical guidance is helping to address this. New facilities should be up to scratch from day one, to avoid any 'bad press' from riders, which may taint their perception of similar facilities in the future.

From a technical perspective, there can be safety issues with both on- and off-road cycle facilities — that is, one is not inherently safer than the other.

(Indeed, it may be the intersection treatments that determine the relative safety.) Obviously, it is desirable that all types of cycle provision are made adequately safe. Even with appropriate design, there may still be some incorrect perceptions by the general public or elected members about the relative merits of some cycle treatments. Education campaigns may be useful to inform these parties of the true characteristics of these treatments in terms of safety, level of service, and so on.

Some of the best solutions for cycling may not involve cycle facilities at all. Streets that are adequately managed to minimise motor vehicle speeds and volumes are likely to be very pleasant environments for cycling, at relatively low cost. The role of lower traffic speeds is also a very important (and under-appreciated) part of protecting people while cycling. Transport planners attempting to provide only one type of cycle treatment throughout a district will probably find situations where an alternative solution would be far more beneficial and/or practical. A 'horses for courses' approach is recommended instead.

It is important to acknowledge that perceived risk may play a large part in acceptance and usage of cycling facilities by a greater number of people, irrespective of actual known risks. To this end, while intersection treatments are often critical to improving the overall safety of people cycling, it may be that attractive mid-block treatments are the key to getting more people to cycle in the first place. User behaviour is just as important as engineering when it comes to best-practice cycle facilities. Campaigns to educate cyclists, motorists and pedestrians alike on how to use various facilities and interact with each other should be considered. Better driver behaviour would make cyclists more comfortable on the road, whilst better path-user behaviour would make them happier off the road.

References

Australian Bicycle Council. (2014). *National cycling strategy 2011-16: 2013 Implementation Report*. Sydney: Austroads. Retrieved 11 August 2015 from http://www.bicyclecouncil.com.au/publication/national-cycling-strategy.

Austroads. (2014). *Cycling aspects of Austroads guides*. Austroads Publication No. AP-G88/14. Retrieved 11 August 2015 from www.onlinepublications.austroads.com.au/items/AP-G88-14.

Beetham, J. (2014). *Re-cycling the streets: Exploring the allocation of public space for transport* (Master of Environmental Studies thesis, Victoria University of Wellington, New Zealand).

Centre for Research & Contract Standardisation in Civil Engineering [CROW]. (2007). *Design manual for bicycle traffic*. Record No. 25. Ede, the Netherlands: CROW.

Charlton, SG, Mackie, HW, Baas, PH, Hay, K, Menezes, M, & Dixon, C. (2010). Using endemic road features to create self-explaining roads and reduce vehicle speeds. *Accident Analysis and Prevention*, 42, 1989-1998. doi: 10.1016/j.aap.2010.06.006.

City of Palo Alto. (1982, December 9). *Bicycle boulevard demonstration study — Evaluation*. Staff report to city council. Palo Alto, USA: City of Palo Alto Transportation Division.

City of Portland. (2010). *Portland Bicycle Plan for 2030*. Retrieved 11 August 2015 from http://www.portlandoregon.gov/transportation/44597.

Cycling Safety Panel. (2014, December). *Safer journeys for people who cycle: Cycling Safety Panel final report and recommendations*. Wellington: New Zealand.

Dearnaley, M. (2012, July 28). Outrage over claim cyclist caused own death. *The New Zealand Herald*. Retrieved 13 August 2015 from http://www.nzherald.co.nz/nz/news/article.cfm?c_id=1&objectid=10822770.

Dill, J, & McNeil, N. (2013). Four types of cyclists? Examining a typology to better understand bicycling behavior and potential. *Transportation Research Record: Journal of the Transportation Research Board*, 2387, 129-138. doi: 10.3141/2387-15.

Erke, A, & Sørensen, M. (2008). *Extended road shoulders on rural roads: A measure for cyclists and pedestrians?* TØI report 961/2008. Oslo, Norway: Institute of Transport Economics.

Fleming (Allatt), T, Turner, S, & Tarjomi, L. (2013, August). *Reallocation of road space*. NZ Transport Agency Research Report 530. Wellington: New Zealand.

Forester, J. (2001). The bikeway controversy. *Transportation Quarterly*, 55(2), 7-17.

Fowler, M, & Koorey, G. (2006, October 8-11). The effects of the pages road cycle lane on cyclist safety and traffic flow operations. *IPENZ Transportation Group Technical Conference*, Queenstown, New Zealand.

Franklin, J. (1999). Two decades of the Redway cycle paths in Milton Keynes. *Traffic Engineering + Control*, 40(7/8), 393-396.

Gardener, R, & Kortegast, P. (2014, March 23-26). Vehicle activated electronic signs — 5 years on. *IPENZ Transportation Group Conference*, Wellington,

New Zealand.

Geller, R. (2009). *Four types of cyclists*. Portland, OR: Portland Office of Transportation. Retrieved 11 August 2015 from www.portlandoregon.gov/transportation/article/237507.

Hancock, K, & Patel, A. (2014, October 29-31). Sharrows — More than just a marking. *2WALKandCYCLE Conference 2014*, Nelson, New Zealand.

Holligan, A. (2013, August 7). Why is cycling so popular in the Netherlands? *BBC News Magazine*. Retrieved 11 August 2015 from http://www.bbc.com/news/magazine-23587916.

Institution of Highways and Transportation [IHT], Cyclists' Touring Club [CTC], Bicycle Association, & Department of Transport. (1996). *Cycle friendly infrastructure: Guidelines for planning and design*. Godalming, UK: Cyclists' Touring Club.

Jacobsen, PL, Racioppi, F, & Rutter, H. (2009). Who owns the roads? How motorised traffic discourages walking and bicycling. *Injury Prevention*, 15, 369-373. doi: 10.1136/ip.2009.022566.

Jensen, SU. (2008). Safety effects of blue cycle crossings: A before-after study. *Accident Analysis and Prevention*, 40, 742-750. doi: 10.1016/j.aap.2007.09.016.

Kingham, S, Taylor, K, & Koorey, G. (2011). *Assessment of the type of cycling infrastructure required to attract new cyclists*. NZ Transport Agency Research Report No. 449. Wellington: New Zealand.

Koorey, GF. (2005, October 14-15). The 'On-again/Off-again' debate about cycle facilities. *NZ Cycling Conference*, Lower Hutt, New Zealand.

Koorey, G. (2007, November 1-2). Are you a cyclist or do you cycle? The language of promoting cycling. *NZ Cycling Conference*, Napier, New Zealand.

Koorey, G. (2011, March 27-30). Implementing lower speeds in New Zealand. *IPENZ Transportation Group Conference*, Auckland, New Zealand.

Koorey, G. (2012, February 22-24). Neighbourhood greenways: Invisible infrastructure for walking and cycling. *2WALKandCYCLE Conference*, Hastings, New Zealand.

Koorey, GF. (2014, March 23-26). Investigating common patterns in New Zealand cycling fatalities. *IPENZ Transportation Group Conference*, Wellington, New Zealand.

Koorey, GF, & Mangundu, E. (2010, January 10-14). Effects on motor vehicle behavior of color and width of bicycle facilities at signalized intersections. *89th Transportation Research Board (TRB) Annual Meeting*, Washington DC, USA.

Koorey, G, Wilke, A, & Aussendorf, J. (2013, April 14-16). Assessment of the effectiveness of narrow separators on cycle lanes. *IPENZ Transportation Group Conference*, Dunedin, New Zealand.

Lahausse, J, van Nes, N, Fildes, B, Langford, J, & Keall, M. (2009, November). *Assessing community attitudes to speed limits: Final report*. Clayton, Australia: Monash University Accident Research Centre.

Land Transport New Zealand [LTNZ]. (2004). *Cycle network and route planning guide*. Wellington: Land Transport New Zealand. Retrieved 11 August 2015 from www.nzta.govt.nz/resources/cycle-network-and-route-planning.

Lee, A, & March, A. (2007). *What is the economic contribution of cyclists compared to car drivers in inner Melbourne's shopping strips?* (Master of Urban Planning Thesis, University of Melbourne, Australia).

Lieswyn, J, Macbeth, A, Wilke, A, Ward, J, Ashford, J, Houghton, R, & Lloyd, W. (2012, February 22-24). An illustrated lexicon of cycle facilities. *2WALKandCYCLE Conference*, Hastings, New Zealand.

McDougall, B. (2011, August 19). Sydney's cyclists ignore their $76 million cycleway network. *Daily Telegraph*. Retrieved 13 August 2015 from http://www.dailytelegraph.com.au/news/nsw/sydneys-cyclists-ignore-their-76-million-cycleway-network/story-e6freuzi-1226117740032.

Ministerie van Verkeer en Waterstaat [MVW]. (2009). *Cycling in the Netherlands*. The Hague, Netherlands: Ministerie van Verkeer en Waterstaat (Ministry of Transport, Public Works and Water Management).

Ministry of Transport [MOT]. (2010, March). *Safer journeys: New Zealand's road safety strategy 2010-2020*. Wellington, New Zealand: Ministry of Transport.

National Association of City Transportation Officials [NACTO]. (2010). *Urban bikeway design guide*. New York, US: National Association of City Transportation Officials. Retrieved 11 August 2015 from http://nacto.org/cities-for-cycling/design-guide.

Parkin, J, & Koorey, G. (2012). Network planning and infrastructure design. In J Parkin (Ed.), *Cycling and Sustainability* (pp. 131-160). Bingley, UK:

Emerald Publishing. doi: 10.1108/S2044-9941(2012)0000001008.

Parsons, J, & Koorey, G. (2013, April 14-16). The effect of cycle lanes on cycle numbers and safety. *IPENZ Transportation Group Conference*, Dunedin, New Zealand.

Patterson, F, Crowther, M, & Solly, P. (2003, October 10-11). From the city to the outback – Next generation bicycle planning in South Australia. *Proceedings, NZ Cycling Conference 2003 — Cycling: Transport for Living* (pp. 109-124). Auckland, New Zealand: North Shore City.

Rosén, E, & Sander, U. (2009). Pedestrian fatality risk as a function of car impact speed. *Accident Analysis and Prevention*, 41, 536-542. doi: 10.1016/j.aap.2009.02.002.

Rosén, E, Stigson, H, & Sander, U. (2011). Literature review of pedestrian fatality risk as a function of car impact speed. *Accident Analysis and Prevention*, 25-33. doi: 10.1016/j.aap.2010.04.003.

State Bicycle Committee. (1977). *Geelong bike plan: For the Victorian government*. Melbourne, Australia.

Stichting Wetenschappelijk Onderzoek Verkeersveiligheid [SWOV]. (2010). *Bicycle facilities on road segments and intersections of distributor roads*. Leidschendam, The Netherlands: Foundation for Road Safety Research.

Templeton, A. (2015, June 24). Adelaide City Council votes make changes to Frome St bikeway to improve peak-hour traffic flow. *The Advertiser*. Retrieved 13 August 2015 from http://www.adelaidenow.com.au/messenger/city/adelaide-city-council-votes-make-changes-to-frome-st-bikeway-to-improve-peak-hour-traffic-flow/story-fni9lkxa-1227412008129.

Transportblog. (2014, January 20). Auckland cycling spend comparison [blog post, Transportblog.co.nz]. Retrieved 11 August 2015 from http://transportblog.co.nz/2014/01/20/auckland-cycling-spend-comparison.

Trumper, H. (2013). *Slow zones: The pedestrian experience* (Master of Engineering in Transportation research report, Department of Civil and Natural Resources Engineering, University of Canterbury, Christchurch, New Zealand).

13 Off-road cycling infrastructure

Narelle Haworth

Introduction

The previous chapter described the spaces for cycling with a focus on on-road facilities and safety issues, including the interface between off-road paths and the road. This chapter moves from the roadway to examine the types of off-road spaces for cycling; who uses them and why; and the influences of these spaces on both cycling participation and safety.

Disagreements abound in the literature regarding spaces for off-road riding. The first level of disagreement relates to what spaces should be included under the term 'off-road'. In this chapter, a practical approach is taken, with off-road spaces encompassing all those which are beyond the roadside kerbs. Under this definition, bicycle lanes with painted (but not physical separators) are classified as on-road spaces, while footpaths (sidewalks in North America) are classified as off-road, whether they are specifically marked for bicycle use or not. In terms of the New Zealand lexicon of cycling facilities introduced in the previous chapter (Lieswyn et al., 2012), the off-road spaces considered in this chapter include:

1. cycle paths — whether Danish cycle tracks or cycle paths at footpath level, called cycle tracks in the European Cycling Lexicon (European Economic and Social Commission, 2011)
2. exclusive or shared paths (beside a road or in a park)
3. footpaths.

Trails (mountain bike [MTB] tracks and shared-use trails) belong to the general category of off-road spaces but are not discussed in this chapter because of the focus of this book on urban cycling.

Disagreements also exist regarding the role and function of on-road versus off-road spaces for cycling. Some cycling advocates argue that all roads should be made safe and convenient for cycling and that there should be no real need or advocacy for off-road spaces. In contrast, some road safety advocates propose that on-road cycling should be allowed in only very restricted circumstances. For example, in describing the Swedish Vision Zero road safety philosophy, Johansson (2009) states that vulnerable road users (cyclists and pedestrians) should be separated from motorised vehicles whose speeds exceed 30 km/h. Similar philosophies have been adopted in the Netherlands, resulting in an extensive off-road network (CROW, 2007). As noted in the previous chapter, government transport departments in some jurisdictions have adopted decision frameworks regarding the type of cycling infrastructure that should be provided, and these decision frameworks are based on a combination of motorised vehicle speeds and motorised vehicle volumes. They generally propose that off-road cycling facilities should be provided in urban areas where the posted speed limit is 80 km/h or greater (regardless of the traffic volume) or where the posted speed limit is 60 km/h or greater if the traffic volume exceeds 5000 vehicles per day. These documents also recommend that segregated facilities be considered where the rare combination of low speeds and high volumes exist. Application of these frameworks results in a very different mix of cycling spaces than would apply under the Vision Zero philosophy or than currently applies in the Netherlands.

There is considerable disagreement in the literature regarding the relative safety of different types of cycling spaces. Much of this disagreement may stem from the mix of cyclists who use different spaces. Cyclists are very heterogeneous in both individual and trip characteristics. Characteristics of the spaces available for cycling affect both the popularity of bicycling and its safety, and therefore comparisons of the safety performance of infrastructure may be confounded by differences in the profiles of cyclists who use them. Several studies have concluded that women choose safer facilities than do men. For example, an observational study in Melbourne (Garrard, Rose, & Lo, 2008) found that female commuters were more likely to use off-road paths than on-road lanes or lanes with no bicycle facilities. Inexperienced commuters also place a greater importance on avoiding motor vehicle traffic (Stinson & Bhat, 2003) and place a higher value on a separate path or bicycle lane than experienced commuters.

There are also a number of issues related to data quality and methodology, which may underpin some of the divergent results reported in the literature. Many writers have pointed out the problems of under-reporting on-road bicycle crashes, but these problems are magnified for off-road spaces because there is often no requirement (or ability) to report these crashes to police. This has led to a reliance on hospital databases, which are very limited in terms of crash location information. Chong, Poulos, Olivier, Watson, and Grzebieta (2010) note that while there is a distinction between traffic versus non-traffic events (the latter being defined as a vehicle accident that occurs entirely in a place other than a public highway) in Australian hospital data, the crash location is coded as 'unspecified' for a large number of injuries; and among the non-traffic events there is no distinction between different off-road spaces (such as footpaths, bicycle paths or shared paths).

Some evaluations of the safety benefits of improvements in cycling infrastructure have measured changes in crashes without directly assessing any increases in cyclist volumes that may have occurred because the new infrastructure is perceived as safer. Yet there are many studies that show that at least some cyclists prefer to ride in off-road spaces. For example, a stated preference experiment in Edmonton, Canada, found that current cyclists judged time spent cycling in mixed traffic to travel to an all-day meeting to be more onerous than time spent cycling on bike lanes or bike paths; but that this difference decreases as level of experience increases (Hunt & Abraham, 2007). In comparison, a more recent study by Shaw, Poulos, Rissel, and Hatfield (2012) observed that within their sample, cyclists spent on average 51% of their time on roads, 17% of their time on shared paths, 15% on bicycle-only paths, 5% on pedestrian footpaths and 3% on other infrastructure.

In many jurisdictions, a significant proportion of all bicycle-related injuries occur in off-road settings (including trails, which are outside the focus of this chapter). In the financial year 2009-10 in Australia, 42.7% of persons admitted to hospital after cycling crashes had been involved in a non-traffic accident (Tovell, McKenna, Bradley, & Pointer, 2012). This is consistent with an earlier interview study of hospitalised riders in Western Australia, which found that the majority (58%) of injuries occurred off-road: on footpaths, driveways, yards, cycle paths, car parks, and bike trails (Meuleners, Lee, & Haworth, 2007). Furthermore, in the Australian Capital Territory [ACT] Pedal study (de Rome, Boufous, Senserrick, Richardson, & Ivers, 2011), 23% of cyclists who presented to emergency departments had been injured on shared paths and 11% on footpaths or other pedestrian areas. Of the cyclists riding on shared paths, 56% had been involved in falls, but 23% had been injured in incidents involving other cyclists and 16% had been involved in incidents involving pedestrians. The estimated average speeds were highest for cyclists riding in traffic (29 km/h); average speed on shared paths was 21 km/h and on the footpath was 11 km/h. While these overall figures suggest that there is a need to improve the safety of off-road cycling, they clearly are not adjusted for the amount of off-road riding that occurs. In some instances, differences between jurisdictions may well represent variations in the availability of off-road paths and corresponding cycling patterns, rather than differences in the relative safety of on- and off-road cycling.

Finally, many comparisons of the safety of on- and off-road riding do not provide useful information about crash severity. This may be crucial in comparing the safety of on-and off-road riding because it may be severity rather than crash or injury rate which distinguishes the two. While it has generally been assumed that off-road crashes should be less severe than on-road crashes because of the lack of involvement with motor vehicles, some studies that have measured severity have questioned this assumption. Studies from the Australian Capital Territory have reported higher injury severity scores (de Rome et al., 2012 — although some cyclists who were severely injured and those who were killed were not included in this study) and a higher average number of hospital bed-days (Richardson & Paini, 2006 cited in de Rome et al., 2012) for cyclists who crashed on bicycle paths compared to in traffic.

The sections which follow will discuss off-road paths which are for the exclusive use of bicycles, and then the particular issues associated with shared bicycle paths and footpaths.

Off-road bicycle paths

The variation in physical and usage characteristics of off-road bicycle paths has hindered general assessments of their contribution to bicycle amenity and safety. Reynolds, Harris, Teschke, Cripton, and Winters (2009) concluded from their review that the evidence regarding the safety of off-road facilities was not consistent

> possibly because this category encompassed a wide variety of facility types. There may have been confounding factors such as whether the surface was paved or unpaved, or for bicycles only or multiple user groups. (p. 60)

Tinsworth, Cassidy and Polen (1994) and Moritz (1997a) concluded that the risk associated with cycling off-road bike paths was lower than on minor roads, but studies that grouped paved and unpaved, bicycle-only and multi-use trails together found elevated risks (Aultman-Hall & Kaltenecker, 1999; Moritz, 1997b; Aultman-Hall & Hall, 1998). With one exception, all the studies assessed risk by examining the collision rates of cyclists. In comparison, Tinsworth et al. (1994) assessed risk in terms of bicycle-related injuries resulting from a collision.

A number of studies have examined the performance of cycle tracks. The traditional Danish cycle track is constructed parallel and adjacent to the road with a kerb to the carriageway and another kerb to the footpath. A before-and-after study of the construction of cycle tracks in Copenhagen by Jensen (2008) concluded that they were associated with a 20% increase in bicycle and moped mileage and a 10% reduction in motor vehicle mileage. There was a non-significant 10% reduction in mid-block cyclist crashes, but a significant 18% increase in crashes at intersections, resulting in an overall 10% increase in crashes. The increase in crashes at intersections appeared to be related to more motor vehicles turning the corners to access back streets because of the removal of on-street parking, which occurred with the installation of the cycle tracks.

Elvik, Vaa, Erke and Sorensen (2009) reported a meta-analysis of 13 studies (mostly from northern Europe) examining the safety outcome of tracks for cycling. They concluded that there was an 11% decrease in bicycle crashes along the road and a 24% increase in bicycle crashes at junctions (both statistically significant), resulting in an overall non-significant 7% increase in bicycle crashes. They noted that this outcome is likely to reflect increases in cycling resulting from the installation of cycle tracks. Based on these results, Sorensen and Mosslemi (2009) conclude that 'tracks for cycling' are a problem treatment because they have a positive effect on subjective safety (as reflected in increased use) but a negative effect on objective safety. This can be further critiqued within the road safety and public health paradigms. Specifically, although it is widely recognised that bicycling is linked to several health benefits (for example, Frumkin, Frank & Jackson, 2004; Oja et al., 2011), it is also linked to a variety of road safety issues, such as bicycle crashes and fatalities (for example, Chong et al., 2010; Elvik et al., 2009). Thus what brings benefits to one area is associated with negative consequences in another.

A more recent study examined bicycle facility guidelines and crash rates on cycle tracks (defined as physically separated, bicycle-exclusive paths adjacent to footpaths) in the United States (Lusk, Morency, Miranda-Moreno, Willett, & Dennerlein, 2013). Some of these may have been equivalent to Danish cycle tracks, while others may have been protected on-road bicycle lanes. The tracks were a mixture of two-way, one-way and contra-flow operations. The authors identified that state transportation department guidelines discouraged or did not include cycle tracks and so their use is not widespread. Their analysis of police-reported crash data and bicycle counts on 19 bicycle tracks in the US found an overall crash rate of 2.3 per million bicycle-kilometres, which they claim is lower than published crash rates on roadways. The authors note that injury severity data was not available, and so it is not clear whether there was a difference in severity between the crashes on cycle tracks and roadways.

An earlier study by the same group (Lusk et al., 2011) compared the crash risk of 6 two-way cycle tracks in Montreal (some of which might be considered to be protected on-road bicycle lanes under the definitions used in this chapter) with one or two reference streets without bicycle facilities that were considered alternative cycling routes. Injury and crash data was sourced from the emergency medical response database (with police-recorded motor vehicle-bicycle crashes used to adjust for crashes on cross-streets) and compared with bicycle volume counts. The analyses found that the relative risk of injury for riding on a cycle track was 28% lower than on a reference street, and that 2.5 times as many cyclists rode on the cycle tracks compared to the reference streets.

A case-crossover study in Toronto and Vancouver (Teschke et al., 2012) found that the injury risk on a cycle track was about one-ninth of that on a major street route with parked cars and no bicycle infrastructure. The estimated injury risk was about 40% lower on bicycle paths than on the major street route, but this difference was not statistically significant. The participants in this study were all adult cyclists recruited from hospital emergency departments.

Danish cycle tracks are not common in Australia, where most bicycle paths are not physically adjacent to roadways.

Design of off-road bicycle paths

The Australasian design guidelines (Austroads, 2014) for bicycle facilities consider bicycle operating speed; horizontal alignment; width; vertical alignment; crossfall and drainage; clearances, batters and fences; and sight distance. These will be outlined further below.

Bicycle speed

Generally, Austroads (2014) recommends that bicycle paths be designed for a speed of at least 30 km/h, wherever possible and desirable given the purpose of the path, and in other cases for the anticipated operating speeds. However, it should be recognised that it may be necessary to adopt higher or lower design speeds in specific circumstances (p. 92).

Horizontal alignment and width

According to the Austroads (2014) guidelines, where a path is not restricted by topography, a generous alignment comprising both straight sections and large radius curves is desirable. In this way, an enjoyable and safe bicycle path can be achieved.

The width of the bicycle path is a major issue, which can have a significant impact on the level of convenience and potential conflict between consumers as well as on the safety of the path (Association of State Highway and Transportation Officials [AASHTO], 1999). An early study of bicycle circulation and safety on the University of California Davis campus by DT Smith (as cited in Gould & Karner, 2012) in this area found that cyclists require a travel lane with a minimum width of 1.2 metres (and double this width for passing), as bicycles are unable to travel in a perfectly straight line. In comparison, the AASHTO Guide for the Development of Bicycle Facilities (1999) recommended a path that is 10 foot wide (approximately 3 metres), increasing to 14 foot if there is a high volume of users (approximately 4.26 metres). The current Austroads (2014) guidelines recommend a minimum width of 2.5 metres for paths which are used exclusively for bicycles; 2.5 to 3.0 metres for shared paths; and 2.0 metres for the bicycle- and 1.5 metres for the footpath-section of a separated path. In comparison to the recommended

Australian guidelines, Jensen (2008) identified that bicycle paths in Denmark are considerably wider, with a one-way path being approximately 2-2.5 metres in width. Considering, though, that bicycling accounts for approximately 1% of all daily trips in Australia, compared with 18% in Denmark (Pucher & Buehler, 2008), part of this variation may be accounted for by differences in the numbers of cyclists. Austroads (2014) does, however, recommend greater widths where the volume of consumers necessitates it.

Vertical alignment

In general, bicycle paths should be as flat as possible. The potential risks for cyclists and other users due to high speeds on steep declines are as important as the difficulty of riding up an incline when deciding maximum gradients on two-way paths (Austroads, 2014). There is also research which suggests that very hilly terrain tends to deter cyclists (Gatersleben & Appleton, 2007; Lehman et al., 2009; Manton & Clifford, 2011).

Crossfall and drainage

As outlined by Austroads (2014), pooled water on bicycle paths can have '... a significant impact on the level of service provided to cyclists as spray leads to grit on both bicycle and rider' (p. 96). Consequently, it is recommended that sealed surfaces should have a crossfall between 2-4%, while unsealed surfaces may require a 5% crossfall to prevent water from pooling on the path. In cases where the path is shared, it is suggested that the crossfall not exceed 2.5%, in order to provide for people who have a disability. Similar recommendations have been made in Ireland (for example, Manton & Clifford, 2011). Drainage should also be adequate enough to prevent water and debris from obstructing the path in the event of heavy rain. In addition to this, Austroads (2014) recommends that paths with high volumes of users should be planned for a flood immunity equivalent to that designed for local roads unless a viable alternate route is easily accessible from the main path.

Clearances, batters and fences

Adequate clearance is an important part of safe bicycle path design. Generally, paths used for commuting and major recreational activity should have a minimum lateral clearance of 1 metre. This is to account for the high relative speed which occurs when cyclists approach one another from opposite directions at speeds of 30 km/h or more. With regards to recreational paths, where it is unlikely that speeds will exceed 20 km/h, a minimum lateral clearance of 0.4 metres is suggested (Austroads, 2014). In addition to this, the installation of a fence at the side of a bicycle path is appropriate in cases such as when there is a steep batter or incline close to the path; when the path is close to a main road; and when there is a bridge or culvert (Austroads, 2014).

Sight distance

Finally, according to Austroads (2014), it is vital that all two-way bicycle paths be planned so as to provide a sight distance between cyclists approaching from opposite directions. This will ensure that cyclists who are overtaking other users can avoid a potential head-on collision.

As highlighted by Manton and Clifford (2011), the proper maintenance of bicycle paths is an important step to ensure the safety of its users. Proper maintenance can also encourage people to view bicycles as a viable mode of transport (Niska, 2011). Unlike cars on roads, bicycles are much more vulnerable to poor path-maintenance quality, which can result in falls or collisions with other users. In Sweden, for example, Niska (2011) reported that approximately 70% of bicycle collisions were single-vehicle collisions and, of these, 40% were due to maintenance issues. To prevent this, key maintenance issues — such as sweeping, surface quality, ponding and signage — need to be adequately maintained (Manton & Clifford, 2011).

Shared paths

Governments in many parts of the world have policies to promote both walking and cycling in order to improve public health, and they provide off-road facilities to increase participation in both activities. Given the limitations of both finance and physical space, this has resulted in the construction of many paths that are signed for shared use by bicycle riders and pedestrians. This is true in Australasia, where the guidelines state that 'off-road bicycle facilities typically take the form of shared pathways for use by both cyclists and pedestrians' (Austroads, 2014, p. 26). Thus a shared pathway is the default design unless there is a strong safety or amenity reason to provide exclusive use for one group or the other. Shared paths are usually considered appropriate when there is a need for both a pedestrian and bicycle path, but where the intensity of the use is not anticipated to be sufficient enough to warrant separate paths. Shared paths may also be appropriate when an existing low-use path can be adequately modified to provide for cyclists (Austroads, 2014). In comparison, paths that are for the exclusive use of cyclists may be necessary in instances such as when there is a significant cycling demand and few pedestrians, or when there is limited motor vehicle access across the path. Finally, separate paths, where cyclists and pedestrians are restricted to selected areas, are used in cases when large numbers of pedestrians and cyclists intend to use the path (Austroads, 2014).

Despite their widespread use, both cyclists and pedestrians have raised concerns about the safety and amenity outcomes of shared paths. Elvik et al.'s (2009) meta-analysis of 16 studies (mostly from northern Europe) examining the safety outcome of tracks for walking and cycling concluded that there was a 2% increase in bicycle injury crashes along the road and a 1% increase in bicycle injury crashes at junctions, contributing to an overall increase of 1% in bicycle injury crashes (none of these differences were statistically significant). In contrast, there was a 35% reduction in pedestrian injury crashes along the road and a 1% increase in pedestrian crashes at junctions, with a resultant 10% overall reduction in pedestrian injury crashes (none of these differences were statistically significant). They noted that this outcome did not control for any changes in the number of cyclists or pedestrians resulting from the installation of the tracks.

Chong et al. (2010) compared the frequency and severity of injuries arising from bicycle-motor vehicle and bicycle-pedestrian collisions in NSW over a five-year period. Most cyclists admitted to hospital were male and injured in collisions with motor vehicles (n = 784). Among females aged 65 and older, less than 5 cyclists were admitted to hospital as a result of a collision with a pedestrian or animal; less than 5 cyclists were admitted as a result of a motor vehicle collision; and 20 were admitted following a collision with a cyclist. The corresponding figures for males aged 65 and older were less than 5, 13 and 46. Of the 163 pedestrians hospitalised due to collisions with cyclists, 72 resulted from a non-traffic accident and 48 were unspecified. The severity of injury was greater for people aged 65 and older, regardless of whether they were a pedestrian in a collision with a cyclist or a cyclist in a collision with a pedestrian or a motor vehicle. Chong et al. (2010) noted the projected increase in the aged population in Australia and concluded that shared bicycle-pedestrian paths may need to be avoided in areas where there are many elderly pedestrians.

Injury is likely to occur when collisions occur between objects which differ greatly in their kinetic energy (a product of mass and the square of velocity). Grzebieta, McIntosh and Chong (2011) point out that the ratio of kinetic energy between a 1.5-tonne car in a 50 km/h zone compared to an adult cyclist riding at 30 km/h in the same direction is about 44:1, which is similar to that of the ratio between the same cyclist and an average-sized pedestrian walking at 5 km/h (that is, 44:1 versus 48:1). For this reason, Chong et al. (2010) support the 10 km/h speed limit for shared paths in most Australian jurisdictions, but many cyclists maintain that riding within this limit is likely to compromise balance and result in increased weaving, thus potentially contributing to collisions with pedestrians or other cyclists. De Rome et al. (2011) provide support for this concern, noting that amongst those cyclists riding shared paths, 19% crashed as a result of avoiding a conflict with pedestrians or other cyclists.

Grzebieta et al. (2011) point out that the potential for conflict on shared paths is heightened by

- the variety of users of shared paths (pedestrians, cyclists, joggers, in-line skaters, skateboards, dogs and so on)
- the variety of purposes the path is used for (recreational, social, sporting, community)
- the use by those on shared paths of electronic devices and/or headphones.

The de Rome et al. (2011) ACT study of riders presenting to emergency departments further highlights the diversity of shared-path users. Specifically, the authors found that commuting was the most common trip purpose for shared paths (55%) and footpaths (56%), as much as for on-road cycling. Recreation was more commonly the trip purpose for those riding on shared paths (32%) than those riding in traffic (23%), with an intermediate value for footpaths (27%).

Despite this heterogeneity with respect to off-road bike path use, there has been relatively little research examining the safety and amenity impact of the diversity of users on shared paths. In one of the few reported studies, Virkler and Balasubramanian (1998) compared the speeds and interactions of walkers (whom they termed 'hikers'), joggers and cyclists on a shared path in Brisbane (with a smooth asphalt surface) with another shared path in the city of Columbia, Missouri (with a crushed-rock surface). They found that, in terms of metres per second [m/s], the mean speeds of joggers (3.34 m/s in Brisbane and 2.87 m/s in the US) were midway between those of hikers (1.56 m/s in Brisbane and 1.59 m/s in the US) and cyclists (5.76 m/s in Brisbane and 5.95 m/s in the US).

Thus cyclists not only overtake walkers but also joggers, and joggers overtake walkers, which can lower the level of service of the path. The mean times taken for an overtaking manoeuvre varied substantially. On the Brisbane path, the mean time taken for a cyclist to overtake a jogger (2.1 s, based on 22 events) was similar to the time taken to overtake a walker (1.9 s, based on 82 events). However, on the US path, the time taken for a cyclist to overtake a jogger (6.5 s, based on 9 events) was substantially greater than to overtake a walker (3.9 s, based on 11 events). The divergent results underline the need for more extensive examination of behaviour on mixed-use paths. Another finding of this study was that the standard deviation of cyclist speeds (which affects cyclists overtaking both cyclists and other path users) was more than double that used in the Dutch manual for designing cycle-friendly infrastructure (CROW, 2007) — which is often cited as the ideal approach.

The Austroads (2014) guidelines also note that bicycles can be threatening and intrusive to pedestrians when used within pedestrian activity spaces, such as city centres. Similarly, research has highlighted that pedestrians, even those who themselves cycle regularly, feel safer when there is a complete separation of pedestrians and cyclists (Bernhoft & Carstensen, 2008; Wennberg, Stahl, & Hyden, 2009). Contrary to this perception, however, an observational study on shared paths in New South Wales, Australia, observed more than 50 000 pedestrians and 12 000 bicyclists but only 5 near misses and no actual contact between bicyclists and pedestrians. The study concluded that the perception of danger of shared paths outweighs the actual level of risk (Roads and Traffic Authority [RTA], 2009).

The specific case of footpath cycling

As previously highlighted, cyclists, particularly those who are less experienced, prefer to avoid motor vehicle traffic (Garrard et al., 2008; Stinson & Bhat, 2003).

Cycling on the footpath is one method of separating cyclists from motor vehicles, but it is illegal for adults in most Australian jurisdictions (except for Queensland, Tasmania and the ACT) unless they are accompanying a child of 12 years of age or younger. These laws appear to stem from concerns about the risks to cyclists related to motor vehicle collisions at driveways and intersections and cyclists presenting as a hazard to pedestrians (Haworth & Schramm, 2011).

Despite this concern, very little research has investigated the topic. A review of primarily North American literature on the issue found that footpaths presented the biggest safety risk of all cycling locations, while appropriate bicycle facilities were associated with the lowest safety risk (Reynolds et al. 2009). An earlier US study by Wachtel and Lewiston (1994), which examined police-reported bicycle-motor vehicle crashes at intersections and driveways, concluded that the increased risk of footpath collisions was almost exclusively related to cycling against the direction of traffic.

Early Victorian studies by Drummond and colleagues produced some of Australia's most important research into the safety of footpath cycling. Drummond and Jee (1988) conducted an observational study of bicyclist exposure patterns on arterial and non-arterial roads and footpaths and compared the results with police casualty crash data in order to produce a crash risk estimate. The study found that the estimated risk of a police-reported casualty crash was higher on the road than on the footpath for riders of all ages. In comparison, the risks of riding on the footpath were approximately double for children and young people than for adults. Based on a Victorian telephone survey asking about the legalisation of footpath cycling and rider behaviour, Drummond (1988) concluded that a crash reduction could occur if footpath cycling was legalised.

Drummond (1989) examined hospital records for admitted patients and those treated in emergency departments at eight hospitals in Victoria. The study identified only two pedestrians who had been injured as a direct result of a collision with a cyclist on a footpath within a 10-month period. The study concluded that pedestrian casualties as a result of a collision with cyclists were not a major cause for concern. It was further noted, however, that the study did not account for the number of pedestrians whose injuries did not require hospital treatment.

More recent Australia-wide data with regards to injuries associated with footpath cycling has been provided by Henley and Harrison (2009). According to their report, in the financial year 2006-07, the number of hospitalised cyclists classed as injured on the footpath was 103, compared with 105 on a bicycle path, 2248 on the road, and 1548 whose location of injury was undetermined. During that same time period, 27 cyclists had to be hospitalised for a total of 59 days as a result of a traffic accident involving a pedestrian or an animal. This is equal to 0.5% of hospitalised cyclists and 0.4% of cyclist bed-days from traffic accidents. Additionally, 42 pedestrians were admitted into hospital for a total of 230 bed-days due to a collision with a cyclist. This is equal to 2.8% of hospitalised pedestrians and 1.0% of pedestrian bed-days from traffic accidents.

Haworth, Schramm and Debnath (2014) reported an observational study of cyclist-pedestrian conflicts at six locations in the Brisbane Central Business District. Only 1.7% of the 4522 cyclists observed were involved in conflicts with a motor vehicle or pedestrian, and no collisions were observed. Increased odds of a pedestrian-cyclist conflict were associated with the following:

- male riders
- riders not wearing correctly fastened helmets
- riding on the footpath
- higher pedestrian density (within 1 metre but not within 5 metres)
- morning peak-hour travel as well as travel between the hours of 2-4 pm (compared with 4-6 pm)
- two-way roads
- roads with more lanes
- higher speed limits
- yellow marked bicycle symbols on the road.

Disentangling the effects of infrastructure, experience and purpose of riding

As has been pointed out in the literature, comparisons of the safety performance of different types of infrastructure may be confounded by differences in the gender or age profiles of cyclists who use these types of infrastructure, or by different levels of skill or risk-taking behaviour (Reynolds et al., 2009). For these reasons, an online survey of 2532 adult riders in Queensland was undertaken to examine the extent to which choice of facility (for example, urban road, sidewalk) is associated with rider experience, purpose for riding, and preference for type of facility. The methodology is described in Haworth and Schramm (2011). Participants were asked about whether they rode regularly for each of the five most recent years. They were classified as *new riders* if they reported riding regularly only in the most recent two years, as *continuing riders* if they rode regularly in all five years, or as *other*.

The study demonstrated that 33.9% of respondents reported riding on footpaths, of whom about two-thirds rode there reluctantly. About one-third of riders who rode on urban roads also reported doing so reluctantly. Most of the riding in other locations occured by choice. A larger proportion of the distance that new riders cycled was on footpaths (6.5%) in comparison with continuing (3.9%) or other (4.5%) riders. However, in terms of the mean distance travelled per week, continuing riders actually rode further on footpaths (3.73 kilometres) than new riders (3.22 kilometres) or other riders (3.10 kilometres). The analysis of riding location and choice found strong differences according to riding purpose. Utilitarian riders were the most likely to ride on the footpath, followed by social and then fitness riders. Regardless of trip purpose, about two-thirds of all riders who rode on the footpath reported doing so reluctantly.

Relative safety of riding in different locations

Of participants' most serious crash-related injuries in the study by Haworth and Schramm (2011), the largest number of crashes took place on urban roads without bicycle markings (38.7%), followed by bicycle paths (14.3%) and footpaths (5.8%). It was further reported that 69.4% of footpath collisions did not involve any other bicycle, pedestrian or animal (and thus were single-vehicle collisions). This figure was higher than for bicycle paths and urban roads, but lower than for off-road/trail collisions, and comparable to rural roads. Collisions most commonly involving pedestrians were on bicycle paths (18.1%), followed by on footpaths (9.7%). Compared to collisions in other locations, footpath collisions ended in less severe injuries than collisions on urban roads. More specifically, injuries to the head, concussion and internal injuries were less frequent in footpath collisions than in collisions in other locations.

Conclusion

This chapter has examined several themes in relation to off-road bicycle spaces, including who uses them and why, and the impact of such facilities on cycling and safety. As a general rule, off-road bicycle paths have been proposed in urban areas where the high speeds or volumes of motorised traffic are considered to necessitate separating cyclists and other road users to improve their safety and amenity. Off-road bicycle paths are considered to play an important role in encouraging cycling among potential and inexperienced cyclists, who perceive off-road bicycle paths to be safer than on-road paths (see, for example, Teschke et al., 2012). Although off-road bicycle facilities do not discriminate between users, this chapter has highlighted that female and inexperienced commuters tend to place a higher importance on separate facilities than do male and more experienced cyclists (Garrard et al., 2008; Stinson & Bhat, 2003). While it is often proposed that off-road spaces are safer and more attractive for children, most of the studies of the safety of off-road riding have been restricted to adult cyclists (possibly because of research ethics).

However, some research challenges the perception that off-road paths provide for the safety and convenience of all cyclists. Some studies have shown that cyclists who were injured off-road received more severe injuries and had a higher number of hospital bed-days than cyclists who were injured on-road (de Rome et al., 2012). Poor design and subsequent maintenance of off-road bicycle facilities can reduce the safety and perception of safety of off-road bicycle paths, and it is important that these are not discounted. While shared paths are the default approach to off-road facilities in Australasia, concerns (and some data) exist that they can endanger both cyclists and pedestrians, and reduce amenity for both groups. Further research on how to avoid conflicts between different users and to improve perceptions of safety is needed.

References

Association of State Highway and Transportation Officials [AASHTO]. (1999). *Guide for the development of bicycle facilities.* Washington, DC: American Association of State Highway and Transportation Officials.

Aultman-Hall, L, & Hall, FL. (1998). Ottawa-Carleton commuter cyclist on- and off-road incident rates. *Accident Analysis & Prevention*, 30(1), 29-43.

Aultmann-Hall, L, & Kaltenecker, MG. (1999). Toronto bicycle commuter safety rates. *Accident Analysis and Prevention*, 31(6), 675-686.

Austroads. (2014). *Cycling aspects of Austroads guides*. Austroads Publication No. AP-G88-14. Sydney: Austroads Ltd.

Bernhoft, IM, & Carstensen, G. (2008). Preferences and behaviour of pedestrians and cyclists by age and gender. Transportation Research Part F: Traffic Psychology and Behaviour, 11(2), 83-95.

Chong, S, Poulos, R, Olivier, J, Watson, WL, & Grzebieta, R. (2010). Relative injury severity among vulnerable non-motorised road users: Comparative analysis of injury arising from bicycle-motor vehicle and bicycle-pedestrian collisions. *Accident Analysis & Prevention*, 42(1), 290-296.

CROW. (2007). *Design manual for bicycle traffic*. Publication No. REC 25. Netherlands: CROW.

De Rome, L, Boufous, S, Senserrick, T, Richardson, D, & Ivers, R. (2011). *The Pedal Study: Factors associated with bicycle crashes and injury severity in the ACT*. Sydney: The George Institute for Global Health.

Drummond, AE. (1988). *Estimation of the safety outcomes of legalising footpath cycling*. Melbourne, Vic.: Monash University Accident Research Centre.

Drummond, AE. (1989). *Pedestrian casualties resulting from collisions with cyclists on footpaths*. Melbourne, Vic.: Monash University Accident Research Centre.

Drummond, AE, & Jee, FA. (1988). *The risk of bicyclist accident involvement*. Melbourne, Vic.: Monash University Accident Research Centre.

Elvik, R, Vaa, T, Erke, A, & Sorensen, M (Eds.). (2009). *The handbook of road safety measures*. Bingley, UK: Emerald Group Publishing.

European Economic and Social Commission [EESC]. (2011). *European cycling lexicon*. Brussels: Section for Transport, Energy, Infrastructure and the Information Society [TEN] and the Visits and Publications Unit [VIP], EESC. Retrieved 8 September 2015 from http://www.eesc.europa.eu/resources/docs/eesc-2011-27-en.pdf.

Frumkin, H, Frank, L, & Jackson, R. (2004). *Urban sprawl and public health: Designing, planning, and building for healthy communities*. Washington, DC: Island Press.

Garrard, J, Rose, G, & Lo, SK. (2008). Promoting transportation cycling for women: The role of bicycle infrastructure. *Preventive Medicine*, 46, 55-59.

Gatersleben, B, & Appleton, KM. (2007). Contemplating cycling to work: Attitudes and perceptions in different stages of change. *Transportation Research Part A: Policy and Practice*, 41(1), 302-312.

Gould, G, & Karner, A. (2012). Modeling bicycle facility operation — Cellular automaton approach. *Transportation Research Record: Journal of the Transportation Research Board*, 2140, 157-164. doi: 10.3141/2140-17.

Grzebieta, RH, & Chong, S. (2008). *Pedestrian-cyclist collisions: Report for the Pedestrian Council of Australia.* Sydney, NSW: NSW Injury Risk Management Research Centre.

Grzebieta, RH, McIntosh, AM, & Chong, S. (2011, September 1-2). Pedestrian-cyclist collisions: Issues and risk. *Australasian College of Road Safety National Conference*, Melbourne.

Haworth, N, & Schramm, A. (2011). How do level of experience, purpose for riding and preference for facilities affect location of riding? Study of adult bicycle riders in Queensland, Australia. *Transportation Research Record: Journal of the Transportation Research Board*, 2247, 17-23.

Haworth, N, Schramm, A, & Debnath, AK. (2014). An observational study of conflicts between cyclists and pedestrians in the city centre. *Journal of the Australasian College of Road Safety*, 25(4), 31-40.

Henley, G, & Harrison, JE. (2009). *Serious injury due to land transport accidents, Australia, 2006-07.* Injury research and statistics series: No. 53. Cat. No. INJCAT 129. Canberra, ACT: Australian Institute of Health and Welfare.

Hunt, JD, & Abraham, EJE. (2007). Influences on bicycle use. *Transportation*, 34, 453-470.

Jensen, SU. (2008, January 13-17). Bicycle tracks and lanes: A before-after study. *TRB Annual Meeting*, Washington DC. Retrieved 28 June 2014 from http://www.ibiketo.ca/sites/default/files/bicycle%20tracks%20and%20lanes.pdf.

Johansson, R. (2009). Vision Zero — Implementing a policy for traffic safety. *Safety Science*, 47, 826-831.

Lehman, R, Lee, D, Reid, I, Barker, N, Zhong, J, Kim, K … Gardland, R. (2009). *Cycling in New South Wales: What does the data tell us?* Sydney, NSW: Parsons Brinckerhoff Australia.

Lieswyn, J, Macbeth, A, Wilke, A, Ward, J, Ashford, J, Houghton, R, & Lloyd, W. (2012, February 22-24). An illustrated lexicon of cycle facilities. *2 Walk & Cycle Conference*, Hastings, New Zealand.

Lusk, AC, Further, PG, Morency, P, Miranda-Moreno, LF, Willett, WC, & Dennerlein, JT. (2011). Risk of injury for bicycling on cycle tracks versus in the street. *Injury Prevention*, 17(2), 131-135.

Lusk, AC, Morency, P, Miranda-Moreno, LF, Willett, WC, & Dennerlein, JT. (2013, May 16). Bicycle guidelines and crash rates on cycle tracks in the United States. *American Journal of Public Health*, e1-9. doi: 10.2105/AJPH.2012.301043.

Manton, R, & Clifford, E. (2011, August 31-September 1). Route selection, design assessment and cost considerations of rural off-road cycleways. *Irish Transport Research Network [ITRN] Conference*, Cork, Ireland.

Meuleners, LB, Lee, AH, & Haworth, C. (2007). Road environment, crash type and hospitalisation of bicyclists and motorcyclists presented to emergency departments in Western Australia. *Accident Analysis & Prevention*, 39(6), 1222-1225.

Moritz, WE. (1997a). Adult bicyclists in the United States: Characteristics and riding experience in 1996. *Transportation Research Record: Journal of the Transportation Research Board*, 1636, 1-7.

Moritz, WE. (1997b). Survey of North American bicycle commuters: Design and aggregate results. *Transportation Research Record: Journal of the Transportation Research Board*, 1578, 91-101.

Niska, A. (2011). *Service levels of cycleways: State-of-the-art focusing on maintenance and operation.* VTI Report 726. Sweden: VTI.

Oja, P, Titze, S, Bauman, A, De Geus, B, Krenn, P, Reger-Nash, B, & Kohlberger, T. (2011). Health benefits of cycling: A systematic review. *Scandinavian Journal of Medicine & Science in Sports*, 21(4), 496-509.

Pucher, J, & Buehler, R. (2008). Making cycling irresistible: Lessons from the Netherlands, Denmark and Germany. *Transport Reviews*, 28(4), 495-528.

Reynolds, CC, Harris, MA, Teschke, K, Cripton, PA, & Winters, M. (2009). The impact of transportation infrastructure on bicycling injuries and crashes: A review of the literature. *Environmental Health*, 8(47), 1-19.

Roads and Traffic Authority [RTA]. (2009, August). *Study of bicyclist and pedestrian safety on shared paths*. Research report. Surrey Hills, NSW: Taverner Research.

Shaw, L, Poulos, R, Rissel, C, & Hatfield, J. (2012, October 4-6). Exploring the application of the Safe System Approach to cycling. *Australasian Road Safety Research Policing Education Conference*, Wellington, New Zealand.

Sorensen, M, & Mosslemi, M. (2009). *Subjective and objective safety: The effect of road safety measures on subjective safety among vulnerable road users*. TØI report 1009/2009. Oslo: Institute of Transport Economics.

Stinson, MA, & Bhat, CR. (2003). Commuter bicyclist route choice: Analysis using a stated preference survey. *Transportation Research Record: Journal of the Transportation Research Board*, 1828(1), 107-115.

Teschke, K, Harris, MA, Reynolds, CC, Winters, M, Babul, S, Chipman, M ... Cripton, PA. (2012). Route infrastructure and the risk of injuries to bicyclists: A case crossover study. *American Journal of Public Health*, 102(12), 2336-2343.

Tinsworth, DK, Cassidy, SP, & Polen, C. (1994). Bicycle-related injuries: Injury, hazard, and risk patterns. *International Journal for Consumer and Product Safety*, 1(4), 207-220.

Tovell, A, McKenna, K, Bradley, C, & Pointer, S. (2012). *Hospital separations due to injury and poisoning, Australia 2009-10*. Injury research and statistics series: No. 69. Cat. no. INJCAT 145. Canberra, ACT: Australian Institute of Health and Welfare.

Transport and Main Roads [TMR]. (2014). *Separated cycleways guidelines*. Brisbane, Qld: Transport and Main Roads.

Virkler, MR, & Balasubramanian, R. (1998). Flow characteristics on shared hiking/biking/jogging trails. *Transportation Research Record: Journal of the Transportation Research Board*, 1636(1), 43-46.

Wachtel, A, & Lewiston, D. (1994). Risk factors for bicycle-motor vehicle collisions at intersections. *ITE Journal (Institute of Transportation Engineers)*, 64(9), 30-35.

Washington, S, Haworth, N, & Schramm, A. (2012). Relationships between self-reported bicycling injuries and perceived risk of cyclists in Queensland, Australia. *Transportation Research Record: Journal of the Transportation Research Board*, 2314(1), 57-65.

Wennberg, H, Stahl, A, & Hyden, C. (2009). Older pedestrians' perceptions of the outdoor environment in a year-round perspective. *European Journal of Ageing*, 6, 277-290.

14 Teaching Australian civil engineers about cycling

Geoff Rose

Introduction

At present over half the world's population lives in urban areas, with that figure expected to rise to two-thirds by 2050 (United Nations, 2014). Accelerating urbanisation along with prevailing urban lifestyles and consumption patterns are placing considerable pressure on planetary systems, with scientific concerns mounting about the risks associated with exceeding the safe operating space for humanity (Rockstrom et al., 2009; Steffan et al., 2015). Even by world standards, Australia is a highly urbanised society with nearly 90% of the population residing in its urban areas (World Bank, 2015) and the national challenges it faces in the context of sustainability firmly in the spotlight (National Sustainability Council, 2013; see also Kingham & Tranter, Chapter Seven, this volume).

While urban areas face many challenges from a sustainability perspective, the issue of transport is of particular concern. Increasing problems associated with urban mobility — including traffic congestion; death and injury from road crashes; vulnerability of energy sources; and adverse environmental impacts, such as poor local air quality and global climate change — are challenging governments around the world. These problems have been magnified because the motor vehicle is the predominant form of urban mobility (Sperling & Gordon, 2010). There is a growing awareness of the need to prioritise moving people rather than cars (Wright, 2001) and a broad range of both supply- and demand-oriented measures are available to address these challenges. Integrating transport and land use planning, expanding public transport and facilitating greater travel by walk and bicycle are seen as key actions (Schiller, Bruun, & Kenworthy, 2010; Tumlin, 2012). While there are no silver bullets, the *National cycling strategy 2011-2016* in Australia notes that 'against the backdrop of a growing population, the highest ever obesity levels and significant environmental challenges — cycling offers a wealth of benefits' (Austroads, 2010, p. 8).

Australia's *National cycling strategy* sets what it acknowledges is an 'aspirational' aim (Austroads, 2010, p. 8) to double the number of people cycling in Australia by 2016, and notes that both

> [d]eveloping high quality networks and facilities for cyclists, as well as ensuring that all local planning and transport plans are fully integrated and address the needs of cycling are … critical. (p. 5)

International research has highlighted the fundamental importance of adequate cycling infrastructure (Pucher, Dill, & Handy, 2010; Buehler & Pucher, 2012) in encouraging cycling, while local research has identified cycling infrastructure deficiencies in the context of Australia's two largest cities, Sydney and Melbourne (Pucher, Garrard, & Greaves, 2011).

Civil engineers play a central role in the development of urban transport infrastructure. As highlighted on the website of Engineers Australia (2014a):

> Much of the physical infrastructure of our modern society is provided by Civil Engineers. Civil Engineers are concerned with all types of structures including dams, bridges, pipelines, roads, towers and buildings. *They are responsible for the design and construction of all our transport systems*, the design and management of our gas and water supply, sewerage systems, harbours, airports and railways. Civil Engineers plan, design and test the structures of private and public buildings and facilities. (Emphasis added)

Clearly Engineers Australia sees civil engineers as central to the development of transport systems. Given the magnitude of the challenges outlined above, and the ambitious targets set for increased cycling, it seems relevant to ask how well Australian civil engineers are being prepared to support the growth of safe cycling. The aim of this chapter is to examine the extent to which civil engineering graduates in Australia are adequately prepared to contribute to the growth of safe cycling.

The literature provides only limited insight into transport in general, or cycling in particular, in the context of the curriculum at a tertiary level. Mateo-Babiano and Burke (2013) reviewed transport planning education in urban planning schools in Australia and found that, when assessed against the Planning Institute of Australia's [PIA] performance outcomes for transport planning, the education programs fell short in a number of areas, including a lack of focus on integration of transport and land use. The PIA course performance outcomes do not mention cycling explicitly, but do include knowledge of various transport modes and their operation, along with the capacity to critique plans and design proposals according to sustainable transport planning principles.

Drawing on a survey of 360 planning professionals in the United States, Handy, Weston, Song, and Lane (2002) measured the gaps between what practising professionals believed was important in their work and what was covered in the university courses they completed. While bicycle and pedestrian planning ranked 10th out of the 25 topics on their survey, nearly half the respondents (42%) indicated that the topic was not covered at all in the university course they completed. Based on the difference in the average scores respondents gave to coverage in their course and the importance of the topic to their job, Handy et al. (2002) prioritised a range of topics for attention in curriculum renewal. Bicycle and pedestrian planning was ranked second in priority, behind public involvement, and ahead of public transport planning (which ranked third).

Dill and Weigand (2010) conducted a survey of accredited planning and civil engineering programs in the United States to examine the extent to which bicycle and pedestrian topics were covered in the curriculum. Of the 451 faculty members who were sent the survey, 20% responded. While that response rate is not atypical for email surveys (Stopher, 2012), Dill and Weigand understandably caution against the potential response bias, with faculty members who were more interested in bicycle and pedestrian topics potentially being likely to complete the survey. Respondents indicated that just over half (59%) of the courses included bicycle or pedestrian topics, and of those about half (52%) included only one to two hours of class time devoted to bicycle and pedestrian topics. This brief review of the literature suggests that, while little is known in the context of Australian tertiary programs, bicycle and pedestrian topics receive limited attention in the curriculum in the United States.

In exploring the extent to which cycling is considered in Australian civil engineering programs, this chapter is structured as follows. The next section outlines the research approach and identifies the three key research questions which guided the research. In turn, the three sections that follow this address those three research questions by progressively exploring, first, the relationship of transport to civil engineering course accreditation; second, the coverage of transport in civil engineering courses; and finally, the extent to which cycling is addressed in the curriculum. A discussion follows, and the final section summarises the conclusions and identifies directions for future research.

It is appropriate at this point to clarify terminology, since terms are not interpreted the same way all around the world. Here in Australia, *course* is used to refer to a program of study — that is, a civil engineering course. Within that course, students enrol in *units*, which a lay person might refer to as a 'subject'. In the US, the units considered here would be referred to as a *class*; in other countries (for example, New Zealand) they would be called a *paper*. A course usually requires the completion of a minimum number of credit points. Each unit corresponds to a certain number of credit points. In many programs, all units have the same credit point value; in others, units vary in size and have corresponding credit point value. Units may be specified as *core*, in which case they must be completed by all students, or as *elective*, where there is a choice of enrolment on the student's part.

Research approach and key research questions

The primary methodology employed in this research is desk auditing of material available on public websites of professional organisations (for example, Engineers Australia and the Accreditation Boards of Engineering and Technology in the United States) and universities. University websites were accessed to obtain information on the structure of civil engineering programs and the outlines of units within those programs.

The research was guided by three key research questions, framed to help achieve the overall aim of the research, as outlined in the previous section, to examine the extent to which civil engineering graduates in Australia are adequately prepared to contribute to the growth of safe cycling. The three key research questions were:

> To what extent is transport a required component of the education of undergraduate civil engineers?
>
> What proportion of civil engineering courses is devoted to transport?
>
> To what extent is cycling considered in the transport units included in civil engineering courses?

Those three research questions effectively structured the research approach, starting broadly and then, rather like increasing the magnification of a microscope, progressively focusing on smaller elements, as illustrated in Figure 14.1.

Transport in the context of civil engineering course accreditation

Engineering degrees in Australia are accredited by Engineers Australia, the professional association representing engineers (Engineers Australia, 2014b). Accreditation offers recognition that the qualification meets national and international benchmarks. Graduates of accredited programs are then eligible for membership of Engineers Australia at the level of a Professional Engineer. They

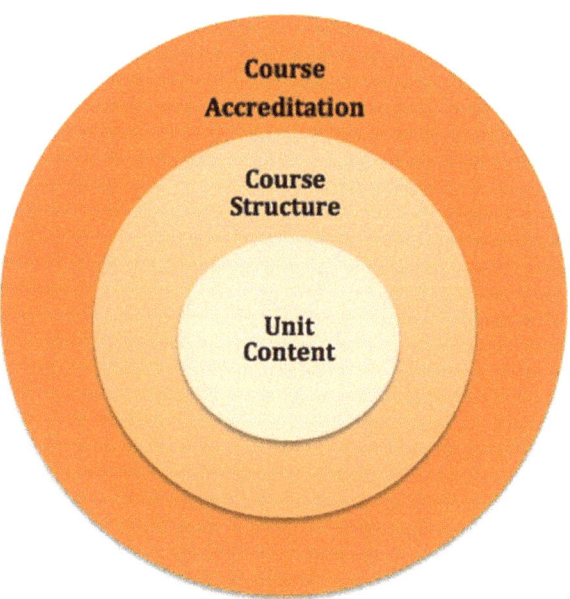

Figure 14.1: Three-level structure of the analysis.
(Source: Author's own work.)

can also benefit from reciprocal arrangements negotiated by Engineers Australia with equivalent professional bodies overseas.

Accreditation reviews are conducted by a panel of appropriately qualified engineers who are appointed by Engineers Australia. The panel has access to comprehensive documentation provided by the educational institution seeking accreditation, and visits the campus to interview a range of stakeholders including staff, students and senior university leaders. The Engineers Australia Accreditation Board is the governing body which considers the recommendations of the panel and makes the final decision on accreditation. Courses that do not meet the required standard are at risk of losing their accreditation or receiving temporary accreditation until such time as identified deficiencies are corrected and appropriately reviewed. Accreditation is for a maximum of five years.

It is not mandatory for universities to submit their engineering degrees for accreditation. However, since accreditation brings professional recognition that graduates who have obtained the degree in question meet the standards required for professional practice, an institution would be at a distinct competitive disadvantage in attracting students if it offered an unaccredited degree. Perhaps not surprisingly, all universities in Australia have sought accreditation of their engineering degrees through Engineers Australia.

To meet the requirements of accreditation, Engineers Australia has developed a set of national generic competency standards. The Stage 1 competency standards which are applied to Bachelor of Engineering courses are those 'deemed to be essential for an individual to commence practice' (Engineers Australia, 2014c); they apply to entry-level positions in the profession, where work is undertaken under guidance. Traditionally, Bachelor of Engineering degrees have been of four years' duration, and a four-year qualification is the minimum time required in order for someone to satisfy Engineers Australia's Stage 1 competencies. In recent years, two universities (the University of Melbourne and the University of Western Australia) have fundamentally changed the nature of their course offerings. Those two universities now offer a limited suite of three-year degrees with students needing to complete a subsequent two-year Masters degree to satisfy the Stage 1 competency requirements.

The Stage 1 competencies are framed in relation to three areas:
1. knowledge and skill base

2. engineering application ability
3. professional and personal attributes.

In each of those areas, elements of competency are identified along with indicators of attainment (Engineers Australia, 2014b). Because the Engineers Australia approach is based on generic competencies, it is not prescriptive of course content. However, engineering has long been recognised as having a central role to play in contributing to a sustainable future (Velazquez, Munguia, & Romo, 1999; Davidson et al., 2010; Karatzoglou, 2013), and sustainability is explicitly mentioned in a number of the competency elements (Engineers Australia, 2014b):

Element 1.5.a — Consider the interaction between engineering systems and sustainable development.

Element 1.6.d — Appreciate the social, environmental, and economic principles of sustainable engineering practice.

Element 2.3.b — Address broad contextual constraints such as sustainable imperatives as an integral part of the design process.

Element 2.3.c — Execute and lead a whole system design cycle approach to systematically addressing sustainability criteria.

Element 2.4.f — Demonstrate commitment to sustainable engineering practices and the achievement of sustainable outcomes in all facets of engineering project work.

As noted in the introduction, transport presents many challenges from the perspective of sustainability, so it is encouraging that sustainability is explicitly mentioned as part of the competency standards. However, there is no specific mention of sustainable transport. Indeed there is no mention of any sub-discipline of civil engineering, because the competency standards are not framed to require a civil engineering course to cover specific areas of civil engineering.

The transport component of Australian civil engineering courses

Now we wind down the microscope to examine the extent to which Australian civil engineering courses have transport content.

Across Australia, 34 universities offer engineering degrees. There are four main groupings of Australian universities. These have been formed to promote the mutual objectives of the member universities. Of particular interest in the context of engineering is the Group of Eight [Go8], which promotes itself as representing those Australian universities that are distinguished by depth and breadth in research (Group of Eight Australia, n.d.). Also of interest is the Australian Technology Network [ATN], which brands itself as bringing together 'five of the most innovative and enterprising universities in the nation' (Australian Technology Network, 2004). Table 14.1 shows the membership of those university groupings.

As shown in Figure 14.2, the Go8 and ATN universities account for approximately two-thirds of the graduates of undergraduate engineering degrees in Australia. The analysis that follows focuses on those two groups of Australian universities, which together account for a substantial percentage of all Australian engineering graduates.

Not all members of the Go8 offer civil engineering courses. Australian National University does not offer a civil engineering specialisation. In addition, two other members of the Go8 do not offer four-year Bachelor of Engineering qualifications. As mentioned above, at the University of Melbourne and the University of Western Australia to be professionally qualified as an engineer, students need to complete a three-year generalist undergraduate degree followed by a two-year Masters. The analysis which follows deals separately with four- and five-year professional qualifications.

Table 14.2 shows the results from an analysis of the content of four-year civil engineering qualifications. Information from publicly available course handbooks

Table 14.1: Australian University Group membership listing.

Group of Eight	Australian Technology Network
• University of Queensland • University of New South Wales • University of Sydney • Australian National University • Monash University • University of Melbourne • University of Adelaide • University of Western Australia	• Queensland University of Technology • University of Technology Sydney • RMIT University • University of South Australia • Curtin University

(Source: Author's own work.)

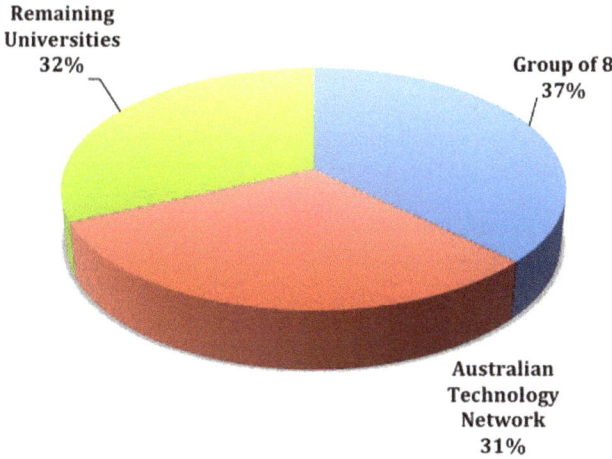

Figure 14.2: Percentage of engineering undergraduate completions (2013) by Australian University group.
(Source: Graph compiled based on data available at http://highereducationstatistics.education.gov.au/Default.aspx.)

was used to compile the summary shown in this table. In addition to summarising the content of the Australian qualifications, results from one program available in the United States are provided as a point of comparison.

Table 14.2 identifies the percentage of the course (in terms of credit points) that is devoted to transport units. Separate results are provided for students who major in transport and those who do not major in transport. For comparison, results are also shown for the percentage of the course that is devoted to structures for students who are majoring in structures. Engineering programs commonly include a final-year research project, and it has been assumed that students undertaking a major in a particular field would choose to do their project in that field. Another feature of civil engineering courses is usually the inclusion of a final-year capstone design unit, where students usually work in teams to undertake a major infrastructure design project. It has also been assumed that students take responsibility for the component of that design which relates to their discipline, and so the credit points of that capstone design project have also been counted towards the student's relevant major.

It is clear from Table 14.2 that the Go8 and ATN universities are fairly similar in their civil engineering course structure. Students who are majoring in transport

Table 14.2: Composition of four-year accredited Bachelor of Civil Engineering degrees.

4-year civil engineering degrees	Percentage of course that is transport		Percentage of course that is structures
	Students majoring in transport	Students not majoring in transport	Students majoring in structures
Go8*	11.3	3.1	30.6
ATN	15.6	3.4	35.0
Average (Go8* & ATN)	13.5	3.3	32.8
Max. (Go8* & ATN)	21.9	6.3	37.5
Min. (Go8* & ATN)	0	0	25
Portland State University, USA	18.5	4.2	31.2

Note: * excluding ANU, University of Melbourne and University of Western Australia.
(Source: Author's own work.)

typically complete about one-sixth of their course in transport, while students majoring in structures complete about one-third of their course in structures. There is on average a quite small (3%) core component of transport which must be completed by students who are not majoring in transport. Importantly, Table 14.2 highlights that some civil engineering programs contain no transport content (shown as minimum content of zero).

As a point of comparison, results are also shown for the civil engineering program at Portland State University in the United States. Portland State has a reputation for emphasising sustainability, and the staff in its planning and engineering faculties are very active in bicycle-related research. It is clear from the results presented in Table 14.2 that the composition of the four-year civil engineering courses in Australia are similar to that at Portland State in terms of the proportion of the course which is devoted to transport.

As noted earlier, at two Australian universities (University of Melbourne and University of Western Australia) students need to complete five years of study to achieve recognition as a Professional Engineer under the engineering accreditation scheme. At each of the institutions offering five-year civil engineering qualifications, there is only one transport unit in each of those programs. The one transport unit is specified as core in the University of Melbourne program, but it is an elective at the University of Western Australia. Students could complete five years of study at the University of Western Australia and graduate with a combination of a Bachelor of Engineering Science and a Masters degree, qualify for recognition as a Professional Engineer by Engineers Australia, practise as a civil engineer and have studied no transport as part of their course. At the University of Melbourne, there is only one core transport unit in the five years of study — accounting for 2.5% of their university studies.

Cycling in transport engineering subjects

As highlighted by the results in the previous section, transport receives relatively little attention in many Australian civil engineering programs. In the transport units which are included, there is a lot of pressure on the curriculum, given the need to cover a broad range of topics such as traffic survey techniques, traffic engineering and management, road design, public transport and transport planning.

An analysis of unit outlines accessible via university websites highlights that it is rare to find bicycles or cycling explicitly mentioned. There are certainly no units devoted to planning and design for non-motorised transport. Where cycling is mentioned as a topic, it is clear that at most about one week of a unit (equivalent to two to four hours of classes) is devoted to the topic. This is not to say that cycling is not mentioned in other parts of the curriculum, even if not explicitly as part of the unit outlines available on the web. To determine the extent to which cycling in particular is mentioned, or considered as part of a broader examination of non-motorised transport, would require more detailed research involving a survey of academic staff.

Discussion

The examination of course accreditation found that there is no requirement under the system for accrediting civil engineering courses in Australia for those courses to include any transport content. For comparison, it is useful to consider the US system. In the United States, where accreditation is undertaken by the Accreditation Boards of Engineering and Technology [ABET], a slightly different approach is taken to that in Australia. Unlike the Australian competency-based approach, ABET emphasises curriculum (Accreditation Boards of Engineering and Technology [ABET], 2013) and specifies separate curriculum criteria for each engineering discipline. For civil engineering, graduates must be able to 'apply knowledge of four technical areas appropriate to civil engineering' (ABET, 2013, n.p.). The four areas typically taught in civil engineering programs in the United States are structural, geotechnical, water, and transport engineering (Agrawal & Dill, 2008). However, since the criteria do not explicitly require transport engineering, a civil engineering program could technically be accredited with no transport content. ABET identifies 11 broad outcomes that programs must demonstrate. One of these 11 outcomes requires students to demonstrate an 'ability to design a system, component, or process that meets sustainability needs' of the future (ABET, 2013, n.p.). However, there is no specific mention of sustainable transport in ABET's framework.

Planners — or 'urban and regional planners', as they are sometimes known — are members of another distinct professional group, whose work can seek to shape the transport system through their roles more generally (see Bell & Ferretti, Chapter Fifteen, this volume). In their examination of transport planning in Australian urban planning schools, Mateo-Babiano and Burke (2013) note that course accreditation requirements specified by the Planning Institute of Australia state that planning programs must advance one or more of five nominated supportive knowledge areas. Those five areas are urban design, social planning, environmental planning, transport planning and economic planning. Therefore, for the two most distinct professions whose work impacts on the transport system, there is no requirement under professional course accreditation for students to have any exposure to transport material as part of their course.

Clearly, despite the importance of sustainable transport in the context of the megatrend of urbanisation, it is afforded little priority in professional course accreditation. Particularly in relation to civil engineering, it is likely that the majority of students select the degree because of career aspirations in other sub-disciplines. In a study of US civil engineering students, Agrawal and Dill (2008) found that three-quarters of all entering civil engineering majors did not know what transportation engineers do, and that students focusing on environmental engineering and structural engineering were more likely to have chosen their focus before starting their university course.

The examination of Australian civil engineering courses found that while some have up to a fifth of the curriculum devoted to transport, there are some institutions where a student can complete a four-year Bachelor of Engineering, or an alternative five-year qualification (as outlined earlier), and complete no transportation-related units. Even in the transportation units which are offered, there is a lot of competition for space in the curriculum. Insight gleaned from university handbooks suggests that in most units there may be one week (that is, two to three hours of classes) devoted to cycling. This is not dramatically different from the results reported by Dill and Weigand (2010), which revealed that about half the civil engineering units covering bicycle and pedestrian topics devoted only one to two hours of class time to that material. However, 62% of those units were electives, so civil engineering students in the United States who are not majoring in transportation appear unlikely to see any course content relating to pedestrians and cyclists — a situation which appears comparable to their Australian counterparts.

Given what little time is devoted to cycling topics in the civil engineering curriculum, it is clearly unrealistic to expect that students will develop deep understanding on the topic over the course of their degree. At best, one might hope that the students would develop a mindset that recognises the role of walking and cycling in the context of sustainable transport, appreciate the role that adequate infrastructure plays in encouraging safe walking and cycling, and know where to turn for further information. Beyond graduation, it is likely to be professional development courses, like those offered in Australia (Salomon, 2014), which have a potentially valuable role to play in upskilling traffic engineers. Ideally, the following learning outcomes — which are specified for the one training course on designing and planning for pedestrians and cyclists which has run in New South Wales, Queensland and the Australian Capital Territory since 2003 (Salomon, 2014) — would be reflected in university courses in the future:

- Recognise the key operating needs and requirements of pedestrians and cyclists.
- Identify the key engineering treatments and facilities available to the planner and designer.

- Understand a wide range of design issues relating to the provision of facilities.
- Recognise the importance of including provision for pedestrians and cyclists.
- Identify the key resource and regulatory documents for facilities provision and policy.

However, it is appropriate to note that there is a substantial challenge associated with the time lags in curriculum renewal. Traditional curriculum renewal can take 15 to 20 years (that is, 3 to 4 program accreditation cycles), and consequently it has been argued (Desha, Hargroves, & Smith, 2009) that rapid curriculum renewal approaches need development and testing, particularly in relation to topics which are associated with sustainability.

Conclusions and research directions

The analysis presented here highlights that civil engineering graduates have limited preparation to enable them to contribute to the growth of safe cycling. Consideration of the three key research questions posed at the start of the chapter has shown that there is no requirement for civil engineering courses to have any transport content, and that while many civil engineering courses enable students majoring in transport to complete about 20% of their course on that major, it is possible for students to graduate with a four- or five-year civil engineering qualification in Australia and be exposed to no transport content in their course. The limited share of existing courses devoted to transport places considerable pressure on the curriculum, with something in the order of two to four hours of class time typically devoted to bicycle- and/or pedestrian-related topics. While progress on curriculum renewal may redress that balance over time, it is clear that professional development courses will continue to have a valuable role to play in upskilling traffic engineers in the field of bicycle transportation.

The work reported here has relied on information available in organisational websites. There would clearly be merit in extending this research to conduct surveys of academic staff involved in teaching transport units in Australia in order to develop a deeper understanding of the content of those units.

All the evidence suggests that the importance of cycling will only grow over time as the policy makers seek to respond to the ever-increasing challenge of enhancing the sustainability of urban transport systems. Civil engineers and planners have an important contribution to make in increasing the uptake of safe cycling. The evidence presented in this chapter suggests that more work will be required to ensure that those professionals are adequately equipped to achieve that outcome for the community.

Acknowledgements

The author gratefully acknowledges the contribution of Chris Piperidis, who compiled some of the data on which this chapter is based.

References

Accreditation Boards of Engineering and Technology [ABET]. (2013). Accreditation. Retrieved 27 January 2014 from http://www.abet.org/accreditation.

Agrawal, AW, & Dill, J. (2008). To be a transportation engineer or not? How civil engineering students choose a specialisation. *Transportation Research Record: Journal of the Transportation Research Board*, 2046, 76-84.

Australian Technology Network of Universities. (2003). Australian Technology Network. Retrieved 27 January 2014 from https://www.atn.edu.au.

Austroads. (2010). *National cycling strategy 2011-2016*. Publication No. AP-C85/10. Sydney, NSW: Austroads.

Buehler, R, & Pucher, J. (2012). Cycling to work in 90 large American cities: New evidence on the role of bike paths and lanes. *Transportation*, 39(2), 409-432.

Davidson, C, Hendrickson, C, Matthews, H, Bridgesc, M, Allend, D, Murphy, C … Austing, S. (2010). Preparing future engineers for challenges of the 21st century: Sustainable engineering. *Journal of Cleaner Production*, 18(7), 698-701.

Desha, CJ, Hargroves, K, & Smith, MH. (2009). Addressing the time lag dilemma in curriculum renewal towards engineering for sustainable development. *International Journal of Sustainability in Higher Education*, 10(2), 184-199.

Dill, J, & Weigand, L. (2010). Incorporating bicycle and pedestrian topics in university transportation courses. *Transportation Research Record: Journal of the Transportation Research Board*, 2198, 1-7.

Engineers Australia. (2014a). What is civil engineering? Retrieved 27 January 2015 from http://www.engineers australia.org.au/civil-college/what-civil-engineering.

Engineers Australia. (2014b). Program accreditation. Retrieved 27 January 2015 from https://www.engineers australia.org.au/about-us/program-accreditation.

Engineers Australia. (2014c). National generic stage 1 competency standards — 2011. Retrieved 27 January 2015 from http://www.engineersaustralia.org.au/sites/ default/files/shado/Education/Program%20Accreditation/140203_foreword_to_stage_1_standards.pdf.

Group of Eight Australia. (n.d.). About GO8. Retrieved 27 January 2014 from https://go8.edu.au/page/go8-indicators.

Handy, S, Weston, L, Song, J, & Lane, KMD. (2002). Education of transportation planning professionals. *Transportation Research Record: Journal of the Transportation Research Board*, 1812, 151-160.

Karatzoglou, B. (2013). An in-depth literature review of the evolving roles and contributions of universities to education for sustainable development. *Journal of Cleaner Production*, 49, 44-53.

Mateo-Babiano, I, & Burke, MI. (2013, October 2-4). Transport planning education in urban planning schools in Australia. *Australasian Transport Research Forum Proceedings*, Brisbane, Australia.

National Sustainability Council. (2013). *Sustainable Australia report: Conversations with the future.* Canberra: DSEWPaC.

Pucher, J, Dill, J, & Handy, S. (2010). Infrastructure, programs and policies to increase bicycling: An international review. *Preventive Medicine*, 50, S106-S125.

Pucher, J, Garrard, J, & Greaves, S. (2011). Cycling down under: A comparative analysis of bicycling trends and policies in Sydney and Melbourne. *Journal of Transport Geography*, 19, 332-345.

Rockström, J, Steffen, W, Noone, K, Persson, A, Chapin III, FS, Lambin, E ... Foley, J. (2009). Planetary boundaries: Exploring the safe operating space for humanity. *Ecology and Society*, 14(2). Retrieved 8 September 2015 from http://www.ecologyandsociety.org/vol14/iss2/art32.

Salomon, W. (2014, May 28-30). Training traffic engineers to see the world from behind the handlebars. *Velocity Global 2014*, Adelaide, Australia.

Schiller, PL, Bruun, EC, & Kenworthy, JR. (2010). *An introduction to sustainable transportation: Policy, planning and implementation*. London: Earthscan.

Sperling, D, & Gordon, D. (2010). *Two billion cars: Driving toward sustainability* (1st ed.). Oxford: Oxford University Press.

Steffan, W, Richardson, K, Rockström, J, Cornell, SE, Fetzer, I, Bennett, EM, … Sörlin, S. (2015). Planetary boundaries: Guiding human development on a changing planet. *Science*, 347(6223), 736-747.

Stopher, P. (2012). *Collecting, managing and assessing data using sample surveys*. Cambridge: Cambridge University Press.

Tumlin, J. (2012). *Sustainable transportation planning: Tools for creating vibrant, healthy and resilient communities*. Hoboken, NJ: Wiley.

United Nations. (2014, July 10). World's population increasingly urban with more than half living in urban areas. Retrieved 9 February 2015 from http://www.un.org/en/development/desa/news/population/world-urbanization-prospects-2014.html.

Velazquez, L, Munguia, N, & Romo, M. (1999). Education for sustainable development: The engineer of the 21st century. *European Journal of Engineering Education*, 24(4), 359-370.

World Bank. (2015). Urban population (% of total). Retrieved 9 February 2015 from http://data.worldbank.org/indicator/SP.URB.TOTL.IN.ZS.

Wright, L. (2001). Latin American busways: Moving people rather than cars. *Natural Resources Forum: A United Nations Sustainable Development Journal*, 25(2), 121-134.

15 What should planners know about cycling?

Wendy Bell and Donna Ferretti

Introduction

Planners have traditionally played an important co-ordination role in planning for urban development by bringing together a range of disciplinary knowledges, including transport knowledges, in determining the suitability of particular forms of development in particular locations. While this has increased planners' understanding of the links between land use, transport and a host of related fields, it has not been conducive to planners seeking out and developing specialised knowledge of particular modes of transport such as cycling. Land use planners in particular have relied on the advice and direction of those with specialised knowledge of transport — namely, transport planners and traffic engineers — in making decisions about cycling without seeking out and actively engaging with knowledges of cycling as a specific mode of urban transport with specific requirements within urban environments.

While the importance of the engineering knowledges that transport planners and traffic engineers use to underpin their practice should not be denied (see Rose, Chapter Fourteen, this volume), there is increasing evidence to suggest that there is a lot more that planners need to know in order to properly plan for cycling as a mode of urban transport. The recent spate of integrated land use and transport initiatives developed across Australia and New Zealand (Auckland

Regional Transport Authority, 2009; Government of South Australia, 2013; Government of Victoria, 2010; New South Wales Government, 2012) attests to the growing recognition of how the nexus between land use and transport planning provides an important mechanism to reshape urban development towards more compact and sustainable urban forms. These initiatives seek to densify the existing urban footprint while boosting the provision of public transport and encouraging active travel modes such as walking and cycling.

In embracing the notion of active travel and its role in creating more sustainable and healthy cities (see Department of Infrastructure and Transport, 2013; Government of South Australia, 2011b; National Heart Foundation of Australia (Victorian Division), 2004; Planning Institute of Australia, Heart Foundation, & Australian Local Government Association, 2009), planners will not only need to broaden their knowledge of specific modes of transport, but also recognise the diverse and sometimes conflicting needs of urban travellers in order to enable greater participation in cycling.

This chapter is fundamentally concerned with the knowledge and skills required by land use planners to enable greater participation in cycling, either for transport or recreation (Figures 15.1 and 15.2). It examines the key strands of land use planning and how the strategies, policies and assessment decisions made by planners can shape the cycling context and the ability of people to cycle in urban areas. The chapter reviews strategic plans created for Adelaide, Melbourne and Sydney in order to determine how cycling is addressed in these plans. It then examines state-level planning policy in South Australia and Victoria to determine how these policies acknowledge and provide for the specific requirements of cyclists. In the final section, a detailed analysis of the 'cycle-friendliness' of two recently constructed public transport sites in metropolitan Adelaide is presented, which identifies the design elements planners should be cognisant of when assessing developments for convenient and safe access by cyclists.

Planning and cycling

The past decade has seen a growing conversation about walking and cycling as key components of active travel. Urban planners have participated in this discussion through examining the environmental, social and economic factors that shape people's decisions to walk and cycle (Department of Infrastructure and Transport, 2013;

What should planners know about cycling?

Figure 15.1: Example of good recreational cycling route.
(Source: Authors' own work.)

Ewing & Cervero, 2010; National Heart Foundation, 2004; Planning Institute of Australia et al., 2009). Some of this discussion is concerned with developing criteria to measure walkability (Clifton, Livi Smith, & Rodriguez, 2007; Ewing & Handy, 2009) and cycle-ability (Wahlgren & Schantz, 2012; Winters, Brauer, Selton, & Teschke, 2013).

Much of the recent discussion examines the relationship between particular urban characteristics and levels of active travel, particularly walking and/or cycling (Adkins, Dill, Luhr, & Neal, 2012; Forsyth & Krizek, 2011; Sick Nielsen, Skov-Petersen, & Agervig Carstensen, 2013). Some researchers (Pucher &

Figure 15.2: Example of good commuting cycling route.
(Source: Authors' own work.)

Buehler, 2006; Pucher, Garrard, & Greaves, 2011) have compared cycling rates in cities with different policies; and other researchers offer speculative pieces on the role of cycling under changing conditions, such as resource scarcity (Burke & Bonham, 2010). While there is widespread agreement in the planning-related literature on the role that cycling can play to address both traditional planning concerns of health and wellbeing as well as more recent concerns of environmental (particularly climate) change, there have been no studies to date that examine how land use planners include cycling in the strategies, policies and assessment decisions they make.

Strategy, policy, assessment

In posing the question of what planners should know about cycling, we have first examined what planners currently 'do' and 'say' about cycling. We have analysed a range of planning and transport texts from predominantly Australian jurisdictions (principally South Australia, Victoria and New South Wales) to examine how these interrelate with broader discussions of urban transport, infrastructure provision, and planning for urban development. State government planning strategies and policy documents have been interrogated with a particular focus on where cycling sits in efforts to regulate urban development.

The questions we have asked of these texts include:
- How has cycling been positioned in the context of broader transport planning objectives (in particular the relationship to motorised forms of urban travel)?
- How has cycling been positioned in the context of planning for urban development?
- How has cycling been positioned in the context of urban design (particularly the design of the public realm)?
- To what extent is cycling seen to contribute to population health outcomes?
- To what extent is cycling seen to contribute to urban sustainability outcomes?

We have supplemented our analysis of planning and transport texts with a case study of two public transport hubs (train stations) in the southern Adelaide metropolitan area.

Strategic planning

Strategic planning encompasses broad objectives to guide the use and development of land. Since the early 1990s, state and territory governments across Australia have developed and adopted strategic land use plans as key instruments to address emergent tensions between environmental, economic and social planning objectives in order to secure the sustainable, productive and equitable city. These plans effectively establish the key directions for future land use change, with the development of more detailed planning policy intended to align with these directions. It is through this strategy-policy linkage that the assessment of individual development proposals is envisaged to bring into effect the desired future development of an urban area.

In contrast to strategies produced in the 1980s-1990s, current metropolitan strategies seek a fundamental change in the trajectory of urban growth: to reshape urban form away from low-density greenfield development towards higher-density, mixed-use development within the existing urban footprint. This shift in strategic direction is a response to the environmental, economic and social problems associated with fringe growth, including the ongoing consumption of productive food-growing land; limited access to key services and facilities; social isolation; and high costs of supplying infrastructure and services at the urban fringe (Berry, 1992; Dodson, 2012; Gleeson, Dodson, & Spiller, 2012). It has also been informed by concerns about the declining health and ongoing car dependency of the urban population, especially those living on the fringes of urban areas, where access to employment and services is difficult (Department of Infrastructure and Transport, 2013).

The transport system occupies a fairly prominent place in metropolitan strategies given its essential role in supporting land use change. In the tranche of strategies developed for Australian metropolitan areas in the 1980s and 1990s, there is little, if any, specific reference to cycling as a mode of transport. Instead, cycling is subsumed within a discussion of private forms of motorised transport (Department of Planning, 1988; Department of Planning and Housing, 1992; Planning Review, 1992). More recent metropolitan strategies give greater weight to active transport modes such as cycling, walking and public transport in order to address the increasing spread of, congestion and pollution within, cities, as well as people's health in cities (Government of South Australia, 2010; Government of Victoria, 2014a; New South Wales Government, 2010).

This change in direction of metropolitan strategies marks a significant shift in the way transport and, in particular, cycling are thought about by land use planners. It also reflects the growing significance of environmental and health discourses in the development of urban planning strategies and policies. However, this shift has yet to be reflected in the ongoing development of urban environments, and there is still much work to do if cycling is to be repositioned and elevated in metropolitan strategies. The development of land use strategies could be informed, for instance, by national, state/territory and local cycling and integrated transport strategies. We would also argue that cycling and transport strategies need to pay greater attention to the role that planning plays in shaping urban mobility options.

At the national level, both the *Urban transport strategy* and *National cycling strategy* note the importance of 'integrated planning', urging state, territory and local governments to address the needs of cyclists when preparing land use and infrastructure plans. However, these two strategies offer little guidance on how these plans might enable more people to take up cycling (Australian Bicycle Council, 2010; Infrastructure Australia, 2013). At the state/territory level, cycling strategies and plans have focused on the provision of cycling infrastructure (Figures 15.3-15.5), cycling networks and increasingly on behavioural change programs to encourage people to cycle. And while these strategies and plans often point to the importance of land use planning in providing safe and convenient spaces for cyclists, there is little consideration of how land use policies or planning practice may need to change in order for this to occur (Government of Victoria, 2012; Government of South Australia, 2006). Planners clearly need to play a stronger role in identifying the land use implications of cycle strategies in collaboration with cycle policy makers, urban designers, asset managers and landscape architects.

At the local level, councils have sought to promote cycling through transport and movement plans, local area traffic management plans, urban design strategies, streetscape guidelines, and recreation and open space plans. Some councils have developed integrated transport strategies that promote an increase in cycling and a reduction in car use. For example, the City of Yarra's Bicycle Strategy has established a goal to double the rate of residents cycling to 15% by

What should planners know about cycling?

Figure 15.3: Shared cycling and pedestrian footpath.
(Source: Authors' own work.)

Figure 15.4: Shared cycling and pedestrian path segregated from vehicular traffic to encourage cycling.
(Source: Authors' own work.)

Figure 15.5: Segregated cycle lane.
(Source: Authors' own work.)

2015, with the city already recording the highest proportion of people who cycle to work in Australia (City of Yarra, 2010). This strategy is a prime example of a shift in emphasis towards cycling by including policies to make cycling, rather than car use, the first choice of transport for residents.

Similarly, *Smart move*, the Adelaide City Council's 10-year transport and movement strategy, has 'safe cycling' as a key objective, and aims for more trips to be made on bicycle, foot and public transport (Adelaide City Council, 2012). This plan acknowledges that there needs to be a shift in emphasis away from motor vehicle use in favour of cycling (Figures 15.6 and 15.7), although — in contrast to the City of Yarra — this shift in emphasis has yet to be adequately incorporated into policy. Neither of these strategies refers to the full range of cycling treatments which could be deployed to enable greater participation in cycling (see Hamnett, Chapter Sixteen, this volume).

Many other councils have prepared cycling plans and strategies to promote cycling.[1] These plans and strategies emphasise the provision of safe and convenient

---

[1] Currently, over 60% of local councils across Australia have a bicycle strategy or plan (Australian Bicycle Council, 2010).

What should planners know about cycling?

Figure 15.6: A shift in emphasis favouring cyclists in the streetscape.
(Source: Authors' own work.)

Figure 15.7: Providing more space for cyclists and pedestrians.
(Source: Authors' own work.)

routes for cyclists, end-of-trip facilities, and, in some cases, bike hire opportunities (City of Melbourne, 2012; City of Sydney, 2007; GTA Consultants, 2007). Planners usually participate in these initiatives, but have not generally considered the implications of this work in strategic and policy planning, development assessment, land division design and public realm development.

Planners also need to incorporate initiatives such as *Healthy spaces and places* into their work. The *Healthy spaces and places* guide and website, produced as a collaborative venture by the Planning Institute of Australia, the National Heart Foundation and the Australian Local Government Association (2009), sets out a number of design principles for creating spaces amenable to cycling, and it offers case studies to demonstrate how the creation of such places can enhance participation in active travel modes. However, as clearly stated in this guide, the application of design principles and creation of healthy spaces requires a strong commitment at *all* stages of the planning process.

In short, information on cycling and the infrastructure that cyclists require is readily available for planners to use in preparing strategic land use plans, so long as planners are willing to apply this knowledge in the ongoing development of the built environment. Planners also have an important role to play in advocating for a greater emphasis on cycling and other active travel modes and ensuring that these modes are at the centre of discussions about the role of transport in shaping urban development. In overseeing land division and structure planning, for instance, planners should play a greater role in co-ordinating the range of disciplines involved in urban design, growth area and renewal area planning, and, more locally, in streetscape planning and design.

In taking a more prominent role, strategic planners are well placed to draw on and extend the transport, environmental and health discourses which promote cycling. This is evidenced by the recent development of *integrated* transport and land use plans and strategies across Australia and New Zealand, which seek to bring together the work of land use and transport planners as a means of producing more efficient, sustainable and liveable cities and regions (Auckland Regional Transport Authority, 2009; Government of South Australia, 2013; Government of Victoria, 2010; Hume City Council, 2011; New South Wales Government, 2012). The emphasis in these plans is to ensure that the transport system supports a more compact urban form and, in particular, helps stimulate higher-density, mixed-use development in inner and middle suburbs. The renewal of these inner- and middle-suburban areas is seen as a way of boosting investment in, and reinvigorating, the economy of a city, but it also requires a significant commitment on the part of state and territory governments to pursue a fundamentally different transport future — one which prioritises cycling and other active transport modes rather than the private motor vehicle.

While the integrated transport and land use plans examined discuss the need to promote cycling and active transport, they fail to acknowledge the degree of shift required to facilitate greater participation in cycling, and how this might be enabled through the land use planning system, or how it might be applied to development through the assessment process. In short, the proliferation of cycling strategies/plans and integrated transport and land use strategies/plans has failed to sufficiently challenge prevailing transport discourses that privilege the private motor vehicle (SQW Consulting, 2008). The question remains: what tools and resources do planners need to effect such a change?

Planning policy

Policy planning involves the formulation of specific policies regulating the use and development of land. These policies are incorporated into planning schemes/development plans, which are applied at the local level and used by land use planners to assess the merit or otherwise of development proposals. It is significant that planning policies are, for the most part, intended to align with, and bring into effect, the land use objectives put forward in strategic plans. For this reason, there are a raft of general policies within planning schemes/development plans concerning transport and related activities such as parking, access and movement, as well as specific transport policies for particular land use zones (such as residential, industrial and commercial).

Most states and territories have developed a suite of standardised planning policies for insertion into local council planning schemes/development plans. The trend is for uniform policies with consistent terminology that can be applied at the local level (although provision is usually made for local variation). Two examples of these state-wide planning policies are the South Australian Planning Policy Library [SAPPL] and the Victorian Planning Provisions [VPP].

In the SAPPL, the 'transportation and access' section (Government of South Australia, 2011a, pp. 107-113) recognises cycling within references to the transport system, but for the most part the policy is aimed at regulating development to accommodate private motor vehicle travel. One objective (of five) acknowledges the importance of active transport in seeking the '[p]rovision of safe, pleasant, accessible, integrated and permeable pedestrian and cycling networks that are connected to the public transport network' (Government of South Australia, 2011a, p. 107). This objective is given further weight through policies on 'movement systems' that ask the following:

- Land uses attracting large numbers of visitors (such as shopping centres, schools, hospitals and medium-high-density residential development) should be located close to public transport while encouraging cycling and walking.
- Development at intersections and crossings should maximise sightlines for motorists, cyclists and pedestrians, in order to ensure safety for all road users.
- Development generating high-traffic volumes should be designed to minimise interference to existing traffic and give priority to pedestrians, cyclists and public transport users (Government of South Australia, 2011a, p. 108).

The last of these provisions is indicative of the enduring focus on maintaining the efficiency of motor vehicle traffic. While new development should accord priority to active travellers, it should only do so if existing motorists are not impeded in any way. Despite the various references encouraging active travel, land use policy in this section of the SAPPL does not go so far as to question or disrupt the privileging of motorised modes of travel.

Nonetheless, the SAPPL does include a dedicated section of policies for 'cycling and walking' (Government of South Australia, 2011a, p. 108). The first policy in this section seeks the provision of safe, convenient and attractive routes for cyclists and walkers, which are connected to local street networks, public transport and activity centres. Here, the emphasis is on encouraging and enabling cycling for short, local trips. The second policy calls for development to provide access for cyclists and walkers to open space networks and recreational trails as well as with Adelaide's principal cycling network, Bike*direct*. While these policies would appear to cover all bases — by accommodating cycling for transport and cycling for recreation — there remains the strong possibility that when these policies are applied to assess development proposals, the 'on-balance test'[2] would see planners support developments that provide access only to recreational cycling routes. The development of safe, convenient and attractive routes for cyclists on local street networks is widely considered to be the responsibility of local councils (specifically local traffic engineers), rather than individual developers. Furthermore, it is worth noting again that neither of these policies anticipates any change to the primary objective of maintaining an efficient transport system for motorists.

The remainder of the 'transportation and access' policies in the SAPPL are focused on access and vehicular parking. For access, the primary objective is to ensure that developments can be safely accessed from the road network without disrupting the flow of traffic (especially on arterial roads). There are no policies at all on bicycle access. In relation to parking, there are some 18 separate policies (and a host of sub-policies) for vehicular parking, as well as a series of tables prescribing the number of car parks that are required for particular forms of development. By way of contrast, there is a single, rather abstract, policy on bicycle parking which calls for the provision of secure bicycle parking facilities that are in prominent, well-lit, signed, undercover and accessible locations. When examining the zone sections of the SAPPL (which are the primary policy provisions used by planners when assessing development proposals), there are scant provisions for cycling and no reference whatsoever in other general sections such as 'infrastructure'.

Turning to the VPP, the overarching planning policy document for Victoria, cycling is similarly recognised in the 'transport' section, particularly in the 'integrated transport' sub-section, which seeks to '… create a safe and sustainable transport system by integrating land use and transport' (Government of Victoria, 2014b, p. 121). Here, the policy provisions promote cycling in relation to co-ordinating urban development with improvements to active transport networks and through the provision of safe, convenient and direct cycling access to activity centres, public transport interchanges and other strategic development sites.

---

[2] In development assessment, planners will apply the on-balance test to those proposals that invoke several different policy objectives, requiring the planner to make a judgement on which objective(s) is/are most relevant or important in assessing the merit of the development.

These provisions are given further emphasis through more detailed policies on 'sustainable personal transport' and 'cycling', which focus on

- encouraging cycling by creating safe and attractive environments
- ensuring that development provides opportunities to create more sustainable transport options, including cycling
- ensuring that cycling routes and infrastructure are constructed early in new developments
- providing direct and connected cycling infrastructure to, and between, key destinations, such as activity centres and public transport nodes
- separating cyclists from motor vehicles
- requiring the provision of adequate bike parking and related facilities when issuing planning approvals for education, recreation, shopping and community facilities
- providing improved facilities (particularly storage) for cyclists at public transport nodes
- ensuring the provision of bicycle end-of-trip facilities in commercial buildings
- development of local cycle networks and new facilities that are linked to, and complement, the metropolitan network of cycle routes (Government of Victoria, 2014b, p. 3 of clause 18).

These policy provisions are noticeably more direct and purposeful in requiring development to specifically accommodate cycling and the needs of cyclists than those within the SAPPL. There is even specific reference to 'incorporating cycling infrastructure in all new road projects', 'facilitating and safeguarding cyclists' access to public transport' and 'considering cycling in providing access to new developments' in the section on the 'transport system' — which is normally the policy area where the efficiency of the transport system for private motor vehicles is prioritised (Government of Victoria, 2014b, p. 2 of clause 18). Moreover, there is a specific policy overlay in the VPP which requires the provision of bicycle facilities — particularly 'secure, accessible and convenient cycle parking spaces and shower and change facilities' — before any new land use can commence or any existing use can be expanded. This overlay also includes detailed guidelines for the design of bicycle spaces, bicycle rails, bicycle lockers and signage (Government of Victoria, 2014b, p. 1 of clause 52.34; see also Hamnett, Chapter Sixteen, this volume).

Taken together, the policies in the VPP actively seek to increase the priority accorded to cycling in the ongoing development of the urban area. Given that these policy provisions are an integral component of all planning schemes in Victoria and that they also require planners to consider other policy documents, such as the Victorian Cycling Strategy, *Cycling into the future 2013-23* (Government of Victoria, 2012), in the assessment of development, it is little wonder that the City of Yarra has successfully enabled a greater number of people to take up cycling.

Moving beyond specific land use policy compendiums, there are various guideline documents available which are intended to shape planning outcomes, including the national *Healthy by design* guidelines (National Heart Foundation, 2004), *Streets for people* compendium (Government of South Australia, 2011b), the Victorian government's *Precinct structure planning guidelines* (Growth Areas Authority, 2013) and *Public transport guidelines for land use and development* (Department of Transport, 2008). These guidelines seek to increase participation in cycling over motor vehicle movement, and have been used to plan and design urban renewal projects and new growth areas on the urban fringe. It is unknown how many councils have adopted these guidelines in local planning schemes/development plans. Anecdotal evidence points to some inclusion of policy to encourage cycling, but there is generally insufficient emphasis placed on the extent of change necessary to enable cycling to become a means of enhancing the sustainability of urban development.

What is known, however, is that new and high-quality facilities attract additional cyclists (SQW Consulting, 2008). Planning practice has the capacity to facilitate greater participation in cycling by ensuring that such infrastructure — including bike routes integrated with wider transport networks, secure bike parking/storage, signage and well-located end-of-trip facilities — is built at an early stage of development. In urban renewal projects, cycling routes can also be integrated with open space networks and streetscapes designed to include bike parking facilities (Figures 15.8 and 15.9).

While reference to these kinds of facilities and infrastructure is apparent in land use planning policies, there is little evidence as yet of them being well integrated into urban development. Not all local councils have adopted cycling

Strategies for change

Figure 15.8: Cycle parking on private sites next to recreational cycle routes.
(Source: Author's own work.)

Figure 15.9: Cycle parking at a railway station.
(Source: Author's own work.)

policies within local planning schemes/development plans, so the capacity of planners to facilitate an increase in cycling in these local areas is slim. For those councils that have adopted cycling policies within local planning schemes/development plans, there appears to be insufficient emphasis placed on these policies during the assessment process. Instead, planners continue to place greater weight on other modes of urban transport when regulating urban development.

The following section interrogates the role of development assessment in shaping urban transport outcomes.

Development assessment

In undertaking development assessment, land use planners are required to apply the strategies and policies described above to development proposals. Although planning systems across Australia are mostly geared towards regulating private development (with special assessment processes usually in place for public development), planners are nonetheless obliged to consider the implications of development on the public realm. To this end, planners, in collaboration with other disciplines within local government, can facilitate upgrades of the public realm arising out of a private initiative or can require a contribution from the developer to such an initiative, which might include, for instance, provision of cycle paths within a land-division development.

From our observations of, and participation in, the development assessment process, planners tend to adopt the 'normal' entrenched approach to transport matters arising from a proposed development — that being deferral to traffic standards established by transport planners and traffic engineers. Typically, this involves reinscribing (through conditions of development approval) car parking standards and access requirements which, as discussed above, are primarily designed to accommodate motor vehicles and facilitate their uninterrupted movement.

Planners tend to apply a similar logic to cycling in the assessment process by focusing primarily on the number of bike parks accompanying a development, rather than considering the range of factors that would enable more people to cycle to access that development. Such factors include where bike parking should be located on the development site, where the site is situated in the transport network, what priority has been given to cycling on surrounding roads and what infrastructure exists to facilitate safe and convenient movement of cyclists to their destination. As cities 'densify', the question of how bicycles are stored within higher-density housing, and whether a proportion of space normally allocated to car parks should be devoted to bicycle parking, will become increasingly relevant. What is needed are detailed guidelines to supplement the policy that planners can refer to when undertaking an assessment.

There are emerging examples, particularly in the central areas of cities, of planning schemes/development plans which include zones or policy areas where development that does not provide vehicular parking spaces and accepts lower than usual rates of parking is supported (see Government of South Australia, 2014; Government of Victoria, 2014b). Such support is usually predicated on developments with good access to public transport and/or a range of facilities and services that residents require. However, if assessment planners continue to give undue weight to established quantitative standards for parking and vehicular access, they will (perhaps unwittingly) reproduce development outcomes that reinforce the marginality of cycling in urban areas.

It would be remiss not to acknowledge the various constraints that planners often encounter in assessing development proposals, including

- the problem of retrofitting existing areas
- the limited role of planners in public realm development, including the planning and design of road reserves and greenways for on- and off-road cycle routes (which are largely the domain of asset managers and engineers)
- the lack of local transport plans that accord sufficient weight to cycling
- the lack of data to substantiate budgets for developing quality cycle infrastructure.

In relation to the development of infrastructure, planners often contribute to the work of engineers, asset managers, project managers and transport planners in designing infrastructure to support urban development and land use change. The following section examines one such case in metropolitan Adelaide.

Case study — The two Seaford Railway Stations

Two new railway stations in southern Adelaide — Seaford Station and Seaford Meadows Station — have recently been developed as an integral part of planning for the growth area of Seaford, incorporating an extension of the southern Adelaide rail line from Noarlunga to Seaford. Both stations are located adjacent to the Coast to Vines cycle trail and have been purposefully designed to accommodate cyclists, primarily through the provision of secure bike parking in the form of 'bike cages'. Seaford Station is located at the end of the rail line and is around half a kilometre east of the Seaford Shopping Centre. Seaford Meadows is located approximately one kilometre north of Seaford and is nestled between an industrial area to the east and a new, developing residential area to the west. Both sites accommodate substantial car parks in order to encourage 'park and ride' patronage.

The location of both stations close to residential and employment lands builds on a number of key objectives of *The 30-year plan for Greater Adelaide* (Government of South Australia, 2010). Of particular relevance is the objective to encourage cycling to and from activity centres and public transport hubs as a means of promoting a shift from private vehicular travel to active travel modes. The location of Seaford Station in close proximity to a mixed-use activity centre, for instance, is envisaged to realise a number of broader planning objectives, such as attracting further investment into that centre, increasing housing densities in and around the centre, and promoting the growth of a transit-oriented development [or TOD]. Seen in this context, these stations are a good case study of how contemporary planning practice has responded to the need to increase participation in cycling, reduce private vehicular use and, in so doing, contain the spread of metropolitan Adelaide.

In assessing these station sites for their capacity to accommodate cyclists, we have adopted four key criteria — namely, access, wayfinding, infrastructure and safety.

Access

This criterion comprises both access to and from the railway station for cyclists from surrounding areas, as well as access to the trains for cyclists wishing to take their bikes on the train.

Access to and from Seaford Station is possible from both the cycle trail immediately to the east as well as the activity centre and surrounding residential area to the west. Poor signage across the station site, however, makes this access quite difficult (Figures 15.12-15.14). When leaving the trail, cyclists must first

Strategies for change

Figure 15.10: Seaford Station and bikecage.
(Source: Author's own work.)

Figure 15.11: Seaford Meadows Station.
(Source: Author's own work.)

What should planners know about cycling?

Figure 15.12: Unclear signage to Seaford Station from the cycle path on the east. (Source: Author's own work.)

determine which direction to proceed in order to access the station and then negotiate steep ramps down to the station entrance. Signage on the trail and at the station entrance is poor. It is written in very small font on small poles, is difficult to read, fails to clearly indicate the direction that cyclists need to travel and is quite inadequate to guide cyclists to either the station entrance or the secure bike storage located on the other side of the railway tracks (Figures 15.12 and 15.16).

In accessing Seaford Station from the north-west (either from the residential area or the activity centre), cyclists can only access the platforms via the station car park (Figures 15.13 and 15.14). There are no paths available from the road to the station for cyclists who

Figure 15.13: Cycles not encouraged to access Seaford Station. (Source: Author's own work.)

Strategies for change

Figure 15.14: Lack of cycle access to Seaford Station from the north-west. (Source: Author's own work.)

Figure 15.15: Lift-only access to Seaford Meadows Station to city, and only for one bike at a time. (Source: Author's own work.)

Figure 15.16: No signage to Seaford Station from the coast path on the east. (Source: Author's own work.)

have to negotiate the car park entrance, often in busy traffic, which is devoid of any directional signage and located some distance (approximately 150 metres) from the station entrance and bike storage area. When accessing the station from the south-west, cyclists can only reach the entrance and bike storage area via a steep ramp which functions as a one-way bus route without any separate route for cyclists other than a footpath.

At Seaford Meadows, there is no direct access to the station from the residential areas to the west. Cyclists must first travel south to access a road that traverses the railway line and then join the bike trail before heading north to access the station entrance. Signage from the bike trail to the station entrance and bike storage area is poor and offers no directional guidance. While accessing Seaford Meadows from the north-east is easier, it is only so because the bike storage area and station entrance is clearly visible and the signage less important. In contrast, when approaching the station from the south, the bike storage area and station entrance are not visible; nor are there signs to give cyclists directions to these facilities until well past the station entrance. Access to the platforms is confusing, and cyclists wishing to access the northbound train to the city can only do so via a lift which can barely accommodate two bikes (Figure 15.15).

According to CROW (2007), the 'directness' of cycle routes (in terms of both distance and time) to access key destinations like railway stations is a key factor enabling people to adopt cycling as a mode of transport. Sadly, the opportunities provided by having a major cycle track located adjacent the southern Adelaide railway line have not been fully realised in terms of allowing direct access to public transport for cyclists.

Wayfinding

Wayfinding is facilitated by the overall design and layout of sites; the visibility of key destinations; the use, location, content and legibility of signage; and the architectural and landscape cues that aid access to, and orientation within, an area.

Wayfinding within each station's environs is clearly geared towards facilitating access by motor vehicle drivers using the car park rather than by cyclists. While facilities are provided for cyclists, such as secure bike cages and bike racks, there are no clear directions to assist their access to these facilities or to the platforms. Indeed, the lack of directional signage to platforms is poor for all users of the stations and indicates a general lack of attention to the importance of wayfinding for people wishing to use public transport. This is especially important given the complexity of both station sites, with multiple levels of platforms and accessways. Unless one is familiar with the layout and location of station facilities and entrances, it would be very easy to access the wrong platform and board a train running in the opposite direction to that intended.

Poor site planning and design for wayfinding at public transport hubs not only increases the inconvenience of using public transport, but also decreases the attractiveness of public transport, and fails to support efforts to shift people's mobility away from private motor vehicles (Russell, 2012). Good signage and wayfinding can make or break efforts to increase public transport patronage and, of particular relevance to this study, to enable cycling to be a means of accessing public transport. For cyclists, what is required is clearly signed routes with symbols and/or colour codes to guide them to the station entrance, bike storage facilities and platforms (Russell, 2012). Such clearly defined routes would also be beneficial for all public transport users.

Infrastructure

The main infrastructure for cyclists at the two stations comprises
- pathways (external to the station) and ramps (accessing the station)
- bike cages (secure storage)
- cycle racks.

At Seaford, the bike cage and racks are located in reasonable proximity to the station entrance (Figure 15.18). In contrast, the bike cage at Seaford Meadows is located some 90 metres away from the ramps leading up to the station entrance (Figure 15.19). Given this distance, it comes as no surprise that at the time we visited there were only three bikes stored in the bike cage at Seaford Meadows (there were five in the bike cage at Seaford), with a further four bikes attached to a fence located closer to the station entrance. There is no apparent reason for the bike cage to be sited so far from the station entrance, as there is ample space available to accommodate this facility. There is also a large, sheltered space beneath the ramps that could easily be used to store bicycles (Figure 15.20).

What should planners know about cycling?

Figure 15.17: No signage from the main cycle path to Seaford Meadows Station. (Source: Author's own work.)

Figure 15.18: Good bicycle cage location at Seaford Station. (Source: Author's own work.)

Figure 15.19: Bicycle cage located far from Seaford Meadows Station. (Source: Author's own work.)

CROW (2007) argues that the attractiveness of cycling infrastructure and its cohesion (meaning the relationship between each component of infrastructure) is of critical importance in enabling people to take up cycling. In the case of the Seaford and Seaford Meadows Railway Stations, the cohesiveness of the cycling infrastructure provided is severely compromised by a number of factors, including inconvenient access, confusing signage, poor wayfinding and excessive distances between bike storage facilities and station entrances. Such disparate connections between pieces of cycling infrastructure all combine to significantly reduce the attractiveness and convenience for cyclists seeking to access these public transport hubs.

Safety

On this criterion, we distinguish between safety from accidents and safety from crime. With regard to the former, access to the Seaford Station from both the southern and the western car park poses serious risks of cyclists coming into conflict with motor vehicles (Figure 15.20). These risks are caused by the lack of direct and clearly marked access routes, with cyclists not knowing how to access the station or bike cage, while motorists are not alerted to the likely presence of cyclists. The steepness of the ramps is also dangerous for cyclists, especially for children riding bikes and for pedestrians who may be using the ramps at the same time. These risks would be amplified on rainy days.

In relation to safety from crime, there is a large body of literature on Crime Prevention through Environmental Design [CPTED] demonstrating that poor wayfinding, together with indirect and difficult access routes, contributes significantly to increased levels of fear (Bell Planning Associates & Gaston, 1995; European Commission, 2006). Although both stations are well lit, neither their surrounds nor main access routes are lit for safe movement by cyclists or pedestrians. Accordingly, cyclists are likely to feel unsafe accessing these public transport facilities, particularly at night, and will be less likely to use public transport as a result. At Seaford Meadows, levels of fear are likely to be compounded by a general lack of surveillance in an area devoid of social activity for significant periods of the day and night (Figures 15.21 and 15.22).

This case study of the Seaford and Seaford Meadows Railway Stations demonstrates that in spite of a raft of strategies and policies supporting the

What should planners know about cycling?

Figure 15.20: Unsafe bicycle route from the south to Seaford Station.
(Source: Author's own work.)

Figure 15.21: The remote location of the bicycle cage at Seaford Meadows may raise fear.
(Source: Author's own work.)

Strategies for change

Figure 15.22: Access from the rear of the bicycle cage is unsafe.
(Source: Author's own work.)

Figure 15.23: Safer alternatives for the bicycle cage at Seaford Meadows Station.
(Source: Author's own work.)

development of appropriate infrastructure and facilities to enable more people to take up cycling, the delivery of these policies and strategies has proven to be problematic at best. Both stations were designed to enhance access to public transport for cyclists. Both sites were located adjacent to the most prominent and well-used cycle track serving the southern Adelaide suburbs. Yet for both sites, access to the stations for cyclists is difficult, inconvenient and, in some circumstances, unsafe. The provision of infrastructure to encourage and enable greater participation in cycling has not been delivered in a sufficiently integrated and cohesive fashion, raising questions about how this infrastructure is provided and about the practices deployed in designing and constructing this infrastructure (discussed below). Little wonder, then, that the stations have yet to attract large numbers of cyclists to use public transport and so contribute to the objective of increasing participation in active travel modes.

Lessons for planners

So what lessons for planners can be gleaned from this interrogation of planning policy and practice as it relates to facilitating cycling in urban environments?

In relation to *enabling cycling*, planners have certainly developed strategies and policies that respond to increasing knowledge of the significance of cycling in planning for sustainable urban futures and healthier urban populations. However, as attested to by the case study, these policies are not sufficiently detailed and their implementation has proven to be more difficult. Planners continue to accord greater significance to supporting motorised modes of urban travel and have not recognised the degree of shift required to get people out of their cars and onto bikes and other active travel modes, even for short, local trips. In a policy context, the privileging of motor vehicle travel is evidenced by the ongoing emphasis on promoting efficient motor vehicle transport, uninterrupted journeys and excessive car parking requirements for individual developments. Until planners understand how this emphasis on motorised forms of travel disadvantages efforts to improve conditions for cyclists and enable more people to take up cycling, we are unlikely to see much change to the current situation.

In relation to *making places*, planners recognise the contribution that cycling makes to the development of convivial and vibrant local places (including public transport hubs), but the design of these places rarely incorporates convenient and accessible cycle routes or the necessary infrastructure to encourage and enable more people to cycle. Knowing how to develop these routes and infrastructure in ways that make it easy, convenient and safe to cycle is of critical importance if planners are serious about their metropolitan planning objectives to both reduce car use and boost participation in active travel. Planners need not only to engage in, and with, the growing body of literature on how to design attractive, convenient and cohesively planned cycling infrastructure, but also to be involved in, and advocate for, the delivery of this infrastructure as planned. This conclusion is timely, given the emerging trend to accord greater statutory weight to the planning and design of the public realm across Australian cities.

In interrogating the delivery of infrastructure for the two case study sites, it was evident that the initial design for Seaford Meadows had the bike cage located close to the station entrance, rather than at its eventual location some 90 metres away. The reason that the final delivery of infrastructure did not match the station design was, according to anecdotal evidence, attributed to a 'project management decision'. Clearly, such decisions run counter to strategic policy objectives to enable cycling, but they are all too common in the final delivery of major infrastructure projects, where motorised modes of transport are continually privileged. This points to the need for planners to be involved not only in the preparation of detailed cycle infrastructure design guidelines but also in the development *and* delivery of such infrastructure to ensure that what gets built matches the initial design. It also reinforces the need for planners to play a stronger advocacy role in promoting cycling and ensuring that cycling infrastructure is built to meet the needs of cyclists. A collaborative process between all disciplines involved in the planning, design and delivery of such public infrastructure projects is required to ensure a high quality of development appropriate to the community that the infrastructure serves.

A holistic approach that includes cultural and behavioural change is needed. Planners can promote this change in practice, but they will require more collaboration with urban designers, asset managers and engineers in the public, private and non-government sectors, all of whom share responsibility for improvements in, and design of, the public realm.

Specific knowledge requirements for planners are summarised in Table 15.1.

What should planners know about cycling?

Table 15.1: What planners need to know to increase participation in cycling.

Writing/ implementing strategy	• how to effectively collaborate with transport planners, urban designers and health professionals • how cycling contributes to urban development and sustainability objectives • the extent of the shift required to challenge prevailing priorities afforded to private motor vehicle travel
Writing/ implementing policy	• how planning decisions often (unwittingly) increase access and convenience for private motor vehicle travel • how to de-prioritise the emphasis on private motor vehicle travel • the range of cycling infrastructure required to properly support development • how to integrate cycling and cycling infrastructure in all movement systems, as well as the public realm more generally • how to provide a better balance between cycling and car parking provision • how to enable access and egress for cyclists between private development sites and the public realm
Assessing development	• how to properly interpret and prioritise policy that enables cycling • how to incorporate cycling in 'on-balance' decisions on individual development proposals • how to challenge existing traffic and parking standards in planning schemes/development plans • how to accommodate cycling in building and public realm design • the requirements to better connect individual sites with the wider cycling networks
Delivering infrastructure	• the extent and range of cycling infrastructure available for private development and the public realm • how to connect cycling infrastructure on individual sites with the wider urban cycling network • how to ensure convenient access to, and use of, cycling infrastructure • how to design infrastructure (such as public transport) for all travellers, not just for motorists • how to ensure ease of movement within, and to and from, sites for cyclists (such as through clear signage) • how to apply CPTED principles in planning and designing for cyclists.

(Source: authors' own work.)

Conclusion

This interrogation of the work of land use planners demonstrates a significant gap in the knowledge of *how* to effectively enable more people to cycle as a regular part of their daily activities within urban areas. While strategic plans and policy provisions articulate the reasons that cycling should be encouraged within urban environments and provide dedicated planning rules to integrate cycling in development, these plans do not challenge the dominance of motor vehicles as the primary means of travelling within urban environments. As a consequence, these plans effectively reinscribe this dominance and the concomitant devaluing of cycling as an alternative travel mode.

Further, it is in the everyday practices of land use planners that this (perhaps unwitting) privileging of motorised travel occurs. The case study demonstrates that, in spite of genuine attempts to integrate cycling into the development of key public transport hubs, planners have failed to adequately support the delivery of convenient, attractive and safe cycling routes and facilities that might enable more people to engage in cycling more often.

A large shift in emphasis and affirmative action is required to change these entrenched practices. Planning has the potential to better integrate cycling into the urban fabric, but planners will need to change not only their approach to urban transport planning, but also the knowledges they deploy in regulating transport and land use. With growing concerns about public health and the ongoing depletion of important environmental assets, it will become increasingly urgent that they do so.

References

Adelaide City Council. (2012). *Smart move — Transport and movement strategy 2012-22*. Adelaide: Adelaide City Council.

Adkins, A, Dill, J, Luhr, G, & Neal, M. (2012). Unpacking walkability: Testing the influence of urban design features on perceptions of walking environment attractiveness. *Journal of Urban Design*, 17(4), 499-510.

Auckland Regional Transport Authority. (2009). *Auckland transport plan*. Auckland: Auckland Regional Transport Authority.

Australian Bicycle Council. (2010). *Gearing up for active and sustainable communities: National cycling strategy 2011-2016*. Sydney: Austroads.

Austroads. (2009). *Guide to road design, Part 6A: Pedestrian and cyclist paths.* Sydney: Austroads.

Bell Planning Associates & Gaston, G. (1995). *Crime, safety and urban form.* Canberra: Australian Government Publishing Service.

Berry, M. (1992). Rediscovering the cities: Prospects for a national urban policy in the 1990s. *Urban Policy and Research, 10*(4), 37-44.

Burke, M, & Bonham, J. (2010). Rethinking oil depletion: What role can cycling really play in dispersed cities? *Australian Planner, 47*(4), 272-283.

City of Melbourne. (2012). *Bicycle plan 2012-16.* Melbourne: City of Melbourne.

City of Sydney. (2007). *Cycle strategy and action plan, 2007-2017.* Sydney: City of Sydney.

City of Yarra. (2010). *City of Yarra bicycle strategy, 2010-2015.* Melbourne: City of Yarra.

Clifton, KJ, Livi Smith, AD, & Rodriguez, D. (2007). The development and testing of an audit for the pedestrian environment. *Landscape and Urban Planning, 80*(1-2), 95-110.

CROW. (2007). *Design manual for bicycle traffic.* Delft: Faculty of Architecture, Delft University Institute of Technology.

Department of Infrastructure and Transport. (2013). *Walking, riding and access to public transport: Supporting active travel in Australian communities.* Canberra: Commonwealth of Australia.

Department of Planning. (1988). *Sydney into its third century: Metropolitan strategy for the Sydney region.* Sydney: New South Wales Department of Planning.

Department of Planning and Housing. (1992). *A place to live, urban development 1992-2031: Shaping Victoria's future.* Melbourne: Government of Victoria.

Department of Transport. (2008). *Public transport guidelines for land use and development.* Melbourne: Government of Victoria.

Department of Transport. (2011). *Public transport for Perth in 2013.* Perth: Government of Western Australia.

Dodson, J. (2012). Transforming Australia's 'housing solution': How we can better plan suburbia to meet our future challenges. In R Tomlinson (Ed.), *Australia's unintended cities: The impact of housing on urban development.* Melbourne: CSIRO.

European Commission. (2006). *Planning, urban design and management for crime prevention handbook.* AGIS — Action SAFEPOLIS 2006-2007. Retrieved

15 September 2015 from http://efus.eu/en/policies/national/italy/public/971.

Ewing, R, & Cervero, R. (2010). Travel and the built environment: A meta-analysis. *Journal of the American Planning Association*, 76(3), 265-294.

Ewing, R, & Handy, S. (2009). Measuring the un-measurable: Urban design qualities related to walkability. *Journal of Urban Design*, 14(1), 65-84.

Forsyth, A, & Krizek, K. (2011). Urban design: Is there a distinctive view from the bicycle? *Journal of Urban Design*, 16(4), 531-549.

Gleeson, B, Dodson, J, & Spiller, M. (2012). Governance, metropolitan planning and city-building: The case for reform. In R Tomlinson (Ed.), *Australia's unintended cities: The impact of housing on urban development*. Melbourne: CSIRO.

Government of South Australia. (2006). *Safety in numbers — A cycling strategy for South Australia 2006-2010*. Adelaide: Department of Transport, Energy and Infrastructure.

Government of South Australia. (2010). *The 30-year plan for Greater Adelaide: A volume of the South Australian planning strategy*. Adelaide: Department of Planning and Local Government.

Government of South Australia. (2011a). *South Australian planning policy library* (Version 6). Adelaide: Department of Planning and Local Government.

Government of South Australia. (2011b). *Streets for people — Compendium for South Australian practice*. Adelaide: Department of Planning and Local Government.

Government of South Australia. (2013). *Draft integrated transport and land use plan*. Adelaide: Department of Planning, Transport and Infrastructure.

Government of South Australia. (2014). *Adelaide (City) development plan*. Adelaide: Department of Planning, Transport and Infrastructure.

Government of Victoria. (1984). *Transport (Road Traffic) regulations 1984*. Melbourne Government of Victoria.

Government of Victoria. (2010). *Transport Integration Act 2010*. Melbourne: Government of Victoria.

Government of Victoria. (2012). *Cycling into the future 2013-23*. Melbourne: Government of Victoria.

Government of Victoria. (2014a). *Plan Melbourne: Metropolitan planning strategy*. Melbourne: State of Victoria.

Government of Victoria. (2014b). *Victorian planning provisions.* Melbourne: Government of Victoria.

Growth Areas Authority. (2013). *Precinct structure planning guidelines: Overview of planning new communities.* Melbourne: Government of Victoria.

GTA Consultants. (2007). *Pick up your bike and go where you like: A bicycle strategy for the Leichhardt local government area.* Sydney: Leichhardt City Council.

Hume City Council. (2011). *Hume integrated land use and transport strategy (HILATS) 2011-2020.* Melbourne: Hume City Council.

Infrastructure Australia. (2013). *Urban transport strategy.* Canberra: Commonwealth of Australia.

Martin, J. (1982). Opportunities for street improvement as part of a local area traffic management package in existing Australian suburbia. *ARRB Proceedings,* 11(4), 103. Melbourne: Australian Road Research Board.

Mees, P. (2010). *Transport for suburbia: Beyond the Automobile Age.* London: Earthscan.

National Heart Foundation of Australia (Victorian Division). (2004). *Healthy by design: A planner's guide to environments for active living.* Melbourne: National Heart Foundation of Australia (Victorian Division).

New South Wales Department of Urban Affairs and Planning. (2001). *Integrating land use and transport, improving transport choice — Guidelines for planning and development.* Sydney: Department of Urban Affairs and Planning.

New South Wales Government. (2010). *Metropolitan plan for Sydney 2036.* Sydney: Government of New South Wales.

New South Wales Government. (2012). *New South Wales long term transport master plan.* Sydney: Government of New South Wales.

Planning Institute of Australia, Heart Foundation & Australian Local Government Association. (2009). *Healthy spaces and places: A national guide to designing places for healthy living — An overview.* Kingston, ACT: Planning Institute of Australia. Retrieved 15 September 2015 from www.healthyplaces.org.au.

Planning Review. (1992). *2020 vision: Planning strategy for metropolitan Adelaide.* Adelaide: Department of Environment and Planning.

Pucher, J, & Buehler, R. (2006). Why Canadians cycle more than Americans: A comparative analysis of bicycling trends and policies. *Transport Policy,* 13(3), 265-279.

Pucher, J, Garrard, J, & Greaves, S. (2011). Cycling down under: A comparative analysis of bicycling trends and policies in Sydney and Melbourne. *Journal of Transport Geography*, 19(2), 332-345.

Rayson, D. (2012). Travelling by bike. *Urban Design Forum*, 99, 4. Retrieved 15 September 2015 from http://www.udf.org.au/wp-content/uploads/2014/07/Edition100.pdf.

Roads and Traffic Authority of New South Wales and Federal Office of Road Safety. (1993). *Sharing the main street*. Sydney: Government of New South Wales.

Royal Dutch Touring Club. (1977). *Woonerf*. The Hague: Royal Dutch Touring Club.

Russell, T. (2012). Signing the way for more cycling in the UK. *TEC Magazine*, UK.

Sick Nielsen, TA, Skov-Petersen, H, & Agervig Carstensen, T. (2013). Urban planning practices for bikeable cities — The case of Copenhagen. *Urban Research and Practice*, 6(1). doi: org/10.1080/17535069.2013.765108.

SKM. (1995). *Trans access guidelines to reduce car dependency (draft guidelines)*. Brisbane: Queensland Transport.

SQW Consulting. (2008). *Planning for cycling — Report to Cycling England*. UK.

Transport for London. (2014). *London cycling design standards — Draft for consultation*. London: Transport for London.

Wahlgren, L, & Schantz, P. (2012). Exploring bikeability in a metropolitan setting: Stimulating and hindering factors in commuting route environments. *BMC Public Health*, 12(168). Retrieved 15 September 2015 from http://www.biomedcentral.com/1471-2458/12/168.

Winters, M, Brauer, M, Selton, EM, & Teschke, K. (2013). Mapping bikeability: A spatial tool to sustainable travel. *Environment and Planning B: Planning and Design*, 40(5), 865-883.

16 Skilling landscape architects and urban designers for design of bicycle parking and network facilities

Hilary Hamnett

Introduction

It will be clear from preceding chapters that the issues around planning and design for sustainable cycling futures are complex and multilayered, requiring input and collaboration from a number of different professions. This chapter addresses the knowledge and skills required by landscape architects and urban designers for best practice design at the beginning and end of cycling journeys, to improve the cycling experience and encourage greater participation in all forms of cycling. It will also consider cycle network design, and demonstrate the core contribution to be made by the two disciplines of landscape architecture and urban design as part of the collaborative, multidisciplinary approach. The chapter provides practical assistance to urban designers and landscape architects who are unfamiliar with designing for cycling. It extracts and further develops key concepts from the plethora of design codes and standards available. The chapter, read in conjunction with Chapter Fifteen by Wendy Bell and Donna Ferretti in this volume, will also assist planners when advising developers on cycling requirements and carrying out development assessment, as well as project managers responsible for the timely completion of developments.

Strategies for change

Landscape architecture has evolved as a profession with a wide-ranging scope, having concern for the health, sustainability and relationships between humans and the natural and built environment. A key feature of landscape architecture is the integration of technical and scientific knowledge with cultural, social and aesthetic sensibilities. Central to the discipline is site planning, a cyclical, unbounded process that builds knowledge to inform the preparation of the plan. Along with the physical site survey and analysis, landscape architects must navigate a network of social decisions and continually monitor, evaluate and revise plans as necessary. They must respond to and manage different viewpoints and potential conflicts between the participants. Despite this, and the many factors to be considered in site planning, cycling has rarely, and only cursorily, been mentioned in the site planning literature dealing with transport issues.

Urban design, meanwhile, is a discipline that transcends the environmental, design and planning professions. There are many definitions of urban design, depending on the perspective of the profession. It is reasonable to say, however, that it is fundamentally concerned with shaping and managing the 'public' environment, understanding movement patterns, social and cultural values and behaviours, and making connections between people and places. It has for a long time been engaged with a focus on non-motorised transport (Forsyth & Krizek, 2011) and with creating 'liveable' walking and cycling environments.

The two disciplines of landscape architecture and urban design intersect with each other, therefore, in their concern for the built environment and shaping cities, towns and communities at the macro- and microlevel. Such work includes street layouts, streetscape improvements, managing the transition between public and private space, and evoking unique qualities and a 'sense of place'. Both disciplines deal with the perception of space as it relates to determining which functions are suitable from a social, cultural, economic and aesthetic perspective for the physical and emotional wellbeing of individuals and communities. Both are involved in mediating conflicts over the use of public space. Fundamental to both is process. Tools include visual assessment and techniques for managing participation, consultation and collaboration. Landscape architects are also versed in water-sensitive urban design and environmental design more generally.

Research for this chapter has included a desktop review of recent urban design studies from various cycling perspectives as well as an examination of some current standards, codes and guidelines for end-of-trip cycling facilities. Forsyth and Krisek (2011) found that there are few academic texts in the urban design and landscape architecture literature which have come to grips with the task of specialised design for cyclists, even though active living and healthy lifestyles are increasingly important in the design of new developments. Within the broader international literature published in the field of urban design, despite a focus on non-motorised travel, cycling has usually been conflated with walking (Forsyth & Krizek, 2011). In the National Heart Foundation of Australia's otherwise valuable document *Healthy by design* (Victorian Division, 2004), cycling is only mentioned once on its own (and only in relation to end-of-trip bicycle facilities) out of 40 references to 'walking and cycling'. When cycling has been addressed, the focus has mostly been on the functionality of network and parking facility design. The 'experiential (perceptual), sensory, visual, temporal or social dimensions', which are central to most urban designers when considering pedestrian activity, have been or more or less completely ignored in the context of cycling (Forsyth & Krizek, 2011, p. 533). But design clearly has an important role to play in supporting and encouraging cycling. As one recent study found, the surveyed cyclists ranked a visually appealing environment as a highly motivating factor in their choice to cycle (Guinn & Stangl, 2014).

Clearly, cyclists differ substantially from pedestrians (notably in their ability to cover much greater distances), and the unique characteristics of cycling warrant further investigation and a differentiated urban design perspective, with the perceptions and experience of the cyclist as important areas for future study. Papers by social and cultural geographers Jones (2005) and Spinney (2006) highlight, amongst other things, the unique experience derived from the sheer physicality of a cycle ride — including speed, steep hill climbing and dodging heavy, motorised city traffic — and the manner in which this experience shapes the perception of our surroundings and spatial relationships. Jones (p. 813) also notes that while some cyclists may enjoy the 'thrills and chills' of urban cycling in Birmingham (United Kingdom), the confronting nature of the daily commute may be less acceptable to a person with, for example, family commitments. Thus the reality of the day-to-day cycling experience may still be a long way from more abstract policies for active travel.

Other papers reviewed for this chapter revealed that generic urban design responses often lack sensitivity to the different demographics and characteristics of cyclists (and the needs of younger and older cyclists), such as children actively commuting to school (Panter, Jones, Van Sluijs, & Griffin, 2010). Preferences and perceptions have a complex relationship to residential layout (Teguh, Mulley, & Nelson, 2013) or indeed to any physical site plan. Considerable differences between the needs of staff and student cyclists at the University of South Australia's Mawson Lakes campus, for example, were identified by Bonham and Koth (2010). Thus the potential for urban design to positively influence the growth in cycling exists, but further evaluation and research is required to tease out the many complexities that influence the choice to cycle, and designers must respond accordingly.

As awareness grows of the influence that aesthetics and quality of experience can have on increasing cycling participation, there is considerable scope for landscape architects and urban designers to contribute to improved cycling network and neighbourhood design. With their broad perspective and multidisciplinary approach, and their understanding of relationships and impacts along the human/environment spectrum, the design disciplines are well placed to evaluate, respond to and manage the design process for improved conditions for cycling.

As indicated at the outset, this chapter briefly discusses aspects of the planning and design of neighbourhood street layouts and cycle networks, but its main focus is on the design of facilities and infrastructure at the origin (home) and destination (away from home) of bicycle trips. For the design practitioner there are numerous codes, standards, design guidelines, action plans, workbooks and resource packs to assist in cycling facility design. Some of these codes and standards are briefly reviewed in this chapter, as they can provide a useful starting point for the principles of active, liveable neighbourhoods, as well as cycle network and parking facility design. However, targeted and site-specific responses are needed, hand in hand with other strategic and policy measures, to meet the intended outcomes (refer to Bell and Ferretti, Chapter Fifteen, this volume). It is impossible to address every aspect of design, so key topics have been identified, including the importance of the following things to encourage the use of the bicycle in preference to other available modes of transport: good design of bicycle storage and parking at trip origin; design of street layouts; access to networks; and aesthetic appeal. The chapter will then discuss design at the trip destination, including parking location, security and signage; additional infrastructure other than the parking arrangements that may be required; workplace facilities; quantity of parking required; cost implications; and who needs to know.

The importance of good design

Good design at the origin and destination of a trip is important not only for the regular cyclist, but can also be a factor influencing the initial decision of a hesitant cyclist to choose cycling in preference to other available transport modes. Convenience is a well-recognised key element in the cycling journey (Bach, van Hal, de Jong, & de Jong, 2006), but we often forget about access to the bicycle itself. The easier it is for the bicycle to be securely stored and accessed, the more likely the journey will be made by bicycle.

Likewise, easy access to a safe, direct route to the destination, a pleasant and attractive network, and safe and convenient parking on arrival will have some influence on the choice. This is especially true of short or frequent 'utilitarian' trips (Bach et al., 2006), but it can also influence the level of recreational cycling amongst less regular or less confident bicycle users. Benefits of good design for the cyclist include less frustration, less weather damage, reduced potential vandalism and theft of bicycles, and reduction in nuisance, conflicts and hazards. The non-cyclist benefits, too, from clear uncluttered paths and lack of conflict, both in the public realm and in transition areas between public and private space; and local authorities and property owners benefit from reduced maintenance costs.

In addition to the brief overview of academic literature on urban design for cycling, research for this chapter looked at selected standards, codes and design guidelines in the United Kingdom and Australia. The aim was to draw on documents that contained robust practical advice for bicycle storage, access, parking and general end-of-trip facilities, based on professional knowledge and skill, personal observation and experience of sites and practices in Australia and the United Kingdom. The Best Practice guidelines for new residential development were taken from the Cambridge City Council in the United Kingdom (Transport Initiatives LLP and Cambridge City Council, 2010) as the most comprehensive advice for bicycle storage at home.

The standards, codes and guidelines were used to test the bicycle facilities at a number of different sites, mostly in the Adelaide metropolitan area, with some examples from Melbourne. Some further examples of good practice are taken from the Netherlands. Where there are legislative requirements, these are noted in the text; however, most of the best practice guidelines are not mandatory.

This chapter seeks to demonstrate the clear benefits of good design. For the developer or property owner, whether in the public or private realm, investment in good planning and design for cyclists at the outset of the development process can lead to significant cost savings in ongoing management and maintenance. In addition, the developer will be making a broader contribution to reduction in car usage and positive environmental, health and social benefits. From the master planning of subdivisions down to the detailed layout of site and building floor plans, design at every scale will have some bearing on a person's choice to use a bicycle. A good process and design can result in benefits for everyone.

Design at trip origin

The first step in the decision to ride the bicycle is taken at home. The Cambridge City Council (United Kingdom), along with Transport Initiatives LLP, provides a detailed guide for planners and developers, *Cycle parking guide for new residential developments* (2010). This section draws substantially on that document. The guide gives excellent diagrams of spatial requirements for bicycle parking, which provide the source for diagrams in the following sections. Some minor changes in dimensions have been made here, to reflect current Australian and New Zealand standards.

A home owner/occupier with cyclists in the household may be able to configure the house and site plan to meet their individual needs and make access to the bicycles as convenient as possible (Figure 16.1).

This may include an accessible, protected and secure space for bicycles, with room for accessories such as a bicycle helmet and clothing, baskets and panniers, maintenance equipment, and maybe a child carrier and/or cargo trailer. However, the space required for bicycle storage and access, even for a single adult bicycle, is quite significant. A typical garage or carport does not allow sufficient room to manoeuvre past bicycles even if there may just be enough storage space. Some home owners may choose to store bicycles in the garage in preference to the car! Whether for an individual dwelling or for multiple-occupancy residences, access to bicycle storage should be at least as convenient as access to car parking

Skilling landscape architects and urban designers

Figure 16.1: Space for storage inside the dwelling.
(Source: author's own work.)

Figure 16.2: Storage outside the dwelling.
(Source: author's own work.)

(Department for Transport, Communities and Local Government, Welsh Assembly Government, 2007). As well as benefiting the cyclist, the prioritising of bicycle facility location sends a broader positive message about the importance of bicycles.

Addressing good design for cyclists at the outset in new developments is the most effective way to achieve a successful outcome. As more people take up cycling, retrofitting existing buildings, developments and neighbourhoods is just as important, but it may be more difficult to achieve in order to meet best practice. Some creativity, negotiation and compromise may be required. Site assessment and consultation is needed to identify the best approach. The context, demographics and type of residence will initially determine the appropriate level and style of provision; and residents, property managers and other users as well as cyclists should also be involved in the design process, with consideration given to the likely age and level of mobility of residents. The selection of a suitable style of storage (for example, a locker, a cage, a rack) and its dimensions and layout are critical to the usability, and therefore success, of the parking.

As a city with high bicycle usage, Cambridge in the United Kingdom has found that good-quality bicycle parking within new residential developments is a positive selling point for developers (Transport Initiatives LLP and Cambridge City Council, 2010).

Planners and urban designers in Australia are starting to include design requirements for bicycle storage as a guide for developers, especially for new medium-density developments. Examples include the *Yarra planning scheme* of the Yarra City Council in Victoria (Department of Transport, Planning and Local Infrastructure, 2014) and the Bowden *Developers' handbook and urban design guidelines* (RenewalSA, 2014). Table 16.1 summarises the best practice for the provision of bicycle parking for new residential developments, adapted from the Cambridge City Council's *Cycle parking guide for new residential developments* (Transport Initiatives LLP and Cambridge City Council, 2010). The principles are also applicable to end-of-trip parking.

Storage design

There are few comprehensive guides available for the design of 'at home' bicycle storage. The most valuable source for this section has been the *Cycle parking guide for new residential developments* (Transport Initiatives LLP and Cambridge City Council,

Table 16.1: Best practice bicycle parking.

Best Practice cycle parking	
Conveniently sited	• in a position that will encourage cycling as the first option for a short trip • as close as possible to building entries/exits • placed so that it does not obstruct passing pedestrians or vehicles • out of pedestrian desire lines[1] (possibly located between other street furniture) • visitor parking should be easy to find and located next to main entrances
Accessible	• easy to get to • avoids steep slopes, detours, narrow access points • does not require dragging or lifting of the bicycles • easy to access for everyone at all ages and life stages
Safe and secure	• well-lit • good natural surveillance • rails should be securely and permanently fixed in place • minimal risk of theft
Protected from weather	• residents' parking should always be covered (also applicable to long-term, away-from-home, parking) • visitor parking should preferably be covered
Fit for purpose	• the rack should provide good support • the rack should allow the frame and at least one wheel, preferably both, to be secured
Well-managed and maintained	• for units and apartments, parking should be adequately funded so that it can be kept clean, well lit and well maintained
Attractive	• bicycle parking areas should be in keeping with surroundings • visible to people with disabilities

(Source: Adapted from Transport Initiatives LLP and Cambridge City Council, 2010, p. 7.)

---

[1] A 'desire line' is the most direct and intuitive route between an origin and destination.

Strategies for change

2010). Some additional material for general bicycle parking has been drawn from *Bicycle parking: Providing bicycle parking facilities* (Bicycle Victoria, 2000)[2] and *Basic principles for designing for bikes: End of trip* (Bicycle Network, 2015).

Individual dwellings

Anyone involved in the development of new residential areas should consider the following guidelines for the provision of bicycle storage and parking. If included in development plans, these guidelines can provide a powerful tool for development assessment planners to leverage greater compliance in bicycle parking provision from developers (see also Bell & Ferretti, Chapter Fifteen, this volume).

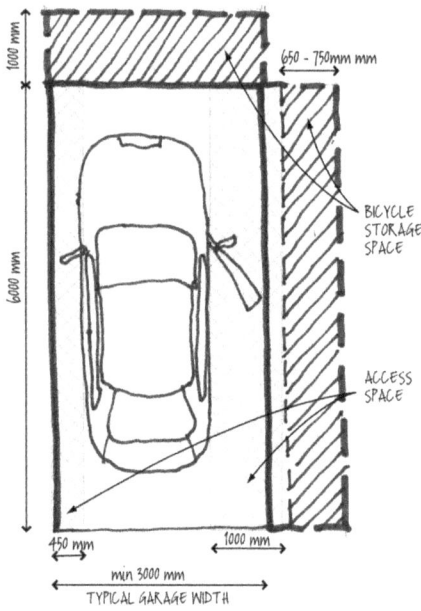

Figure 16.3: Proposed bicycle storage for a typical single garage.
(Source: Based on Transport Initiatives LLP and Cambridge City Council, 2010. Dimensions adapted for typical Australian garage.)

Bicycle parking should preferably be near the front of the property in a secure, covered and lockable enclosure, either within the footprint[3] of the house or the garage, or in an easily accessible shed close to the rear of the house. The design should be appropriate to the street setting. If bicycle storage is in a garage, residents should be able to remove bicycles without first having to move the car. If possible, the bicycle parking should be at the front of the garage so it is easy to remove.

If storage is located at the rear of the garage, there should be enough space to manoeuvre past the vehicle (Figure 16.3).

To access storage, a person pushing a bicycle requires at least

---

[2] At the time of writing, this document was in the process of being updated but the principles are still relevant.

[3] The area of ground within a site covered by the built structure, usually the slab.

1100 mm width. For storage of an average adult bicycle, planners and designers should allow a length of 1800 mm and a width of 700 mm, including the handlebars. If two bicycles are stored side by side, a length of 2000 mm and a width of 800 mm are needed so that handle bars do not clash.

If parking is not available in the house or garage and has to be located at the rear or side of the property, then enough space is required to walk beside the bicycle. Access width of 1500 mm to the store should be provided. Gates should be 1200 mm wide. Doors must be at least 1000 mm wide, so that residents are able to walk through alongside the bicycle. Door closers are useful, as they allow time to get through the door or gate with the bicycle. The shed or locker should be at least 1400 mm wide and 2000 mm long to allow for two bicycles. The enclosure needs to be covered, well lit and constructed of materials sympathetic to the design of the property. On-site parking and storage should always be provided where possible. Bicycles stored outside in the street are subject to theft, damage and vandalism, as well as deterioration from weather (Figure 16.4).

Multiple-occupancy dwellings

Residents of apartments and units, especially if they are renting, have less control over bicycle storage than single dwelling home owners, and even in recent developments they may have to make do with arrangements that are inconvenient and unsatisfactory both for the bicycle owner and other residents (Figures 16.4, 16.5, 16.6 and 16.7). Bicycles may be banned from certain areas such as foyers, corridors, against railings or under stairwells; hooks, racks and pulleys attached to walls are also likely to be prohibited. If a family has to carry bicycles up and down two flights of stairs in a three-storey walk-up, or even carry them up to a second floor, the incentive to ride is diminished from the outset.

Recommendations for multiple-occupancy dwellings become more complex as the number and diversity of occupants increase. Issues include the management of the interface between the public and private domain. Sensitivity to non-cyclists' needs must be considered and, especially where there may be small children, elderly residents and people with mobility issues or other impairments, a best fit should be found between all residents' needs.

Individual apartment parking should be at ground-floor level and internal to the building so that there is direct access from the parking to the building. Lifts are not

Strategies for change

Figure 16.4: On-street home parking.
(Source: author's own work.)

Figure 16.5: Storage requires the bicycle to be lifted up steps. (Note the bicycle behind the hedge, secured to a pole).
(Source: author's own work.)

Figure 16.6: Bicycles stored on a disability access ramp at affordable housing apartments, Adelaide.
(Source: author's own work.)

Figure 16.7: Bicycles stored in a car park at affordable housing apartments, Adelaide.
(Source: author's own work.)

a satisfactory solution, as there can be numerous problems associated with their use. Many lifts are not large enough to accommodate more than one bicycle at one time; controls may be awkward or difficult to operate, especially with loaded panniers or with children and bikes in tow; lifts may be difficult to manoeuvre in and out of, and are unusable when out of service or when occupied at peak times. In addition, there will be physical wear and tear to the lift, which may present an ongoing maintenance problem for asset managers and even for other residents. Proximity and provision for cyclists should be at least as good as resident car parking, closer than the nearest non-disabled parking, within 20 metres of the relevant entrance and well lit. If ground level provision is not possible, it must be serviced by a lift large enough for at least one bicycle and rider — preferably two. It must also be possible to get quickly and easily from the street to the lift with the bicycle, thus minimising the possibility of damage to walls, doors and other property. The lift dimension should be at least 2000 mm deep X 2000 mm wide, with a minimum door opening of 1200 mm.

If parking has to be external to the building, it should be overlooked by other dwellings, not screened by planting, and it should be covered by CCTV security cameras if provided. Visitor parking should be provided at each public entrance. Connections from parking to bicycle paths and roads should have hard surfaces and be well lit.

Options for storage in apartment developments include shared access to communal cages with fixed rails using a key, pincode or swipe card, or individual lockers for one or two bicycles. Table 16.2 indicates some of the advantages and disadvantages of each type of storage.

Small blocks of units

Each dwelling should preferably have an individual storage space, such as a locker, located within the building footprint. If this is not possible, a secured space with a rack for each bicycle should be provided. If located outside, the parking should be within a well-lit, covered and lockable enclosure. Locker parking is the most secure form of storage space (Figure 16.8); however, it is also the most expensive to provide.

Medium or large blocks of units

With larger blocks of apartments, a higher level of management and co-operation is required to maintain the facilities in good, clean condition with safe locks and

Table 16.2: Advantages and disadvantages of communal cages and lockers.

Storage type	Advantages	Disadvantages
Communal cage	• cost-effective • economical in use of space • additional small lockers can be provided for personal items • passive surveillance from regular users may be an advantage and give a sense of personal safety	• lower level of security • keys may be shared around and copied • less convenient for personal items which are either less secure in the cage, or have to be removed or placed in a separate secure place. • gates may be left open
Bicycle locker	• provides a higher level of property security • single-person lockers are easier to manage	• expensive to provide • requires more space • some users find them 'creepy'

(Source: author's own work.)

functioning lighting. Parking should, as for small units, be at ground level. If access has to be via steps, at least one wheel ramp should be provided. Two ramps are preferable, one at each side of the steps, to allow for cyclists to pass. Ideally, the ramp will be incorporated into the step construction (Figure 16.10), but it can be as simple as retrofitting a piece of guttering (Figure 16.11). Bicycle parking must be distributed throughout the site to meet the proximity requirements outlined above.

Where parking has to be accessed via consecutive corridors and doors, additional sweep space is needed for cyclists to negotiate the bicycle around corners and for them to be able to access doors, which should preferably be automatic. In addition, secure communal parking areas should always be separate from car parking to avoid cars encroaching on the bicycle parking space.

Bicycle rail design

The most common 'fit for purpose' rail style for storage of a standard adult bicycle is the 'flat top' rail (Figure 16.12). It is cheap, durable, easy to install and suitable for a variety of situations.

Figure 16.8: Residents' locker parking, Delft, the Netherlands.
(Source: author's own work.)

Figure 16.9: Apartment residents' storage, secure but uncovered.
(Source: author's own work.)

Skilling landscape architects and urban designers

Figure 16.10: Integrated bicycle access ramp.
(Source: author's own work.)

Figure 16.11: A simple wheel ramp installed alongside steps.
(Source: author's own work.)

Strategies for change

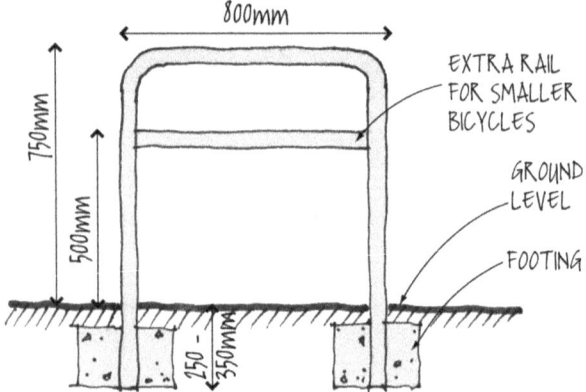

Figure 16.12: 'Flat top' rail dimensions.
(Source: Sketch based on the Australian Standard AS2890.3-1993 Part 3 — Bicycle parking facilities; for more information, see Standards Australia International and Standards New Zealand, 1993. Extra rail adapted and incorporated from Transport Initiatives LLP and Cambridge City Council, 2010.)

Other styles are available for floor or wall mounting, suitable for different applications depending on the amount of space available and level of security required. There is also a rack available for placement above the car bonnet for small garages. Two-tier racks are not generally acceptable, as they require lifting of the bicycle, which may not be possible for all residents. While two-tier racks can increase the capacity at high-usage sites where lifting may not be considered to be an issue, the increase in heavier bicycle styles such as step-through, mountain, hybrid and touring bicycles means lifting is rarely an option. Although some two-tier racks incorporate hydraulic or spring-loaded lifting mechanisms, they are more costly to provide and maintain, and can be awkward or difficult to operate. If two-tier racks have to be provided, detailed instructions for their use should be clearly posted to ensure the safety of the user as well as to prevent damage to the bicycle.

Rails need to be selected and spaced to make efficient use of the space, but should also, where possible, allow for flexibility of use. It is important to allow sufficient space for cyclists to be able to walk beside the bicycle, pass others with bicycles and avoid damaging other bicycles while parking. Typical minimum dimensions for setting out multiple rails are shown in Figure 16.13.

Material selection is important. Both the durability of the rail and protection of bicycle paintwork should be considered. Galvanised steel is effective and one of

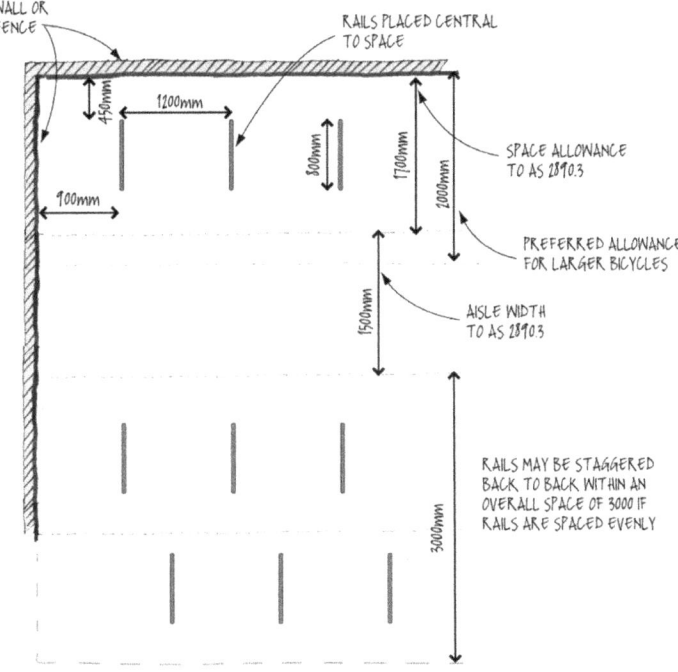

Figure 16.13 Layout dimensions for bicycle parking rails.
(Source: Adapted from Standards Australia International and Standards New Zealand, 1993.)

the cheapest materials. Stainless steel and black nylon coating may be considered more aesthetically pleasing. These are durable but add cost. Painting to customise rails also adds cost and can be difficult to maintain if it gets damaged. Powder-coating is a simple way to customise rails to a local theme, but it is costly to fix if it gets deeply scratched, as the rails must be removed for hot-dipping in order to retain the high-quality finish.

Standards, codes and statutory requirements

Standards

The *Australian Standard AS 2890.3-1993 Part 3 — Bicycle parking facilities* (Standards Australia International and Standards New Zealand, 1993)[4] sets out the

---

[4] Since writing this chapter, a second edition of this standard, AS 2890.3:2015, has been published which addresses some of the issues raised in this and subsequent sections.

minimum requirements for the design of parking facilities. The assumption is that the Standard is for facilities at the trip destination. However, it has some relevance for residential applications covering minimum bicycle storage area requirements and dimensions, floor slopes, protection from vehicular encroachment, location and clearances, signing, lighting, weather protection, maintenance, security, access and ease of use. Appendices to *AS 2890.3-1993 Part 3* cover dimensions of a typical adult bicycle and parking facilities. Developers and designers should be aware of these when designing bicycle parking for apartments and multi-occupancy residential complexes.

Minimum standards are, however, just that. They should not always be equated with desirable standards. *AS 2890.3-1993 Part 3* is also over 20 years old, and there have been significant changes in cycling in that time which need to be accommodated. As with changes in car sizes, the range of bicycle styles has increased and the minimum dimensions may be inadequate for some applications. Where space is limited, in contrast, closer spacing of racks may be acceptable. It is important to note that this standard is currently under review. Designers must always be aware of the currency of relevant standards, and the possible implications if circumstances demand a departure from the standard.

Codes

Many planning authorities now have some form of acknowledgement of bicycle provision planning, whether in the form of a policy, code or guidelines (see also Bell & Ferretti, Chapter Fifteen, this volume). Grants may also be available for complying projects, such as the Perth Bicycle Network Grants Program, part of the *Western Australia bicycle network plan 2014-2031* (Department of Transport, 2014, p. 4). Development may be required to conform to the relevant codes, as well as to any Acts and Standards, to qualify for funding. The depth of detail provided will vary depending on the authority. Where the Standard is deemed to be inappropriate (if, for example, it is quite old or inadequate) the code may take precedence.

If suitable pre-existing facilities are available, a developer may not be required to provide bicycle parking to the same level. Examples range from the extensive and detailed code of the Australian Capital Territory [ACT] Planning & Land Authority *Bicycle parking general code* (2013, p. 1) — which has, as its first objective: *'To reduce the barriers to cycling by ensuring safe and convenient end-of-trip facilities are available at residences as well as common commuting and recreational destinations'* — to the more concise six-page document of the City of Rockingham's *Bicycle parking and end-of-trip facilities policy* (2011).

Statutory requirements

Local authority development plans may have specific requirements for bicycle parking provision, such as Yarra City Council's *Statutory Planning Scheme* (Department of Transport, Planning and Local Infrastructure, 2014, p. 731: Section 50, Particular provisions, Clause 52.34: Bicycle Facilities), which aims to

- encourage cycling as a mode of transport
- provide secure, accessible and convenient bicycle parking spaces and associated shower and change facilities.

The scheme includes location of parking provision as well as level of provision for various land uses, design of rails, lockers and signage. Even when considering structures such as sheds, and setbacks for bicycle storage, the provisions of the relevant development plan or planning scheme must be met. A minimum quantity of bicycle parking for different types of development may also be specified. If these are inadequate, recommendations should be made to incorporate bicycle-friendly requirements in future updates of planning provisions.

For local authorities that have no existing policies and are considering improvements to their local bicycle networks and facilities, the *Bicycle plan workbook* (Rev. 1), produced by the Bicycle Network (2011), gives step-by-step guidance for 'a plan that reflects their context, their aims, their culture and capabilities' (p. 3). This is not a template but it provides assistance on such aspects as processes; who best to do the work; what data may be required and how it can be collected; what questions need to be asked; and community engagement, evaluation and endorsement.

How much parking

The amount of bicycle parking for residential development will depend on the housing density and the nature of the development. A typical level of provision is given in the *Adelaide (City) Development Plan*'s Bicycle Access: Principle of

Development 233 (Adelaide City Council, 2015, p. 75; see also Table Adel/6: Bicycle Parking Provisions, pp. 372-373). This requires one resident bicycle parking space per dwelling/apartment of less than 150 square metres of total floor area in low-scale residential development, and two bicycle parking spaces in medium- to high-scale developments with more than 150 square metres of total floor area. Visitor bicycle parking is one for every ten dwellings. However, whether or not there are statutory requirements, levels should, at a minimum, align with the local authority's projected cycling targets, and should be consistent with cycling, transport and integrated movement strategies and plans. A site assessment will determine the appropriateness of existing parking, but the provision of better facilities may increase the demand, and providing more than the minimum should be considered to allow for future growth.

Network design

Subdivision and neighbourhood design

Subdivision and neighbourhood design may encourage or deter bicycle use. Urban design studies frequently highlight the contribution that good cycling and walking environments can make to the success and wellbeing of the neighbourhood. Good neighbourhood design focuses on accessibility, and aims to create convenient, comfortable, safe and enjoyable environments for cycling and walking. A grid street pattern is preferable to a hierarchical network with cul-de-sacs, as it distributes traffic evenly, thus reducing the overall impact of traffic. It is also more permeable and accessible, and increases the level of choice of route (Figure 16.14).

Visual permeability of the grid is important so that users can easily identify the choices available to them to enable them to move through the neighbourhood. In new developments, some cul-de-sacs may be included over and above the grid if they provide more direct access and greater choice for cyclists and pedestrians. Cyclists will tend not to use routes for short convenience trips that do not go directly to the destination. Street networks should be designed to give equal or greater consideration to cyclists and walkers, and to discourage unsafe and unnecessary use by motor vehicles.

Medium-density housing with compatible mixed land use development shortens the distance and increases accessibility to services. Larger apartment and multiple-occupancy developments that incorporate dedicated bicycle and walking networks between buildings will allow for greater permeability through the site (Figure 16.15).

In addition to the main street network, dedicated and well-managed cycling and walking paths will increase the permeability but must still meet the criteria of a safe, attractive environment.

It is more difficult to retrofit good cycling networks into existing hierarchical developments that have not allowed for cycling and walking access. Acquisition of properties to improve connections is one possible solution. The issue of poor cycling surfaces and their maintenance, meanwhile, can be partially addressed by good initial planning and design. Giving thought to the location of service pits (i.e. *not* placing them in bicycle lanes) and to the selection of suitable surfacing materials can minimise hazards and ongoing maintenance costs.

Cycling routes should be provided to meet the needs of the different types of cyclist. What is convenient for a fast commuter may not be suitable for children travelling to school, so alternative route options may be required for different riding practices. A study of school children's 'active commuting' — that is, walking or cycling — found that the studied group avoided direct routes, possibly because they encountered busier traffic (Panter, Jones, Van Sluijs, & Griffin, 2010). All routes should link into the wider bicycle networks and city-integrated transport systems.

Cycle paths through 'green' corridors reserved for services such as stormwater disposal are to be encouraged, but will not attract more frequent utilitarian trips unless they are designed to easily connect to services such as schools and shopping centres. Bike trails in terrain that is steep or difficult to develop for other reasons, in leftover space or drainage corridors, may be suitable for some types of recreation trail but not for regular short trips.

Water-sensitive urban design, shade and aesthetics must now be given equal weight to convenience and safe access to services in the design of new cycling routes, in order to attract a greater number of regular cyclists. With an increasing emphasis on enhancing the cycling experience, landscape architects and urban designers are well placed to contribute their skills and knowledge, which include consultation with stakeholders and undertaking site and visual assessment, as well as site planning, environmental and culturally sensitive design, and the application of water-sensitive urban design principles.

Strategies for change

Figure 16.14: The density of bicycle routes in Bowden (grid street pattern) and Greenwith (cul-de-sac hierarchy) in the Adelaide metropolitan area.
(Source: Adapted from Bikedirect maps in Department of Planning, Transport and Infrastructure, 2011.)

Figure 16.15: Cycle and pedestrian access through an apartment building, Hiuzen, the Netherlands.
(Source: author's own work.)

Design at trip destination

Convenience and well-designed end-of-trip bicycle facilities (away from home) have been identified as key issues for encouraging cycling. Sources for this section include *The bicycle parking handbook* (Bicycle Victoria, 2004)[5], *Basic principles for designing for bikes: End of trip* (Bicycle Network, 2015) and 'Section 11 — Bicycle parking and end of trip facilities' in *Cycling aspects of Austroads guides* (Levassuer, 2014), in addition to the author's own observations.

Some commuter trips of up to 15 kilometres may now be almost as quick by bike as by car (Royal Automobile Association of South Australia [RAA], 2014). However, for distances of over 5 kilometres the journey may take longer for many cyclists, and convenience and the quality of bicycle parking will be a major consideration in selecting the bicycle as the mode of transport (Bach et al., 2006). Poorly located, designed and maintained facilities will be underutilised and may lead to inappropriate bicycle parking with potentially hazardous conditions for pedestrians, as well as greater uptake of other transport modes to access facilities. Poor signage can also contribute to underuse if cyclists are unaware of the parking options available.

Destinations

Trip destinations include any type of development and service to which it is possible to cycle. The *Bicycle parking general code* (ACT Planning and Land Authority, 2013, p. 4) lists a number of developments that require end-of-trip cycling facilities and hence must meet the provisions of the code. In addition to some more obvious developments such as 'outdoor recreation facility' and 'shop', it includes 'special care hostel', 'defence installation' and 'bulky goods retailing'.

Bicycle parking facilities required for different land uses will vary greatly. It is critical to understand the context and to ensure that products and arrangements are appropriate to the application. A primary school will have very different needs to a university or an aged care facility, and consultation and consideration must be given to all potential users of cycling facilities, such as staff and visitors as well as the principle occupants. Questions — such as whether the bicycle has to be lifted,

---

[5] At the time of writing this chapter, this document was in the process of being updated but the principles are still relevant.

whether it can be parked by one user, and whether there is room for a trailer — should be asked.

The range of bicycle types that may need to be accommodated (see Figures 16.16 and 16.17), depending on the situation, will include a standard adult bicycle, small child's bicycle, mountain bicycle, bicycles with panniers and baskets, cargo bicycle, bicycle with child carrier (front or trailer), adult tandem, adult and child tandem, tricycle, and a recliner.

As with provision at the trip origin, the designer and/or developer must be aware of the relevant standards, codes and statutory provisions and comply with mandatory requirements. Other standards may be relevant and should be referred to where appropriate.

The *Australian Standard AS 2890.3-1993 Parking facilities Part 3 — Bicycle parking facilities* (Standards Australia International and Standards New Zealand, 1993) is possibly even more important at the destination due to the broader implications for the possible impact of poor design in the public domain. Signage, surveillance and typical location of bicycle parking facilities on a footpath must be considered. The Standard classifies bicycle parking according to the level of security provided, Class 1 — the highest level — having fully enclosed lockers, and Class 3 — the lowest level — being a facility to which a frame and wheel can be locked (p. 4). This classification is a useful starting point but, as with at the trip origin, the Standard is a minimum rather than a desirable level of provision (and is under review). The Standard only cursorily addresses safety for the user who may be accessing a locker alone and/or at night. Personal safety demands a higher level of passive surveillance than described in the Standard. The designer must also assess and achieve a balance between what level of security is acceptable in order to maximise the number of parking places. Class 1 provision, for example, provides the highest level of security but is expensive, is not very efficient in the use of space, and limits the quantity of bicycle parking which can be provided. It can also be argued that Class 2 cages are more secure due to passive surveillance.

On its website, BicycleNetwork (2015) publishes a discussion of end-of-trip facilities including current applications for Australian Standard Classes, some limitations of various guidelines and proposed changes to the Australian Standard. The *London cycling design standard* (Transport for London, 2014) includes procedures and methods for assessing demand as well as criteria to

Skilling landscape architects and urban designers

Figure 16.16: Long rail accommodates larger bicycles and trailers.
(Source: author's own work.)

Figure 16.17: Cargo bicycles require more storage space.
(Source: author's own work.)

Strategies for change

Figure 16.18: Australian Standard Class 1 locker.
(Source: author's own work.)

Figure 16.19: Australian Standard Class 2 communal locked cage.
(Source: author's own work.)

Figure 16.20: 'Flat top' placed end to end for narrower footpaths.
(Source: author's own work.)

Figure 16.21: 'Flat top' rails stacked, with room for two bicycles with panniers at each rail.
(Source: author's own work.)

Figure 16.22: Rail placed too close to adjacent pole.
(Source: author's own work.)

Figure 16.23: Supportive and visually pleasing rail for low-volume use.
(Source: author's own work.)

support different uses such as public transport interchanges and schools. It also discusses management options that may be employed to minimise the cost of additional infrastructure to the client while remaining acceptable to users. The second edition of the Austroads publication *Cycling aspects of Austroads guides* also

Figure 16.24: Space-efficient rack that does not support the frame.
(Source: author's own work.)

Figure 16.25: Cheap, easily installed rack that provides no frame support and can damage bicycle wheels.
(Source: author's own work.)

provides comprehensive coverage in 'Section 11 — Bicycle parking and end-of-trip facilities' (Levassuer, 2014).

Bicycle rail design

As with bicycle parking and storage at home, the 'fit for purpose' guidelines apply, and at a minimum the rail should provide good support and allow the frame and at least one wheel, preferably both, to be secured. For street parking the 'flat top' (Figures 16.2 and Figures including 16.20, 16.30 and 16.36) is, again, the commonly preferred style, as it meets the above criteria for support and security and is economical to supply and install. It is efficient in use of space and adaptable to different layouts depending on the width of the footpath or configuration of the streetscape, as long as it is correctly installed.

Other styles may add more interest to a streetscape and an assessment must be made as to the priority of efficiency, level of provision and cost over aesthetics and/or meeting a minimum standard. Some rails may be cheap for the provider to supply and install, but can damage the bike if the only support is for one wheel, and such rails are less efficient in the use of space, as each rack only supports one bicycle (Figure 16.25).

Custom-designed bicycle rails

Designers may want to create custom designs for bicycle parking rails which are unique to the site or development. Rails may be designed and/or manufactured by local artists or as part of community workshops. This can be a valuable place-making exercise, which in turn may induce more people to ride bicycles. A number of cities, such as Adelaide and Portland, Oregon, have established bicycle art trails incorporating custom-designed bicycle parking which can also serve to differentiate neighbourhoods, make a statement about a place or identify a business. The rails should, however, be 'fit for purpose'. Depending on the rail style, cyclists may not realise the purpose or may be inhibited from using a rail for fear of damaging it as a piece of art (Figures 16.27, 16.28 and 16.29).

Parking location and security at destinations

The best location for bicycle parking is a place where cyclists want to park. In a study of Sydney suburban railway stations, it was found that in some cases cyclists

Strategies for change

Figure 16.26: One car park equals space for ten bicycles.
(Source: author's own work.)

Figure 16.27: Canberra, Lake Burley Griffin.
(Source: author's own work.)

Figure 16.28: Bike Art Trail, Adelaide Botanic Gardens.
(Source: author's own work.)

Figure 16.29: Bike Art Trail, Adelaide Zoo.
(Source: author's own work.)

used fences and poles for parking despite the availability of bicycle parking closer to the station (Arbis, Rashidi, Dixit, & Vandebona, 2013). The level of surveillance is a critical factor, especially for long-stay bicycle parking. At stations with a higher frequency of trains, cyclists were able to rely on the high level of pedestrian activity and the proximity of shops and bus stops to provide an adequate level of security. At stations that were less frequently used, cyclists were prepared to walk further if secure locker or cage parking was available, rather than parking closer in the open and with less security. The study revealed that it is inadequate just to rely on generic classes of parking as described in the Australian Standard and that it is important to consider the local conditions in selecting the type and placement of cycling facilities. At large concentrated developments, such as shopping centres or stadia with multiple entrances, distributing a number of smaller clusters of parking rails around the access points and close to entrances (Figure 16.30) is better than placing them in one central space that is difficult to get to or too remote. Street parking for short-term stays serving a single destination should generally be no more than 15 metres from an entrance, or 25 metres where there are a number of possible destinations. Parking should always be visible and located where there is good natural surveillance (Figure 16.31).

Where a high level of street parking is not feasible, or where it is difficult to provide parking associated with a particular business or a street of small shops, city-centre bike parking stations are a good alternative. Such parking stations are common in Dutch cities and towns such as Rotterdam, Breda and Houten. These parking stations usually offer a choice of free parking with a lower level of security, or more secure parking for a nominal fee (Figure 16.33).

Long-term parking (four hours or more) requires a secure, undercover area no further than 70 metres from the main entrance. Arbis et al. (2013) argue that cyclists are prepared to walk further and pay for parking if it is a more secure type of parking — for example, an individual locker or a parking station with a high level of security such as CCTV.

It is important for parking areas to be well signed. If the cage is only accessible by a prepaid swipe card, signage should include information on obtaining the card. Sources for prepaid cards should be located nearby and the cards available from an automatic dispenser or a corner store/kiosk with reasonable opening hours, including normal business hours and weekends. Secure end-of-trip facilities such

Figure 16.30: Protected cluster parking, Adelaide Oval.
(Source: author's own work.)

Figure 16.31: Priority parking at the supermarket, North Fitzroy, Melbourne.
(Source: author's own work.)

Strategies for change

Figure 16.32: Priority parking at a fitness centre with a choice of rail or locker. (Source: author's own work.)

Figure 16.33: Parking options and availability, Rotterdam Central Station. (Source: author's own work.)

as cages or lockers are often placed out of sight, in which case signage is essential. The assumption often seems to be that cages are only used by regular commuters or locals who will pre-purchase a swipe card and know where to find the cage. Some local governments have installed secure cages and undercover bicycle parking in their public car parks. However, they often fail to provide directional signage or clear indication of how to access the cages — which may explain why they appear to be under-utilised (Figures 16.34 and 16.35). A visitor or tourist wanting to securely park their bicycle and belongings would have difficulty finding out where or how to park.

All types of bicycle parking should be available in the public domain so that cyclists can choose the level of security, service and payment that suits their needs. Therefore, cycle parking locations must be well signed with clear payment and operational instructions.

All street-side parking should be easy to access with minimum conflict between pedestrians and motorists. Ideally, cyclists should not have to dismount in the carriageway (Figure 16.36). If there is a kerb, an easily accessible kerb ramp should be provided, separated from pedestrian access ramps to avoid conflict. Where cyclists and pedestrians have to share kerb ramps, they must be wide enough to accommodate both, with the ramp section at least as wide as the path (Figure 16.37). This is especially important at locations where high volumes of pedestrian and cycling traffic may be expected at certain times, such as sporting and entertainment venues where large crowds exit from events at one time.

Additional facilities

At busy transit hubs, facilities such as showers and repair and maintenance services are a further incentive for people to choose the bicycle over other modes of transport. At the Houten train station in the Netherlands, parking facilities are located directly beneath the platforms (Figure 16.38). In addition, well-signed repair, servicing and bicycle hire are available at the station entrance (Figure 16.39). This kind of extensive facility has to be planned at the outset of a development. However, small repair hubs are a useful low-cost initiative to service popular and busy locations. The 24/7 public work station at tram stop 15 in Glenelg, South Australia, has covered parking and a drinking fountain as well as a pump and multiple tools (Figure 16.40).

Strategies for change

Figure 16.34: Cage parking located inside an enclosed car park, with no directional signage.
(Source: author's own work.)

Figure 16.35: Under-used cage parking.
(Source: author's own work.)

Skilling landscape architects and urban designers

Figure 16.36: Accessible parking at street level.
(Source: author's own work.)

Figure 16.37: Long stretches of kerb ramp help reduce pedestrian and cyclist conflict.
(Source: author's own work.)

Strategies for change

Figure 16.38: Houten station, bicycle parking.
(Source: author's own work.)

Figure 16.39: Houten station, one-stop maintenance, repair and hire.
(Source: author's own work.)

Skilling landscape architects and urban designers

Figure 16.40: Parking shelter and workstation, Mike Turtur Bikeway.
(Source: author's own work.)

Figure 16.41: Workstation, Mike Turtur Bikeway.
(Source: author's own work.)

Some destinations may require more specific infrastructure. Transport hubs such as railway platforms, where access may be needed to several levels, should provide at least one lift, and preferably two, stopping at each level. The lifts should be large enough to accommodate two bicycles at one time, with the riders standing to the side. In addition, a wheel ramp should be provided alongside flights of steps, so that there is an alternative form of access if the lifts are occupied or out of service (Figure 16.10). Drinking water and fountains should be located at all transport hubs, parks and reserves.

E-bicycle charging hubs will be in increasing demand and should be considered for all major destinations. They should be easy to find and use, and clearly signed, especially as e-bicycles offer mobility to a wide range of people, some of whom might not otherwise use a bicycle.

Bicycle-friendly work places

New buildings and developments should ideally meet Green Star rating[6] for bicycle provision, even if not required to do so under statutory regulations. The cost to the developer will be a very small percentage of the overall building development budget.

Purpose-built bicycle parking, showers and lockers are a good addition, but there are other ways to make the workplace bicycle-friendly. Under-utilised space may be available for bicycle storage, or existing secure bicycle parking may be available in a nearby car park. If the building does not have showers, an arrangement may be possible with a nearby gym to use their facilities. Repair facilities and a pump may be kept at the office for staff use.

Quantity of bicycle parking

While it is not possible to definitively say what quantity of parking is required without looking at the unique circumstances of each site, there are currently general guidelines available for calculating an increase to existing bicycle parking facilities, and these guidelines can form a starting point (Table 16.3). The following table is adapted from *The bicycle parking handbook* recommendations (2004. p. 5).

---

[6] Green Star is a voluntary sustainability rating system for buildings, administered by the Green Building Council of Australia.

Table 16.3: Recommended quantity of bicycle parking for retrofitting existing buildings.

Bicycle parking situation	Recommended quantity of parking
When increasing existing bicycle parking facilities	• 1 bicycle parking space* for every 10 long-term users of the location (over 4 hours) • 1 bicycle parking space for every 25 short-term users of the location
When no facilities currently exist	• 1 bicycle parking space for every 20 long-term users of the location • 1 bicycle parking space for every 50 short-term users of the location
If clothing storage, showers and change rooms are appropriate, then the following should be provided as a minimum	• 1 clothes locker per bicycle parking space • 1 shower for the first 5 bicycle parking spaces • 1 shower for every 10 subsequent bicycle parking spaces • 1 change space for each shower, or direct access to a communal change space

* A space must contain a bicycle parking rail or bicycle locker.
(Source: Adapted from Bicycle Victoria, 2004.)

The importance of providing adequate facilities in public spaces cannot be overstated. If the cycling facilities provided are of sufficient quality, demand for parking is likely to increase, so a higher level of provision should be considered at the outset.

With high levels of risk management and duty of care in public places, there may be negative impacts on the level of bicycle use from the consequences of informal parking unless sufficient acceptable parking is provided. Despite the capital costs for the property owner for providing well-designed bicycle parking, maintenance cost savings will be achieved as a result of reduced property damage and inconvenience to non-cyclists caused by unplanned bicycle storage. The initial cost of a more generous allowance for future growth is also likely to pay for itself over the long term for the same reasons. With bicycle lockers offering the highest level of security, and being preferred for long-term parking, they may also be cost-effective over time. If cyclists are prepared to pay for the increased security, the revenue can contribute towards ongoing upkeep and maintenance.

Wayfinding and signage

'Wayfinding' describes a design approach to facilitate navigation of the built environment from various perspectives such as cycling, walking and driving, and for building occupants, locals or visitors (Apelt, Crawford, Hogan, & Cooperative Research Centre for Construction Innovation, 2007). It encompasses both interior and exterior environments, including public streets, complex developments and sites such as transit hubs and commercial centres. Wayfinding is about effective communication delivered by sensory cues — visual, auditory, tactile and olfactory. Visual cues come from good site planning and spatial organisation, including logical and rational sequences of travel. Signage is an important part of wayfinding for cyclists. Well-designed signage provides useful information and sends a positive message that cycling is a legitimate and welcome activity (Figure 16.42).

A site dominated by car parks that preferences motor vehicles, lacks signage directed at cyclists and provides outdated and poorly maintained cycling infrastructure, as found at the University of South Australia's Mawson Lakes campus, 're-positions cycling as a marginal mode and the cyclist as abnormal' (Bonham & Koth, 2010, p. 99). All signage must, however, be meaningful. Overuse should be avoided to reduce clutter and ensure that messages are clear and easily conveyed.

Signage falls under various headings such as directional and way-marking, safety and caution, naming and information, and interpretive. Wayfinding signs have to be unique to the site if they are to function correctly; the best placement and orientation must be determined before the sign content is prepared, and the position of the viewer, which should always be shown, can only be marked once placement has been determined. This adds cost but is an essential part of good communication and design.

Signage design is an area of expertise claimed by many disciplines but involving a diversity of skills and knowledge which is rarely found in one person. Behavioural psychology, graphic design, written content, and placement in terms of location and orientation are all important to the understanding of what needs to be conveyed, and how, when, where and to whom. There is considerable scope for undertaking further investigation into signage appropriate for cyclists which is also visible to, and able to be interpreted by, others such as motorists and pedestrians.

Some signage can be purely celebratory but is a great way to encourage more cyclists (Figure 16.43).

Who needs to know?

As has been discussed earlier, bicycle infrastructure is best developed collaboratively with input from a range of stakeholders. The most powerful players include developers, financiers, designers and elected members, but the often unheard users (current and future) must also be considered as part of the network for successful decision making. Developers need to provide more site and floor plan options which allow for usable bicycle storage with capacity for future expansion. They must be aware of the

Figure 16.42: Sign on the Mike Turtur Bikeway.
(Source: author's own work.)

Figure 16.43: 'Amsterdam loves cycling' — Celebrating the bicycle.
(Source: author's own work.)

responsibilities in meeting statutory requirements; however, these requirements must be updated to meet growing and changing demand. Development Assessment planners need to be aware of best practice bicycle provision and be skilled in assessing the compliance of development applications. Designers must work collaboratively with clients and colleagues in associated professions to think beyond their immediate discipline and anticipate cyclists' needs at the outset of projects. Disciplines may include urban, social, health and transport planners; landscape architects and urban designers; traffic, civil and hydrological engineers; and anyone involved in development and environmental design. Project managers responsible for the delivery of projects must have sufficient knowledge to effectively implement bicycle infrastructure; building and asset managers and maintenance staff need to understand the impact that good bicycle facility design has, in both practical and financial terms.

Conclusion

There has been much published literature that focuses on generic principles of planning for bicycle networks, and minimum quantitative requirements for storage and parking facilities. It is a more complex matter, however, to determine the qualitative aspects of the range of cycling experiences and the design inputs which can trigger the choice to ride. A greater understanding of user preferences and a commitment to investing in well-planned treatments and infrastructure are needed. Urban design studies that are directed towards environments that encourage active, healthy living must address the significantly different needs for cycling from other modes of active travel, and the needs of different types of cycling and cyclist. With a larger pool of shared knowledge and better integrated-design processes, landscape architects and urban designers can apply their professional knowledge and skills to help further the growth of cycling as a preferred choice for active travel.

References

Adelaide City Council. (2015, September 3). *Adelaide (City) development plan*. Adelaide: Government of South Australia.

Apelt, R, Crawford, J, Hogan, D, & Cooperative Research Centre for Construction Innovation. (2007). *Wayfinding system audit*. Brisbane:

CRC for Construction Innovation. Retrieved 11 January 2015 from http://www.construction-innovation.info/images/pdfs/Publications/Industry_publications/CRC0001_CRC_Wayfinding_Audit.pdf.

Arbis, D, Rashidi, T, Dixit, V, & Vandebona, U. (2013, October 2-4). Analysis and planning of bicycle parking for transport interchanges. *Australasian Transport Research Forum 2013 Proceedings*. Retrieved 24 August 2015 from http://atrf.info/papers/2013/2013_arbis_rashidi_dixit_vanderbona.pdf.

Australian Capital Territory [ACT] Planning and Land Authority. (2013). *Bicycle parking general code*. Canberra: ACT Government. Retrieved 9 August 2014 from http://www.legislation.act.gov.au/ni/2008-27/copy/94067/pdf/2008-27.pdf.

Bach, B, van Hal, E, de Jong, M, & de Jong, T. (2006). *Urban design and traffic: A selection from Bach's toolbox*. Ede, the Netherlands: CROW.

Beer, A, & Higgins, C. (2000). *Environmental planning for site development: A manual for sustainable local planning and design* (2nd ed.). London & New York: Spon.

Bentley, I, McGlynn, S, Smith, G, Alcock, A, & Murrain, P. (1985). *Responsive environments: A manual for designers*. London: Routledge.

Bicycle Network. (2011, December). *The local government bike plan workbook: How to develop a great bike plan* (Rev. 1). Retrieved 8 July 2015 from https://www.bicyclenetwork.com.au/general/for-government-and-business/3371.

Bicycle Network. (2015). *Basic principles for designing for bikes: End of trip*. Retrieved 7 August 2015 from https://www.bicyclenetwork.com.au/general/for-government-and-business/2879.

Bicycle Victoria. (2000). *Bicycle parking: Providing bicycle parking facilities*. Victoria: Government of Victoria. Retrieved 16 August 2015 from http://www.bikeparking.com.au/general/bike-parking-experts/409/.

Bicycle Victoria. (2004). *The bicycle parking handbook*. Victoria: Bicycle Victoria. Retrieved 7 August 2015 from https://www.bicyclenetwork.com.au/general/bike-parking-experts/409.

Bonham, J, & Koth, B. (2010). Universities and the cycling culture. *Transportation Research Part D, 15*(2), 94-102.

Carmona, M, Heath, T, Oc, T, & Tiedsell, S. (2010). *Public places, urban spaces: The dimensions of urban design*. London: Architectural Press.

City of Newcastle. (2012). *Newcastle cycling strategy and action plan.* Newcastle: City of Newcastle. Retrieved 22 June 2014 from http://www.newcastle.nsw.gov.au/data/as sets/pdf_file/0007/203020/Final_Newcastle_Cycling_Strategy_and_Action_Plan.pdf.

City of Rockingham. (2011). *Planning policy 3.3.14: Bicycle parking and end-of-trip facilities.* Rockingham: Government of Western Australia. Retrieved 24 August 2015 from http://www.rockingham.wa.gov.au/getmedia/45fd8388-c831-4d6d-90b8-c88abf8e631a/PD_Planning-Policy-3-3-14-Bicycle-Parking-and-End-of-Trip-Facilities.pdf.aspx.

Department for Transport, Communities and Local Government, Welsh Assembly Government. (2007). *Manual for streets.* London: Telford Publishing. Retrieved from https://www.gov.uk/government/uploads/system/uploads/attachment_data/file/341513/pdfmanforstreets.pdf.

Department of Planning, Transport and Infrastructure. (2011). Bike*direct* bicycle maps. Adelaide: Government of South Australia. Retrieved 13 January 2015 from http://www.sa.gov.au/topics/transport-travel-and-motoring/cycling/cycling-maps.

Department of Transport. (2014). *Western Australian bicycle network plan 2014-2031.* Perth: Government of Western Australia. Retrieved 7 August 2015 from http://www.transport.wa.gov.au/activetransport/25720.asp.

Department of Transport, Planning and Local Infrastructure. (2014). *Yarra planning scheme.* Victoria: Government of Victoria. Retrieved 24 August 2015 from http://planningschemes.dpcd.vic.gov.au/schemes/yarra.

Forsyth, A, & Krizek, K. (2010). Promoting walking and bicycling: Assessing the evidence to assist planners. *Built Environment Volume,* 36(4), 429-446. Retrieved 10 October 2015 from http://kevinjkrizek.org/wp-content/uploads/2012/04/Bltenv.pdf.

Forsyth, A, & Krizek, K. (2011). Urban design: Is there a distinctive view from the bicycle? *Journal of Urban Design,* 16(4), 531-549.

Green Building Council Australia. (n.d.) Retrieved 10 August 2014 from https://www.gbca.org.au/green-star.

Guinn, J, & Stangl, P. (2014). Pedestrian and bicyclist motivation: An assessment of influences on pedestrians' and bicyclists' mode choice in Mt. Pleasant, Vancouver. *Urban Planning and Transport Research: An Open Access Journal,* 2(1), 105-125. doi: 10.1080/21650020.2014.906907.

Jones, P. (2005). Performing the city: A body and a bicycle take on Birmingham, UK. *Social & Cultural Geography*, 6(6), 813-830.

Levassuer, M. (2014). *Cycling aspects of Austroads guides* (2nd ed.). Sydney: Austroads. Retrieved 16 August 2015 from https://www.onlinepublications.austroads.com.au/items/AP-G88-14.

Lynch, K, & Hack, G. (1984). *Site planning* (3rd ed.). Cambridge, MA: MIT Press.

Mongard, J. (2006, May). Networks not lines: Toward a long term cultural realm in the landscape architectural project. *IFLA Conference*. Retrieved 13 October 2014 from http://mongard.com.au/assets/articles/Networks_Not_Lines_JMongard_2006.pdf.

National Heart Foundation of Australia (Victorian Division). (2004). *Healthy by design: A planners' guide to environments for active living*. Victoria: National Heart Foundation of Australia. Retrieved 14 October 2014 from http://www.heartfoundation.org.au/SiteCollectionDocuments/Healthy-by-Design.pdf.

Panter, J, Jones, A, Van Sluijs, E, & Griffin, S. (2010). Neighborhood, route, and school environments and children's active commuting. *American Journal of Preventive Medicine*, 38(3), 268-278.

Renewal SA. (2014). *Developers' handbook & urban design guidelines, Bowden*. Bowden: Government of South Australia. Retrieved 14 October 2014 from http://lifemoreinteresting.com.au/wp-content/uploads/Bowden-Urban-Design-Guidelines.pdf.

Royal Automobile Association of South Australia [RAA]. (2014, December 12). Adelaide commuters urged to jump on a bus, bike, train. Retrieved from http://www.raa.com.au/community-and-advocacy/media-releases/1047.

Sick Nielsen, TA, Skov-Petersen, H, & Carstensen, TA. (2013). Urban planning practices for bicycleable cities — The case of Copenhagen. *Urban Research & Practice*, 6(1), 110-115.

Spinney, J. (2006). A place of sense: A kinaesthetic ethnography of cyclists on Mont Ventoux. *Environment and Planning D: Society and Space*, 24(5), 709-732.

Standards Australia International and Standards New Zealand. (1993). *AS 2890.3-1993 Parking facilities — Part 3 Bicycle parking facilities*. Sydney: Standards Australia.

Teguh Aditjandra, P, Mulley, C, & Nelson, J. (2013). The influence of neighbourhood design on travel behaviour: Empirical evidence from North East England. *Transport Policy, 26,* 54-65.

Transport for London. (2014). *London cycling design standards: Chapter 8 — Cycle parking.* Consultation draft. London: Transport for London. Retrieved 9 August 2014 from https://consultations.tfl.gov.uk/cycling/draft-london-cycling-design-standards/user_uploads/draft-lcds---all-chapters.pdf.

Transport Initiatives LLP and Cambridge City Council. (2010). *Cycle parking guide for new residential developments* (1st ed.). Cambridge: Environment and Planning, Cambridge City Council. Retrieved 9 June 2014 from https://www.cambridge.gov.uk/sites/www.cambridge.gov.uk/files/docs/CycleParkingGuide_std.pdf.

17 Cycling and Australian law

Margaret Grant

Introduction

Readers may expect this chapter to discuss laws about wearing a helmet, having lights and a bell, stopping at red lights and pedestrian crossings, using bicycle boxes, defined passing distance laws and other road safety rules. Some of these issues are mentioned, but they are not the focus of the discussion. Rather, the chapter is concerned with the law in relation to 'making space for cycling', and it is specifically aimed at those working on sustainable transport systems; academics responsible for designing courses about urban planning and transport; cycling and health promotion organisations; lobby groups; cycling advocates; and individuals interested in cycling safety. This chapter does not provide legal advice or information that can be relied upon in any legal situation.

The objective of this chapter is to stimulate thinking and provoke conversations by relevant stakeholders about the interface between the regulatory frameworks established by Australian law and the policy initiatives aimed at promoting sustainable transport and reducing death and injury of cyclists. This chapter argues that the current and future laws that apply to design and management of roads as well as road safety are key considerations in designing a road safety regulatory framework that makes space for sustainable and safe cycling in Australia. After a brief discussion of relevant concepts in

Australia's legal system, the chapter examines some case studies to illustrate the current limitations of the law when cycling-related matters are dealt with by the courts. It introduces some of the laws that impact on cycling and then explores the role of the law in making space for cycling and the potential for reform in work health and safety laws to inform future regulatory frameworks in the context of cycling.

Fundamental concepts in Australian law

The legal system in Australia is a *common law* system, wherein laws are generally made through judges' decisions (common law) and through legislation (statutory law) passed by the relevant parliament.

Two areas of law in the Australian legal system are most relevant to death and injury of cyclists — criminal law and civil law. Broadly speaking, criminal law matters arise from the set of rules that regulate the behaviour of individuals in the community and lead to penalties for individuals who break those rules. These rules include road traffic laws and road rules. Civil law matters arise from private interactions between two or more individuals and include claims for financial compensation for personal injury and damages following cycling-related accidents.

There are fundamental differences in the ways laws are made and applied in Australia and in European countries. European countries such as France, the Netherlands and Germany do not have judge-made laws. Broadly speaking, their laws are based on a *Civil Code* and applied through a *civil law* system. Although the same words are used, the area of law known as 'civil law' within Australia's common law system is entirely different to the meaning of 'civil law' in European legal systems. Australian law is applied through an adversarial system, whereas European countries use an inquisitorial system.

Because of these fundamental differences, caution must be taken in advocating the application of legal approaches in European countries (for example, liability laws in Netherlands) in the Australian context.

Application of criminal law and civil law in Australia in cycling-related matters

Criminal law

Criminal law is important in making space for cycling because it establishes the rules about road-user behaviour, including the use of bicycle boxes, bicycle lanes and, where relevant, minimum passing distances for motorists overtaking cyclists.

In most states and territories, there are three categories of criminal offences — summary (or simple) offences, minor indictable offences and major (or serious) indictable offences. The category of an offence determines how it is dealt with by the legal system. Broadly speaking, summary offences are less serious than indictable offences, and both the severity of the penalty and the way the penalty is imposed reflect the category of the offence. An example of a summary offence is drink driving, whereas an example of a major indictable offence is drink driving causing death. The penalty for drink driving might be a fine imposed on the spot, whereas the penalty for drink driving causing death might be imprisonment imposed by a court.

Most offences related to cycling are summary offences covered by road traffic laws, including regulations made under road safety and road traffic acts. More serious offences (indictable offences) involving death or injury due to reckless or dangerous driving are described in the crimes legislation that applies in the relevant state or territory.

A criminal offence is described in terms of the acts, omissions or events that the law prohibits (the *physical element*) and the state of mind of the accused (the *fault element*). Generally, the physical and fault elements must be present at the same time to constitute a criminal offence — that is, an individual must be in the relevant state of mind at the time they carry out the relevant act. Broadly speaking, if a criminal matter is tried in court, the prosecution must prove each and every element, and a court must be satisfied 'beyond reasonable doubt' that an offence has been committed before the accused individual is found guilty and convicted of the offence. These legal requirements are one reason that few cycling-related criminal matters are tried in court and, when they are, the accused is sometimes found not guilty.

A recent example of a criminal law case where the accused was found guilty of an indictable offence in the context of cycling is *Director of Public Prosecutions v Leddin*.[1] This case was initiated by the State of Victoria through the Director of Public Prosecutions [DPP]. The DPP acted in this case on behalf of the community of Victoria.

In this case, Eamonn Francis Leddin (the defendant) was charged in January 2013 with culpable driving causing death under section 318 of the Victorian *Crimes Act 1958*. In December 2013, at the County Court of Victoria Warrnambool Criminal Division, the defendant pleaded guilty to this charge and was sentenced by His Honour Judge Taft to 4 years and 3 months' imprisonment, to serve a minimum of 2 years and 3 months. The defendant subsequently applied to the Supreme Court of Victoria, seeking leave to appeal against the sentence. The grounds for the application included that Mr Leddin was a young offender of good character and that the term of the sentence was manifestly excessive. The application was heard in the Supreme Court of Victoria Court of Appeal before three Judges of the Court of Appeal.[2]

The judges noted in paragraph 6 that the collision occurred on a straight stretch of road, and that the weather was fine and visibility was good. They took into account that the cyclist was wearing a pink high-visibility top and there was a roadside sign warning of cyclists. Mr Leddin was not alleged to have been speeding, distracted by other circumstances or affected by drugs or alcohol. Despite these factors, the cyclist was killed. The judges noted that it was possible the driver was fatigued. The appeal court judges agreed unanimously to dismiss the application.

One of the judges, in paragraph 25 of his judgement, described this case as one

> … of real and significant culpability in terms of the driving. The applicant had a clear view of the cyclist, who was highly visible. He saw a sign warning him of the presence of cyclists. He did actually see the cyclist well before the collision. His passenger also saw the cyclist and called out to the applicant a hundred metres before the impact. Yet the applicant collided with the cyclist without taking any evasive action.

---

[1] [2013] VCC 2074.

[2] *Eamonn Francis Leddin v The Queen* [2014] VSCA 155.

This case highlights the vulnerability of cyclists when their space is shared with motor vehicles. One of the judges, in paragraph 28 of his judgement, described this case as one that demonstrates

> … the terrible two-fold character of these tragedies. A wife and mother is dead, leaving a family distraught and with what could be a life sentence of grief. A young, law abiding person, who is of good character and not in any sense a criminal, is condemned to spend time in gaol. He too may suffer life long consequences.

This chapter will discuss the potential that regulatory reform of road safety has to contribute to a reduction in the incidence of death and injury of cyclists and, in doing so, its potential to avoid such life-changing tragedies.

Civil law

If an accident has caused injury or damage to property, the person who suffered the injury or has incurred expenses to repair damage will generally seek to be compensated financially. This compensation is referred to in law as *damages*. A claim for damages falls within civil law and involves the person who suffered injury or damage and the person they consider responsible for paying compensation. Liability for the accident generally needs to be established prior to a claim for damages being determined.

In the context of cycling-related civil cases, the injured party often seeks compensation for personal injury and damages by bringing an action against another person on the grounds of negligence. For example, if a cyclist was injured in an accident caused by an open car door, the person opening the door or leaving the door open could be liable under civil law. The cyclist could be entitled to compensation and damages but, depending on the state or territory, they might need to take legal action to establish liability, even where an insurance company would cover the compensation and damages under compulsory third party insurance.[3] In a civil law case, each individual (referred to as the *plaintiff* and *defendant*) presents evidence to support their argument, and the judge needs to decide if the person

---

[3] In this example, a claim for damages through civil law is a private law matter between individuals and is unrelated to any infringement notice or court penalty imposed if the person opening the car door was in breach of the road rules that apply in the relevant state or territory.

opening the door is liable. Then, subject to that being established, the judge would quantify the amount of compensation and damages.

Unlike the criminal case outlined above, the judge in a civil matter generally has limited capacity to explore factors that might have compromised the defendant's actions or contributed to the accident. In this type of case, the focus is on the actions of the individuals involved in the case. The judge can only decide the liability of the defendant or defendants named by the plaintiff. Although the evidence may show that road infrastructure contributed to an accident involving a cyclist, the judge cannot find the person responsible for the infrastructure liable unless they are named in the plaintiff's claim.

A recent example of a civil law action that highlights this limitation is *Nettleton v Rondeau*.[4] Bruce Nettleton (the plaintiff) had claimed damages associated with an accident between him (as a cyclist) and a car driven by Jocelyn Germaine Rondeau (the defendant). The case was heard in the Supreme Court of New South Wales before the Honourable Justice Hoeben Chief Judge at Common Law (the judge). The accident occurred when the defendant drove her car out of a driveway and emerged from behind parked cars into the lane in which the plaintiff was cycling. The plaintiff collided with the car and was rendered a complete T10 paraplegic. At the time the judge heard the matter, the plaintiff was in a relatively early stage of his rehabilitation and the court had previously ordered that the question of liability be separately determined from the question of damages in this matter.[5]

The arguments put forward by both the plaintiff and the defendant described significant infrastructure issues that impacted on their actions. In the absence of these infrastructure issues, it is likely the accident might not have happened.

One of the key issues in the plaintiff's case was that the defendant did not have a clear view of the road because cars were parked quite close to her driveway. The allegation of negligence included that the defendant could have improved her view of the road by entering the road via an adjacent bus stop rather than emerging straight into the lane in which motor vehicles and cyclists were travelling. A key assertion in the defendant's case, meanwhile, was that the

---

[4] [2014] NSWSC 903.

[5] See *Nettleton v Rondeau* [2013] NSWSC 1321.

plaintiff's actions contributed to the accident because he should have been using an off-road bike path instead of riding on the road.

In considering whether the defendant was negligent, the judge noted in paragraphs 52, 58 and 65 of his decision:

> The defendant owed the plaintiff and other road users a duty to take reasonable care to avoid a foreseeable risk of injury arising from her use of her motor vehicle.
>
> I have concluded that in the circumstances of this case the defendant did breach the duty ... because ... despite having lived in the premises for three years ... every time she drove from the premises onto the westbound lane when there were cars parked to the west of the driveway, she was accepting the risk that drivers using the eastbound lane might be speeding or not keeping a sufficient lookout so as to avoid a collision. A reasonable driver in the position of the defendant would have looked for a safer way of driving onto Lauderdale Avenue from those premises.
>
> ... Not only was the risk of a collision foreseeable, but ... the likelihood of it occurring was high and the consequences potentially catastrophic. In the circumstances, a reasonable driver in the position of the defendant would have taken the course which the plaintiff suggested, i.e. turning to the east when cars were parked to the west of the driveway. The burden of taking such a precaution was modest in the circumstances and would have given rise to no more than a temporary inconvenience.

The judge heard evidence from two experts, whose reports noted design and construction problems with the shared pedestrian/bicycle path that the defendant claimed the plaintiff should have been using at the time of the accident. The problems with the path included that sections of the path were narrower than minimum standards required, had a downhill grade that exceeded the maximum available under the relevant Austroads Guide (Austroads, 2009)[6], had insufficient clearance of fixed objects beside the path, provided cyclists with insufficient sight distance through corners, and had an uneven surface.

---

[6] Austroads is the association of Australasian road transport and traffic agencies. Austroads publishes guides that contain their members' agreed methods and processes for the design, construction, maintenance and operation of the road network in Australia and New Zealand.

The judge rejected the proposition that it was negligent for the plaintiff to ride his bicycle on the road rather than on the shared bicycle/pedestrian path. The judge also heard evidence from two pedestrians who were walking on the footpath adjacent to the road at the time of the accident. One pedestrian reported that the plaintiff was looking at them a short time prior to the accident. The judge found that this distraction delayed the cyclist from starting to brake in an unsuccessful attempt to avoid the collision. The judge accepted the defendant's submission that, given the plaintiff was riding near parked cars and there were driveways leading onto the road, it was negligent for him not to pay attention to the road.

Because the judge found that both the driver and the cyclist were negligent, they shared liability for the accident, and damages were reduced by 25% to take account of the plaintiff's contributory negligence. The judge noted in paragraphs 81-83:

> The defendant, as the driver of a motor vehicle, who had a choice of utilising the bus stop and turning left out of the drive was in control of the situation. Had she taken that option, a dangerous situation would not have eventuated and it would not have mattered if the plaintiff had been momentarily distracted. Her decision to enter the eastbound lane in the way in which she did, brought about the potentially dangerous situation. Accordingly, I regard the causal potency of the defendant's negligence as greater than that of the plaintiff. In relation to moral culpability, I also find that it weighs more heavily against the defendant than the plaintiff. The defendant having lived in the premises for three years, was well aware of the danger associated with driving into the eastbound lane in circumstances where she could not see vehicles approaching from the west. This is to be contrasted with the plaintiff's relatively brief lapse in concentration. Taking those matters into account, I would apportion liability as to 75 percent against the defendant and 25 percent against the plaintiff.

This case highlights the limitations of the current road safety regulatory framework within Australia's adversarial court system. Although the plaintiff and defendant both submitted evidence of infrastructure issues that compromised their actions, the judge had limited ability to address these issues as contributing factors. Instead, he considered what actions the defendant might have taken to overcome her limited vision of the road and found it was reasonable for the cyclist to choose not to ride on the cycling path. No action was taken to reduce the risk of another 'potentially dangerous situation'.

Limitations of the Australian law in cycling-related matters

The two cases discussed above are used to demonstrate how the Australian law is applied when a cyclist is injured or killed in a motor vehicle accident. The judges in each case comment upon infrastructure issues relevant to the cycling space. The laws that apply in the current framework that regulates safety in the context of cycling do not extend to infrastructure issues.

If the regulatory framework for road safety included infrastructure issues, the judge in the civil case might have recommended that the cycling path be replaced by one that complied with design standards, that signs be erected to alert cyclists to emerging cars and to alert emerging cars to cyclists, or that a 'no parking' area be introduced to improve the vision of the road for motorists emerging from the driveway.

The potential to reform the currently complex and diverse range of laws and initiatives related to road safety in Australia to enable issues such as these to be addressed by an evidence-based regulatory framework is explored later in the chapter. This type of framework would aim to establish safe and sustainable space for cycling in Australia.

The diversity and complexity of current road safety laws and related initiatives

The most obvious laws that impact on cyclist safety in Australia are the road rules legislated in each state and territory. These laws regulate the behaviour of motorists and of cyclists on the road, but, as demonstrated by the cases outlined earlier, they do not prevent death or injury of road users. Governments in Australia have supported the development of a range of initiatives to complement road safety laws, reduce death and injury, and promote sustainable transport. Examples include the *National Road Safety Strategy 2011-2020* (Australian Transport Council, 2011), the *National Road Safety Action Plan 2015-2017* (Transport and Infrastructure Council, 2014) and the *National Cycling Strategy 2011-2016* (Austroads, 2011). These initiatives are not currently part of the formal regulatory framework for road safety in Australia.

Austroads has published guides for a range of aspects of road and related infrastructure design such as cycle paths (Austroads, 2009). State and territory road authorities have agreed to use these guides as their primary road design guide

(Austroads, 2009). A recent publications highlights the scope and complexity of the rules, regulations and guidelines which engineers, planners and designers must consider when working on infrastructure projects that impact directly or indirectly on cyclists (Austroads, 2014).

The potential for these disparate road safety laws and initiatives to inform development and implementation of a more effective regulatory framework for road safety is considered later in the chapter.

The Australian Road Rules

The Australian Constitution, based in its federal history, requires each of the eight state and territory parliaments to make the laws that establish the road rules for that state or territory. In an effort to reduce variation and improve consistency in laws, the states and territories have committed, through an intergovernmental agreement, to national consistency in the regulation of roads and transport. The Australian Road Rules are an example of the benefits and challenges of this type of arrangement between governments.

The Australian Road Rules (National Road Transport Commission, 2012) are not laws in their own right, but the states and territories use the Australian Road Rules as the basis for the part of the road safety laws their parliament makes for the relevant jurisdiction. As a result, despite the Australian Road Rules, some road rules (even those with the same numbers) vary between the states and territories — for example, there are variations in the rules that apply to cyclists riding on the footpath, to motorists passing cyclists on the road, and to cyclists wearing helmets.

Riding on the footpath

In Queensland[7], Tasmania[8], the Australian Capital Territory[9] and the Northern Territory[10], cyclists of any age are allowed to ride on the footpath unless a 'no

---

[7] *Transport Operations (Road Use Management — Road Rules) Regulation 2009* (Qld) s250.

[8] *Road Rules 2009* (Tas) r250.

[9] *Road Transport (Safety and Traffic Management) Australian Road Rules Incorporation 2013 (No 1)* ACT r250.

[10] *Traffic Regulations 1999* (NT) reg85.

bicycles' sign indicates that this is prohibited. In the other states, unless a cyclist is under 12 years old, they are not permitted to ride on the footpath. Some exemptions from the laws are available to cyclists over this age in Victoria[11], New South Wales[12] and South Australia[13].

Passing cyclists on the road

The introduction of laws specifying a minimum passing distance for motorists when overtaking cyclists on Queensland roads was the first of its kind in Australia.[14] This legislative change, introduced for an initial two-year trial in April 2014, is an example of the role of states and territories in making road rules that apply in their own jurisdiction, without the need to wait for a change in the Australian Road Rules. To assist motorists to comply with the prescribed minimum distance when passing cyclists, the Queensland laws also permit drivers to cross centre-lines (including double unbroken centre-lines), to straddle lane-lines and to drive on painted islands if necessary, provided that the driver has a clear view of any approaching traffic and that it is safe to do so.[15]

At the time of writing this chapter, a new law with regards to minimum passing distances is due to commence in the ACT on 1 November 2015 (Belot, 2015). Bills to establish minimum passing distances for motorists when overtaking cyclists have been tabled in the State Parliaments of South Australia[16], Victoria[17] and Western Australia[18]. The Tasmanian Government has not legislated a minimum passing distance, but amended the road rules.[19] These amendments permit drivers to cross centre-lines (including double unbroken centre-lines), straddle lane-lines

---

[11] *Road Safety Road Rules 2009* (Vic) r250.

[12] *Road Rules 2014* (NSW) r250.

[13] *Road Traffic (Road Rules — Ancillary and Miscellaneous Provisions) Regulations 2014* (SA) reg33.

[14] *Transport Operations (Road Use Management — Road Rules) Regulation 2009* (Qld) s144A.

[15] *Transport Operations (Road Use Management — Road Rules) Regulation 2009* (Qld) ss132, 137, 138 139A, 147.

[16] *Road Traffic (Overtaking Bicycles) Amendment Bill 2013* (SA).

[17] *Road Safety Road Rules 2009 (Overtaking Bicycles) Bill 2015* [private member's bill] (Vic).

[18] *Road Traffic Amendment (Keeping Safe Distances from Bicycles) Bill 2014* (WA).

[19] *Road Amendment (Overtaking and Passing Bicycles) Rules 2015* (Tas).

and drive on painted islands when passing cyclists, provided that the driver has a clear view of any approaching traffic and that it is safe to do so. This approach is intended to provide motorists with the ability to observe a minimum distance when passing cyclists.

It is interesting to note that although minimum passing distance legislation creates a statutory space for cyclists, the laws are not accompanied by mandatory changes in infrastructure to accommodate this space. The absence of changes in infrastructure to increase the space available means that motorists' space is potentially compromised. If the regulatory framework for road safety included infrastructure as well as road users, unintended risks and consequences associated with a compromise such as this might be identified and addressed as part of the introduction of minimum passing distance legislation.

Australia's helmet laws

In July 1990, Victoria became the first state in Australia to introduce laws that mandated the wearing of helmets by cyclists. Over the next three years, mandatory helmet laws were introduced and enacted in the other states and territories. Road rule 256(1) of the current Australian Road Rules specifies that 'the rider of a bicycle must wear an approved bicycle helmet securely fitted and fastened on the rider's head, unless the rider is exempt from wearing a bicycle helmet under another law of this jurisdiction' (National Road Transport Commission, 2012). There are some minor differences in helmet laws between the states and territories. In the Northern Territory, adults cycling along footpaths or on cycle paths are exempt from wearing helmets.[20] Some exemptions from the laws on religious grounds are available to cyclists in Queensland.[21]

There are also laws that regulate the safety standards of bicycle helmets and apply to manufacturers, distributors and retailers who deal with bicycle helmets in Australia.[22] The interaction of these product safety laws and road rule 256(1) means that a cyclist must wear a helmet that complies with Australian and New

---

[20] *Traffic Regulations* 1999 (NT) reg86.

[21] *Transport Operations (Road Use Management — Road Rules) Regulation* 2009 (Qld) s244B.

[22] *Australian Trade Practices (Consumer Product Safety Standards) Regulations 2001 — Bicycle Helmets* (Cth).

Zealand safety standards. This is an example of how a regulatory framework for cyclist safety can be created by the integration of related legislation.

Other cycling-related laws

There are other regulatory frameworks which create the obligations and rights of relevant individuals and entities in relation to cycling in Australia. These range from the product safety standards applying to manufacturers, distributors and retailers to ensure the quality of bicycles[23] through to road management and infrastructure laws in each jurisdiction in Australia.[24]

Despite the range of regulatory frameworks and rules established by the law, the fact that cyclists continue to be killed and injured on Australian roads means the space for cycling is not safe. This leads to two broader questions — first, what is the role of the Australian law in making space for cycling? Second, are there opportunities to modify the road safety regulatory framework to make space for cycling?

What is the role of the Australian law in making space for cycling?

On the face of it, the role of the law in making space for cycling may appear to be to establish rules about cyclists' obligations and rights, particularly in the context of cyclists as road users. Some may consider the role to be to protect cyclists as vulnerable road users by creating rules about motorists' obligations and rights. Such perspectives are limited to the role of the law in relation to cyclists and motorists as road users, and they may arguably fail to consider the role of the law in establishing broader regulatory frameworks relevant to cycling. The basis for this view is that the current laws that have an impact on cycling are not limited to the rules for road users. As outlined earlier in this chapter, they include a range of other regulatory frameworks and rules. It seems that an important role of the Australian law — not only in making space for cycling but also in road safety

---

[23] *Trade Practices Act 1974 — Consumer Protection Notice No. 6 of 2004 — Consumer Product Safety Standard: Pedal Bicycles: Safety Requirements* (Cth).

[24] These laws are often set out in more than one piece of legislation in each state and territory. For example, relevant laws in Queensland include the *Transport Infrastructure Act 1994* (Qld), *Transport Operations (Road Use Management) Act 1995* (Qld) and the *Transport Planning and Coordination Act 1994* (Qld).

and sustainable transport more broadly — is to address the shared responsibility for safety across a range of people, including those responsible for the design and management of roads and related infrastructure.

There is limited literature directly related to the role of laws about the design and management of roads and related infrastructure in making space for cycling in Australia. Within Australia's federal system, responsibility for the design and management of roads and related infrastructure rests with the three different levels of government as follows. The Australian Government is responsible for allocating resources for infrastructure, including safety-related initiatives, across the national highway and local road networks. The eight state and territory governments' responsibilities include planning, designing and operating their respective road networks, regulating road-user behaviour and establishing (and enforcing) road rules and other laws. The local (municipal or regional) governments' responsibilities generally include planning, designing, operating and funding road networks within their respective area.

A recently published review (Austroads, 2015) of the Australian *National Road Safety Strategy 2011-2020* [NRSS] (Australian Transport Council, 2011) found a correlation between infrastructure improvements and improved safety for cyclists. This finding and legal cases such as those outlined earlier in this chapter support the proposition that laws about road management and infrastructure play an important, but unfulfilled, role in making space for cycling. One challenge in implementing reforms to fulfil this role is that there is no current national regulatory framework that links these responsibilities with road safety laws.

Are there opportunities to modify the road safety regulatory framework to make space for cycling?

Regulatory frameworks in Australia

Australians live in a highly regulated community where, broadly speaking, the law regulates activities that are likely to harm individuals, specific groups or the community as a whole. Consequently, a range of legislative and policy frameworks have been established and implemented to regulate potentially harmful behaviour across a range of contexts. These frameworks include environmental law, corporations law, taxation law, privacy law, aviation law, medicines law, occupational licensing law, work health and safety law, and food safety law. In recent years, the policy and legislation underpinning these frameworks have been updated to improve safety outcomes. Recent reforms in work health and safety provide an example of how a comprehensive safety strategy such as the *National Road Safety Strategy* can achieve improved outcomes if it is integrated within a framework that includes 'whole of system' legislation.

The recent reforms to work health and safety in Australia address the shared responsibility for workplace safety across a range of people including workers, employers and owners of workplaces by establishing duties of care in all Australian work health and safety legislation. Safe Work Australia states that 'these duties reflect the philosophy that workers should be given the highest practical level of protection against harm to their health and safety from hazards and risks arising from work' (2012, p. 4).

The *Australian Work Health and Safety Strategy 2012-2022* [AWHSS] provides a framework to drive improvements in work health and safety in Australia and promotes a collaborative approach between the nine governments and key stakeholders to achieve the vision of *healthy, safe and productive working lives* (Safe Work Australia, 2012). The AHWSS identifies the following four outcomes to be achieved by 2022:

- 'a reduced incidence of work-related death, injury and illness achieved by
- reduced exposure to hazards and risks using
- improved hazard controls supported by
- an improved national work health and safety infrastructure' (p. 6).

Safe Work Australia identifies that to achieve these outcomes by 2022 it needs

- a responsive and effective regulatory framework
- the knowledge and skills of all parties with a role in work health and safety
- a robust evidence base (2012, p. 5).

Reform of the road safety regulatory framework

The AWHSS and the *National Road Safety Strategy* (NRSS) both aim to reduce the incidence of death and injury. Although the NRSS is a comprehensive strategy, it does not translate into a comprehensive national regulatory framework. As highlighted by the civil court case provided earlier, the NRSS has limited regulatory impact because there is a disconnect between the policy framework and the legal system. In that case, although the judge identified infrastructure issues that contributed to the accident — the parked cars near the driveway, and the design and structure of the shared pedestrian/bicycle path — he was not able to recommend infrastructure improvements to reduce the risk of injury or death of another cyclist in a similar incident. The approach to work health and safety reform supports the proposition that a reform of the road safety regulatory framework might assist in making space for cycling.

There may be opportunities to use outcomes of the NRSS to leverage reform of the current road safety regulatory framework. The NRSS is firmly based on principles of a 'Safe System' that has the goal of establishing a system in which human mistakes do not lead to death or serious injury of road users (Australian Transport Council, 2011). The recommendations from a recently published review of the NRSS (Austroads, 2015) include an increased focus on establishing this Safe System for vulnerable road users. Establishing a Safe System requires a 'whole of system' approach, which accepts that humans will make mistakes, and considers the interaction between roads, vehicles, speeds and road users. It is possible that reforming the regulatory framework could contribute to establishing a Safe System, in particular by integrating regulation of the interactions considered by the Safe System.

The case of *Nettleton v Rondeau* cited earlier in this chapter highlights the potential to reduce accidents by strengthening the current regulation of the interaction between roads, vehicles and road users in the context of the Safe System principles. If a framework that reflected some of the principles of work health and safety regulation applied in the context of road safety, local governments might then have a statutory responsibility based on reasonableness in any given situation.

In addition to more clearly identifying obligations and rights, the regulatory framework may establish a system of penalties. The work health and safety laws offer a model for offences and penalties that apply to anyone who fails to comply with a health and safety duty. Importantly, the penalties are proportional to the risk of injury or death and to the level of control a person has for work health and safety. The legislation provides for on-the-spot fines, and details action to be taken if a fine is not paid. The work health and safety laws also offer a model that reduces the time, cost and stress of personal injury claims.

The road safety regulatory framework needs to be responsive, as well as effective. Many of the regulatory frameworks in Australia are underpinned by regulatory philosophies that draw upon the basic principles of 'responsive regulation' (Wood, Ivec, Job, & Braithwaite, 2010). Existing policy frameworks such as the NRSS and its associated action plan align with the principles of responsive regulation. It is acknowledged that the current regulation of activities such as driving cars and cycling has some of the hallmarks of responsive regulation, insofar as it encourages individuals to behave in a way that minimises the risk of harm and reserves punitive measures for serious offences such as the criminal case outlined earlier in this chapter. Many of the underlying principles of responsive regulation discussed by Braithwaite (2011) are relevant to implementing a regulatory framework to support establishment of a Safe System for vulnerable road users.

The introduction of a responsive road safety regulatory framework similar to the work safety framework would not of itself affect the availability of civil action by injured parties to claim loss and damages. Nor would it affect the bringing of criminal charges where relevant.

Another regulatory approach that provides the potential application of learning is that applied to breaches of environment protection laws. Regulators, or in some cases members of the community, can use civil enforcement to bring action against someone who breaches environment protection laws. These cases are enforced through the civil courts, so the standard of proof is 'on the balance of probabilities'.[25] The civil enforcement includes imposition of penalties aimed to compensate for, and prevent, environmental damage.

Imagine a regulatory framework for road safety based on learnings from frameworks such as those outlined above. Such a framework could only operate if it was part of a strategy that covered the entire scope of stakeholders with obligations and rights related to road safety. Given the complexity and enormity of that scope across eight states and territories, the development of such a framework may prove to be too challenging. A staged approach may reduce the complexity and enormity

---

[25] This is a lower threshold than the criminal court standard of 'beyond reasonable doubt'.

sufficiently to at least start a conversation about drawing on the principles. It may be that the co-ordinated commitment of key stakeholders, including all levels of government, to implement initiatives such as the *National Road Safety Strategy 2011-2020* (Australian Transport Council, 2011), the *National Road Safety Action Plan 2015-2017* (Transport and Infrastructure Council, 2014) and the *National Cycling Strategy 2011-2016* (Austroads, 2010) provides a useful opportunity for dialogue about the potential to develop a more effective and responsive regulatory framework.

Conclusion

Whilst international experiences are of interest, laws are applied within a particular culture and legal system. Future opportunities for the law to have a positive impact on cycling and cyclist safety in Australia require an Australia-specific focus, not a mimicking of international laws.

Current and future laws that apply to the planning, design, construction and management of roads as well as road safety are key considerations in making space for cycling. For example, if governments use the law to create minimum passing distances that motorists must observe when overtaking cyclists, laws about the design of roads may need to take this into account, in order to make sure that there is sufficient space for all road users. Similarly, if a space for drivers and passengers to open the doors of parked cars is created alongside bicycle lanes, roads may need to be widened to continue to comply with recommendations in Austroads guides. This may require changes to planning and infrastructure laws.

Law has a part to play in making space for cycling by providing a regulatory framework with shared responsibilities across a range of people including cyclists, drivers and infrastructure agencies. The framework must provide for regulation of a range of factors including, but not limited to, cycling behaviour, driver behaviour, infrastructure laws and planning laws. A sound regulatory framework requires the law and policy makers in these areas to interact with each other.

References

Articles/Books/Reports

Australian Transport Council. (2011). *National Road Safety Strategy 2011-2020*. Canberra: Australian Transport Council. Retrieved 17 September 2015 from https://infrastructure.gov.au/roads/safety/national_road_safety_strategy.

Austroads. (2009). *Guide to road design: Part 6A — Pedestrian and cyclist paths*. Austroads Publication No: AGRD06A-09. Sydney: Austroads. Retrieved 17 September 2015 from https://www.onlinepublications.austroads.com.au/items/AGRD06A-09.

Austroads. (2011). *The Australian National Cycling Strategy 2011-2016*. Austroads Publication No. AP-C85/10. Sydney: Austroads. Retrieved 17 September 2015 from https://www.onlinepublications.austroads.com.au/items/AP-C85-10.

Austroads. (2014). *Cycling aspects of Austroads guides* (2nd ed.). Austroads Publication No. AP-G88-11. Sydney: Austroads. Retrieved 17 September 2015 from https://www.onlinepublications.austroads.com.au/items/AP-G88-14.

Austroads. (2015). *Review of the National Road Safety Strategy*. Austroads Publication No. AP-R477-15. Sydney: Austroads. Retrieved 17 September 2015 from https://www.onlinepublications.austroads.com.au/items/AP-R477-15.

Belot, Henry. (2015, Sept. 21). Trial to keep Canberra motorists one metre away from cyclists. Retrieved 1 October 2015 from http://www.canberratimes.com.au/act-news/trial-to-keep-canberra-motorists-one-metre-away-from-cyclists-20150917-gjp1c4.html.

Braithwaite, J. (2011). The essence of responsive regulation. *UBC Law Review*, 44(3), 475-520. Retrieved 17 September 2015 from https://www.anu.edu.au/fellows/jbraithwaite/_documents/Articles/essence_responsive_regulation.pdf.

National Road Transport Commission. (2012). *Australian Road Rules*. Melbourne: National Transport Commission. Retrieved 17 September 2015 from http://www.ntc.gov.au/roads/rules-compliance.

Safe Work Australia. (2012). *Australian Work Health and Safety Strategy 2012-2022*. Canberra: Safe Work Australia. Retrieved 17 September 2015 from http://www.safeworkaustralia.gov.au/sites/swa/about/publications/pages/australian-work-health-and-safety-strategy-2012-2022.

Safe Work Australia. (2014). *The second progress report on the Australian Work Health and Safety Strategy 2012-2022*. Canberra: Safe Work Australia. Retrieved 17 September 2015 from http://www.safeworkaustralia.gov.au/sites/swa/about/publications/pages/second-progress-report-australian-whs-strategy.

Transport and Infrastructure Council. (2014). *National Road Safety Action Plan 2015-2017*. Canberra: Transport and Infrastructure Council. Retrieved 17 September 2015 from https://infrastructure.gov.au/roads/safety/national_road_safety_strategy.

Wood, C, Ivec, M, Job, J, & Braithwaite, V. (2010, June). Applications of responsive regulatory theory in Australia and Overseas. Canberra: Regulatory Institutions Network Occasional Paper 15, The Australian National University, Canberra. Retrieved 17 September 2015 from http://regnet.anu.edu.au/research/publications/2701/no-23-applications-responsive-regulatory-theory-australia-and-overseas.

Case Law

Director of Public Prosecutions v Leddin [2013] VCC 2074.
Eamonn Francis Leddin v The Queen [2014] VSCA 155.
Nettleton v Rondeau [2013] NSWSC 1321.
Nettleton v Rondeau [2014] NSWSC 903.

Legislation

Australian Constitution.
Australian Trade Practices (Consumer Product Safety Standards) Regulations 2001 — Bicycle Helmets (Cth).
Road Amendment (Overtaking and Passing Bicycles) Rules 2015 (Tas).
Road Rules 2009 (Tas).
Road Rules 2014 (NSW).
Road Safety Road Rules 2009 (Vic).

Road Safety Road Rules 2009 (Overtaking Bicycles) Bill 2015 [private member's bill] (Vic).

Road Traffic Amendment (Keeping Safe Distances from Bicycles) Bill 2014 (WA).

Road Traffic (Overtaking Bicycles) Amendment Bill 2013 (SA).

Road Traffic (Road Rules — Ancillary and Miscellaneous Provisions) Regulations 2014 (SA).

Road Transport (Safety and Traffic Management) Australian Road Rules Incorporation 2013 (No 1) (ACT).

Trade Practices Act 1974 — Consumer Protection Notice No. 6 of 2004 — Consumer Product Safety Standard: Pedal Bicycles: Safety Requirements (Cth).

Traffic Regulations 1999 (NT).

Transport Infrastructure Act 1994 (Qld).

Transport Operations (Road Use Management) Act 1995 (Qld).

Transport Operations (Road Use Management — Road Rules) Regulation 2009 (Qld).

Transport Planning and Coordination Act 1994 (Qld).

Victorian Crimes Act 1958 (Vic).

18 Evaluating cycling promotion interventions

Jan Garrard

Introduction

Research and evaluation play a crucial role in providing the evidence base for effective action to increase the bicycle mode share of transport in countries such as the United States, United Kingdom and Australia, which currently have low levels of utilitarian cycling. The terms 'research' and 'evaluation' are often used interchangeably, and while they share the common goal of answering questions based on data and evidence, there are also some important differences. A great deal of cycling research focuses on monitoring trends in cycling participation over time or across countries, and identifying factors that influence cycling behaviour. This type of *problem*-focused research is useful for understanding the nature of the 'problem' (that is, low levels of cycling) and its determinants (that is, supports and constraints on cycling) as a basis for taking action to address it.

Evaluation, on the other hand, is *solution*-focused research (Robinson & Sirard, 2005). It asks important questions about whether interventions aimed at increasing cycling participation are having the desired effects, and what can be done differently to improve our efforts. Currently, the cycling promotion literature focuses on the determinants of cycling, with relatively few evaluations of policies and programs designed to increase cycling. The deficit is particularly marked for evaluations employing the more rigorous evaluation designs, although, as outlined in this chapter, some innovative study designs are currently being developed and applied to address this deficit.

This chapter focuses on the evaluation of interventions aimed at increasing cycling participation in low-cycling countries such as the United States, United Kingdom and Australia. It is not a review of the effectiveness of cycling interventions, as several of these have been published elsewhere (Möser & Bamberg, 2008; Hosking, Macmillan, Connor, Bullen, & Ameratunga, 2010; Pucher, Dill, & Handy, 2010; Yang, Sahlqvist, McMinn, Griffin, & Ogilvie, 2010; Martin, Suhrcke, & Ogilvie, 2012). Nor is it a comprehensive 'how-to' manual for evaluating cycling promotion initiatives. The chapter includes some elements of cycling promotion evaluation designs, methods and findings, but the focus is on the key issues associated with the evaluation of cycling interventions. These are illustrated using examples from the cycling promotion evaluation literature. The overall aim of the chapter is to facilitate reflective practice in cycling intervention evaluation, especially in relation to critically examining evaluation practice; interpreting evaluation findings; and considering the implications of evaluation findings for cycling promotion policy, practice and advocacy.

The chapter focuses on cycling for transport, as this form of cycling has multiple benefits that include, but extend beyond, the health benefits associated with physical activity (Pucher & Buehler, 2010; Garrard, Rissel, & Bauman, 2012). The chapter covers:

- the importance of evaluating cycling promotion interventions
- evaluation purposes and approaches
- measuring and understanding change
- evaluation opportunities and challenges
- conclusions and recommendations for future evaluations.

Why evaluate cycling promotion interventions?

Cycling for transport addresses a number of important public policy objectives, including

- improving health
- improving transport efficiency and reducing traffic congestion

- improving air quality and reducing noise pollution
- reducing greenhouse gas emissions
- improving the liveability and amenity of urban environments (Litman, 2013).

These public policy objectives are primarily the responsibility of national, state and local government authorities, which operate within the overarching aim of providing policies, programs, services and infrastructure as effectively and efficiently as possible. Evaluation is a key tool for assessing whether or not (and *why*) interventions are achieving their desired objectives. Evaluation therefore plays a crucial role in the policy/program cycle illustrated in Figure 18.1.

The monitoring and evaluation component of the policy/program cycle has the dual roles of (a) measuring change, and (b) fostering understanding of why change occurred (or failed to occur), as a means of improving the effectiveness and efficiency of interventions. For example, knowing that a program aimed at increasing the number of students cycling to school led to an *average* 10% increase in the number of students riding to school at least once a week across 20 participating schools is useful information. However, understanding *why* there was no change in cycling rates in some schools, while others exceeded 10%[1] is even more valuable information. Understanding critical success factors is a crucial component of *evaluation to improve*. If we are to achieve substantial, sustained increases in utilitarian cycling for diverse population groups across a range of settings, we need to ask not just, 'Did the program work (on average) — yes/no?', but rather, '*What* worked (that is, what program factors) for *whom* (that is, which population groups) under what circumstances (that is, what settings and contexts)?' This is the basis of the Realistic Evaluation model, which is well suited to measuring and understanding change for multi-component programs in diverse socio-environmental settings (Pawson & Tilley, 1997; Pawson, 2006; Ogilvie et al., 2011), as is the case for many cycling promotion interventions (Ogilvie et al., 2011).

Producing evidence of what works in promoting utility cycling is an important contribution to securing the resources required to increase the bicycle mode share of travel. As noted by Hembrow (2010), there is a positive correlation between bicycle mode share of travel and investment in cycling. However, it is

---

[1] Variation in outcomes across sites is a common finding in the evaluation of multi-site programs.

Strategies for change

Figure 18.1: The program cycle.
(Source: author's own work.)

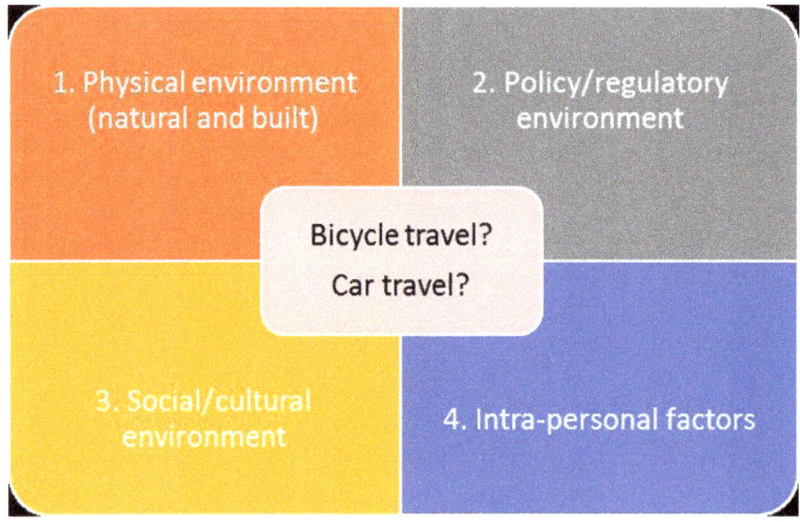

Figure 18.2: Social-ecological model of cycling for transport.
(Source: adapted from Gebel, King, Bauman, et al., 2005.)

also important to keep in mind that frequently, data does not 'speak for itself', particularly in car-oriented countries with a long-established history of investing in car travel and neglecting bicycle travel. The concept of *path dependence* has been used to explain how investment in certain developments (for example, personal mobility based on car travel) excludes alternative options (such as cycling and walking). Over time, through processes akin to 'habit', resistance to adopting alternatives such as prioritising bicycle travel for short- to medium-distance trips accumulates (Low, Gleeson, & Rush, 2005; Curtis & Low, 2012). Path dependence helps to explain why, in many instances, bicycle infrastructure projects with very favourable benefit-cost ratios [BCR] are denied funding, while road projects with unfavourable BCRs are funded (Garrard, 2012).

While rarely effective as a stand-alone measure, evaluation can assist in challenging the status quo of continued irrational over-investment in private motor vehicle travel (Litman, 2013), thereby contributing to more rational, balanced investments in transport infrastructure. It is thus important to acknowledge that an important ancillary purpose of evaluating cycling interventions is to provide evidence to assist in advocating for appropriate investment in cycling promotion which is commensurate with the resulting benefits.

Evaluation designs and methods

Cycling interventions span a range of disciplines and sectors including health, transport, urban planning and the environment. Cycling promotion measures therefore include several different types of interventions, which can be categorised according to the four quadrants in Figure 18.2. Quadrant 1 includes the provision of bicycle infrastructure; Quadrant 2 includes road rules designed to improve cycling safety; Quadrant 3 includes efforts directed at changing social norms and travel habits that currently make car travel the default travel mode for trips that are potentially 'bikeable'; and Quadrant 4 includes behaviour change programs aimed at changing people's travel behaviour through awareness raising, motivation, education, skills or incentives. This model is also an important reminder that factors across these four domains have an impact on car travel as well, and therefore on people's decisions about whether to drive or cycle.

Diverse cycling promotion interventions require differing evaluation designs and methods. Hierarchies of evidence generally place experimental designs at the top of the design hierarchy, due to their ability to both measure change and attribute any change to the intervention itself rather than to other, extraneous causes of change.

However, for many interventions it is not feasible or practical to use experimental study designs. Alternative designs exist, though they may not be considered as methodologically rigorous, and therefore may not provide definitive evidence. For example, bicycle counts on newly constructed bicycle paths or lanes frequently demonstrate an increase in the number of cyclists using the path compared with the number of cyclists using the route before the path was built (for instance, see City of Sydney, 2014). However, these may not be 'new' cyclists, as the new path may attract cyclists who previously used an alternative route. Comparison locations can sometimes be included in the study design, but identifying well-matched comparison locations can be difficult (Goodman, Sahlqvist, Ogilvie, & iConnect Consortium, 2014). Intercept surveys may help to answer the question of whether new path users are indeed new cyclists, though these are considered less accurate than observational counts, due to the potential for sampling and non-response biases.

The recent evaluation of the United Kingdom's iConnect program — which assessed the effects of providing new traffic-free walking and cycling routes on the overall levels of walking, cycling, and physical activity in three UK municipalities — faced the usual difficulties in obtaining suitable comparison sites for the evaluation. Instead, the study used a graded-exposure approach, by using distance from the Connect2 intervention sites as a marker of exposure and then comparing changes observed in participants living nearer to the sites with those observed in participants living further away (Goodman et al., 2014). The evaluation found that, at the two-year follow-up mark, people who lived closer to the infrastructure walked and cycled more (15.3 additional minutes/week walking and cycling per kilometre nearer), and had higher levels of overall physical activity (12.5 additional minutes/week of total physical activity) than those living further away.

Another example of an intervention that is thought to increase cycling, but for which there is little definitive evidence, is motor vehicle speed reduction (Killoran, Doyle, Waller, Wohlgemuth, & Crombie, 2006; Mackie, Charlton, Baas, & Villasenor, 2013). Lack of consistent evidence is partly due to the fact that few studies of traffic-calming measures actually measure cycling levels as an outcome variable (most focus on injury reduction), and partly due to methodological challenges. In addition, most of the studies that have been conducted in low-cycling countries such as the United Kingdom and New Zealand have assessed the impacts of traffic-calming measures in selected streets or short zones. Methodologically, it is easier to measure the impacts of reduced speeds for short distances (for example, a residential street, a 500-metre shopping strip or a 250-metre school zone) than for area-wide speed reduction, such as a default 30km/h speed limit in residential areas. However, relatively short sections of traffic calming may be insufficient to encourage more cycling, as most utilitarian cycling trips are longer than 1 kilometre (Australian Bureau of Statistics, 2012). These trips require the area-wide traffic calming that occurs in the high-cycling countries in Europe, and also in Japan, where most residential areas have speed limits of 30 km/h or less (Fildes, Langford, Dale, & Scully, 2005).

It is more difficult to measure the impact of these area-wide low-speed zones, though the observation that most developed countries with high levels of utilitarian cycling have extensive traffic-calmed areas points to their importance. Precisely *how* important reduced speed is for increasing cycling is difficult to quantify because it is rarely a stand-alone measure. Most high-cycling countries and cities also have networks of high-quality bicycle infrastructure, and road rules that place a high degree of responsibility on drivers to avoid collisions with people on bicycles (Pucher & Buehler, 2012).

This dilemma — of possibly the most effective cycling promotion measures being the most difficult to evaluate using rigorous, controlled evaluation designs — was highlighted in a review of policies and programs to increase cycling (Pucher et al., 2010). In addition to reviewing evidence for the effectiveness of specific cycling promotion measures such as the provision of bicycle infrastructure or travel behaviour change programs, the authors also included case studies of 14 cities that had increased cycling levels by implementing city-wide strategies incorporating packages of measures from across all four quadrants in Figure 18.2, directed at both bicycle use and car use. By monitoring changes in cycling levels over time, and identifying commonly used measures in the case study cities, the authors developed a set of 'key lessons' for cycling promotion (Pucher et al., 2010; Pucher & Buehler, 2012).

This type of overall policy evaluation has several advantages over the evaluation of specific measures, though evaluations of specific measures are often technically more rigorous. The main advantage is that macrolevel policy evaluation can capture the impacts of the multi-component interventions that appear to be effective for increasing the mode share of cycling in large areas such as cities (Pucher et al., 2010). An important feature of ecological models such as the one depicted in Figure 18.2 is that the multiple components are mutually interactive, with the impact of the overall package being substantially greater than the sum of the impacts of the individual measures, were they to be implemented alone.

An example of this interactive effect is the interaction between encouraging cycling and discouraging car use. The high-cycling industrialised countries do both, but in many low-cycling countries, cycling promotion measures such as installing bicycle paths fail to achieve their full potential because car use continues to be prioritised and heavily subsidised (Public Transport Users Association, 2010; Glazebrook, 2009). Many of the 'tacked-on' or 'squeezed-in' bicycle lanes that have been built in cities such as Sydney and Melbourne are substandard and provide a poor level of service for cyclists, as a result of trying to provide for cycling while not impacting on motor vehicle speed, volume and flow. The relationship between cycling and car use was demonstrated in the evaluation of the iConnect study, which found that the effects (increased walking, cycling and physical activity for people living nearer the intervention sites) were larger for people without a car (Goodman et al., 2014).

It is also more difficult to choose to cycle rather than to drive when 'free' or cheap car parking is readily available (Shoup, 2005; Glazebrook, 2009); when motor vehicle manufacturing, road infrastructure and motor vehicle fuels are heavily subsidised; when residential and service areas have high speed limits; and when road rules prioritise motor vehicle speed and driver safety over cyclist amenity and safety. Once again, the experience of the high-cycling countries is that removing incentives for car travel (many of which are indirect and effectively 'hidden') contributes to increased cycling by establishing a more level playing field for travel mode choices — that is, one that no longer favours car travel for all trip distances and purposes.

Few evaluations have assessed the effect of these measures on cycling behaviour. However, a recent review of the use of positive and negative financial incentives (such as the provision of free bicycles to employees, and increased fuel taxes or congestion taxes) concluded that '… financial incentives may have a larger role in promoting walking and cycling than is acknowledged generally' (Martin et al., 2012, p. e45). This evaluation deficit may contribute to the neglect of policies that disincentivise car travel as a means of increasing cycling, as policy attention is usually focused on what is commonly measured — namely, the effects of cycling promotion interventions rather than measures aimed at curbing car use.

The main disadvantage of macrolevel policy evaluation is not knowing definitively which specific components of the policy package are most effective, or indeed whether individual measures are likely to have an impact. This issue frequently arises when governments are motivated or persuaded to do *something* to support cycling, but lack the commitment to invest in an overall package of measures, or the political courage to adopt measures that might be seen as disadvantaging car drivers. They may therefore be interested in which individual cycling measure(s) should be prioritised for immediate action.

Implementing trials or pilots of the potentially unpopular measures that are required to establish a more level playing field for bicycle-car mode choices and evaluating their impacts (including acceptability) may provide a useful mechanism for initiating and maintaining effective and acceptable measures for increasing cycling. This strategy has been effectively implemented in New York, where traffic-calming measures designed to make New York streets more walkable and bikeable were implemented on a trial basis, evaluated and ultimately sustained (Sadik-Kahn, 2014). Similarly, in 2010, Bayside and Kingston City Councils, which are home to the very popular Beach Road cycling route in suburban Melbourne, implemented a trial clearway zone along Beach Road between 6 am and 10 am on weekends in the face of strong and protracted opposition from many residents and mass media outlets. Following implementation and evaluation, the 'trial' has been extended several times, most recently in July 2014, with little opposition from residents or bad press from the media (Murphy, 2014).

Measuring and understanding change

As outlined above, a wide range of evaluation designs have been used to assess interventions aimed at increasing cycling. Similarly, a range of data collection methods have been used. Commonly used methods for programs that encourage travel behaviour change include

- travel diaries (Department of Transport, 2009)
- surveys asking about travel behaviour 'in the previous week', 'usually' or 'in an average week/month/etc.'

- 'hands-up' school surveys (Hinkson, Duncan, Kearns, & Badland, 2008)
- observational counts (such as manual, video or sensor counts of cyclists at various locations; children riding to school; or bicycles in the school grounds)
- wearable cameras (Kelly et al., 2014)
- personal GPS devices (Mavoa, Oliver, Witten, & Badland, 2011; Madsen, Schipperijn, Christiansen, Nielsen, & Troelsen, 2014).

Each of these data collection methods has advantages and disadvantages. Self-reported cycling behaviour is sensitive to survey purpose and the wording of questions, with recent cycling surveys conducted in Australia (Rissel, Munro, & Bauman, 2013) producing widely divergent self-reported rates of people stating they have cycled in the past year (ranging from 6.5% to 29.7%). Manual and automated bicycle counts avoid the biases associated with self-reported data, but the data is site-specific and cannot readily be used to measure area-wide (for example, national, state or city) levels of cycling. Nevertheless, such counts can produce good pre- and post-intervention data (Rissel et al., 2010), and can also monitor bicycle volumes (for example, on bicycle paths and lanes) over time (VicRoads, 2014). The use of personal GPS devices is a promising development for objectively measuring bicycle trips, though constraints include costs and user errors, such as failing to record changes in travel mode from, for example, cycling to walking.

Some evaluations of cycling interventions have used a form of data triangulation to deal with the inability of one data collection method alone to provide valid and reliable measures of bicycle use. If a number of different and individually imperfect data collection methods produce consistent findings, we can be more confident of the outcome than we can by relying on one data source alone. For example, the evaluation of the pilot phase of the Victorian Ride2School program used pre- and post-program observational counts of children cycling to school, counts of bicycles in the school grounds, and self-reported 'hands-up' survey data in two programs and two matched comparison schools (Garrard, Crawford, & Godbold, 2009). The study reported consistent evidence of an increase in active travel to school in the inner-suburban primary school relative to the matched comparison school; but no consistent evidence of an increase in active travel to school in the outer-suburban primary school relative to the matched comparison school (Garrard, Crawford, & Godbold, 2009). Additional observational and qualitative data conducted as part of the concurrent process evaluation of the program provided insights into possible reasons for the different outcomes in the two program schools. The authors concluded that

> the promotion of active travel to school appears to be facilitated within supportive built and transport environments, within schools with an interest in active travel to school and able to commit time and resources to the promotion of active travel to school. (Garrard, Crawford, & Godbold, 2009, p. 4)

As described above, measuring change associated with cycling interventions is methodologically challenging in terms of both study design and data collection methods. Interpreting and understanding evaluation findings, as well as considering the policy implications of the findings, are equally challenging. A common over-simplification is to rely on metrics such as the percentage of individuals who cycled more frequently post-intervention. Bicycle skills training programs for adults often produce impressive increases in the number of program participants who cycled more frequently after participating in the program. A recent review of bicycle skills training programs found that, across programs, the proportion of participants who reported cycling more frequently after attending courses ranged from 24% to 71% (Garrard & Fishman, 2013). It might therefore be concluded that bicycle skills programs represent an effective intervention for increasing cycling. However, these evaluation findings need to be interpreted in the context of two important caveats.

First, many program participants are already motivated to cycle more, and this is the reason they self-select to attend the program. The generalisability of the evaluation findings to the wider population is therefore limited. Second, the number of program participants is generally small, usually between 10 and 100 (the latter for training conducted with multiple groups of about 10), so a large percentage increase represents only a small number of people. In contrast, interventions with wider population reach (such as traffic-calmed residential areas) might only increase cycling in the neighbourhood by a few percentage points (for example, from 6% of trips to 8% of trips), but the difference of 2 percentage points represents a much larger number of people than a 71% increase in cycling among 100 cycle training program participants.

In general, it appears to be easier to achieve behaviour change for cycling promotion interventions that target individuals and groups in specific settings than it is to change the bicycle mode share of travel at an aggregate level (for example, in a city, state or country). For instance, active school travel programs can lead to increased levels of active travel in participating schools, but in countries like Australia, which have low rates of cycling for transport, there is little evidence of an overall mode shift from car to bicycle travel to school at the wider community level. A recent analysis of school travel data found few statistically significant changes in young people's modes of travel to and from school in Victoria between 2006 and 2009, and in the greater Sydney Metropolitan area between 2005 and 2008 (Garrard, 2010), despite the implementation of several active school travel programs in both states.

Similarly, Cycling England's 'Cycling Demonstration Towns' project showed an increase in cycling in program (primary) schools but little community-wide increase. Pooled data from Hands Up surveys (conducted in 2006-07 and 2007-08) of students in 'Bike It' schools (primary schools which received the intensive support of a 'Bike It' officer) showed an increase in the proportion of students cycling to school every day or 'once or twice a week' of 20.4% (from 8.7% to 29.1%). By comparison, school census data (all schools in the town, for students up to 15 years old, 2006-07 to 2007-08) reported an increase of 0.1% (1.5% to 1.6%) in the number of students for whom cycling is the usual mode of travel to school (Sloman, Cavill, Cope, Muller, & Kennedy, 2009).

Similar patterns are evident for utilitarian cycling among adults. Between 2007-08 and 2009-10, daily average bicycle volumes on several inner-Melbourne bicycle routes increased by 18.2% (VicRoads, 2014), while data from the Victorian Integrated Survey of Travel and Activity (2014) showed that the bicycle mode share of travel for the greater Melbourne Metropolitan area and selected Victorian regional cities remained virtually unchanged (1.7% in 2007-2008; 1.6% in 2009-2010). In Sydney, bicycle counts, conducted twice a year at 100 intersections across central Sydney, showed a 113% increase in bike trips between March 2010 and late 2013 (City of Sydney, 2014), while for the greater Sydney area, according to the New South Wales [NSW] Bureau of Transport Statistics (2013), there was little change in bicycle mode share of travel (0.6% in 2010; 0.5% in 2012).

It is sometimes argued that, in the interests of demonstrating the cost-effectiveness of cycling promotion interventions, programs should target 'low-hanging fruit' in the form of low-cost, easy-to-implement interventions with people, and in locations, that are most amenable to change. There is nothing inherently wrong with this strategy, but it is important to acknowledge its limitations. In countries such as the United States, United Kingdom and Australia with bicycle mode shares of travel of around 1-2%, the majority of the 'fruit' is not low-hanging, so the bulk of the population is left unchanged, and the multiple societal benefits of a widespread mode shift from driving to cycling are largely unrealised.

The health benefits of cycling for transport are well established and apply to most people, including those who already participate in leisure-time physical activity (Sugiyama, Merom, Reaves, Leslie, & Owen, 2010). Public health 'success stories' such as tobacco control, child immunisation and road safety are successful because they have been implemented at the population level and are able to demonstrate effectiveness at an aggregate level. Low smoking rates, high child immunisation rates and reduced road fatalities in only small pockets of the population in selected communities would lead to intensified action rather than to congratulations. The benefits of a mode shift from inactive to active transport, including cycling for short- to medium-distance trips, warrant a similar perspective. If it is worth doing — and a large body of evidence indicates that it is (Götschi, Garrard & Giles-Corti, 2015) — it is worth intervening as effectively and efficiently as possible at the population level.

In summary, evidence from several sources indicates that in order to achieve the multiple and substantial benefits of cycling for transport at the population level, an integrated package of measures from across the four domains in Figure 18.2 is required to make active travel choices easy for all population groups for multiple trip purposes in diverse settings and locations (Pucher & Buehler, 2012).

Evaluation opportunities and challenges

Ideally, evaluation should be built into program planning and implementation, rather than 'tacked on' at the end of the intervention, as often happens. Concurrent program and evaluation planning will benefit both the program and the evaluation. Planning a program with evaluation in mind provides a focus for developing appropriate program objectives, realistic program activities and achievable program impacts and outcomes.

Program logic models are often used to provide a diagrammatic overview of the 'logical' links between the resources, activities, and outcomes of a program

(Brousselle & Champagne, 2011). A program logic model aims to provide answers to key questions:

a) What resources are available to conduct the program?
b) What activities will be implemented, when, and with whom?
c) What outcomes are expected and when (short-, medium- and long-term)?

The 'if-then' [causal] relationships between the elements of the program can then be interrogated. Can the planned activities be conducted with the available resources? Are the planned activities likely to achieve the expected outcomes? While the key focus of evaluation is usually on program outcomes, systematic examination of all steps in the causal pathway contributes to the development and implementation of a program that is more likely to achieve the desired program outcomes.

Program logic models are also valuable for interpreting evaluation findings. For example, if a program fails to achieve its intended outcomes, it is important to understand why. 'Failure' can occur at each of the steps in Figure 18.3 — namely, lack of appropriate resources; poor implementation of program activities; or 'program failure', in the sense that the intervention itself, despite being well resourced and well implemented, is unable to bring about the desired outcomes. Examples of this type of program failure would be a behaviour change program encouraging students to ride to school in a neighbourhood with few safe routes to school; or constructing a bicycle path that does not connect people's homes with common travel destinations.

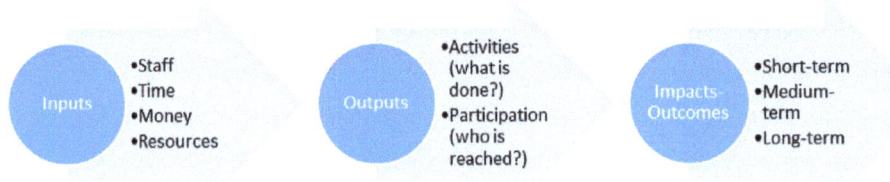

Figure 18.3: Program logic model.
(Source: author's own work.)

The requirement for cycling promotion interventions to be adequately resourced applies equally to program evaluations. While it is tempting to allocate available (often limited) resources to 'doing' rather than 'measuring', failure to evaluate is a lost opportunity to achieve the multiple benefits of evaluation described earlier. Appropriate evaluation budgets depend on the type of program and evaluation. A distinction is often made between *evaluation research* and *program/policy evaluation*.

Evaluation research often takes the form of an intervention trial, where the aim of the overall project is to assess the efficacy of the intervention. In intervention trials, the intervention and evaluation are integrated, with each shaping the other, and the evaluation budget can be up to 50% of the total cost of the overall project. In contrast, in program/policy evaluation, the focus is on implementing the program or policy, and the evaluation accommodates the program rather than the program being shaped by the measurement requirements of the evaluation (as in intervention trials).

Program/policy evaluations typically require a budget of about 10-20% of the cost of the program being evaluated. These evaluations are often methodologically constrained because they need to fit in with program activities and timelines. For example, due to program requirements, it is not always possible to conduct rigorous baseline measures before the program commences, or to include comparison groups in the evaluation design. In the evaluation of the Victorian Ride2School program, the evaluators were unable to include comparison schools in the before-after evaluation design because insufficient comparison schools could be recruited in time to conduct baseline measures of students' modes of travel to school before the program commenced. Instead, multivariate regression analysis was used in an attempt to control for non-program influences on before-and-after rates of students cycling to school (Crawford & Garrard, 2013).

Recently, *natural experiments* have been conducted as a form of methodological middle ground between intervention trials and program evaluations (Goodman, Panter, Sharp, & Ogilvie, 2013). Goodman et al. (2013) used a 'controlled before-after natural experimental study' to investigate the impacts of town-wide cycling initiatives (incorporating bicycle infrastructure and cycle skills training) in six Cycling Demonstration Towns and twelve Cycling Cities and Towns in England. The study used English census data to compare trends in rates of cycling to work in the intervention towns with changes in three comparison groups comprising matched towns, unfunded towns and a national comparison group. The study reported that the prevalence of cycling to work rose from 5.8% in 2001 to 6.8% in 2011 in the intervention cities and towns, representing a significant increase relative to all three comparison groups. The study also reported the common finding of substantial variations in effect size between intervention sites (that is, in this study, cities and towns).

Studies such as these, which opportunistically make use of 'naturally occurring' interventions, highlight the importance of collaboration between the people and organisations that implement cycling promotion interventions and those with an interest in, and the capacity to conduct, evaluation studies. Knowing that an intervention is being planned provides an opportunity for researchers to incorporate cycling-specific evaluation into the intervention. Historically, traffic calming, complete streets and road diets[2] have been evaluated for their injury prevention impacts, but, increasingly, their impacts on walking and cycling behaviour are starting to be included in evaluation studies (Mackie et al., 2013). The benefits of practitioner/evaluator collaborations are two-fold: practitioners and policy makers obtain useful evaluation data, and the close collaboration between researchers and practitioners is likely to assist with the process of knowledge transfer that facilitates putting evidence into practice in future initiatives.

The role of evaluation in policy advocacy

Cycling advocacy, in its many forms, is crucial for creating the conditions that support increased utility cycling. While travel mode choices (such as, 'Will I ride my bicycle to work, shops, social activities, etc, or drive my car?') are individual behavioural choices, they are 'choices' that are strongly influenced by a range of socio-environmental factors.

Widespread, sustained, effective action to increase rates of cycling requires change in the factors that shape bicycle/car travel behaviour as modelled in Figure 18.2. Recognising that behaviour change occurs via change in the environmental,

---

[2] Road diets reduce the number of traffic lanes on selected roads, and use the additional space to widen footpaths, introduce or widen roadside landscaping, or construct bicycle lanes.

social and regulatory factors that shape behaviour shifts the focus from exhorting individuals to change their behaviour to lobbying decision makers to create the socio-environmental conditions that support, rather than constrain, people's capacity to choose to cycle rather than drive. Individuals cannot build bike paths, or change road rules that currently prioritise motor vehicle mobility over the safety of people riding bicycles. These changes, which require action at the political and policy level, highlight the importance of cycling advocacy.

Evidence obtained from cycling research and evaluation is integral to effective cycling advocacy in its many forms. For example, in the last few years, cycling advocates (organisations and individuals) have made numerous written submissions and have appeared as witnesses in several Australian federal and state government inquiries related to cycling and cycling safety. These include:

- Review of the Australian Road Rules and Vehicle Standard Rules (National Transport Commission, 2011)
- Development of the National Road Safety Strategy 2011-2020 (Department of Infrastructure and Regional Development, 2011)
- Speed Limit Review (Victoria) (VicRoads, 2011)
- Inquiry into Serious Injury (Victoria) (Road Safety Committee, 2014)
- Queensland Parliamentary Inquiry into Cycling Issues (Queensland) (Transport, Housing and Local Government Committee, 2013)
- Inquiry into Vulnerable Road Users (ACT) (Standing Committee on Planning, Environment and Territory and Municipal Services, 2014).

Access to, and use of, supportive research and evaluation data have been integral to these submissions and hearings, including economic data that demonstrates high returns on investments in cycling interventions (Cavill, Kahlmeier, Rutter, Racioppi, & Oja, 2008). In recent years, evidence-based cycling advocacy has been supported by the development of a number of new tools and methods for the economic evaluation of cycling interventions. These include the World Health Organization's Health Economic Assessment Tool [HEAT], an online tool for estimating the value of reduced mortality that results from regular cycling (Rutter, Cavill, Dinsdale et al., 2011).

Reduced mortality is an important contribution to the favourable benefit-cost ratios associated with many cycling interventions, but it is not the only benefit.

Litman (2013) has developed a more comprehensive framework for evaluating the multiple benefits and costs of active transport. The framework includes the monetisation (where possible) of the following factors:

- health
- traffic congestion
- road and parking facility costs
- vehicle expenses
- crash risk
- pollution emissions
- cost savings for lower income users
- user enjoyment
- option value
- support for equity objectives
- more compact and accessible land use development (smart growth)
- economic development
- improved community liveability
- habitat preservation.

Litman (2013) argues that conventional transport economic evaluations ignore many of these benefits of cycling and walking, and that their inclusion in economic assessments of transport initiatives supports investment in cycling and walking.

Conclusions and recommendations

Cycling promotion and evaluation are natural allies in ongoing efforts to establish more balanced transport planning that reflects the multiple personal and social benefits of more people making more short- to medium-distance trips by bicycle rather than by car. More and better quality evaluations will continue to provide leverage for challenging the unhealthy and economically irrational car dependence that has developed in many industrialised countries in the last half century.

Classically rigorous evaluation designs are not possible for many cycling interventions, but innovative evaluation approaches (such as realistic evaluation), designs (such as natural experiments) and data collection methods (such as personal GPS devices) have been developed recently to address this constraint on establishing a good evidence base for cycling promotion. In addition, mixed-methods evaluations, which combine process and impact measures, are providing greater insights into *why* interventions succeed or fail — thereby contributing to continuous improvements in policy and practice.

This chapter has emphasised the key role that evaluation plays in establishing an evidence base for action to increase utilitarian cycling at the population level, including using evidence to advocate for the establishment of cycling-friendly cities, suburbs and towns. Evaluation can also be used to investigate cycling advocacy processes and outcomes, but few such evaluations have been conducted. Pucher and Buehler (2012), Pucher et al. (2010) and others have identified *what* has been done to increase cycling in small and large cities, but less common in the cycling research and evaluation literature are comprehensive investigations of *why* and *how* these measures came to be implemented in these cities. The existing literature does, however, include a number of accounts of the establishment of more cycling-friendly cities such as Copenhagen, London and New York (for example, Pucher, de Lanversin, Suzuki & Whitelegg, 2012); a more detailed case history of Davis, California (Buehler & Handy, 2008); and historical and contemporary examinations of cycling advocacy (Wray, 2008; Aldred, 2012).

This chapter therefore concludes with recommendations for continued methodological innovation in the challenging field of cycling promotion evaluation; more, and adequately resourced, evaluation studies; greater collaboration between evaluators, practitioners, policy makers and cycling advocates; and more systematic evaluations of cycling advocacy.

References

Aldred, R. (2012). The role of advocacy and activism. In J Parkin (Ed.), *Cycling and sustainability* (pp. 83-108). Bingley, UK: Emerald Group Publishing Limited.

Australian Bureau of Statistics. (2012). *Environmental issues: Waste management, transport and motor vehicle usage*. Cat No. 4602.0.55.002. Canberra: ABS.

Brousselle, A, & Champagne, F. (2011). Program theory evaluation: Logic analysis. *Evaluation and Program Planning*, 34(1), 69-78.

Buehler, R, & Handy, S. (2008). Fifty years of bicycle policy in Davis, California. *Transportation Research Record: Journal of the Transportation Research Board*, 2074, 52-57.

Cavill, N, Kahlmeier, S, Rutter, H, Racioppi, F, & Oja, P. (2008). Economic analyses of transport infrastructure and policies including health effects related to cycling and walking: A systematic review. *Transport Policy*, 15(5), 291-304.

City of Sydney. (2014). City count reveals record bike trips. Retrieved 30 July 2015 from http://www.sydneymedia.com.au/city-count-reveals-record-bike-trips.

Crawford, S, & Garrard, J. (2013). A combined impact-process evaluation of a program promoting active transport to school: Understanding the factors that shaped program effectiveness. *Journal of Environmental and Public Health*. doi: 10.1155/2013/816961.

Curtis, C, & Low, N. (2012). *Institutional barriers to sustainable transport.* Farnham, England: Ashgate.

Department for Transport (UK). (2013). *National Travel Survey: 2012.* Retrieved 30 July 2015 from https://www.gov.uk/government/uploads/system/uploads/attachment_data/file/243957/nts2012-01.pdf.

Department of Economic Development, Jobs, Transport and Resources. (2014). *Victorian Integrated Survey of Travel and Activity [VISTA].* Melbourne: Department of Economic Development, Jobs, Transport and Resources. Retrieved 30 July 2015 from http://economicdevelopment.vic.gov.au/transport/research-and-data/statistics/vista.

Department of Infrastructure and Regional Development. (2011). *National Road Safety Strategy 2011-2020.* Canberra: Department of Infrastructure and Regional Development. Retrieved 17 September 2015 from https://infrastructure.gov.au/roads/safety/national_road_safety_strategy/index.aspx.

Department of Transport. (2009). *Victorian Integrated Survey of Travel and Activity 2007 (VISTA 07): Summary report.* Melbourne: Department of Transport.

Fildes, B, Langford, J, Dale, A, & Scully, J. (2005). *Balance between harm reduction and mobility in setting speed limits: A feasibility study.* Sydney: Austroads Inc.

Garrard, J. (2010). *Active school travel research project: Final report.* Melbourne: Victorian Department of Planning and Community Development.

Garrard, J. (2012, June 12). Cutting cycling funding is economic non-sense. *The Conversation*. Retrieved 30 July 2015 from https://theconversation.com/cutting-cycling-funding-is-economic-non-sense-7547.

Garrard, J, Crawford, S, & Godbold, T. (2009). *Evaluation of the Ride2School Program: Final report*. Melbourne: Deakin University.

Garrard, J, & Fishman, E. (2013, March 10-13). Adult cycling proficiency courses: Do they assist more people to cycle more often? *Asia-Pacific Cycling Congress*, Gold Coast, Queensland.

Garrard, G, Rissel, C, & Bauman, A. (2012). Health benefits of cycling. In J Pucher, & R Buehler (Eds.), *City cycling* (pp. 31-55). Cambridge, MA: The MIT Press.

Gebel, K, King, L, Bauman, A, Vita, P, Gill, T, Rigby, A, & Capon, A. (2005). *Creating healthy environments: A review of links between the physical environment, physical activity and obesity*. Sydney: NSW Health Department and NSW Centre for Overweight and Obesity.

Glazebrook, GJ. (2009). Taking the con out of convenience: The true cost of transport modes in Sydney. *Urban Policy and Research*, 27(1), 5-24.

Goodman, A, Panter, J, Sharp, SJ, & Ogilvie, D. (2013). Effectiveness and equity impacts of town-wide cycling initiatives in England: A longitudinal, controlled natural experimental study. *Social Science and Medicine*, 97, 228-237.

Goodman, A, Sahlqvist, S, Ogilvie, D, & iConnect Consortium. (2014). New walking and cycling routes and increased physical activity: One- and 2-year findings from the UK iConnect study. *American Journal of Public Health*, 104(9), e38-46.

Götschi, T, Garrard, J, & Giles-Corti, B. (2015). Cycling as a part of daily life: A review of health perspectives. *Transport Reviews*, 1-27. doi: 10.1080/01441647.2015.1057877.

Hembrow, D. (2010, March 31). Beauty and the bike: What happened next? [blog post, *A view from the cycle path* blog]. Retrieved 30 July 2015 from http://www.aviewfromthecyclepath.com/2010_03_01_archive.html.

Hinkson, E, Duncan, S, Kearns, R, & Badland, H. (2008). *2008 School Travel Plan evaluation: 2007 school year*. Auckland: Auckland Regional Transport Authority.

Hosking, J, Macmillan, A, Connor, J, Bullen, C, & Ameratunga, S. (2010). Organisational travel plans for improving health. *Cochrane Database* of *Systematic Reviews*, 3, Art. No.: CD005575. doi: 10.1002/14651858. CD005575.pub3.

Kelly, P, Doherty, A, Mizdrak, A, Marshall, S, Kerr, J, Legge, A, & Foster, C. (2014). High group level validity but high random error of a self-report travel diary, as assessed by wearable cameras. *Journal of Transport & Health*, 1(3), 190-201.

Killoran, A, Doyle, N, Waller, S, Wohlgemuth, C, & Crombie, H. (2006). *Transport interventions promoting safe cycling and walking: Evidence briefing*. London: National Institute for Health and Clinical Excellence.

Litman, T. (2013). *Evaluating non-motorised transportation benefits and costs*. Victoria, BC, Canada: Victoria Transport Policy Institute.

Low, N, Gleeson, B, & Rush, E. (2005). A multivalent conception of path dependence: The case of transport planning in metropolitan Melbourne, Australia. *Environmental Sciences*, 2, 391-408.

Mackie, HW, Charlton, SG, Baas, PH, & Villasenor, PC. (2013). Road user behaviour changes following a self-explaining roads intervention. *Accident Analysis and Prevention*, 50, 742-750.

Madsen, T, Schipperijn, J, Christiansen, LB, Nielsen, TS, & Troelsen, J. (2014). Developing suitable buffers to capture transport cycling behavior. *Frontiers in Public Health*, 2, 61. doi: 10.3389/fpubh.2014.00061.

Martin, A, Suhrcke, M, & Ogilvie, D. (2012). Financial incentives to promote active travel: An evidence review and economic framework. *American Journal of Preventive Medicine*, 43(6), e45-e57.

Mavoa, S, Oliver, M, Witten, K, & Badland, HM. (2011). Linking GPS and travel diary data using sequence alignment in a study of children's independent mobility. *International Journal of Health Geographies*, 10, 64-73.

Möser, G, & Bamberg, S. (2008). The effectiveness of soft transport policy measures: A critical assessment and meta-analysis of empirical evidence. *Journal of Environmental Psychology*, 28(1), 10-26.

Murphy, T. (2014, July 29). Bayside Council extends Beach Road clearway on weekends. Retrieved 30 July 2015 from http://www.reviewproperty.com.au/Local-News/406012/Bayside-Council-extends-Beach-Road-clearway-on-weekends/?mode=buy.

National Transport Commission. (2011). *Review of the Australian Road Rules and Vehicle Standards Rules: Discussion Paper October 2011*. Melbourne: NTC.

Retrieved 17 September 2015 from http://www.ntc.gov.au/Media/Reports/(A4CA5CEA-FE90-E625-D305-039068E43FEA).pdf.

New South Wales [NSW] Bureau of Transport Statistics. (2013). *Sydney cycling survey 2012: Methods and findings*. Sydney: Transport for NSW.

Ogilvie, D, Bull, F, Powell, J, Cooper, AR, Brand, C, Mutrie, N, & Rutter, H. (2011). An applied ecological framework for evaluating infrastructure to promote walking and cycling: The iConnect study. *American Journal of Public Health*, 101(3), 473-481.

Pawson, R. (2006). *Evidence-based policy: A realistic perspective*. London: Sage Publications.

Pawson, R, & Tilley, N. (1997). *Realistic evaluation*. London: Sage Publications.

Public Transport Users Association. (2010). Common urban myths about transport: Motorists pay more in taxes and fees than is spent on roads. Retrieved 30 July 2015 from http://www.ptua.org.au/myths/petroltax.shtml.

Pucher, J, & Buehler, R. (2010). Walking and cycling for healthy cities. *Built Environment*, 36(4), 391-414.

Pucher, J, & Buehler, R. (2012). Promoting cycling for daily travel: conclusions and lessons from across the globe. In J Pucher, & R Buehler (Eds.), *City cycling* (pp. 347-364). Cambridge, MA: The MIT Press.

Pucher, J, de Lanversin, E, Suzuki, T, & Whitelegg, J. (2012). Cycling in megacities: London, Paris, New York and Tokyo. In J Pucher, & R Buehler (Eds.), *City cycling* (pp. 319-345). Cambridge, MA: The MIT Press.

Pucher, J, Dill, J, & Handy, S. (2010). Infrastructure, programs and policies to increase bicycling: An international review. *Preventive Medicine*, 50 (Jan Suppl 1), S106-125.

Rissel, C, Munro, C, & Bauman, A. (2013). Assessing cycling participation in Australia. *Sports*, 1(1), 1-9.

Rissel, C, New, C, Wen, L, Merom, D, Bauman, A, & Garrard, J. (2010). The effectiveness of community-based cycling promotion: Findings from the Cycling Connecting Communities project in Sydney. *International Journal of Behavioral Nutrition and Physical Activity*, 7, 1-11.

Road Safety Committee. (2014). *Inquiry into serious injury*. Melbourne: Parliament of Victoria.

Robinson, TN, & Sirard, JR. (2005). Preventing childhood obesity: A solution-oriented research paradigm. *American Journal of Preventive Medicine*, 28(2S2), 194-201.

Rutter, H, Cavill, N, Dinsdale, H, Kahlmeier, S, Racioppi, F, & Oja, P. (2011). *Health economic assessment tools (HEAT) for cycling*. Copenhagen: WHO Regional Office for Europe.

Sadik-Khan, J. (2014, May 27-30). How New York City made room for bikes. *Velo-City Global Conference*, Adelaide. Retrieved 31 July 2015 from http://www.adelaidecitycouncil.com/inside-adelaide/article/janette-sadik-khan-how-new-york-city-made-room-for-bikes.

Shoup, D. (2005). *The high cost of free parking*. Chicago: Planners Press.

Sloman, L, Cavill, N, Cope, A, Muller, L, & Kennedy, A. (2009). *Analysis and synthesis of evidence on the effects of investment in six Cycling Demonstration Towns*. England: Department for Transport and Cycling England.

Standing Committee on Planning Environment and Territory and Municipal Services. (2014). *Inquiry into vulnerable road users*. Canberra: ACT Legislative Assembly. Retrieved 18 September 2015 from http://www.parliament.act.gov.au/in-committees/recent-reports/?a=602200.

Sugiyama, T, Merom, D, Reaves, M, Leslie, E, & Owen, N. (2010). Habitual active transport moderates the association of TV viewing time with body mass index. *Journal of Physical Activity and Health*, 7, 11-16.

Transport, Housing and Local Government Committee. (2013). *A new direction for cycling in Queensland*. Report No. 39. Brisbane: Queensland Parliament.

VicRoads. (2011). *2011-2012 Victorian speed limit review*. Melbourne: VicRoads.

VicRoads. (2014). *Cycling data and statistics*. Retrieved 31 July 2015 from https://www.vicroads.vic.gov.au/traffic-and-road-use/road-network-and-performance/road-use-and-performance.

Wray, JH. (2008). *Pedal power: The quiet rise of the bicycle in American Public Life*. Boulder, USA: Paradigm Publishers.

Yang, L, Sahlqvist, S, McMinn, A, Griffin, SJ, & Ogilvie, D. (2010). Interventions to promote cycling: Systematic review. *British Medical Journal*, 341, c5293.

Electronic Index

This book is available as a free fully-searchable ebook from
www.adelaide.edu.au/press

www.ingramcontent.com/pod-product-compliance
Lightning Source LLC
Chambersburg PA
CBHW042033100526
44587CB00029B/4407